A HISTORY OF SOVIET RUSSIA

A HISTORY OF SOVIET RUSSIA

ADAM B. ULAM
Harvard University

HOLT, RINEHART AND WINSTON
New York Chicago San Francisco Atlanta
Dallas Montreal Toronto London Sydney

Photographs on the following pages are reproduced by permission of: Magnum: 240 (© Brian Brake magnum), 301 (Burt Glinn); Novosti from Sovfoto: 15, 91; Sovfoto: 29, 97, 109, 129, 157, 165, 176, 219; Tass from Sovfoto: 23, 51, 184, 214, 258; Wide World Photos: 70, 73, 140, 205, 245, 281.

Published in the United States of America in 1976
by Praeger Publishers, Inc.
A division of Holt, Rinehart and Winston

Library of Congress Cataloging in Publication Data

Ulam, Adam Bruno, 1922–
A history of Soviet Russia.

Includes index.
1. Russia—History—1917–   I. Title.
DK266.U5   947.084   73–16896
ISBN 0–275–89260–3

Printed in the United States of America

234567890 038 0987

Preface

This book tells the story of communism and Soviet power in Russia since the Revolution of 1917. While my main emphasis has been on internal and foreign policies, no history of the USSR would be worthy of its name without describing the vast social and economic changes which Russian society has undergone during the last sixty years; and alluding at least to intellectual and artistic trends, which in Russia, perhaps more than anywhere else, have always possessed political significance.

My thanks go to the personnel of the Russian Research Center at Harvard with which I have been associated for more than twenty years, especially to the executive assistant to the director, Miss Mary Towle, and my secretary, Mrs. Christine Balm.

Denise Rathbun has been a most helpful and patient editor.

A.B.U.

Contents

1.
1917: Two Revolutions

The Search for Authority

The strikes and street manifestations that afflicted Petrograd during the last week of February 1917 could not have filled the authorities or partisans of the old regime with undue apprehension at first. Compared with the "Bloody Sunday" of January 9—the shock that ushered in the Revolution of 1905—the current disorders, caused in the main by food shortages and the ravages of inflation, did not appear too ominous. And unlike the previous occasion, when revolutionary strife spread with electric rapidity throughout the empire, this time the trouble seemed to be confined mainly to the capital. Some civil disorders were not unexpected in this third year of a bloody, inconclusive, and, for Russia, generally unsuccessful war. But within five days such comforting reflections were exposed as illusory; the Tsarist regime had collapsed.

The immediate reason lay in the demoralization of the army, especially of its rear units. In 1905 the soldiers, when called upon to suppress revolutionary manifestations, usually obeyed. But now the garrison of Petrograd, composed mostly of recent draftees and staffed largely by reserve officers drawn from the intelligentsia, many with radical or liberal sympathies, refused to succor authorities in putting down the disturbances, and soldiers would occasionally fire upon the police rather than the demonstrators. On February 23, ninety thousand men were on strike in Petrograd. The next day the number grew to two hundred thousand. The nerve center of the empire was paralyzed.

A self-confident, energetic government might have been able to cope with the emergency through a mixture of concessions and firmness. But the Tsar was away at field headquarters in the Ukrainian town of Mogilev, having unwisely assumed the supreme command of the army. Though the actual direction remained in the hands of the chief of staff, General Alexeyev, by this step Nicholas II had associated himself more directly with Russia's military failures in the eyes of the public. His cabinet was composed of nonentities. This time there was no statesman of the caliber of Witte or Stolypin to step into the breach and save the monarchy by political and social reforms. The monarch's immediate reaction was to strike at the body he still might have conciliated, the parliament, where for over a year his regime had been vilified for incompetence, if not worse, in the conduct of the war. On February 26, he ordered the Duma prorogued. But this once predominantly promonarchist assembly refused to obey: on February 27, it elected a provisional committee which would try to grasp the authority slipping out of the hands of the Romanovs. Its representatives sought to persuade the now utterly discredited Emperor to abdicate in order to save his dynasty. Most of the front-line commanders lent their support to this initiative of the parliamentarians. On March 2, Nicholas resigned the throne in favor of his brother. Grand Duke Michael in turn refused the onerous charge, leaving the decision on the country's form of government to the future Constituent Assembly. Russia ceased to be a monarchy without becoming a republic. (Not until the waning moments of its existence in August did the Kerensky regime proclaim the republic.)

This snapping of the links with more than three hundred years of Russia's past represented by the House of Romanov was far from unimportant for the future course of events. During the previous two years the monarchy might have been largely discredited among the educated classes, the Emperor recognized as weak, his wife the subject of scandalous gossip on account of both her German origin and her sponsorship of Rasputin. Still, in the country where parliamentary and other representative institutions were of a very recent and fragile nature, where the army's esprit de corps had been damaged through defeats and the high commanders' repudiation of their sovereign, the abrupt liquidation of the monarchy meant the disappearance of the last potential source of political legitimacy and national cohesion. Both the antecedents of the collapse of the imperial house and its ignominious manner meant in turn that the Romanovs could not, even after the Bolshevik coup in October, have become a rallying point for political moderates. Only the barbarism of the Civil War, not political necessity, was responsible for the Bolsheviks' execution of Nicholas and members of his family in July 1918.

The story of the Russian Revolution thus becomes, as of March 1917, the story of the search for authority to fill the vacuum left by the collapse of the monarchy. It is symptomatic that between March and October Russia was to have no head of state in the proper sense of the word. It soon became clear that the Duma could not effectively provide the source of political legitimacy. Elected in 1912 on the basis of a very undemocratic franchise and composed of a motley of parties *then* of a predominantly moderate to conservative hue, Russia's parliament was a crucial factor in the destruction of the old order but could not become the foundation upon which to build a new one. Moved by the momentum of the Revolution, the Duma gave birth to a government it was incapable of endowing with undisputed authority, and then to all purposes, vanished from the scene.

The very words "undisputed authority" would, to a Russian contemporary, have sounded incongruous, for from the very beginning of the revolutionary sequence political power was shared by two bodies. The nature of their future coexistence could already be partly divined from their initial proclamations: "The Provisional Committee of the Duma has found itself compelled to take into its own hands the restoration of state and public works." But against this language, under the circumstances conventional, another declaration on the same day, February 27, struck a new note: "The Soviet has set for itself as its main task to organize the popular forces and to fight for the consolidation of political freedom and popular government."[1]

The Soviet was the creation of a group of socialist leaders of various denominations (with as yet not a single Bolshevik among them), who, hearkening back to the traditions of 1905, proceeded to reinstitute those workers' committees of action that had played such an important role in the first Russian revolution. This time soldiers were going to be joined with the workers' deputies. Thus with the beginning of March there began the fateful bifurcation of political power that was to endure until October. The Duma's child, the Provisional Government, was to be, insofar as the law and foreign states' recognition were concerned, the official successor to the regime of Nicholas II. But by its side stood the Petrograd Soviet of Workers' and Soldiers' Deputies, with similar soviets soon springing up all over the land.

This division reflected both pragmatic considerations and some dogmas of long standing within politically conscious segments of Russian society. The Provisional Government, even in the opinion of its own members, lacked a popular mandate. But by the same token

[1] *Documents of Russian History,* ed. F. A. Golder, New York, 1927, pp. 281, 287.

the socialists and radicals who dominated the Petrograd and other soviets believed that, according to the canon of Marxism, Russia was not ready for socialism, the working class neither numerous enough nor prepared to assume power. Hence it should be a "bourgeois" government—i.e., one that would usher in a democratic era for Russia—and democracy *in due time* would create economic and social conditions for socialism to take over. But could the bourgeois government, like the present one composed of bankers, industrialists, and professors, be fully trusted and unconditionally obeyed? No, the same doctrinal reasoning urged that "revolutionary democracy"—i.e., the soviets—should exercise stern control and have veto power over the actions of the rulers.

Hardly had it been organized when the Executive Committee of the Petrograd Soviet issued its Order No. I, calling upon all military and naval units to form their own soldiers' councils—soviets. Each military detachment was to be now, in matters not pertinent to actual fighting, under the authority of the Petrograd Soviet and its own soldiers' council. The latter was to control all weapons, arbitrate any differences between the rank and file and the officers. The old forms of saluting and address between the soldiers were abolished.

The people who composed and approved this startling directive, bound to demoralize any army let alone one that had suffered huge casualties, were at the time far from wishing for Russia's defeat or even defection from her allies. But again, history and their doctrine taught them that the greatest danger to a revolution lay in the possibility of a military coup. Hence their order, which, though it had no legal authority, did in fact destroy much of what remained of the army's fighting spirit and discipline and led to that politicization of the rank and file without which the subsequent development of the Revolution, including the Bolsheviks' seizure of power, would have been inconceivable.

Order No. I did not lead, as might have been expected, to a sharp clash between the government (one must resist the temptation to put this word in quotation marks) and the Soviet. One tends to forget nowadays that initially the February Revolution led not only to democratic but also to patriotic elation and produced an impression of national unity which only gradually turned out to be a mirage. It was fondly believed that, freed from the encumbrance of the imperial house with its dynastic connection with Germany and of the incompetent and corrupt tsarist bureaucracy, Russia, like the revolutionary France of yore, would astound the world; the army of a free people would repulse the forces of German militarism and help secure democracy for all of Europe. Few, even among the leaders of the Soviet, antimilitarist though they were, questioned the necessity of continuing the war to a victorious end, and even those who did rejected the possibility of Russia's concluding a separate peace. As for the Provisional Government, it was composed for the most part of people for whom the tsarist expansionist war aims retained their full validity.

That the personalities pushed by the first impetus of the Revolution to the forefront of the political stage were, for the most part, ill prepared for their historic role was perhaps less a reflection on their capacity than on the conditions of prerevolutionary Russia, where politicians' training could be only in rhetoric rather than in running affairs of state. Prince George Lvov, a liberal nobleman and erstwhile head of the association of local governments, became (a most ineffective) prime minister. The long-time leader of the left wing of the Kadets (Constitutional Democrats), Professor Miliukov, held the portfolio of foreign affairs. A former president of the Duma, Guchkov, Octobrist by party affiliation and industrialist by profession, headed the army and war ministry. None of the three, men cast to be parliamentarians rather than leaders in a revolutionary situation, enjoyed any considerable political following. And the swift current of the Revolution was soon to engulf both the Kadets and the Octobrists. Representing bodies of opinion of the liberal intelligentsia and of the moderate conservatives, respectively, rather than organized political forces, as did their socialist rivals, the two parties would be unable to gain any support whatsoever among the soldiers and workers, those segments of the population that would count most at the decisive turns of the Revolution.

Revolutionary democracy—i.e., the Petrograd Soviet and its imitations, which sprang up all over the land—did in contrast appear to have not only grass-roots support among the masses but also real party organizations hardened under the conditions of their largely clandestine pre-1917 activity. The original Soviet was dominated by the Mensheviks and the Socialist Revolutionaries, as demonstrated by the affiliations of its leaders. Nicholas Chkheidze, a Georgian Menshevik, was chairman; his deputies were M. I. Skobelev, a fellow Menshevik, and the Socialist Revolutionary Alexander Kerensky, a thirty-five-year-old lawyer who since 1912 had enjoyed a national reputation for defending radicals and revolutionaries. At first the Bolsheviks' role in the revolutionary assembly, which in eight months they would use as one of the main instruments in seizing power, was insignificant. In the vote by the Soviet on whether to accept the Provisional Government, the Bolsheviks' negative motion could command but nineteen votes against four hundred. Their leaders, Shlyapnikov and Molotov, were invited to sit on the Executive Committee more as a courtesy to fellow revolutionaries than as a recognition of their faction's strength.

And thus the Revolution organized itself. But this recital of bare facts is hardly sufficient to convey, first, the feelings of exaltation with which it was greeted, and, then, the unavoidable rush of disappointments and the kaleidoscopic transformation of the initial mood of relief and national unity into one of increasing political polarization and growing exasperation with the war. The very structure of post-revolutionary politics—the government, which shouldered the responsibility for the management of the country but which could not govern effectively because of the Soviet; the latter, which, while it disclaimed any responsibility for the conduct of affairs, yet had arrogated to itself a considerable slice of power; and finally, the proliferation of local and army soviets, usually but not always taking their cue from the Petrograd one—was a blueprint for anarchy. The only way to avoid that condition would have been the creation of a new, undisputed source of legitimacy and authority through the convocation of a universally and democratically elected Constituent Assembly, the step to which both the Provisional Government and the Soviet were solemnly pledged. But as we shall see, by the time this body was to assemble, anarchy, having eroded both legitimate authority and democracy, had cleared the path for dictatorship.

Some, to be sure, began to cast around for the proverbial "strong man" to save Russia from chaos. The likeliest candidate appeared to be the one man who had defied the socialists' agreement on nonparticipation in the "bourgeois" government, Minister of Justice Alexander Kerensky. A talented, if at times florid, orator, he soon outshone both the ephemeral premier Prince Lvov and the lackadaisical head of the revolutionary democracy, Chkheidze. Kerensky, to many of his countrymen, seemed to have the qualifications for the kind of democratic dictator who would lead Russia out of the wilderness, preserve the newly won liberties, and secure peace. But quite apart from the exorbitant nature of such expectations and his own very considerable shortcomings, Kerensky suffered from one basic political weakness. He was in no sense *the* or even *a* leader of his own party, his ties with the Socialist Revolutionaries being quite recent and tenuous. And much as oratory and charismatic personality were to count in the development of the Revolution, they could be effective only if their possessor had behind him a disciplined party.

Such a party began to be forged in April. Prior to Lenin's return from Switzerland, the Bolsheviks did not seem much different from other socialist parties, whether it came to cohesion or uncertainty as to what policies they were to pursue. Certainly, Lenin's position since the beginning of the war had pushed his party to the extreme left of the socialist spectrum. By the same token, witness the initial composition of the Soviet: the Bolsheviks' antiwar stand had contributed to their isolation and numerical weakness on the eve of the Revolution. In the middle of March two senior Bolsheviks, Joseph Stalin and Lev Kamenev, returned to Petrograd from their Siberian exile and, after a brief altercation with Shlyapnikov and Molotov, took over the leadership of the Bolshevik faction. The new arrivals steered their party in a more moderate direction, moderated the antigovernment and antiwar stand, and opened negotiations with the Mensheviks, looking toward a reunification of the two factions of the Russian Social Democracy. But then on the night of April 3, Lenin, after his trip through Germany, arrived in Petrograd.

On hearing of the Revolution while still in Switzerland, Lenin exclaimed that Russia had become the freest country in the world. But the dazzling new developments—political amnesty, legalization of all parties, fullest freedom for propaganda and agitation—were for him no reason to collaborate with and acquiesce in the new order. They were opportunities to put into action the concept of the revolutionary party that had been in his mind ever since he wrote *What Is to Be Done* in 1902 and the revolutionary program that germinated in 1914: the imperialist war had to be turned into a civil one. And on April 4, before a joint session of the Bolsheviks and Mensheviks, Lenin loosed his famous April Theses. No compromise with the Provisional Government—*all* power was to go to the soviets; an immediate confiscation of landed estates and their transfer to poor peasants; no reunion with the Mensheviks—on the contrary, *his* party should change its name to Communist and help establish a new militant Marxist International, devoted to world revolution. Though by now he was prudent enough not to advocate an immediate peace—the general mood was still patriotic, and those Bolsheviks who returned through enemy territory were rumored to be German agents—he still called for intense antiwar propaganda and for encouraging the front-line soldiers to fraternize with their German and Austrian foes.

This program, which seemed to fly in the face of Marxism ("Russia was not ready for a socialist revolution"), as well as of the political realities of the moment, at first aroused violent opposition among his own followers. But within a few days Lenin's position prevailed, and the Bolsheviks adopted it as their own. It was not only the matter of Lenin's prestige within his party, which he had led since 1903, but of the almost daily demonstration that the mood of the masses was growing more radical and that the dual structure of the authority erected in February was incapable of coping with the situation. The majority of the Soviet, while still against Russia's unilateral withdrawal from the war, was now demanding a peace without annexation and indemnities. The radicalization of the soldiers and (especially) the sailors was proceeding apace. By the end of April, the Bolsheviks' membership, from perhaps some twenty thousand before February, leaped to eighty thousand. What had seemed madness in the first days of April now appeared a daring but not unreasonable political gambit. If the present trend continued, the soviets would come under the domination of the Bolsheviks and their allies. The rank and file of the army, mostly peasants, was bound to be impressed by the fact that, of all parties, only the Bolsheviks urged an immediate and free distribution of the landlords' estates.

The Provisional Government faced impossible dilemmas. It was committed to continue the war at the side of Russia's allies, and yet it could, or dared, do nothing to arrest the army's growing demoralization. The government believed it could not, while at war, embark on a far-reaching program of economic reform to offset the effect of the Bolsheviks' slogan "All land to the peasants." Another fundamental problem—that of the non-Russian nationalities of the erstwhile empire—was also being exploited by the extremists. The Bolsheviks proclaimed the right of every ethnic group to secede from Russia if it so desired. But how could responsible leaders of a country at war concede independence or far-reaching autonomy to Finland or the Ukraine? Though other socialist parties half perceived the demagogic nature of the Bolsheviks' slogans, both the Mensheviks and the Socialist Revolutionaries were themselves, in view of their own traditional stance on those issues and the fear of being outflanked on the left, being pushed toward a more radical position.

The inevitable clash between the Provisional Government and the "revolutionary democracy" came as early as May. Miliukov's reiteration of the tsarist government's war aims led to a challenge by the Soviet. Prince Lvov felt constrained to dismiss both his foreign minister and Guchkov. The reconstructed Provisional Government now received a somewhat socialist tinge. Menshevik Skobelev assumed the ministry of labor, the Socialist Revolutionaries' leader, Victor Chernov, became minister of agriculture. And Kerensky, now clearly the key figure, took over the ministry of war. Theoretically, the old duality between the government and the Soviet was removed or at least attenuated, and the regime included representatives of parties with mass support among workers, peasants, and politically active soldiers. Had these been normal times, Russian democracy might well have lived happily ever after, with the Bolsheviks remaining an impotent minority. But with the coalition government incapable of solving the two outstanding problems, those of war and economic distress, the Bolsheviks would become beneficiaries of their socialist rivals' identification with the government's increasingly unpopular policies of continuing the war and failing to tackle the land question. In the First All-Russian Congress of the Soviets, which met in early June, the Bolsheviks and their allies had about 130 delegates of the total 777, a dazzling accession of strength since February. Lenin's party felt confident enough to risk a test of strength with the authorities: an inflammatory proclamation of June 9 called upon the people of Petrograd to take to the street, to demand an immediate peace and the resignation of the "ten capitalist ministers." But the Congress banned all demonstrations, and on June 10, the Bolsheviks called off what would have been at least a rehearsal for an armed uprising.

The June fiasco was soon compounded by a more serious one. In the same month the Lvov-Kerensky government authorized a Russian offensive. A victorious advance, it was believed, could be the only effective antidote to the increasing demoralization that inactivity (with the February Revolution, the Germans and Austrians had suspended major operations on the Eastern front) and defeatist propaganda (emanating mostly from the Bolsheviks) were bringing to the troops. The offensive, as might have been expected, soon faltered. On July 3–4, part of the Petrograd garrison, in imminent danger of being ordered to the front, mutinied. They were joined by pro-Bolshevik workers. Lenin and his lieutenants were presented with the dilemma of whether to encourage the uprising their slogans had inspired or to try to stop it. Rather halfheartedly, they chose the former. Armed sailors from the Kronstadt base, by now the most reliable supporters of the party, were brought to Petrograd. And thus the incongruous spectacle of the Bolshevik supporters besieging the Tauride Palace, seat of the Executive Committee of the Soviet, demanding that its leaders, still mostly Mensheviks and Social Revolutionaries, should take over full power. But the befuddled uprising soon dissipated. Front-line units loyal to the Provisional Government were summoned to the capital. The military strength behind the Bolsheviks evaporated in thin air, the sailors fleeing Petrograd or surrendering to the government forces.

The uncertain and confused bid at seizing power appeared for the moment to bring the Bolsheviks an irretrievable disaster. Their party headquarters were seized, their organ, *Pravda,* banned at the order of the Executive Committee of the Soviet. Lenin and his then chief lieutenant, Zinoviev, went into hiding. Other leaders—Kamenev, Anatole Lunacharsky, Trotsky (officially not yet a party member but already on Lenin's side)—were placed under arrest. Rumors now were rife that Lenin and his followers were in German pay, and on July 7, a government order authorized his arrest.[2] On July 11, the Bolsheviks'

[2] We now know that the substance but not the implication of the charges was correct. The Bolsheviks did receive funds from Germany, but in no sense could Lenin and his followers be described as Berlin's agents; their aim was a revolution in Germany as well as in their own country. See *Germany and the Revolution in Russia,* ed. Z. A. Zeman, London, 1958.

leader fled Petrograd; he was not to reappear there until the eve of the momentous events of October.

And yet by the end of the very same month, far from being shattered, the Bolsheviks were to exhibit increased strength. There were several reasons for this amazing development. Leaders of the revolutionary democracy stopped short of complete repression of the Bolsheviks. To them, as to the most prestigious figures among the Mensheviks, Lenin and his followers were fellow, if misguided, socialists. A real threat to the Revolution could come only from the right; for all their undemocratic behavior, the Bolsheviks still expressed the real grievances of the proletariat. Hence the proper response to the July imbroglio, Martov, a Menshevik leader, and his ilk believed, would be the adoption of needed reforms, and then, having been "morally isolated," the Bolsheviks would mend their ways and abandon their un-Marxist adventurist tactics.

The worsening of the general situation also helped revive the Bolsheviks' fortunes. The Russian offensive launched in June ground to a halt in the first days of July and soon, through a German counteroffensive, turned to retreat. With the defeat there evaporated that residue of discipline and patriotism within the regular army that had made possible the routing of the July insurrection. Desertion now became endemic, and, short of a miracle, a complete dissolution of the army could be only a question of time. A new government crisis brought Kerensky to the helm. His cabinet had a socialist majority, but time was running out on the non-Bolshevik left, and the new premier, once considered the man of destiny of the Revolution, had been compromised by his responsibility for launching the disastrous offensive.

It is thus understandable how the Bolsheviks' Sixth Congress, which met at the end of July, witnessed a reborn and strengthened party. Its membership stood at close to 250,000, half of it in Petrograd and Moscow. In the leader's absence the party's affairs were being run skillfully by Jacob Sverdlov[3] and Stalin. The Congress authorized the admission into the party of Trotsky and his so-called interfaction group of socialists. And thus the man whose role in the subsequent struggle and conquest of power was to be second only to Lenin's became officially a Bolshevik.

The assembled delegates kept in contact with their absent leader, still hiding and still sought, but not very energetically, by the government authorities. It was with his concurrence that the slogan "All power to the soviets" was now dropped. The July events having demonstrated that the Menshevik and SR leaders of the soviets were not

[3] An old Bolshevik who acted as the party's main administrator and was to be Soviet Russia's closest approximation to the head of state until his death in 1919.

going to facilitate or tolerate the Bolsheviks' aim of overthrowing the Provisional Government, the party's new motto called for the seizure of power by "the workers and poor peasants." (The residue of orthodox Marxism in the Bolshevik ideology precluded a plea for dictatorship pure and simple by their party. This was not just a matter of tactics: before October most of the Bolsheviks, if not Lenin, would have been genuinely shocked had they realized that the road they traveled led to a one-party dictatorship and the suppression of other socialist groups.)

But it was not political formulas, however ingenious, nor even the Bolsheviks' superior political maneuverability that set the stage for October. The second phase of the Revolution was being prepared by ever-widening social and political anarchy. A wave of peasant disorders and seizures of landlords' estates was spreading all over Russia. Industrial production had fallen off catastrophically in comparison with the pre-1917 level. Inflation was rampant. By October, the number of army deserters would reach incredible proportions. Barring a political miracle, such as an immediate peace, Russia's experiment in democracy initiated in February was clearly drawing to an end.[4] Perhaps this end would have been postponed or taken a different form had not yet another blow struck the tottering regime in August.

Following the July defeats, Kerensky had appointed General Lavr Kornilov as the commander-in-chief. The new head of the army enjoyed a widespread popularity. Unlike most regular tsarist officers, he came "from the people," being a son of a poor Cossack, and had distinguished himself by daring exploits in the course of the war. He expected the government to help him restore the army discipline and authority of officers, expectations which, almost superfluous to say, were unfulfilled. Disgruntled, Kornilov began to heed those in the officer corps and outside it who hoped for a military dictatorship to save Russia from traitors and Bolsheviks. Yet Kornilov, a "man with the heart of a lion, brains of a sheep," as characterized by a fellow general, did not conspire to seize power, but rather stumbled into a futile plot. Kerensky asked him to have a cavalry corps ready to march on Petrograd to smash a possible Bolshevik uprising. The general took this as an intimation that the prime minister wanted him, Kornilov, to become dictator. He informed Kerensky's emissary that

[4] The Provisional Government has often been criticized for not taking Russia out of the war. Yet such criticisms overlook the following: (1) In the opinion of most democratic leaders, Russia's defection and a peace on the order of the subsequent one of Brest Litovsk would have meant German victory in the European war and Russia's becoming a virtual satellite of the Central Powers. (2) It would have required a minor miracle for the government even to open peace negotiations with Germany and Austria without being overthrown. The Bolsheviks and other left-wing forces demanded peace but would have cried out in outrage had Kerensky proposed to deal with the Imperial German and Austrian governments.

he was quite ready to assume supreme civil as well as military authority, and he proposed to retain Kerensky as minister of justice. On being then ordered to lay down his command, the unfortunate general refused and issued a declaration repudiating the Provisional Government, while dispatching troops to seize the capital.

But the Revolution was not destined to have a Napoleonic finale. A defeated and demoralized army does not become a ready instrument of a coup d'etat unless indeed it is directed against its own command. The march on Petrograd disintegrated; Kornilov's forces, uncertain of why and against whom they were being sent, mutinied in their turn against their officers. The would-be dictator and his chief aides were put under arrest.

At the first news of Kornilov's move the government released imprisoned Bolshevik leaders and permitted a reconstruction of their private army, the Red Guards. Thus the Bolsheviks were the principal beneficiaries of the tragicomedy of errors associated with Kornilov's name. In contrast, the abortive revolt was a veritable coup de grace to Kerensky. He lost whatever support he had had in the army, even those officers who had not sympathized with Kornilov viewing the prime minister and his regime with loathing. The moderate left now stood utterly discredited: it was unable to conduct the war or to bring it to an end; it was incapable of dealing with the other pressing problems of the day. In a sense forces of the right, including a majority of regular army officers, hated Kerensky and his motley crew of liberals and right-wing socialists more passionately than they did the Bolsheviks: the latter, it was held, knew what they wanted and pursued the goal of power; the Provisional Government and its supporters foundered in indecision and phrase-mongering while anarchy was engulfing Russia.

The soviets, their members having no set term of office but being elected and recalled at irregular intervals, reflected the shifting mood of the masses of workers and soldiers. By September this mood was becoming pro-Bolshevik. And thus, the majority of the Petrograd Soviet having become Bolshevik, Trotsky was elected its leader. With the Provisional Government impotent and the soviets being conquered by Lenin's supporters, the stage was being set for a decisive turn in the Revolution. The Second All-Russian Congress of Soviets was to assemble in October. It was easy to foresee that it would displace the current Executive Committee with one predominantly Bolshevik.

It was at this point that a dispute developed within the Bolshevik ranks as to the tactics they were to pursue. From his Finnish hideout Lenin bombarded the Central Committee of his party urging the necessity of an armed take-over of power without waiting for the Congress. Several Bolshevik leaders, most notably Zinoviev and

Kamenev, were shocked at this suggestion: the Bolsheviks would risk a repetition of their July disaster. It was folly to risk everything on an armed coup when their party had an excellent chance of securing a majority in the Congress of Soviets and thus of legally obtaining a share of power. Such sentiments make us realize how far the Bolsheviks were as yet from the disciplined, militant body they would become in a few months and how slow in dying were their last democratic scruples. By the same token, Lenin's frantic insistence on an act of force reflected his conviction not only that this was the moment to seize power, but also that such an act was a psychological necessity if his wing of the Russian Social Democracy was to be reborn as the Communist Party, an organization devoted to world revolution, one that would leave behind the last vestiges of "bourgeois legality" and democratic scruples.

The conflict might well have split the party except for Trotsky's tactical genius. Embracing Lenin's idea about the necessity of an armed uprising, he still had the perception that its chances of success would be immeasurably strengthened if it was undertaken in conjunction with the meeting of the Second Congress of Soviets. The Congress' pro-Bolshevik majority would cast a cloak, if not of legality, then of ideological justification over the armed coup. Many non-Bolshevik socialists, while opposed to violence, would still hesitate to support the bourgeois government against the party that expressed the will of the majority of the proletariat. The same insight led Trotsky to entrust the actual planning of the insurrection to the Military Revolutionary Committee of the Petrograd Soviet, with himself its actual leader. The uprising would not thus carry a purely Bolshevik label.

October, 1917

The final decision to attack was taken at a meeting of twelve members of the Bolshevik Central Committee which took place on the night of October 10. Even at this late date it required all of Lenin's force and persuasiveness to prevail over his lieutenants' fears and hesitations. (He had returned to Petrograd on the third of October but would not emerge from hiding until the twenty-fourth.) Two of them, Zinoviev and Kamenev, remained opposed to the uprising and, when outvoted, leaked the news of the Bolsheviks' intention to the press. But nothing now could stir the Provisional Government from its coma and the leaders of the Mensheviks and the SR's from their indecision. On October 23, the government brought itself to some feeble countermeasures: it ordered the closing down of the Bolshevik newspapers. But this dying gasp brought only fresh protests from the non-Bolshevik left. The surrogate parliament improvised by Kerensky some time before, the Council of the Republic, passed on October 24 a motion condemning both the Bolsheviks and Kerensky and asserting that any coup d'etat, though impermissible, would still be the result of the government's reactionary policies. And with this resolution Russian democracy passed into history.

October 25, though one of the great dates of history, does not mark the real beginning of the Soviet *state*. What transpired on this day was the seizure of the city of Petrograd by forces under the command of the Military Revolutionary Committee. The hollow shell of political authority which the Provisional Government had become collapsed with barely a whimper. Kerensky fled. The Winter Palace where the remaining ministers huddled was occupied by the Red Guards with hardly any casualties. And, as Trotsky had anticipated, the All-Russian Congress of Soviets, 390 of its 650 members Bolsheviks, threw its support behind the revolutionary deed, thus paralyzing the will of the anti-Bolshevik left. But the sum total of the day's events spelled out the collapse of one regime without a definite birth of another. Only in February–March of 1918, when the new rulers demonstrated their ability to conclude peace and to take their country out of the war, did they give a convincing proof that theirs would not be just an ephemeral reign.

October 25 was, however, a decisive step in the transformation of the Bolsheviks into a new type of party, one that, against all the previous assumptions of Marxist ideologists, whether Russian or foreign, would assume exclusive authority over its country, extirpate all, even socialist, opposition, and in the process itself lose all the vestiges of democracy within its own structure. Against doubters and skeptics among their own followers, Lenin and Trotsky demonstrated that the question of power could be solved through force rather than political coalitions and constitutional and ideological formulas. It was this lesson and its psychological consequences that give the day its greatest historical significance.

Having pushed out the ghost of the Provisional Government, the Bolsheviks set out about the infinitely more difficult task of securing power. Their strength among workers and soldiers was to secure them the main urban centers, though in many, as in Moscow, there was, in contrast to the almost bloodless take-over of Petrograd, some really hard fighting. But armed force was less important in the Bolsheviks' ability to preserve and expand their power than their skill in propaganda and revolutionary tactics.

On October 26, Lenin read two "decrees" to the Congress of Soviets. One was the declaration of peace: a grandiloquent plea to all warring

A column of soldiers demonstrating under the slogan, "Communism," during the October Revolution, Moscow, 1917.

peoples and governments to enter into immediate negotiations for a peace without annexation and indemnities. But into this rhetoric the Bolsheviks injected a practical and, to a country fed up with war, appealing note: they were "willing to consider any other conditions of peace, insisting only that these be presented as quickly as possible by one of the fighting countries." Unlike their predecessors, they were ready to do something to secure immediately *any* peace, and this would bring them enhanced support among millions of soldiers.

And, in the same vein, the Decree on Land: Private ownership of land was abolished, but the working peasants would retain free use of their holdings. (Thus not until the collectivization drive of the late twenties would the mass of peasants realize that *legally* their holdings had been nationalized.) With one stroke of the pen Lenin cut the

Gordian knot that had bedeviled his socialist opponents when they tried to cope with the peasants' hunger for land: state, church, and landlords' estates were to be seized and distributed by the village councils to poor peasants. The land decree flew in the face of Marxism, which proclaims the necessity and economic benefits of large-scale agricultural cultivation. Under the existing conditions, Lenin's drastic step was bound to deepen the chaos in the countryside and worsen the already desperate food situation. But the measure was an absolute necessity of the moment if the Bolsheviks were to hang on, for it assured them, if not of support, then of the benevolent neutrality of the peasant masses. It was, as a Bolshevik contemporary admitted, "a weapon of the revolution which had still to conquer the country."

The army would now dissolve completely as a fighting force, food shortages in cities would become endemic, but the Bolsheviks would gain a few weeks to establish their power.

The decrees were approved by the Congress of Soviets (from which the majority SR's and the Mensheviks stomped out, assured by the exultant Trotsky that they were politically bankrupt and marching straight "to the rubbish heap of history"), as was the composition of the new government. The bourgeois nomenclature of ministers was eschewed, again at the inventive Trotsky's suggestion, in favor of commissars. Lenin, of course, became the chairman of the Council of Commissars; a few of its members would make subsequent history: Trotsky, commissar of foreign affairs; Alexei Rykov, of interior; Alexander Shlyapnikov, of labor; the list closing with the name of the man who would destroy the preceding as he would so many others, Joseph Dzhugashvili-Stalin, commissar of nationalities.

Like its predecessor, this was proclaimed a provisional government, for its mandate was to be reviewed by the Constituent Assembly representing all the people of Russia and not, like the Congress, just workers and soldiers. Under the circumstances, elections and the convocation of this assembly could not be avoided by the Bolsheviks, even in the face of the virtual certainty that they would find themselves in a minority with the peasants' party, the SR's, very likely to be the dominant body. But for all this bowing to the still strong democratic ethos of the Revolution, Lenin and most of his followers did not propose to be dislodged by any votes or assemblies.

To some of his followers, the idea of a one-party government, not to mention a one-party state, still appeared not only undemocratic but un-Marxian. If the doctrine could be stretched to permit the forcible eviction of a bourgeois government, then there was nothing in Marx nor, for that matter, in pre-1917 Lenin to warrant the exclusion of other socialist parties. Many SR's and Mensheviks had been compromised by their collaboration. But there were also, as the phrase went, "internationalist Mensheviks," such as Martov, whose views on policies, if not on tactics, did not differ much from Lenin's. And the Left Socialist Revolutionaries had fought at the Bolsheviks' side. The more moderate among the latter, Kamenev, Zinoviev, and Rykov, pleaded for a governmental coalition of all left-wing socialist forces. They urged practical as well as doctrinal reasons for their demands: how could a party of three hundred thousand members run single-handedly a country of 150 million? The powerful Railwaymen's Union threatened a strike unless Lenin heeded the plea for a coalition of all genuinely proletarian forces. But for Lenin this was a test of strength like the one that had preceded October. A revolutionary party and, even more, a revolutionary government could not afford the luxury of dissent, of endless discussions and compromises, which a coalition would inevitably portend. And, as on the previous occasion, his view prevailed: Zinoviev, Kamenev, and Rykov submitted to their leader—yet another important step toward an outright dictatorial concept of the party and the state. Having won on principle, Lenin knew now to compromise on details: some representatives of the Left Socialist Revolutionaries, a group then not posing a challenge to Bolshevik primacy, were coopted into the Council of Commissars.

Revolutionary Democracy

Yet the most basic problem concerned not so much the distribution of ministerial portfolios but how any political authority could be restored to the country which had not known political legitimacy since February, any effective government since at least June, and which now in the last weeks of 1917 was experiencing deepening social and political anarchy. The news of October increased the already strong centrifugal tendencies in non-Russian and borderland areas of the former empire. The Ukraine and Finland became virtually independent. National separatism was sweeping the Caucasus. Army officers were streaming south where they would seek the support of the Cossacks, the one segment of the population that retained sentimental links to Old Russia in mounting a rebellion against the Red usurpers. But even in the areas that acknowledged or acquiesced in the new regime the restoration of any effective authority appeared to be an impossible task. The notion of any centralized government, the habit of civil as well as military obedience, of adherence to the laws—they had all virtually vanished in the course of the last eight months. The machinery of the state was shattered: most civil servants would not serve the body that called itself the Council of Commissars. Industrial production was grinding to a complete halt, the workers in many cases evicting their managers as well as proprietors and workers' committees trying to run factories, usually with disastrous results. The Bolsheviks, it seemed in November and December, would not be overthrown; they would simply be swept aside by the rising tide of anarchy they themselves had done so much to thrust upon Russia.

That they were not to be would be due to a variety of factors, among which luck and mistakes and division among their opponents were to play a prominent part. But one must give the new rulers their due: the survival of the Bolshevik regime during those first crucial months has also to be explained by Lenin's political skill and the energy and resourcefulness of his followers. Revolutionary anarchy, he perceived, could not at first be conquered through a frontal attack. It would have been political suicide to order workers to return factories to the bosses, to try to reimpose military discipline upon what remained of the army, to deny in principle the right of self-determination for non-Russian nationalities, to demand that a local soviet obey unquestioningly an edict issued in Petrograd. He eschewed a direct identification of his regime with the Bolsheviks. His government, though Bolshevik in composition, was ruling Russia not on behalf of a party or a doctrine, but on behalf of the Revolution. Even in the present distress, the idea of the Revolution to most Russians who were not members of the pre-1917 privileged classes retained something of the magic incantation it had conveyed in February: the synonym for future freedom and social justice. And the Revolution's child, "soviet," had also acquired a meaning going far beyond its literal translation, council; it came to express the idea of grass-roots democracy, of political power emanating not from a distant government and bureaucrats, but from the people. And so the Bolsheviks' government became *soviet* power.

This successful appropriation of the symbolism of revolution and the language of democracy enabled the new rulers to present, most of the time convincingly, any opposition to their usurpation as being directed not against their party but against the Revolution, as a bid to restore not democratic freedoms but the pre-February order of things. Even an intellectual challenge to their authority would be denounced and punished (as it still is in the Soviet Union of today) as counter-revolutionary activity. Only at the end of the Civil War did the country and, for that matter, many Bolsheviks themselves come to realize that while defending the Revolution they had established a one-party dictatorship.

The main reason for the Bolsheviks' seizing and harnessing the Revolution lay in their sense of mission. The craving of power for power's sake was not as yet the dominant motivation. Whatever the disputes or personality clashes that divided their ranks, most of them genuinely felt they were the advance guard of the world revolution, and their personal ambitions were still submerged in that grandiose aim. If Russia with her sparse proletariat and numerically weak socialist movement shook off bourgeois power, could a revolution be far away in highly industrialized Germany? in France, which in 1917 had experienced a series of military mutinies? and in other war-weary countries? And for the sake of that wider revolution, the Bolsheviks had to cling to power, for the success of the socialist experiment in Russia was to arouse the working masses of Germany and other belligerent nations. This sense of mission goes far in explaining the ease with which the Bolsheviks suppressed their ideological scruples, made a bid for power in a country the Marxist canon proclaimed not ready for socialism, and then, when in power, departed from the orthodoxy on such issues as land, the use of terror against political opponents, etc. One could not bother with the fine print of the doctrine while pursuing its principal objective: the world revolution.

It was the problem of securing peace that was first to challenge, then to destroy this happy symbiosis of millennarian expectations born out of the doctrine with the harsh realities of preserving power. At first the Bolsheviks clung to their pre-October position: the Revolution and its effects on the working and soldier masses in the West would force all the belligerent governments to seek a "people's peace," with no annexations and indemnities. But within a few days after the Decree on Peace it became obvious that Russia's allies would not recognize her new government, still less heed this band of usurpers' plea for general peace negotiations. And nothing as yet indicated the imminence of a German or French October or even February. Hence the ineluctable first lesson in political realism: Revolutionary Russia would have to conclude a separate peace and that not with the German and Austrian workers but with the imperial governments of those enemy countries. It would mean for Russia a harsh and humiliating peace of the defeated.

The actual negotiations between the Soviet government and representatives of the Central Powers began in Brest Litovsk on December 9. They were to be concluded with an agreement, if such it can be called, on March 3, 1918.

The intervening three months marked a basic transformation of the Bolsheviks' attitudes on power and on the relationship between their obligations as the vanguard of the international revolutionary movement and their role as the rulers of Russia. It is that role which in March emerged as the dominant one in the Bolsheviks' behavior: their self-interest as the ruling group and that of their state now began to outweigh ideological and international obligations.

The first set of German demands required Russia to cede its Polish and Baltic provinces. (For all the formal participation of other Central Powers, it was the German high command which in fact called the shots in Brest Litovsk.) This demand was not, explained General Hofmann, who represented the High Command, in any conflict with his government's previous acquiescence in the Soviet "no annexation" postulate. On the contrary, the freeing of those areas was in accord with the Bolsheviks' oft expressed adherence to the principle of national self-determination. The prospect of pushing *their country's* frontiers to where they had been some hundred and fifty years before brought out the strong, if for the most part unconscious, *Russian* nationalism of the Bolsheviks. One member of their delegation wept. The first session of the negotiations adjourned inconclusively.

The second round, which opened in late December, saw Trotsky at the head of the Soviet delegation. It was hoped that his diplomatic and rhetorical gifts would enable the Soviets to prolong the parley indefinitely, for its immediate conclusion either in an unfavorable peace or through a renewal of war would spell ruin for the Bolshevik regime, which now, in addition to everything else, had to be apprehensive about the Constituent Assembly scheduled to meet on January 5. But though Trotsky managed to drag out the negotiations, German conditions, far from having softened, now escalated. To his previous demands Hofmann now added independence for the Ukraine. As with similar demands in respect to Russian Poland and the Baltic countries, this would mean, in effect, that the Ukraine would become a satellite of Germany. A delegation of Ukrainian nationalists was at Brest seconding the Germans' demands. After ten days of inconclusive deliberations, marked by Trotsky's brilliant though often irrelevant oratory, the conference again adjourned on January 5.

On the same day the Constituent Assembly met in its first and only session. The Soviets' task in dealing with this inconvenient apparition was facilitated by the fact that they did not have to encounter it after signing a shameful treaty or with the German armies on the march. As expected, the Assembly had an anti-Bolshevik majority, the regular SR's, still the most popular party in the countryside, having won more than half the seats. The Bolsheviks' showing was respectable: they carried most of the cities and larger towns, securing a bit less than one-fourth of the popular vote—more than that, if one adds their allies the Left SR's. A few weeks before, certainly as late as October, it would have been inconceivable for any party or government to have dared to dissolve by force the first democratically elected organ of the Russian people. But now it was even more inconceivable that Lenin's government would meekly lay down its powers for the disposal by the Assembly or, even in the absence of an outright challenge to its authority, tolerate the existence of a legislature it could not control. And so at four o'clock the following morning armed sailors compelled the remaining delegates to disperse, the Bolsheviks and Left SR's having walked out earlier. Apart from a noisy demonstration in the streets of Petrograd, no force appeared to support the majority of the elected representatives of the Russian people. Once again the non-Bolshevik left had demonstrated its impotence in coping with its ruthless rivals.

For the moment the supreme danger to the Soviet power was to lie in the rulers' own division and conflicts—not concerning the treatment dealt out to the Assembly: the Bolsheviks' democratic scruples had by now atrophied; but the question of war and peace could not be resolved by force or oratory. Lenin was convinced that the Germans' last proposals, disastrous as they were in their implications, must be accepted. But for the moment he was in a minority within his own group. It was pointed out that, once the news of this capitulation to German militarism spread, the Bolshevik regime was doomed. Even if it was not overthrown by a popular revolt, what remained of Soviet Russia would be at the enemy's mercy—like the Ukraine or Lithuania, very likely to become a German satellite. And why should the Germans tolerate for long a political system pledged by its ideology to seek the overthrow of their as of every other European government?

This reasoning by the opponents of capitulation to Germany could not be faulted for logic. But their conclusion—that Russia should go on fighting—met with Lenin's equally ineluctable logic: there was nothing and nobody to fight with. Those soldiers who miraculously had failed to desert would still refuse to fight, and there was no one to lead them. Officers who had tried to resist the Bolsheviks' take-over had either been murdered (the fate of the last commander-in-chief, General Dukhanin) or been forced to flee. The current commander of the army, in a manner of speaking, was the Bolshevik former ensign Krylenko, but the only orders he could issue with any hope of being obeyed pertained to demobilization. The opponents of peace refused to concede the brutal facts. Perhaps the regular army would not fight, but would not the masses respond to an appeal for the revolutionary war against the invader? Trotsky, while dubious about the possibility of the revolutionary war, advocated yet another position: "neither peace nor war"; without accepting German conditions, Russia would simply announce that she would not continue to fight. The German generals would not dare order their troops to continue war upon a peaceful and disarmed people. Stalin stated Lenin's position on such chimerical reasoning, though less diplomatically than Lenin himself would have: "The position of Comrade Trotsky represents no policy at all. . . . In October we talked about the sacred revolutionary war because we were promised that one word, peace, would bring a revolution in the West. But that has not come to pass."[5] At the January 8 meeting of the Bolshevik notables, Lenin's demand for immediate peace secured only fifteen votes as against sixteen for Trotsky's "neither peace nor war" and thirty-two for the proponents of the revolutionary war, led by one of the party's most popular leaders, Nikolai Bukharin.

Power brought out the diplomat in Lenin (prior to 1917 he was widely considered a fanatic incapable of political compromises). Now he agreed to let Trotsky go back to Brest to try out, if everything else failed, his fatuous formula. But in return he exacted a promise from his second-in-command that, should his policy fail, he would not oppose the conclusion of peace on any terms.

And so on January 17 the Brest parley resumed. But the Germans, especially their generals, were in no mood to procrastinate. They concluded a separate peace with Ukrainian nationalists, and their armies would occupy the Ukraine on behalf of the latter. On January 28 Trotsky loosed what he hoped was a bombshell: His government would not traffic in people and lands; it was ending the war without signing the peace. The novelty of the gesture did bring some confusion among the enemy representatives. But their confusion and the Bolsheviks' exultation that they had tricked the greedy imperialists did not last long; within five days, on February 16,[6] the Germans terminated the armistice and the next day began an offensive. As Lenin had foreseen, there was no resistance nor even an attempt at organized retreat: whole Russian regiments would surrender to a handful of enemy soldiers. On February 18, Lenin prevailed on the Bolshevik Central Committee to authorize an appeal for peace. But now it seemed questionable whether the enemy would even bother to answer, or merely continue its virtually unopposed march to the gates of Petrograd. The danger brought out yet another proof of Lenin's pragmatism: If the Germans did not desist, he was ready to seek help from France and Britain. The proponents of the revolutionary war were shocked at this readiness to seek assistance from the imperialists. Lenin was unperturbed: "Please add my vote to those who are in favor of receiving food and weapons from the Anglo-French imperialist robbers."

But the Germans relented. On March 1, the Soviet delegates, led by Sokolnikov (no leading Bolshevik was willing to go on the shameful errand—Trotsky resigned as foreign commissar though he agreed to keep his resignation secret for the moment), returned to Brest. The

[5] See the author's *The Bolsheviks*, New York, 1965, p. 393.

[6] On February 1 Western style—the Russian calendar jumped thirteen days to conform with Western usage.

A battlefield, 1915. World War I took a heavy toll of Russian lives.

treaty, which was signed two days later, on the face of it sanctioned what constituted an irretrievable disaster for the Bolshevik regime and the undoing of three centuries of Russian expansion. The treaty stripped Russia of one-third of her population: the Ukraine, Finland, the Baltic and Polish provinces were wrested away. Territorial concessions were also made to Turkey (in the Caucasus). Soon Bessarabia would be seized by Rumania. Russia pledged to pay Germany a considerable indemnity, part of it in gold. In the course of the next few months the German high command was to give every indication that it considered the treaty of Brest as just the first step in the parceling out of the old empire and in the subjugation of Russia proper, and such undoubtedly would have been the future course of events had not Imperial Germany, and with it the provisions of the Russo-German treaty, collapsed in November 1918.

The treaty had been signed, but it still had to be ratified. On March 6 assembled the Seventh Congress of the Bolshevik Party. The proponents of the revolutionary war, now dubbed Left Communists, were far from giving up their struggle. The majority of the rank and file of the party was opposed to ratification. Rumors were rife, and evidently there was some substance to them, that the Left Communists and the Left SR's contemplated a coup against Lenin and the pro-treaty faction of the government. But Lenin's speech at the Congress, probably the best and most decisive of his career, sobered up many delegates. The country was in no condition to carry out any war, any resistance. He would have been ready, he said, to sign a peace even worse than the one before them. The remedy could come only with time. "Learn to be disciplined . . . otherwise you will continue to be under the German heel . . . until the nation learns to fight, until it can create an army which will not run away but which will be capable of enduring the most extreme hardships." Of course, he continued, they would not feel obliged to adhere to the treaty provisions that forbade revolutionary propaganda among the German soldiers. Despite his readiness to sacrifice vast provinces and population, Lenin's speech exuded strong if not fully articulated nationalism: come what may, the Soviet state, the *Russian* state, must be preserved and strengthened if the shameful capitulation was to be undone in the future. And so in a sense March 6 marks the prelude to the policy that under Stalin became known as socialism in one country.

The momentous if still hidden significance of the occasion was underlined by the party's changing its name. The Bolshevik faction of the Russian Socialist Democratic Party became the Russian Communist Party (b), the "b" standing for "of bolsheviks," as had been Lenin's wish ever since 1914. And so we shall speak of "the Party," for the body having seized power, it now more than just dominated the Russian state, it came in a sense to absorb it.

Insofar as there were constitutional proprieties in Soviet Russia, they were satisfied by the Congress of Soviets' ratifying the treaty of Brest Litovsk by the vote of 784 to 261. The Left SR's and the handful of other socialists still in the Soviets voted against; the former also left the government, which from then on would be comprised exclusively of the Party. With the signing of the treaty taking Russia out of the war, the anarchic phase of the Revolution came to an end. From the most anarchic of all revolutions there now emerged the most authoritarian state modern history has known.

2.
War Communism and Civil War

The fact that the building of the Soviet state took place under conditions of civil war was to leave an indelible imprint on the character of the state and on the nature of Soviet politics to this very day. We have seen how the process of seizing and then preserving power led to the gradual attrition of democratic principles and scruples among the Bolsheviks. Now during three years of struggle against domestic and foreign enemies this process not only continued but intensified and extended beyond politics to practically every sphere of social life. The mentality of the state of siege, the feeling of "who is not with us is against us," became part of the psychology of communism. Terror, from being an instrument of the class war and then of preserving the victorious revolution, would grow into an administrative routine. Repression of all, even intellectual, dissent—a usual feature of most civil wars—would continue and become intensified when peace finally came to the land. It was not Marxian formulas or bargaining but force that had to be employed in dealing with the most pressing economic and social problems. And, having acquired the habit, the Communists would not lose it when the fires of the fratricidal conflict receded.

Even the first Soviet constitution, adopted in 1918, marked the encroachment of the realities of power and of the struggle to preserve it upon those principles in the name of which the Communists had sought power. The constitution "guaranteed" the usual democratic freedoms, but even on paper they were reserved for the "toiling masses." Members of the former exploiting classes, a wide category covering businessmen, clergy, officials of the tsarist government, etc., were barred from voting and holding public office. In the election to the supreme legislature, the All-Russian Congress of Soviets, the workers' vote was weighted, as against that of the peasants, in the proportion of five to one. The idea of "soviet power," with its implication of grass-roots democracy and local autonomy, still remained the regime's most effective propaganda slogan, but even the letter of the constitution called for a highly centralized state. The unwieldy pyramidal structure of soviets, culminating in the huge Congress which would meet at long intervals, guaranteed that all effective authority would remain in the hands of the executive, the Council of Commissars—officially appointed by the Presidium of the Central Executive Committee of the Congress; in fact, designated by the Party's Central Committee. Thus, from the beginning, though not to the extent it was to assume later, the Soviet constitutional structure was to bear a decorative character, the real locus of power being the Communist Party.

As in the dispute about the peace treaty, the latter was still far from being a monolithic body ruled unconditionally by one man or even a single faction. Although Lenin's authority was clearly dominant, on occasion he had to plead or negotiate the solving of intra-Party disputes. But already, during the Civil War and perhaps because of it, the Party was going through some of the same process it was imposing upon the country: increasing centralization of authority and its growing, all-encompassing character. Though Party congresses elected by the mass of the membership met every year during Lenin's life, actual policies and decisions increasingly came to be shaped by an oligarchy—the Central Committee. And with the numerical growth of the latter, another organ, theoretically its subcommittee, in effect arrogated to itself the Central Committee's powers and became the collective leader: the Politburo, first elected in 1919, Lenin, Trotsky, and Stalin among its original full members.

"We shall now proceed to the building of socialism," declared Lenin on the Bolsheviks' accession to power. But no more than any other Marxist could he then believe that Russia was ready for socialism. Unlike their fellow Marxists, the Mensheviks, the Bolsheviks did believe that one could give history a push. Profiting from the war situation, socialists should take over power and then create the conditions needed for the transition to socialism: an advanced level of industrial output; large-scale units of production, including those in agriculture; a powerful, class-conscious, and *disciplined* industrial working class. But as we have seen, the imperative necessity of preserving power made the Bolsheviks enact or tolerate policies and tendencies that clashed head on with the ideologically prescribed conditions for an orderly march toward socialism. Industrial production fell as the workers' committees took over factories, often chasing out the managers. The Decree on Land enhanced the tendency to small-scale agricultural holdings. One need not discuss to what extent the Russian industrial worker of 1917–18 could be described as disciplined, able, and willing to do everything in order to increase industrial production, the main prerequisite for laying down the material conditions for socialism.

It would have been impossible for the Bolsheviks to declare upon coming to power that the very slogans and policies they had advocated before were no longer relevant, that in many cases a hundred-eighty-degree turn had to be made if the country was to emerge from social and economic anarchy, let alone begin its journey toward socialism. Again the precarious condition of the Communist regime between 1918 and 1921 meant that it had to pursue a circuitous rather than a direct path out of the chaos to avoid a clash with the very forces that had enabled the Bolsheviks to come to power. The workers would not return the factories to the bosses, and so the government, though the Marxian canon would not authorize such a measure at Russia's current stage of development, felt constrained to nationalize all industry without compensation. The workers' feelings having been appeased, it was hoped that they would tolerate control of production by the state with the former proprietor or manager, now renamed "bourgeois specialist," remaining in charge of the technical side of the factory or business.

The argument that the foodstuffs large estates produced were essential to save the country's cities from famine could not restrain the peasants from helping themselves to the large estates as authorized by the Decree on Land. The government sought a solution through force: peasant households were required to turn over their surplus foods to the state so it could feed the Red Army and city workers. With rampaging inflation which brought the economy back to the barter stage, the only way of enforcing the law was through armed requisitions and fanning the class struggle in the villages. Armed detachments would descend upon the countryside to seize from the peasants all the food above their families' needs. Poor peasants were encouraged and rewarded for denouncing their richer neighbors, real and alleged hoarders. To prevent a united front of the peasantry against communism, the regime sanctioned the formation of "committees of poor peasants" to assume the responsibility for repression in the countryside.

If we add to the preceding the official ban on private trade and a system of rationing for distribution of whatever goods still remained, we begin to get the picture of what became known as war communism

—Russia's economic system in the years 1918–21. The term is somewhat misleading, for war communism was far from being a conscious effort to bring full national ownership of the means of production, economic equality, and other features of an advanced socialist society; it was equality brought about by the utter economic chaos, and government control exercised not through orderly planning but through the sporadic resort to violence and the deliberate instigation of the class war.

It might well be asked how a regime confronted by such disastrous economic conditions not only did not collapse but managed to prevail over a multiplicity of domestic and foreign enemies. A major part of the answer must be found in the new spirit of realism and resolution born out of the travails of Brest Litovsk. The Communists sought to implement Lenin's command, "Learn to be disciplined, to introduce severe discipline . . . create an army which will not run away but which will be capable of enduring the most extreme hardships." With anarchy and lawlessness still rife in society at large, those goals would not be fully realized, whether in the case of the Red Army or the Communist Party itself. Desertion would be widespread among the Red troops (so widespread that recaptured deserters were allowed to reenlist; only the second attempt to defect was punished by death). Severe political and personal conflicts would afflict the Communist ranks throughout the Civil War. But as the war progressed, the Communist movement gained in discipline and cohesion while its enemies foundered amidst indecision and disunity—a replay on a different stage of the drama of 1917. Lenin's by now unchallenged supreme authority, his clear domination of the whole politico-military apparatus, Trotsky's inventiveness and organizational talent, the audacity and ruthlessness of other Communist leaders, the still-strong revolutionary zeal among the rank-and-file Communists—these were the elements that in combination with their enemies' mistakes brought about not only the regime's survival but also its inheritance of most of the multinational empire that once had been under the sway of the tsars.

The creation of the Red Army had begun in February–March 1918. Even before the signing of the treaty of Brest, the Communists realized that their old postulate, a people's militia instead of a professional armed force, was a dream, and a dangerous one at that. Even those military units that helped the Bolsheviks seize power in October—the Red Guards, the sailors—were but armed rabble, almost as ready to turn against the new masters if they tried to introduce military discipline as they had been to chase out the Provisional Government. The new army had to be built from the ground up. The voluntary principle was soon abandoned, and soldiers would be drawn through conscription among the workers and poorer peasants. The initial Soviet concept of command demanded professionally trained leadership at the top, a transparent device against a would-be Russian Bonaparte. But the post-Brest spirit urged the imperative necessity of a single direction of military affairs. And so in March, the man whose name is (though not in the current Soviet literature) indelibly associated with the creation and first triumphs of the Red Army, Trotsky, was appointed the commissar of war.

The great revolutionary orator soon showed himself to be a brilliant administrator and a ruthless disciplinarian. Professionalism rather than revolutionary rhetoric would be his guiding principle in building the Soviet military edifice. Officers would not be elected by their men, as had become the custom in the past October days, but appointed from above. And since the Revolution could not leisurely train its own officer corps, Trotsky resorted to the employment of former tsarist

Soviet Defense Minister Leon Trotsky crossing Red Square to inspect troops during war games, 1921.

officers. A few of the latter were brought over to the Communist side by genuine ideological conversion (such as the former tsarist lieutenant and future Soviet marshal Mikhail Tukhachevsky), more by the hope that in leading Soviet troops they could still serve Russia's national interest, and some, finally, for purely professional reasons. To secure this alien element's loyalty, the Communists took over and developed the already existing system of political commissars: every military unit in addition to its regular commander had a Party representative who would have to countersign the officer's order as well as to watch over the political education of the men. But while taking those steps to keep the officers in line (their families, they were also made to understand, were hostages for their good behavior), Trotsky showed himself an uncompromising defender of their authority against the more unruly of the Communists, who resented and fought the employment of the hostile class elements. When in August 1918 the Red Army faltered in one of the first major engagements of the Civil War, at Svyazhsk, Trotsky decided that the fault lay with the political apparatus: the local military commissar and twenty-six other Party workers were ordered shot for insubordination. The battle was turned around. The imperious War Commissar ordered that in cases of mass desertion or disobedience to orders, it would be the commissar who would be shot first. Trotsky's insistence on discipline and efficiency often made him clash with other Communist potentates. In the fall of 1918 he demanded and finally procured the recall of Stalin from Tsaritsyn, where the future dictator had dealt barbarously with military officers and disobeyed the orders of the front commander. Trotsky's uncompromising methods, his assistants' skill in conjuring up munitions and other supplies for the troops, the combination of professional competence at the command level with the still strong revolutionary enthusiasm—they all bore their fruit: within a year of its creation the Red Army was, at least for the purposes of a civil war, a formidable fighting machine. But the memory of the War Commissar's highhanded ways, of his readiness to sanction the shootings of Communists, was to weigh heavily on Trotsky's subsequent political career. At the Eighth Party Congress (March 1919) a group of delegates, the so-called military opposition, demanded the curtailment of the function and prerogatives of the former tsarist officers. But Lenin's authority was, as in most such encounters, thrown behind the War Commissar, and the military opposition, despite the wide support it enjoyed among the rank-and-file Communists, was defeated. As he himself was to write: "I elbowed away those who interfered with military success or in the haste of the work trod on the toes of the unheeding and was too busy even to apologize." Some fifty thousand former officers served with the Red Army during those decisive years, and that they contributed decisively to the victory in the Civil War is one thing on which both the Communist and anti-Communist sources are agreed.

Most Soviet historians have no compunction in asserting that next to its political leadership (i.e., Lenin) and the Red Army, the Revolution—the Communist regime—owed its survival most to revolutionary terror. But as with the army, so with terror: most of its post-October manifestations were potentially as dangerous to the regime as to the class enemy. Mobs of armed sailors and soldiers roamed the streets; occasionally they would break into prisons and even hospitals to lynch political prisoners, looting and robbing anybody who could even vaguely qualify as a former "exploiter" and in some cases turning their rifles against those Soviet officials who attempted to restrain them. Before the Revolution the average Bolshevik would have rejected as unworthy slander the notion that socialist Russia would build a centralized political police which would dwarf in its size and functions the infamous tsarist Okhrana. But just as the realities of power dealt a death blow to the idea of a volunteer army, so what might be called amateur terror had to give way to the state-organized security apparatus which in a systematic, "professional" way would suppress counterrevolution—and, soon, any and every form of dissent. This was the idea behind the organization on December 7, 1917, of the notorious Cheka (from the Russian initials of the Extraordinary Commission to Combat Counterrevolution and Sabotage), the lineal ancestor—down to the present KGB—of the successive organs of political police in Soviet Russia. To be sure, the new institution's projected and actual sphere of work went beyond political repression. It also dealt with speculation and hoarding of vital goods, hooliganism, and banditry, as well as with corruption and abuse of authority among the Communists themselves. "Dealt with" in those early years could most often be taken as a euphemism for the shooting, sometimes even without the formality of a brief trial by a revolutionary tribunal, of the accused and those apprehended on suspicion. As the Soviet authorities proceeded to draft a regular civil and criminal code, there was no thought among the Communists, certainly not in Lenin's mind, that regular legal procedures would enable the regime to dispense with arbitrary repression in the foreseeable future. The Communists felt themselves to be a garrison amidst the largely hostile population. Terror was not only to be the means of destroying the declared foe, it was also to serve to intimidate *potential* enemies of the regime, to purge the Communists' own ranks of criminals and careerists. And so, from a weapon of the class war, terror was to become a regular administrative technique designed to root out corruption and inefficiency as well as opposition. It would be hypocrisy for them to pretend, wrote Lenin to his commissar of justice, that the new criminal code would obviate the need for terror. And on occasion Lenin would approve even the "old-fashioned" type of terror. When the Communist boss of Petrograd, Zinoviev, tried to curb lynchings and lootings directed against the former middle class, Lenin wired him: "I protest that we should be meddling with the completely correct revolutionary initiative of the masses."

The first head of the Cheka was Felix Dzerzhinsky, a man subsequently elevated to the stature of a Communist saint, a "knight without fear or blemish," as almost every Soviet biographer of him feels constrained to repeat; Dzerzhinsky died in 1926, thus avoiding a close association with the atrocities of Stalinism. But while utterly incorruptible and above the use of his dread office for personal preferment, Dzerzhinsky was still a fanatic who without any compunction presided over summary shootings of thousands of people. It was he as much as Lenin who was instrumental in developing a veritable mystique of terror: the ultimate goal of communism is the abolition of all forms of coercion, indeed of the state itself, but as long as the state, and with it class conflicts, exists, terror must remain as an indispensable weapon of the class war.

"Power comes out of the mouth of the gun," the leader of another Communist revolution was to write. Well, the history of the Russian Civil War offers only a partial justification of this maxim: power was retained by the Bolsheviks because of their superior political skill. But their re-creation of the instruments of coercion—the professional army and the security police—made it certain that the political future of Russia would be resolved through an armed conflict; unlike Kerensky's, Lenin's regime would not fight its enemies with just slogans and proclamations.

Before tackling its outright enemies, the Revolution had to be purged of its own unruly and anti-Communist elements. During the October coup the Bolsheviks profited by the assistance not only of the Left Social Revolutionaries but also of the anarchists. The latter represented a conglomeration of people ranging from criminal elements to believers in philosophical anarchism, rather than a political party in the true sense of the word. In any case, the anarchists' basic opposition to an organized form of authority made their coexistence with the Communists unthinkable. In April 1918 lightning Cheka raids destroyed the anarchists' centers in Moscow (which as of March 10 had replaced Petrograd as the capital). The stage was set for a confrontation with the Bolsheviks' most dangerous internal enemies, the Left SR's.

The latter, though still represented in the Soviets and participating in some government agencies, including, surprisingly, the Cheka, could hardly be described as the loyal opposition. They strenuously attacked all policies—such as the reintroduction of the death penalty and the employment of "bourgeois elements" in the army and industry—looking toward the strengthening of the state and never ceased their agitation against the peace with Germany. And a party with a long terrorist tradition of its own could not be expected to remain content with verbal protests and agitation.

The Left SR's staged their coup in July. It is unclear how far its various threads had been planned beforehand by the Central Committee of their party and how much, if any, advance knowledge the Communist government had of their erstwhile-allies-turned enemies' plans. The opening of the Fifth Congress of the Soviets witnessed a violent attack on Lenin by the Socialist Revolutionary members of that body. Two days later two conspirators contrived to gain entrance to the German Embassy and assassinated Ambassador Count Mirbach. Simultaneously with the murder, the Left SR members of the Cheka staged a revolt and imprisoned their Communist bosses. Other SR-sponsored revolts broke out simultaneously in provincial cities, and a Red Army commander with ties to the rebels, Muraviev, tried to subvert his troops.

But the rebellion proved abortive. The Left SR's, skilled in individual terrorism, lacked the ability for the kind of concerted politico-military planning that had brought about October. Their main expectation had been that Germany, provoked by the murder of the ambassador, would react with military measures and that the fires of the revolutionary war would consume the Communist regime. But the Germans, then in the last throes of the war on the western front, were in no position to mount an offensive in the east. The Moscow revolt was suppressed the very same day; the mutinous Cheka members were executed. Elsewhere the Bolsheviks' hold also proved too strong; local insurrections were put down in a matter of days. Muraviev, failing to carry his troops with him, ended a suicide. There now ensued a wave of terror: executions, taking of hostages, etc., directed not only against the actual rebels and other Left SR's but also against former middle-class and peasant elements entirely unconnected with the attempted coup. The Left SR's, a party in many respects to the left of the Communists, were proclaimed by the government as having acted in the interests of monarchists and international capital.

The abortive revolt marks yet another milestone in Soviet history. Of course, individual terrorist acts and local insurrections by left-wing elements did not cease after that date.[1] But the July events offered convincing proof of the Communists' now tenacious hold on

[1] On August 30, Fanny Kaplan would shoot and seriously wound Lenin, while on the same day another Communist dignitary was killed in Petrograd—his assassin, like Kaplan, a person with a revolutionary past. The government answered these two acts of individual terror with mass terror on a scale used in suppressing the July outbreaks. In Moscow alone about six hundred people were executed by the Cheka, even though Kaplan's deed was never proved to involve any party or organization.

power; they could not be overthrown by the means they themselves had employed in October—a revolutionary coup. The Soviet state was and would remain a Communist one, until and unless it was defeated and conquered by a superior military force.

Yet in the summer of 1918 no Communist would have denied the possibility if not the probability that such a force would come into being. Indeed, by the end of the summer *eighteen* governments or movements existed over the vast space of Russia challenging the Communist one in Moscow. (This is not counting five "independent" governments under German occupation—e.g., in the Ukraine—nor the ones more genuinely independent like those in Georgia and Finland.) The approaching German defeat in the war promised not so much a relief for the Bolsheviks as a new and overwhelming danger. The victorious Western powers would be able to deal at their leisure with the regime that had stabbed them in the back by concluding a separate peace, had canceled Russian international debts and nationalized foreign property (measures especially resented by France, the main prewar lender to tsarist Russia), and beyond that had proclaimed itself the vanguard of the international revolutionary movement.

The Allies Intervene

The Allies' intervention began in the spring of 1918, with the British landing in the northern ports of Murmansk and Archangel, and the Japanese in the Far East in Vladivostok. The United States, the most reluctant interventionist power, was to follow suit as well as France. The initial rationale of intervention was a military rather than political one: Allied troops were needed on Russian soil to prevent military supplies in these ports from being surrendered to Germany. But inevitably the British and French were drawn to provide encouragement and then outright material and military support to anti-Communist movements. Japan, Russia's long-time rival in the Far East, had obvious expansionist aims concerning Siberia. And with the disintegration of what had been the Russian Empire, it was natural and not too unreasonable for the Communists to believe that the British, once their hands were free, would proceed to establish a sphere of influence in Transcaucasia and Central Asia.

But even within the interior of Russia a foreign army helped set off the flares of the Civil War. The old Russian army had had a Czechoslovak corps, the liberation of fellow Slavs having been one of the professed tsarist war aims. After the Revolution the Bolsheviks agreed that this corps, some forty thousand strong, should be evacuated through Vladivostok to the western front, there to join the Anglo-

French armies. In the spring this force was thus in the process of transit on the Trans-Siberian railway. A series of incidents (and perhaps German demands) led the Communist regime to order forcible disarmament of the Czechoslovak camp. This incautious decision led to the Czechs' uprising: they seized the railway and extended armed support to anti-Communist movements, eventually leading to the establishment of anti-Soviet regimes at Omsk in Siberia and in Samara in the Volga region. Needless to say, the Czechs' actions were approved by the Western powers.

What was to become the most dangerous front of the Civil War had opened in the south the preceding winter. There some former tsarist generals assembled a sizable number of members of the old officer corps and, profiting by the proximity of the now independent Don and Kuban Cossacks' areas, organized the so-called Volunteer Army. This army became the nucleus of the strongest anti-Communist military force and the basis of a regime with the professed aim of liberating all of Russia from the Communist yoke. After the death in action of its first head, General Kornilov, who had fled south after the Bolshevik coup, the army and the South Russian regime were headed by General Anton Denikin.

To an outsider the position of the Soviet regime on the first anniversary of October (now, under the newly adopted calendar, November 7) must have appeared well nigh hopeless. The collapse of Germany on November 11 lifted the threat, so real earlier in the year, that Soviet Russia might be overthrown by or become a satellite of the Kaiser's Reich. But the number of enemies of the Soviet power and of the resources at their disposal appeared to grow daily. The White armies (the generic name of the anti-Red forces, in itself something of a psychological handicap: white had been the color of the dress tunic of officers of the imperial army—this seemed then to strengthen the insinuation of Soviet propaganda that a victory by the Whites would mean the return of tsarism and the landlords) in the south, north, and east were threatening the central Russian heartland of Soviet power. Poland, now independent, would soon make a bid for the Ukrainian and Byelorussian lands that had belonged to the Polish state before its partition in the eighteenth century. Northern Caucasus and Transcaucasia were ruled by independent nationalist regimes and appeared irreparably lost not only to Communism but also to Russia. Eastern Siberia seemed destined to come under Japanese rule. Mention has already been made of the desperate economic situation of the territories under the Soviets' authority which still remained their enemies and which, though afflicted by food shortages, economic collapse, and epidemics, could still look confidently for help from the victorious Allies.

And yet, as Lenin was to say, looking back on this period, "Weak, torn apart, downtrodden Russia . . . turned out victorious" against "the rich mighty countries which rule the world." And he provided the main reason why: ". . . because among those powers was not a shadow of unity because all of them worked at cross purposes." This explanation applies to the failure not only of foreign intervention but also of the internal White foe—the opponents of communism lacked unity and a common sense of purpose.

The foreign powers' anti-Communist policies were beset by basic contradictions: Japan and the newborn states, especially Poland and Finland, viewed a Communist Russia as a lesser evil, less threatening to their vital interests, than a conservative Russia, which could claim all the territories that had been the tsars' before 1914. France wanted the rebirth of a strong (White) Russia to offset any future German threat. Some British politicians eyed longingly the riches of the Caucasus. Others, like Mr. Churchill, foresaw the mortal danger that victorious communism would pose to the British Empire. But the now influential Labour Party would oppose any intervention in Russia's internal struggle. The United States watched suspiciously Japan's designs in Siberia; in fact, American military detachments were sent there mainly to keep an eye on Tokyo's activities in the area. To decide the issue, foreign intervention would have had to be massive in terms of soldiers. But after four years of the (till then) bloodiest of all wars and in the face of the serious social ferment in their own countries, how could the democratic governments of France and Britain dispatch large armies to fight in a distant land and for a cause that was alien and confusing to their own people? There had been warning signs—e.g., a mutiny on board French naval vessels sent to the Black Sea. And small-scale, piecemeal military help to the Whites was, in terms of popular reaction, probably more harmful to their cause than to the Reds'.

Whatever rivalries and dissensions existed in the Communist camp paled in comparison with those on the White side. The White generals did not trust each other; their politicians were a motley crowd of Socialist Revolutionaries, liberals, and monarchists, unable to agree on a political program that would gain them popular support. There were constant coups and government changes within the White regimes. Thus the Siberian government was at first a coalition between the right SR's and moderates, but almost immediately dissensions within it led to its overthrow and the establishment of a dictatorship by Admiral Kolchak, who adopted the title the Supreme Ruler. In little more than a year the Supreme Ruler (his armies having been driven back to Siberia), was in turn overthrown, to end up before a Red firing squad. The anti-Communist parties active in the White areas had learned nothing from their 1917 experience; to them, and this was especially true of SR's, doctrinal and policy issues still loomed more important than the task of defeating communism. And the bulk of the White officers viewed moderate and left-of-center politicians not so much as their allies in a common cause but as the very people who through their undermining of the monarchy and ineptitude had brought about Russia's current and parlous condition. The military mind grasped but with difficulty the need for a political program that would appeal to the masses and thus offset the Communists' slogans and propaganda. Thus, though by the middle of the Civil War the peasants had lost most of their illusions concerning the Communists, they would not for the most part support the Whites, whose victory, it was feared, would bring back the landlords. And so, in addition to the Red and White armies' fighting over and devastating the unhappy land, there now appeared the so-called Green guerrilla forces, recruited mostly from among peasants, led sometimes by anarchists and sometimes by soldiers of fortune, but in each case looting and indulging in banditry as well as fighting the political authority in the given region, whether White or Red. The most notorious of the Green chieftains, Nestor Makhno, collaborated intermittently with the Communists, shooting out of hand captured White officers; occasionally he would clash with the Red forces, and then it would be captured political commissars who were executed. This in a sense epitomized the peasant's weird logic: he was still for Soviet power—it had given him more land; he was against the Communists who then came and took his grain and cattle. In the Ukraine the White or Green capture of towns and cities, whose populations were largely Jewish, was often followed by pogroms. Anti-Semitic feelings ran high among the Whites. They were fed both by the traditional anti-Jewish feeling among the city lumpen proletariat and the peasants and by the fact that a high percentage of the Communist elite was of Jewish origin. But so were many SR's and Menshevik leaders, and thus the Whites' depradations, vainly discouraged by their responsible leaders, made it all the more difficult for them to secure the support of the non-Communist left.

One of the most decisive advantages enjoyed by the Bolsheviks lay in their flexible and skillful nationality policy. Even so, by 1918 much luster had rubbed off the famous doctrine of "national self-determination"—the more perceptive could see that the Communists would not voluntarily surrender any non-Russian territory that had been part of the old empire. But there was still an enormous propaganda appeal in the Soviet declaration that every nationality within the Communist state should enjoy autonomous or, if it so wished, independent political and cultural existence.

In contrast, the White leaders, for all their ambivalent declarations on this issue, could hardly conceal their passionate attachment to "Russia great and undivided," which members of the minority nationalities took to mean that non-Communist Russia would seek its frontiers of 1914 and might pursue nationality policies not much different from those of the tsars. And so the new national states born out of the debris of the empire would not help the Whites at the decisive points of the Civil War when their intervention might have made all the difference. When General Yudenich's armies stood on the threshold of Petrograd in May and then again in the fall of 1919, Finland, with its frontier so close to Russia's second capital, offered them no assistance. Even more decisive and deliberate was Poland's inactivity during Denikin's summer offensive in 1919, the one military effort by the Whites that came closest to turning the tide of the war.

In fact, the entire fortune of Denikin's regime in South Russia, the most viable and at one time the most promising among the White forces, was fatally affected by its failure to be more resilient on the nationality issue. His government was in constant conflict, at times verging on warfare, with the Caucasian nations in the rear and the Ukrainian nationalists. Even his allies, the Don and Kuban Cossacks, resented his rigid Great Russian nationalism and the refusal to pledge that Russia, once freed from the Reds, would become a federation with a wide latitude of local self-government for groups like theirs. The Whites always declared that the political questions could be resolved only *after* the military issue had been decided and when the people of Russia could have their say through freely elected representatives. Constitutionally this was correct, but politically it was disastrous. People will not willingly fight and die for an uncertain goal. The Whites realized that the restoration of monarchy, utterly discredited between 1914 and 1917, could not be such a goal,[2] but they were enough men of the old Russia to abhor those principles of the Revolution that still retained their hold on the masses. The Bolsheviks, on the contrary, while laying down the foundations of an absolute state, fought and won in the name of the principles of February as well as of October.

Thus 1919—the year of decision: in the spring Kolchak crushingly defeated; in October Denikin's offensive grinding to a halt not far from Moscow; by the end of the year, on every front the Red Army in pursuit of the Whites. The saga of Kolchak and the Siberian anti-Communist forces ended tragically in February 1920 when the Supreme Ruler and his lieutenants, abandoned by the Czechoslovaks,

[2] Nicholas II, his family and personal attendants were executed by the Communist authorities in Ekaterinburg in the Urals on July 16, 1918. Even among conservatives there was no enthusiasm to enthrone a new Romanov.

were turned over to the Soviet authorities and executed. In the meantime the southern Whites, driven back, were forced to evacuate their army to the Crimea. From there their new commander, General Wrangel, probably the ablest, both militarily and politically, among the White generals, still managed to harass the Soviet forces in southern Russia. But with the end of the Polish war his situation became hopeless. By the end of 1920 the remnants of the White forces left Russian soil.

Militarily the reasons usually adduced for the Communists' victory stress their domination of the center of the country, with relatively short interior lines, while their enemies were on the outside, their main armies separated from each other, with great distances to march before they could come to grips with the Red forces. The Whites' offensives were not so much defeated as exhausted in long marches through partisan-infested territory, with long communication lines, lack of supplies, and epidemics (especially typhus) taking toll of their armies even before they could tackle the enemy. But the main key to the Communists' success was in politico-psychological rather than in purely military factors.

The Polish war concluded what in the Soviet annals is described as the heroic period of the Revolution. Hostilities between Poland and Soviet Russia flickered off and on from the rebirth of the Polish state in November 1918. But, for reasons spelled out above, the head of the Polish state and army, Joseph Pilsudski, would not launch a major attack so long as it appeared that the Whites had a chance of succeeding. Once there could be no fears on that count, in April 1920, the Polish armies struck.

Behind the Polish attack lay Pilsudski's broad geopolitical scheme of weakening the Russian state in perpetuity by detaching from it the Ukraine and Byelorussia. They, while independent, would enter into a close association with Poland as well as with some other succession states, such as Lithuania. Russia's domination of eastern Europe, her ever present threat to the central and southern parts of the continent, which had been the key to her position as a world power ever since Peter the Great's time, would thus come to an end.

Within two weeks the Polish army swept through the Ukraine, capturing Kiev on May 7. But then the same factors that had fatally affected the Whites' chances were to lead to the undoing of Poland's military and political enterprise. Pilsudski's armies stretched their communication and supply lines to the danger point. The population of the Ukraine failed to respond to the appeals of Poland's Ukrainian ally, Petliura. The Ukrainian peasants, while not enchanted with the Communists, were exhausted from the years of warfare that had rolled over their unhappy land, and they were fearful that Polish alliance would mean Polish domination and that the latter would bring back the landlords. (A sizable proportion of major landowners before the Revolution was Polish.) In June the Soviets began their counteroffensive. Soviet cavalry under the famed Civil War leader Semyon Budenny cut the thin and vulnerable communication lines of the Polish armies. The Polish campaign, like the Civil War, was a war of movement. With the armies on both sides poorly equipped, their soldiers hastily trained, a victory might turn into a rout at the first threat from the rear. And so Budenny's attack turned the whole campaign around: the Poles' retreat became as rapid as had been their advance.

With the Ukraine reconquered, the Red Army reached the line corresponding to the ethnic frontiers of Poland by the end of July. The dilemma confronted by the Communist leaders at this point reflected both their revolutionary hopes and their recent political experience. The Western powers proposed an armistice with the line between the two armies running roughly along the ethnic frontier—the famous Curzon line, first proposed as the border between the two countries in 1919 by the then British foreign secretary. For Lenin, however, the prospect of an advance upon Warsaw and of the conquest of Poland for communism appeared irresistible. Communism and the Red Army would then reach the frontiers of Germany, still in political and social turmoil, lend encouragement and perhaps more than that to the German Communists. Some other Soviet leaders had heeded the lesson of the Civil War: in order to foist a political system upon a country, one had to have considerable popular support. And it was unlikely that the Communist appeal to the Polish workers would overcome their traditionally anti-Russian and nationalist sentiments. Said Stalin, "The rear of the Polish armies is monolithic and nationally united . . . the dominant sentiment is the feeling for the Fatherland." Trotsky also expressed misgivings about the desirability of a further advance into Poland. But as on most occasions, Lenin's position prevailed. The Soviet conditions for an armistice were drafted so as to be unacceptable even to a state undergoing a military debacle. The Red Army advance continued while the provisional Polish Revolutionary Committee, including such Soviet notables of Polish origin as Dzerzhinsky and his Cheka deputy, Unschlicht, was set up to administer communism in the conquered country.

In some ways the 1920 events offer a preview of what would happen in 1944–45 when the victorious Soviet army *did* install a Communist regime in Poland. But there was one basic difference: The Soviet army at the end of World War II was a powerful military machine capable of subjugating areas bled by the German occupation; the Red Army of World War I vintage was still a hastily improvised and primitive force, formidable under the anachronistic conditions of the Russian Civil War, but hardly equal to the task of imposing a regime upon a hostile population. Inherent in Lenin's gamble was the conviction that Polish communism already represented a considerable force and that local uprisings by workers and poor peasants would facilitate the Red Army's task. Yet there was but feeble response to the ideological propaganda that accompanied the Red Army's foray into Poland. On the contrary, the Polish Peasant and Socialist parties joined in a government of national unity and called upon all classes to resist the invader. Even had the Red Army succeeded militarily, it is most doubtful that Soviet Russia was as yet strong enough to conquer and impose a Communist system on a nation of twenty-five million. And as to Lenin's ultimate goal—the sovietization of Germany—it was clearly beyond Russia's capacity, any attempt at it being bound to bring massive military intervention by France and Britain. That such ideas could even be entertained by realistic men with three years of experience with the hard facts of politics is convincing proof of how slow in dying were the millennarian hopes of October.

Buoyed by the apparent ease with which they were beating the Poles, the Soviet military commanders grew overhasty and imprudent. A dangerous gap opened between the two main Soviet armies, one commanded by Tukhachevsky and the southwestern group marching on the important city of Lvov. On August 11, the Soviet commander-in-chief Sergei Kamenev ordered Yegorov to detach Budenny's First Cavalry Army and to send it north to protect Tukhachevsky's left flank. But Kamenev, a former tsarist officer, was not in a position to enforce his orders upon Party bigwigs. Stalin, then the political commissar with Yegorov's group, refused to countersign the order for the transfer of Budenny's cavalry. And so, when the Poles counterattacked on August 16, their most damaging blow came on Tukhachevsky's left flank. The battle turned into a rout with the Red armies fleeing in disorder. An armistice came in October. The subsequent peace treaty between Poland and the Soviet republics (the Ukraine and Byelorussia were, on paper, independent Soviet republics and remained such until the formation of the USSR in 1922) established the Polish frontier considerably to the east of the Curzon line. Far from having become a Soviet republic, Poland would now contain a considerable Ukrainian and Byelorussian population, a fact of tremendous importance in European politics between 1921 and the end of World War II.

By 1921 the most improbable consequence of the Bolshevik Revolution had come to pass: the Soviet government had reconquered the vast majority of multinational territories that had constituted the Russian Empire. The last forcible reincorporation was that of Georgia. In 1920, during the first and unsuccessful phase of the Polish war,

Lenin's government recognized the independence of that socialist-ruled Caucasian republic. But in February 1921, its hands free, the Red Army invaded and occupied Georgia, which shared the fate of her Caucasian neighbors, Armenia and Azerbaijan, by becoming a Soviet republic. In the Far East, as long as the Japanese occupation and threat persisted, the Soviets thought it advisable to tolerate the existence of an independent Far Eastern republic. When the Japanese, largely under pressure from the United States, withdrew from the Siberian mainland, the Far Eastern republic acceded to Soviet Russia. The process of regathering the pieces of the old empire was completed in 1925 when Japanese troops evacuated northern Sakhalin.

And thus, territorially, the balance sheet of the Revolution and the Civil War showed losses only in the West, where the Baltic states and Poland became independent and Bessarabia remained within Rumania. In Transcaucasia, the Turkish republic retained the territories Russia had conquered from the Ottoman Empire in 1878 and which the infant Soviet state surrendered in Brest Litovsk. The Soviet empire, already united through the agency of the Russian Communist Party, its edicts as effective in Kiev and Tiflis as in Moscow, received formal unity through the creation in 1922 of the Union of Soviet Socialist Republics.

The laboratory for the Communist experiment was thus to be not a small country but a vast, multinational empire. And the ideas of communism, far from being discredited through the disintegration and partition of the state, on the contrary gained increased international resonance as the ruling creed of a country covering one-sixth of the earth's surface.

The other side of the Communists' prodigious achievement was that, by preserving most of the old Russian state's territory, they became heirs of the *Russian* national tradition. Ironically, it was this band of devotees of a supranational ideology, many of their leading figures non-Russian, that fulfilled the White generals' pledge of "Russia great and united." That the new Soviet state was essentially Russian could not be perceived clearly during the tumultuous years of the Revolution. The new rulers' legal enactments and rhetoric breathed internationalism and the condemnation of Russian chauvinism. And by their own lights most of the Communist leaders undoubtedly thought of themselves as the advance guard of world revolution rather than as rulers of a predominantly Russian state. But even at this most ideological and internationalist phase of its history, communism assumed some specifically Russian characteristics, even though its exponents might not have been fully aware of this latent transformation. Already there were occasions when an appeal to Soviet and even Russian patriotism became quite explicit. During the most crucial period of the Polish war the main strain of Communist propaganda was still ideological: the enemy's conquest of the borderlands would mean the return of landlords and other exploiters. But there was also an unmistakable note of undiluted nationalism: here was the traditional enemy of the Russian state trying once more to wrest away the lands that were Russia's by tradition and right. And as early as 1919, Lenin reprimanded a critic of his nationality policy: "Scratch a Russian Communist and you will find a Russian chauvinist." For the moment most of the leaders were unaware that there could be a conflict between their duties as international revolutionaries and as rulers of a state. They fought to save or conquer the Ukraine and Georgia for communism and not merely for the Soviet state. But those two roles could not always be so easily reconciled or synchronized.

The Communist Party and the Soviet State

Quite apart from the inherent conflict between nationalism and internationalism which the Communist system portended, there were even more basic questions about the future: Having developed from a conspiracy into the ruling party, would the Communists allow any element of popular control or rule? And the Party itself, whose hierarchical and armylike structure and spirit had in the past been excused by extraordinary circumstances—first its illegal existence, then the requirements of the struggle for power and survival—would it, now that victory was won, develop along democratic ways, or would power serve to strengthen its inherent oligarchical structure and dictatorial ways?

We have already seen the answer to the first question. Terror and centralization of all decision making within the Communist Party made genuine constitutionalism unthinkable. Until 1921 some representatives of non-Communist socialist parties were tolerated within the soviets. (The majority of the Mensheviks supported the Communist regime against foreign intervention and in the Polish war.) But with the end of the Civil War the Communists would not tolerate any, even loyal, opposition. Most prestigious Menshevik leaders, such as Martov and Dan, were forced to leave Soviet Russia; some joined the victorious Party. With the soviets no longer containing even a sprinkling of representatives of other political groups, their function became purely decorative; they would vote the laws decided by the Party beforehand, put a populistic varnish over the edifice of the one-party dictatorship. It was the Party Congress that debated and settled policies and not the All-Union Congress of Soviets or its Executive Committee, which merely ratified them. The local Party secretary was the political boss of the district, not the chairman of the given soviet, whose province was that of routine administration and who was anyway, except in most rural districts, a Party member bound by its discipline.

But while the Communists, having won the war, found it easy to dispose of the remnants of the revolutionary democracy of pre-October days and to consolidate the dictatorship of the Party, the task of preserving this Party's unity was to prove much more difficult and complex.

Here it is necessary to go back in time. The Bolsheviks were an outgrowth of the Russian Social Democracy, and, while they were disciplined and united for the purpose of seizing power, it was natural that once in power there would be a certain recrudescence of the democratic instincts and practices of pre-1914 European Marxism. Although, as Trotsky's and Dzerzhinsky's measures demonstrated, members of the ruling Party could be and were shot for corruption or disobeying military orders, it was still unthinkable and would remain so until the middle twenties that a Communist could be seized for disagreeing with the leadership or even for criticizing Lenin or the Central Committee. Democratic centralism still retained, and would, insofar as the Party was concerned, until 1921–22, its literal meaning: the Party Congress elected by the mass of membership was the sovereign body that elected the highest Party organs. It was unlikely but not entirely inconceivable that the Congress could overrule a policy of Lenin's, refuse to elect Trotsky or Stalin to the Central Committee, etc. And as it was becoming more certain that the Communists would not be dislodged, it was natural that clashing viewpoints would emerge as to the direction the Soviet state should take and that the unity forged by the common task and danger would begin to dissipate and give way to factional disputes and personal conflicts.

What should be the nature of the Communist state? While in hiding after the July 1917 debacle, Lenin wrote his *State and Revolution,* devoted precisely to this question. The answers he gave were in agreement with the semianarchist mood of the moment rather than in accordance with the traditional teaching of Marxian socialism. The old state with its bureaucratic and coercive appurtenances had to be smashed. The new state would from the beginning be based on egalitarianism. No need for material incentives in the form of disparities of pay: all officials, managers, etc., would be paid the worker's wages. All citizens would be employees of one vast national syndicate. No need for a special administrative or managerial class: with some on-the-job training, workers could speedily learn to run production, soldiers to command armies, etc.

While he was never to repudiate the extravagant promises of *State and Revolution,* Lenin *the ruler* found its simple precepts unacceptable. Not only the practical necessities of the moment but his Marxian beliefs urged him that socially and economically Russia was not ready for that far-reaching egalitarianism which in the heat of the battle he had preached so fervently a few months before. To bring Russia out of chaos, never mind instituting socialism, one had to revert to many of the old capitalist practices. "State capitalism would be a step forward for us," he had said back in 1918. And in 1921: "Can any worker administer the state? Practical people know that that is a fantasy. . . . After they [the workers] spend years in learning, they will know how." As we have seen, Lenin and his lieutenants could not and would not dare to try to undo in one fell swoop the effects of their revolutionary rhetoric. But as the Communist rule progressed, it became increasingly evident to the rank and file of the Party that much of the rhetoric that had brought them into the struggle was now, in the eyes of their leaders, as Lenin himself said, "syndicalist nonsense . . . to be thrown into the wastebasket."

Opposition to Lenin's policies had already manifested itself during the most precarious moments of the Revolution. The Left Communists, as their name indicated, were not only opposed to Brest Litovsk but wanted a fuller implementation of the egalitarian and anti state slogans of October. The "military opposition" of 1919 was directed primarily against the former tsarist commanders, now officers in the Red Army, but was also motivated by the perception, quite correct, that their employment, though an emergency measure, was the portent of the Soviet state abandoning many of its "left" slogans and policies, and acquiescing in and encouraging disparities of status and pay, and creating a professional bureaucracy drawn largely from the previous middle class.

But these had been but preliminaries to the major intra-Party struggle that erupted in 1920–21 concerning some basic issues affecting the character and future of the Communist state. Two groups challenged Lenin's policies. They did not aim to remove him but wanted a basic alteration of the course on which he had steered the Party and the state. One opposition group, or, as the defeated intra-Party groups are called in Communist parlance, "deviation," became known as Democratic Centralists. They protested the increasingly authoritarian and oligarchic direction of political and economic affairs. Though the Party life of the Lenin era, when compared with that of Stalin, appears an exemplary democracy, the Democratic Centralists detected the existence and growth of the tendencies that were to culminate in Stalinism: the focus of decision making was shifting from the Party Congress to the Politburo and the Council of Commissars; Lenin's style of leadership was becoming increasingly authoritarian, the old spirit of camaraderie and equality that had characterized the Bolsheviks was now being replaced by distinctions of rank and political power. The Communist Party, in theory the vanguard of the working class, was acquiring the typical characteristics of a ruling caste. But the Democratic Centralists lacked a real remedy for all those disquieting phenomena. They were beguiled by the same dilemma that would confront every opposition within the Communist ranks: How can a party that rules undemocratically and through repression preserve or achieve democracy within its own structure?

Another and more important deviation sought to provide an answer, but it was an answer unacceptable to the Party elite. The Workers' Opposition also concentrated its fire on the elitist character of Communist policies, the growing inequality of status and pay, and Lenin's authoritarian ways. "Comrade Lenin," said one exasperated oppositionist at a Party Congress, "do you think that the only salvation of the Revolution lies in mechanical obedience?" The Opposition demanded that the workers and not the government or the Party should run industry. The economy should be controlled by the trade unions, and they in turn should have their leaders genuinely elected rather than, as increasingly was the case, having them imposed by the Politburo or the Central Committee. Other ideas and proposals of the Workers' Opposition smacked of what today would be classified as Maoism: the Party was to be purged of all "careerists," i.e., people of nonworker and nonpeasant background who had joined it after 1918; every Party member, no matter what his position, should spend three months a year as a rank-and-file industrial or rural worker!

But the spirit of October was far behind. The Workers' Opposition was attacked head on by Trotsky. At the Ninth Party Congress in 1920 the War Commissar chose to be brutally explicit: It was nonsense to prattle about proletarian democracy when Russia's economy was in ruin and the country required military methods to get going again. Marxism, he reminded his hearers, does not promise economic equality until the final stage of socialism-communism, with its material abundance, is reached. At present, when Russia's economy and society were in shambles, material incentives and industrial discipline were desperately needed to restore production. Just as the Civil War could not have been won without nonproletarian military specialists, so the campaign for industrialization, the basic prerequisite for socialism, could not be waged without managers and engineers.

Trotsky's uncompromising and brutal language, much as he had both common sense and Marxism on his side, could not but have aggravated the situation. As had the Left Communists in 1918, in all likelihood the Workers' Opposition had behind it the majority of the Party rank and file. But, as before, Lenin's prestige and persuasiveness were brought into play to save the leadership from defeat. He eschewed Trotsky's violent language and drastic proposals. (The War Commissar would have abolished the trade unions' autonomy there and then.) No, said Lenin, trade unions should preserve their autonomy vis-à-vis the Party; they should function, he said soothingly, as "schools of socialism." But it would be anarcho-syndicalism to allow workers to control industry; its direction must remain in the hands of the government. And to ensure economic reconstruction, it was necessary to put up, for a while at least, with disparities in pay, with higher remuneration for managers and engineers. The Ninth and Tenth Party congresses endorsed Lenin's position; the opposition's leaders, Alexandra Kollontay and Alexander Shlyapnikov, were warned and reprimanded. (Kollontay was famous also as a strenuous advocate of women's rights. Subsequently a long-time diplomat, she was one of the few old Bolsheviks to escape liquidation under Stalin.)

But the task of defending his policies through parliamentary means and oratory had wearied Lenin. He now looked toward administrative methods to ensure Party discipline and to prevent deviations from constantly raising their heads. The Tenth Congress passed a rule designed to curb future challenges to the official (i.e., Lenin's) Party line: a disobedient Communist dignitary could be excluded from the central organs and even the Party itself by a two-thirds' vote of the Central Committee.

If the realities of power constrained the Communist leadership to tighten up intra-Party discipline, then the overall situation in the country at large compelled them to reassess their economic policies. With the end of the Civil War, the effects of war communism could be seen as similar to those of a drug that temporarily keeps the patient from a collapse but whose continued use must lead to a fatal deterioration of his condition. Industrial production stood at a fraction of the prerevolutionary figure, that of food less than a half. Food shortages grew into the disastrous famine of 1921–22, which, though alleviated through foreign help—most notably by the American relief mission under Herbert Hoover—still led to widespread starvation and mass migration from the worst-stricken region. (To enlist foreign support, the government's committee to fight famine included members of former political parties such as Mensheviks and even Kadets, the last occasion when representatives of non-Communist political circles were allowed on an official Soviet body. With the extreme emergency over, the committee was dissolved and some of its "bourgeois" members arrested.) The widespread social and economic distress, the now quite obvious fact of one-party dictatorship, led to a number of popular uprisings. In the Tambov province a peasant rebellion erupted in 1920; the back of the revolt was broken in 1921 by the Red Army under Tukhachevsky, using methods reminiscent of the Civil War at its most gruesome: the families of insurgents were held hostage and often executed unless their menfolk turned themselves in. But anti-Soviet partisan activities continued for several years. Even more symptomatic was the uprising of the sailors of Kronstadt, during the Revolution one of the main centers of Bolshevik influence. The sailors rose to demand the fulfillment of the pledges of October: political freedom for all socialist and anarchist parties, real elections to the Soviets, an end to the oppression of the peasants. Here again the regime acted speedily and ruthlessly: the Red Army stormed across the ice and seized the fortress. The captive sailors were shot in droves. The Kronstadt rebellion, a truly grass-roots, confused movement of protest against hunger and Communist dictatorship, was portrayed by Lenin as the result of a plot involving White generals, the Kadets, and the Western powers.

The Communists were too intelligent to rely only on repression or to fail to realize that Tambov and Kronstadt would be repeated unless they tackled the root cause of the crisis. And so, at the Tenth Congress, which coincided with Kronstadt, the government announced a series of measures that were to become known as the NEP, the New Economic Policy.

The NEP could more correctly be described as an *old* economic policy. War communism was buried; as Lenin frankly confessed, "It was a fantastic idea for a Communist to dream that in three years you could drastically change the economic structure of our country." And so the profit motive was rehabilitated as a legitimate instrument of socialist economic policy. Private trade was legalized. With the government reserving for itself the "commanding heights" of the economy, what there was of heavy industry, banks and railways, private ownership would be tolerated in the case of smaller industrial enterprises. The most basic change concerned agricultural policies. Arbitrary food requisitioning by the state was given up. The Communists are seldom inhibited about condemning their own *past* abuses, and so Lenin was outspoken in describing how the policy of requisitioning of the peasants' surpluses had actually worked: "They would come and take two and three times over from the peasant, leaving him in an unbearable position; the most efficient producers suffered worst; any possibility of stable economic conditions was destroyed." Now, the peasant would pay a tax in kind; only a *scheduled* proportion of his crop would be required from him by the state. He would thus have again an incentive to produce over and above his family's needs; no armed detachments will come to ransack his barn and confiscate his surplus.

The NEP, said Lenin, answering an unspoken question in the minds of both partisans and enemies of communism, was "meant seriously and for a long time." Whatever "long time" meant in the vocabulary of the Party, which within five years had effected such cataclysmic social and political changes, the common assumption at the beginning of the NEP was that the era of war communism—an attempt to transform Russia's economy, and especially her agriculture, through sheer coercion—would not return. In any case, in the seven years that were to be allotted to it, the new-old economic policy largely accomplished its purpose; Russia's industrial and agricultural production returned pretty much to its prerevolutionary level. For a socialist this could hardly be a splendid achievement: prerevolutionary Russia was for him a barbarous and economically backward society. Nor could a follower of Marxism look with complacency at the state of Soviet agriculture: the vast number—over twenty million—of small holdings, the peasants' primitive methods of farming (the use of the wooden plow was still widespread), strip cultivation[3]—all those features of rural Russia clashed head on with the absolute prerequisite for a socialist economy of large-scale production units where mechanized, labor-saving instruments of cultivation can be employed. The inherent conservatism of the peasant was also seen as a political danger. While proclaiming the NEP, Lenin in his paradoxical way stressed the danger inherent in the existing structure of agriculture: "Petty production gives birth to capitalism and the bourgeoisie every day, every hour, spontaneously and on a mass scale." Thus for all of its benefits the NEP was seen by most Communists as a retreat, in turn to be succeeded by a new advance toward socialism. The timing and character of this advance would be the principal and the most contentious issue of the politics of the 1920's.

The NEP in any case provided Russia with a viable economy. It served to blunt the charge rife among the opponents of the Soviet system at home and abroad that the Communists' repressive and utopian schemes were bound to cripple the economy permanently, bringing nothing but famine and industrial stagnation. Some of the Communists' opponents among the intelligentsia concluded that the regime was now done with doctrinaire policies, that the national interest of the country was its primary goal. This conclusion led many engineers, economists, and others with previous Menshevik, Kadet, or even conservative political affiliations to offer their help to the Soviet state. Their services contributed significantly to the improvement of the Soviet economy and administration, but with the end of the NEP most of them fell victim to political persecution.

[3] The village commune, in retreat ever since Stolypin's reform, received a new lease on life with the Revolution; most of the "separators"—i.e., those who had chosen to leave the communes and to consolidate their holdings under the Stolypin reforms—were forced by their fellow peasants back into the communes.

It proved beyond Lenin's resources, however, or perhaps it was incompatible with the logic of the Soviet system, to ensure a commensurate measure of political stability. To be sure, after 1921 there was no major political or military challenge to the rule of the Party. But no resolutions or tightening up of the inner discipline could preserve the Party in Lenin's last years from renewed factional strife and ever more severe personal rivalries. The erstwhile revolutionaries were rapidly developing into a privileged caste, at least insofar as the leaders were concerned. This in turn bred increasing resentment among the rank and file. Lenin's great prestige to some extent contained the intra-Party strife and restrained the struggle for power among his lieutenants. But in 1921 his health took a turn for the worse, and it became at least problematical how long he would be able to retain active leadership. And with *the* maker of the revolution dead or incapacitated, with the Party having lost much of the revolutionary zeal and sense of mission that had carried it through the ordeals of the past two years, how long would the Communists be able to preserve that élan and unity which enabled them, a tiny minority, to rule a vast country? Would they, like the Russian Social Democracy at the beginning of the century, split into openly hostile factions or parties? Then the whole socialist experiment would come to an abrupt end.

During the last years of Lenin's active leadership, he groped desperately for some institutional device to check the divisive tendencies within the Party and preserve it from degeneration. The authoritarian in him rejected resolutely the logical solution, the licensing of opposition and/or freedom of the press. No, the answer had to come within the framework of the Party's rule.

In 1919 the Commissariat of the Workers' and Peasants' Inspection was created. In 1920 Lenin sanctioned the institution of a network of control commissions within the Party. The Commissariat, commonly known from its initials as the Rabkrin, was to watch over ministries and state commissions, register citizens' complaints, combat abuses and bureaucratism. Stalin was its first head and remained as such until 1922. The Party control commissions were to perform the parallel function as far as the ruling body was concerned. To preserve their members from involvement in factional politics, they were barred from sitting on the corresponding legislative and executive bodies of the Party—thus a member of the Central Control Commission, elected by the Congress, could not simultaneously sit on the Central Committee. In theory, the control network was to watch and restrain administrators and politicians, be a stern censor of the official morals and practices.

In fact, the history of these organs offers a convincing illustration

Lenin and Stalin in the village of Gorky, 1922.

of how an authoritarian regime can seldom hope to cope with its own abuses. Created to restrain oligarchical abuse and bureaucratic tendencies by the Party's elite, the control organs soon became an ally of this elite in putting down opposition and criticism. The Rabkrin itself grew into a bureaucratic monster employing twelve thousand officials. The Party control organs concentrated their attention not on the misdeeds of the ruling group but on transgressions, real and imaginary, of the partisans of the Workers' Opposition and other critics of Lenin's leadership. And, as we shall see, Stalin was able to defeat his opponents and grasp the main threads of power, even with Lenin still alive, largely through clever use of the control organs.

But the main impetus to Stalin's inheriting Lenin's mantle and the subsequent evolution of the new style of dictatorship was given by the appointment of the future tyrant in April 1922 as the general secretary of the Party's Central Committee. The "general" part of the title was a novelty, though the Party secretaryship, thought of hitherto mainly as an administrative office and hence eschewed by most prominent Communists, had officially existed since 1919. Already a member of the two most important bodies within the Central Committee—the Political and Organizational bureaus—Stalin would now have the Secretariat in his hands, and he would use this office as the chief ladder for his ascent to absolute power. It was far from Lenin's intention that the General Secretary should be his successor as *the* leader of the Party. But by appointing Stalin, he hoped to achieve the aim that had hitherto eluded him—to introduce order and discipline within the Party apparatus, to curb the opposition which, undaunted by its previous defeats at the Ninth and Tenth congresses, erupted again at the Eleventh and came close to defeating the leadership on some crucial issues. The expulsion from the Party of Shlyapnikov and Kollontay had to be abandoned; only some less well-known oppositionists were expelled. An efficiently organized Secretariat, it was hoped, would be able to coordinate (i.e., to control) the activities of the local Party organizations, uphold the center's policies, and prevent the appearance of large blocs of opposition-minded delegates at Party congresses. Stalin's designation appeared fairly logical in view of his then reputation: hard-working and efficient, even if somewhat coarse; unlike many of the first-rank leaders, not overly involved in the policy disputes that had divided the Party between 1919 and 1922. As of the date of his momentous appointment, few thought of the Georgian as being capable or desirous of stepping into Lenin's shoes; he did not arouse the envy or resentment a considerable number of Party notables felt against Trotsky and Zinoviev—both thought, and correctly, to be overly ambitious. There was another, and in Lenin's mind probably a very important, consideration: son of a shoemaker and a peasant woman, Stalin was one of the very few top leaders who came from "the people" rather than from the intelligentsia.

But events soon confounded expectations that Stalin could or would serve merely as the Party's chief administrator. Lenin's stroke on May 26, 1922, culminated a long period of ill health. Except for a few months in the fall he would be unable to resume the helm. With him incapacitated, with the leadership rent by personal rivalries, and with considerable turbulence among the rank and file, the Communist regime had passed the point of no return: it could either disintegrate or grow more totalitarian. The rule by one party which had preserved some vestigial remnants of democracy in its inner procedures would within a few years give way to personal dictatorship and then to outright tyranny.

With the end of the Lenin era, it is appropriate to take a look at the international situation and the problems of the Soviet state. Still weak and economically backward, this state represented a new and unique phenomenon in international politics. While endowed with the traditionalist trappings of statehood, communism had not forsaken its universalistic goals and ambitions. Brest Litovsk and then the defeat in the Polish war made Lenin and his comrades abandon their belief in the imminence of world revolution; it did not make them alter their faith in its eventual inevitability. The concrete embodiment of this faith was the Communist or Third International (the Comintern), born officially in Moscow in March 1919. While its first congress was a hastily improvised affair, with most of the non-Russian delegates having dubious credentials or representing communist or socialist parties that as yet existed only on paper, it still was a momentous breach with the concept of international socialism that had existed prior to the World War. This concept, embodied in the Second International, a loose confederation of socialist parties with programs ranging from reformism to violent revolution, was now specifically rejected by the fathers of the Comintern. The new International was to be a cohesive, ideologically monolithic, and militant organization. Though tactics of the individual parties were to be adjusted to the political and economic circumstances of their countries, there was to be no latitude concerning the revolutionary strategy or its eventual aim: "The conquest of the majority in the soviets constitutes our main task in the countries where Soviet power has not as yet conquered." Thus the Russian example was to serve as the obligatory model for foreign Communists both before and after the conquest of power in their own lands.

When the Second Congress assembled in July 1920, this formula was spelled out in more detail. The congress laid down twenty-one conditions of membership in the Comintern. Each party was to have an illegal as well as (when possible) legal apparatus. International communism was to combat "systematically and ruthlessly not only the bourgeoisie but its helpers, the reformists of all shades." The Comintern was to be strongly centralized, the resolutions and directives of the Comintern's congresses and of the Executive Committee of the Third International being binding on all individual parties. It was clear even in those early days that this centralization, combined with the fact that the seat of the Comintern was in Moscow, would lead to the domination of the international Communist movement by the Soviet government, though nobody in Lenin's era could suspect how absolute this domination would become in Stalin's. But already in the twenty-one conditions one finds an explicit statement that the duty of every Communist party was to lend every possible assistance to Soviet Russia.

The creation of the Third International was a challenge to every other existing form of government in Europe. There was no attempt to conceal this fact. Again it was stated explicitly: "In those countries where the Communist deputy enjoys some parliamentary immunity, he should use it in order to help the Party organization in its illegal work." There was likewise no real attempt to conceal the intimate connection between the organization devoted to the overthrow of all other existing governments and the Russian government. One of the leading Soviet dignitaries, Zinoviev, became the head of the Comintern's Executive Committee; Lenin and Trotsky were among its members.

Thus from the beginning there was a bifurcation in the international character of the Soviet state. On the one hand it was a "normal" state claiming diplomatic recognition, seeking trade agreements, etc., with the outside—i.e., largely capitalist—world. But at the same time the Soviet state not only stood at the head of the international Communist movement, but considered that its members owed primary loyalty to the movement—in effect, to the Soviet Union. Although in theory the Russian Communist Party was itself subject to the edicts of the Comintern, this fiction clashed revealingly with reality as early as 1922, when a group of oppositionists headed by Kollontay and Shlyapnikov complained to the Executive Committee of the Comintern about the internal policies of Lenin. The Executive then condemned the petitioners for providing grist for the mill of the "enemies of Communism and of the proletarian dictatorship." On the face of it, the Comintern was an amazing challenge to the whole concept of international relations between sovereign states as it has existed for at least three hundred years. What added poignancy to it was that the leaders of the Soviet state officially professed to see no incongruity in their dual position: as rulers of an established state, they sought and had the right to be treated by France, Britain, etc., in the light of the established rules of international law and comity; as interpreters of a universal ideology and chiefs of a world movement they had the right and duty to urge the French, British, etc., workers to fight against their own governments. Further than that, since, according to the theory laid down by Lenin as early as 1916 in his *Imperialism,* the colonial problem was the Achilles heel of world capitalism, anti-Western propaganda in the still vast colonial possessions of Britain and France was one of the earliest leitmotivs of both (if indeed the two could be distinguished) Soviet policy and Communist propaganda.

That the Soviet state got away with such a drastic challenge to the whole concept of the international community was due to several factors. First, and paradoxically, was Soviet Russia's weakness, both militarily and economically. The Soviet-Communist threat to the international order was felt by the Western powers to be clear but hardly serious, in view of Russia's weakness and the similar weakness of the British, French, and other Communist parties as of 1920–22. The recent experience of intervention in the Civil War argued against an attempt at a new anti-Soviet crusade. In fact, this experience was held among the socialist and progressive circles in the West as an explanation and partial justification of the Soviet-Communist aggressive rhetoric: the capitalist world had tried to choke off the infant Communist state. If diplomatic recognition and trade relations were extended to the Soviets, they would in due time get over their fear of the capitalist encirclement and behave in a more normal fashion. The economic dislocations and crises of the postwar world made influential circles, especially in Britain, look longingly and unrealistically at the possibility of large-scale trade with Russia. France, whose financial circles suffered most on account of the Soviet cancellation of foreign debts and confiscation of foreign investments, was in a less forgiving mood. The political and economic realities of the postwar world precluded the possibility of any joint front vis-à-vis the infant Communist state, even among the victorious powers.

But if it was the collapse of the European order as manifested through World War I that enabled communism to come to power, then it was the failure to restore the prewar rules and stability of international life that was the main reason for communism's and the Soviet state's ability to survive at the period both of their greatest weakness and of their most blatant defiance of the established norms of international polity. The Western state system, the basis of that albeit imperfect world order which had prevailed between 1815 and 1914, had been fatally disrupted. The League of Nations, weakened from the beginning by the abstention of the United States, would be unable to provide a surrogate of a new order. Germany lay crippled and resentful of the limitations imposed upon it by the Treaty of Versailles. What was to become known as the Third World was already showing signs of turbulence and of growing anti-Western feelings.

Both their ideology and common sense urged the Soviet leaders to take advantage of the elements of division and conflict in international life. The League of Nations, "the league of imperialist robbers" in Communist parlance, was from Moscow's perspective a sort of capitalist international rather than an organization to preserve peace and lay the foundations of an international order. Germany, humbled and impoverished, was the country where communism could become a contestant for power and, even under a non-Communist government, a natural ally against the European *status quo* as laid down by Versailles. Nationalist aspirations in colonial and semicolonial areas would be endorsed by the Soviet state and supported by communism because they weakened and preoccupied British and French imperialism, made it more difficult for the main capitalist countries to mount a joint anti-Soviet front, whether military, political, or economic.

In 1922 the Soviets scored a diplomatic breakthrough. Though still unrecognized by Britain and France, Soviet Russia was invited to the Genoa conference of the major European powers, called for the purpose of reconstructing the economy of Europe. As such, the Genoa conference came to nothing, like most of those interwar conferences designed to restore the pre-1914 Europe through a revitalization of trade and world economy. But in the neighboring spa of Rapallo, on April 16, 1922, German and Soviet representatives signed a formal treaty initiating normal diplomatic and commercial relations. The two pariahs of European politics reached an agreement which for both of them marked an end to the diplomatic isolation in which they hitherto had found themselves.

On the face of it, the Rapallo treaty contained nothing sensational: just the restoration of normal relations between two powers which in theory (since Brest Litovsk had been annulled) had not had them since 1917. But following Rapallo, the military and political contacts and negotiations that had been going on since at least 1921 finally fructified into actual collaboration. Military bases in Russia would be put at the disposal of the Reichwehr, which would thereby be able to experiment with advanced techniques and weapons prohibited to Germany by Versailles. Germany would in turn erect armament and other heavy industry factories in the Soviet Union. The two countries would exchange military plans and instructors. It was in fact an alliance, though a strange one. The Soviet Union would collaborate with Germany diplomatically, economically, and militarily, and this collaboration would last until Hitler's coming to power. But the Soviet leaders would not give up their goal; in fact, within a year of Rapallo they would license the German Communists to try to overthrow the bourgeois regime of the Weimar Republic. The still weak and vulnerable Soviet state was reentering the world diplomatic stage on its own terms. Who in the nineteenth century would have conceived of normal diplomatic relations, let alone an alliance, between two states, one of which would openly advocate and work for the overthrow of the other's government?

Diplomatic recognition by Germany followed that by Russia's eastern neighbors. And immediately after the Revolution Lenin's government hastened to establish relations with independent Asian states. They, Afghanistan, Iran, China, and Turkey had traditionally been the sphere of competition between Imperial Russia and Britain. Now the nature of this competition would be greatly changed by the appearance of Communist Russia: the Soviet government renounced those special rights and privileges the age of imperialism had bestowed on European powers in their dealings with weak Oriental states. By renouncing such unequal treaties, Soviet diplomacy hoped to (and to a large extent did) establish the picture of Soviet Russia as free from the taint of imperialism, a natural ally of the nations of the East in their struggle against European domination, whether in its outright colonial form or through their spheres of influence.

In the fifth year of the Soviet era Russian communism had reached an apparent accommodation with the realities of world politics. Stymied in its endeavor at expansion in Europe, it responded in a twofold fashion. To a large extent, the Party turned its attention inward: it would try to lay the foundations for a socialist economy within Russia. In the East, which, unlike postwar Europe, remained in a state of ferment, Soviet policies, both "official" and those of the Comintern, would support any and all national emancipation and revolutionary movements directed against the great powers, and especially Britain, held to be the bastion of world capitalism.

Both the internal and external paradoxes of Soviet policies could find their rationale in the doctrine that, while world revolution and socialism are inevitable, there is no precise timetable for their achievement. And so the stabilization of European capitalism would be but temporary; in due time new crises and imperialist wars would disrupt the Western world and enable Communism to resume its forward march. Until then, the Soviet state had to attempt to reconstruct its economy and, both for internal and external reasons, seek normal diplomatic and trade relations with its ideological enemies. (Trade agreements with the main capitalist countries antedated the resumption of diplomatic relations, thus the Anglo-Soviet trade treaty of 1921. Despite the cancellation of foreign debts of Russia and the confiscation of Western-owned enterprises, the Soviet government assiduously sought foreign credits, indicating at times that it would allow and guarantee new foreign investments for the development of Russia's natural resources. This motif of Soviet economic policy reappeared in the 1970's.) At the same time the Comintern stood as the obvious proof that the realities of power had not eroded the Communist leaders' sense of mission and revolutionary goals.

Yet 1922 marked a significant stage in the process that had been unfolding since Brest Litovsk: the Soviet leaders were now, first of all, rulers of their state; world revolutionaries, second. Imperceptibly as yet, the Comintern had become an auxiliary branch of the state apparatus for the purpose of furthering the interests of the Soviet state. And internally, the hierarchical, disciplined structure of the Party, which had been rationalized by the necessities of the struggle for power, not only remained now that power was in the Communists' hands, but was enhanced: with the designation of Stalin as the general secretary, a new phase began to unfold; with the last vestiges of intra-Party democracy destroyed, the rule by the oligarchy would increasingly give way to that of the Party *apparat*-bureaucracy and finally to the despotism of the man who both created and epitomized this bureaucracy.

3. The Era of the New Economic Policy

Stalin's Rise to Power

Stalin's rise from the Party's chief administrative officer to absolute dictator coincides almost exactly with the NEP era—1921–28. (In some official Soviet historiography the New Economic Policy is stated to have been concluded only in 1936, when Stalin announced that socialism had been established in the Soviet Union, but such chronology is, as we shall see, absurd.) It was as an advocate of moderate social and economic policies that Stalin widened his political base within the Party. This in turn enabled him, along with gaining control of the administrative machinery, to defeat his rivals in the mid-twenties—Trotsky, and then Zinoviev and Kamenev. With power firmly in his hands, he would embark on the mass forcible collectivization that spelled out an abrupt end of the NEP and ushered in the period of the veritable "war against the nation."[1] The dictatorship was then transformed into untrammeled despotism.

Lenin's stroke on May 26, 1922, removed him from the political scene, at first for four months, and threatened the Party with the revival of internal dissensions and personal rivalries. The Soviet system of government could at this time be characterized as oligarchy dominated by one man. Lenin's primacy depended not so much on his position as chairman of the Council of Commissars as on his un-

[1] A phrase from a poem by a contemporary Soviet poet, Yevtushenko.

equaled prestige and the utter inconceivability that with him well anyone else could head the regime. The decision and policy-making organ was by now clearly the Politburo. In 1922, it included—in addition to *the* leader—Kamenev, Trotsky, Stalin, Zinoviev, Rykov, and Tomsky as full members, and four alternates, among them Bukharin and Stalin's main lieutenant in the Secretariat, Molotov. The Politburo overshadowed its parent body, the Central Committee. Some of its members held ministerial posts—Trotsky was still at the War Commissariat, Rykov was deputy chairman of the Council—but even they derived their power mainly from their standing as members of the Party's inner group rather than as administrators. Others, in addition to their Party preeminence, occupied prestigious positions in other spheres of Soviet life: Zinoviev was chairman of the Executive Committee of the Comintern; Tomsky headed the labor unions; Bukharin was recognized as the leading publicist and, next to Lenin, the preeminent theoretician of communism. It was difficult to conceive that, in the absence of Lenin, those powerful and ambitious men in the prime of their lives would be able to work together or to avoid the resurgence of opposition to the elite as a whole, opposition that had manifested itself as recently as the Eleventh Party Congress. The Council of Commissars could hardly aspire to fill in the vacuum created by Lenin's debility. Its members, unlike Party potentates, in their own right were thought of mainly as executors rather than as makers of policy. Thus Georgi Chicherin, who headed the Commissariat of Foreign Affairs, and Leonid Krasin, commissar of trade, were, for all the importance of their jobs, considered mainly as technicians rather than as members of the ruling elite. The titular head of the state, Mikhail Kalinin—whose official title was chairman of the Presidium of the Executive Committee of the Supreme Soviet—was likewise, though an alternate member of the Politburo, not a Party figure of the first rank.

Lenin's illness was thus bound to lead to political combinations and intrigues within the ruling elite. No single leader was as yet strong enough to step into his shoes. To the world and to the country, Trotsky appeared as the second giant of communism. But the brilliant comaker of the Revolution did not enjoy popularity commensurate with his fame or ability. It was remembered that he was but a recent (1917) adherent to bolshevism, and Party members also resented his authoritarian ways both in wartime and during the trade union dispute. Still, he had devoted followers among the rank and file, and though he could not count on the undivided support of the Red Army, his commissariat provided him with a certain political base.

Fear of Trotsky was a contributing factor in the political alliance of Stalin with Zinoviev and Kamenev; thus in the summer of 1922 was created the intra-Politburo nucleus, *troika* (triumvirate), which remained the collective leadership of the Party and the state until the end of 1924. To the average Party member, the main figure in this arrangement was Zinoviev: for long Lenin's closest lieutenant, the boss of the Party organization in Petrograd as well as the head of the Comintern, Zinoviev was a bitter enemy of Trotsky's. Kamenev was one of Lenin's deputies in the Council of Commissars and dominated the Communist organization of Moscow. A man of an academic rather than political temperament, he, unlike Trotsky and Zinoviev, lacked both fervent followers and bitter enemies. The General Secretary, of whom but few could conceive as Lenin's successor, was still thought of mainly as an administrator. As such, he complemented Zinoviev's rhetorical flair and Kamenev's Marxist erudition. The new alliance was ostensibly not directed against any other leaders: it was simply, the partners piously proclaimed, a provisional arrangement to ensure the Party's direction and cohesion during Lenin's temporary absence.

Though Lenin's condition soon improved and on October 2 he was able to resume his official duties, it was clear that the days of his leadership were over. On December 16 came another major stroke, and from then till the end he remained an invalid. Whether it was the natural irritability of an ailing man or a belated realization of the true character of the person whom he had entrusted with the "straightening out" of the Party, Lenin's attitude toward Stalin now underwent a drastic change. Equally belated was his realization that the Party had traveled far on the road to bureaucratization and oligarchy and that there were violent divisions and personal enmities within the high command of communism.

Bedridden and forbidden by doctors to engage in politics, Lenin succeeded in the last days of December in composing a message to the next Party Congress with his recommendations on how to save communism from degeneration and ruinous struggle between the oligarchs. This so-called Testament of Lenin contained characterizations of some of his chief lieutenants. Stalin, he said, had accumulated vast powers in his hands and could not be counted on to use them wisely. Trotsky, the most capable man in the current leadership, was too prone to behave in an authoritarian way. He recalled the faint-hearted behavior of Zinoviev and Kamenev on the eve of the Revolution. Thus informing the Party, though diplomatically, about the frailties of his would-be successors—two others, Bukharin and Pyatakov, are also characterized in this "able but would not do" vein—Lenin hoped to warn it against dictatorship, either by an individual or a clique. But his one concrete suggestion as to how to thwart this danger was singularly ineffective: the Central Committee's membership was to be increased from its present number of twenty-seven to fifty or even a hundred, most of the newcomers to be rank-and-file workers rather than Party politicians. On January 4, incensed by another report of Stalin's authoritarian ways, the sick man added a postscript to the Testament: Stalin was too rude and had to be removed as General Secretary.[2]

While reserving this blow for the next Party Congress, the invalid also criticized its main targets, Stalin and bureaucracy, publicly, but in a more veiled form. In February, during the temporary improvement in his health, Lenin wrote an article for *Pravda* castigating the Rabkrin, until recently Stalin's ministry, for its wasteful and inefficient ways. And then he again launched a more direct attack against his erstwhile protégé. Stalin's lieutenant, Ordzhonikidze, was acting in a high-handed way as the virtual overlord of Soviet Transcaucasia, and the Georgian Communists complained about the extent to which their republic was run by Moscow or, more precisely, by the Secretariat. In January Lenin had dictated a memorandum on the nationality question in which he wrote wrathfully that the Russian-dominated central apparatus of the Party (as epitomized by the russified Georgian Stalin) was making a mockery of the rights of the non-Russian nationalities, the Soviet constitution being unable to protect them from the "invasion of their rights by this typical Russian man, the chauvinist, whose basic nature is that of a scoundrel and repressor—the classical type of Russian bureaucrat." Now in early March he wired the Georgian dissidents that he was on their side and was appalled by "Ordjonikidze's coarseness and the connivance of Stalin." Copies of the telegram and pleas to do something about the matter were sent by Lenin to Kamenev and Trotsky.[3] But the proposed political offensive against the General Secretary never developed, for on March 7 Lenin's condition worsened and on the tenth paralysis of his right side ensued as well as loss of speech, which he would never recover. With Lenin in a hopeless condition (though reassuring communiqués about his health were issued up to his death), neither Kamenev nor Zinoviev could pick a quarrel with their partner, and no other leader, not even Trotsky, found the moment opportune to challenge the powerful trio. The Twelfth Party Congress held in April witnessed but feeble op-

[2] The Testament had a curious history. With Lenin dead, it was turned over by his widow, Krupskaya, to the Central Committee on the eve of the Thirteenth Congress in May 1924. It was decided not to make it public but to acquaint only select members with its contents. And so, though whispered about and published abroad, Lenin's Testament was not released to the Soviet public until the Khrushchev era.

[3] The nationality memorandum and the telegram were also suppressed during the Stalin era, as was Lenin's personal letter of March 5 to Stalin, in which he demanded the latter's apology for his rudeness of Krupskaya and threatened to break off personal relations until a full apology was offered to his wife.

position to the ruling *troika* and solidified still further Stalin's position as the master of the Party apparatus.

The new leadership thus weathered successfully the first challenge to its unity and power. Stalin, it was felt, was too valuable an organizer to be sacrificed to a sick man's whim. And wasn't Lenin himself, when well, a vigorous proponent of centralization and a defender of the leadership's prerogatives? When at the Thirteenth Congress Stalin, after the Party's notables had been acquainted with the Testament, offered his resignation as general secretary, the Central Committee unanimously rejected it.

Even before Lenin's death Stalin began to emerge as a statesman as well as an administrator. Taking into account both his natural coarseness and his future lack of restraint, it is remarkable how in the mid-twenties he succeeded in establishing a reputation for prudence and moderation. In foreign policy at first he avoided intruding his views. Very much a home-grown Communist with no knowledge of foreign languages, the Georgian wisely preferred to leave the initiative in such matters to people like Zinoviev, with their more cosmopolitan background and connections. Yet even here at an early date he showed that he disapproved the adventurism of his senior colleague (as Zinoviev then was). In 1923, the Comintern made a halfhearted attempt to promote a Communist coup in Germany. The French occupation of the Ruhr strained the fragile fabric of the Weimar Republic and ruinous inflation combined with political unrest to create seemingly favorable conditions for a revolutionary enterprise. In August the German Communists were encouraged by the Comintern to seek power through a general strike and armed action. Trotsky and Zinoviev indulged in revolutionary heroics, both of them offering to go to Germany to lead a German October. Stalin indicated his skepticism. The coup was finally called off, but not before the Communists rose in Hamburg and were suppressed after two days' fighting. The incident could not but increase Stalin's political stature. For the moment, most Communists were tired of foreign adventures and eager to get on with the solution of domestic problems.

Internally, the growing power of the Secretariat was rapidly becoming the number-one political issue. On October 15, forty-six prominent Communists issued a statement attacking the "intolerable regime within the Party," the serried ranks of local secretaries who tried to suppress criticism and pack the Party gatherings. Their criticism was subsequently endorsed by Trotsky. This precipitated the first open clash between the War Commissar and the triumvirate. The dissidents' main point—the growing restriction on freedom of speech within the Party—was obscured by the fact that they also criticized the current economic policies: the NEP was popular with rank-and-file Communists. And while some already began to perceive that the unassuming General Secretary had the makings of a dictator, the main danger in this direction was still thought to come from Trotsky. And so the Thirteenth Party Conference in January 1924 censured Trotsky and forty-six others for engaging in factional activity and expressing "the petty bourgeois deviation" with only three votes cast against the resolution.[4]

The public reprimand to Trotsky and other malcontents was followed by an event that removed a hitherto always present danger to the triumvirs' power: Lenin died on January 21, 1924. Ever since the preceding April it had been out of the question that he would resume the helm, but even his partial recovery could have meant a fatal setback to Stalin. The latter's and other Communist notables' funeral orations emphasized, of course, the theme that no single leader could or would presume to inherit the mantle of the creator of communism. He would be succeeded by the collective brain of the Party, the "Leninist Central Committee"—which by now met but once every two or three months. The funeral ceremonies contravened not only what would have been Lenin's last wishes, but also the revolutionary ethics in such matters: the pomp of the proceedings, the preservation and permanent exhibition of the dead leader's remains in the Lenin Mausoleum laid the foundation of the "personality cult," hitherto alien to the Communist code. To a degree, this expressed political deliberation on the part of Stalin and his partners. They had been enthroned in Lenin's life, and the average Party member had no inkling about the deceased's true feelings toward one of his main successors. And by bestowing upon Lenin a superhuman stature, by insinuating his infallibility, Stalin was laying the foundations for his own cult and of the story soon to gain currency that he was Lenin's favorite disciple and chosen successor.

If the opponents of the *troika* made a serious tactical error in combining a challenge to their domination of the Party with economic policy issues, then the same mistake was soon duplicated by Zinoviev and Kamenev. By the end of 1924, belatedly it became clear to them that Stalin, far from being content with a junior partner's status and with executing *their* policies, was in fact making a bid for primacy. He further irked his two colleagues by refusing to go along with the sanctions they proposed against Trotsky. It suited his strategy to oppose, for the moment, Trotsky's removal from the Politburo. (In Jan-

[4] The Party Conference was a less formal version of the Party Congress, assembling members of the Central local bodies of the Party. "Deviation," in the Communist vocabulary, had come to mean an erroneous interpretation of and departure from the ideologically correct policy, but as yet a mere tendency rather than a basic betrayal of the ideology.

uary 1925, however, Trotsky was dismissed as war commissar.) As Stalin was to describe it after he had broken off publicly with Zinoviev and Kamenev, "They did want blood—dangerous and contagious; today you cut off one, tomorrow a second, and then a third. Who would remain in the Party?" This puts in full relief an observation of a contemporary who found Stalin a master of the art of political timing. When Zinoviev and Kamenev turned against Stalin in 1925, Trotsky stayed on the sidelines.

Along with his skill in timing political moves, Stalin excelled in the art of alliances. With the growing estrangement between him and the other two triumvirs, he sought support in what was to be described subsequently as the Party's right wing.[5] The chief representatives of this wing or tendency were the Party's most talented publicist, Nikolai Bukharin, and Alexei Rykov, who succeeded Lenin as chairman of the Council of the People's Commissars. They, along with Stalin, were to become the new ruling *troika,* which governed between 1925 and 1928, but this time it was unmistakable that it was the General Secretary who was the senior partner. A close ally of the new triumvirs was Mikhail Tomsky, head of the Soviet labor unions and a man with great popularity among the rank and file.

The issue that united the new ruling team was its determination to carry on moderate social and economic policies. Also, Bukharin's and Rykov's feelings about Zinoviev were not too dissimilar from the latter's about Trotsky. They still saw Stalin's ambitions as limited in their scope: to be sure, he was now number one, but certainly he would not seek to become an absolute dictator as would Trotsky or Zinoviev. And the General Secretary, they also and fallaciously believed, was an economic moderate; he would not jettison the NEP prematurely.

Their expectation of and alliance with Stalin were seemingly solidified in April 1925 when the Party adopted a series of measures intended to conciliate the peasant still further. The tax on agricultural holdings (now collected partly in cash and partly in kind) was reduced. Since the inception of the NEP, the better-off peasants had tended to lease land beyond their own allotment and to hire labor, practices that, though tolerated, were, strictly speaking, illegal as they contravened the Marxist canon against exploitation and the

[5] Designations "right" and "left" wing within communism have to be used with extreme caution since they usually reflect the victorious factions' semantics rather than their opponents' consistent ideological position. The correct position is always centrist—eschewing the left's alleged adventurism and the right's "opportunism," i.e., lack of socialist fervor. And so, though with forced collectivization Stalin was to adopt radical policies going beyond the wildest dreams of Trotsky or Zinoviev *circa* 1925, they were officially still the centrist—that is, ideologically correct—position.

growth of capitalism in the countryside. Now the Party openly sanctioned them. Bukharin rationalized the new policy: The Party's slogan to all peasants should be "Enrich yourselves."

Zinoviev and Kamenev now thought they had an ideological issue in their struggle against Stalin and his new allies. According to the Communist semantics, the peasantry was divided into three subclasses: the kulak (the "tight-fisted one") the top layer of peasants who leased additional land and hired his poorer neighbors and was thus an exploiter; the "middle peasant," engaged in family farming; and the "poor peasant," whose land and income were insufficient to feed his family and who subsequently had to hire himself out to the kulak. The classification was hardly precise. The average kulak could not be considered prosperous by the standard of the West European, not to mention the American, farmer. Quite often he was simply the more efficient producer and as such the key to the farm surplus that went to feed the cities and for exports. According to the classical formulation laid down by Lenin, the poor peasant was the natural ally of Soviet power; the "rich" peasant, its natural enemy who one day would have to be tackled. Thus the key to the ideologically correct policy in the countryside was for the Party to win over the middle peasant. The Marxist purists among the Communists felt that the new agricultural policy represented a betrayal of the ideology and might lead to a serious political and social danger. The kulak would be strengthened, and the principle of individual enterprise in agriculture might become so entrenched that the Party would never be able to reorganize agriculture along socialist lines.

The new or, as it was sometimes called, the Leningrad opposition (the Leningrad Party organization, still under Zinoviev's thumb, refused to submit to domination by the Secretariat) made its bid at the Fourteenth Party Congress, which assembled in December 1925 and was to be the last such gathering to witness a real political debate and contest. The stakes were loaded against the Zinoviev-Kamenev faction. The Congress had been carefully "prepared" by the Secretariat; apart from the solid bloc of Leningraders, only a handful of other delegates were ready to follow the two ex-triumvirs in their attack upon Stalin and his new partners. Trotsky, still with some, though dwindling, following in the Party, preserved silence and neutrality at this phase of the struggle—his hostility toward Zinoviev did not abate even after the latter's break with Stalin. And Kamenev and Zinoviev were equally blind: they still underestimated the General Secretary and concentrated their fire on Bukharin, the alleged inspirer of the non-Marxian rightist policies on agriculture. "Comrade Stalin has become the prisoner of that false policy whose creator and main representative is Comrade Bukharin," said Kamenev from the tribune of the Congress. This was yet another tactical error: Bukharin was personally very popular within the Party.

Kamenev went on to compound this error by mounting an attack upon the Secretariat not in the name of intra-Party democracy but in the narrow interest of the old-guard oligarchy: "We are for an organization of our high command in which you have an all-powerful Politburo uniting the leading politicians of the Party, to which the Secretariat would be subordinate as a mere technical organ." It was a new and unheard-of thing to introduce into communism the notion of the supreme leader: "I am deeply convinced that Comrade Stalin is incapable of uniting the Bolshevik guard." The motives of the new opposition were thus transparent: they wanted the Party and the state run by a narrow circle headed by Zinoviev and Kamenev. Their ideological posture was an afterthought: hadn't they gone along with the NEP as long as their leaders remained in the driver's seat? Stalin and his lieutenants easily parried their thrusts: to attack the kulak now meant to interrupt the recovery of agriculture and to risk a civil war. No, pleaded the Stalin-Bukharin faction, they certainly did not propose to set up a one-man dictatorship. "The Party never has gotten and never will get on its knees before Stalin, Kamenev, or anyone else," said Rykov. The resolution affirming the correctness of official policies passed by a vote of 559 to 65.

Stalin's victory was followed by personnel changes in the high command. His lieutenants, Molotov, Voroshilov, and Kalinin, were made full members of the Politburo; Kamenev was demoted to alternate member. A special mission to Leningrad headed by Molotov wrested its Party organization away from Zinoviev. The latter's turn came in July 1926 when the Central Committee expelled him from the Politburo and his supporter, Lashevich, was removed as deputy war commissar.

Too late, the fallen greats decided to combine their dwindling strength in an assault upon the General Secretary and Bukharin, whom they still considered Stalin's ideological mentor and without whom they felt the untutored Georgian could certainly not preserve and enhance his leadership. In the spring of 1926 Trotsky joined hands with Zinoviev and Kamenev. The combined opposition concentrated its assault on Stalin's new slogan, "Socialism in One Country." As such the slogan was not as yet accompanied by concrete policy proposals—this would come in 1928–29. But on the face of it, the Socialism in One Country formula again seemed to clash with the doctrinal teaching. How could agrarian, backward Russia acquire by her own endeavors that advanced industrial economy on which alone, as Marx had taught, socialism could be built? Yet by the same token, it was, as long as the terrible sacrifices involved in its accomplishment were not spelled out, an attractive political slogan. The Russian Communists would not wait until the distant moment when a revolution in a more advanced country would enable them to obtain foreign help. The current international situation warranted little hope of a revolutionary situation developing in Europe in the immediate future. Capitalism appeared to have overcome its postwar crises. The Dawes Plan in 1924 had laid down the basis for German economic stabilization. Germany now acknowledged and began to pay war reparations but would be provided with substantial credits from Western, mainly American, sources. Political accommodation followed in the form of the Locarno agreement in 1925. The Weimar Republic pledged to observe its Versailles frontiers with France and Belgium but in return was readmitted to the European community, entered the League of Nations, and received a permanent seat on the Council, thus signifying Germany's return as a Great Power. Politically as well as economically, Europe appeared on the road toward stability and reconciliation. The Weimar government did not abandon collaboration with the USSR. The Treaty of Berlin of April 1926 between the two powers reaffirmed Rapallo and pledged neutrality in the case of an attack upon either of them by a third state. But the vision of Germany, whether Weimar or Communist, as an outright ally in the struggle against the European status quo had now to be given up. Therefore it made ample sense for the regime to proclaim that, without giving up its ultimate goal of world revolution, it proposed to do something to advance socialism in Russia rather than marking time until the distant moment when red flags waved over Berlin and Paris. And it could argue that the pledge of Russia becoming industrialized, implicit in Stalin's slogan, met Trotsky's and Zinoviev's earlier criticism of the economy's continuing at a standstill and of Stalin and Bukharin's acquiescing in an indefinite continuation of the NEP.

But the opposition interpreted Socialism in One Country as meaning the repudiation of the international goals of communism. Trotsky picked up the theme of the Communist Thermidor: Just as, with the overthrow of Robespierre in 1794, the French Revolution had passed its radical and ideological phase and turned right, so now a similar danger threatened the Soviet Union. With the bureaucratic degeneration of the Party proceeding apace, with the abandonment by its leadership of Leninist internationalism, another dictator—and it was not difficult to divine whom he meant—stood in the wings to usurp the legacy of the Revolution.

The intra-Party struggle now reached its most bitter phase yet. Though the ruling group had clearly an upper hand—it enjoyed the support of the majority of the rank and file and by now also solid control of the apparatus—some of Stalin's lieutenants scorned no weapons in their countercampaign against the falling greats. Trotsky and his two main partners being Jewish, an anti-Semitic note was injected in the attacks upon them. The Party's control organs had by now become a preserve of Stalin's faction, and joint meetings of the Central Committee and the Central Control Commission were employed to swamp whatever opposition there still remained in the Central Committee. In October 1926 such a joint meeting ejected Trotsky and Kamenev from the Politburo. There followed Zinoviev's removal as chairman of the Executive Committee of the Comintern. Foreign Communist parties were already being subjected by the new leadership of the Comintern, headed by Bukharin, to the process of "bolshevization," which in practical terms meant their being purged of the followers of Trotsky and Zinoviev.

The Fifteenth Party Conference, which assembled at the year's end, put its seal of approval upon the formula of Socialism in One Country. As Stalin put it: "Yes, we can and we ought to conquer the capitalist elements in our economy; we can and must build socialist society in our country." He was careful to add that this victory could not be secure so long as Communist Russia was surrounded by the capitalist world: "To win fully, to win definitely, we must see to it that the current capitalist encirclement is changed to a socialist one; we must strive for the proletariat's winning in at least a few other countries. Only then will our victory be full and final." Trotsky's and Zinoviev's speeches were greeted with hostility and derision. The left opposition, the delegates to the conference voted unanimously, had been guilty of the social democratic deviation.

The left opposition, though decisively trounced, was not dealt with by Stalin in a manner which in a few years would become familiar: Only political sanctions were applied, some of the followers of Trotsky and Zinoviev being consigned to honorable exile—diplomatic and trade posts abroad. The two leaders were retained on the Central Committee. It would have been prudent for them to bide their time and defer any further political move on their part until, as already seemed inevitable, Stalin clashed with his current allies, Bukharin and Rykov. But Trotsky and Zinoviev were temperamentally incapable of such restraint. Their followers in turn could not as yet believe that Lenin's closest lieutenants had been definitely eclipsed.

In 1927 the left opposition made its last gesture of political protest. Nothing in the political picture at home warranted the belief that it would be any more successful than the previous attacks on what now had to be called the Stalin regime. But a series of international setbacks for the Soviet Union and communism served to inspire the rebels with the hope that the Party would finally realize that the General Secretary was leading it on the road to disaster.

Over the years since the Revolution there had grown a belief, somewhat illogical in view of Soviet Russia's still considerable economic and military weakness, that the performance of the Soviet regime had to be measured not only by its record at home but also by the ups and downs in the fortunes of international communism. The removal of Zinoviev from the leadership of the Comintern ended the bifurcation of Soviet policy making: the situation in the international as well as the domestic sphere could be attributed to decisions by Stalin and Bukharin. To a student of international politics 1927 appeared the most peaceful year yet since 1913. By the same token, the illusory stabilization of the world situation which it portended meant an apparent setback to the Communist thesis of the insurmountable "inherent contradictions of capitalism" setting the stage for an advance of communism.

The opposition pinpointed two failures of communism as springing from the Stalin regime's departing from the ideologically correct path. In 1925 his ally, Tomsky, was instrumental in establishing an Anglo-Russian trade union committee. Even then the Trotsky and Zinoviev wings of the Party objected that the British trade unions were largely "reformist" in their character and that it was foolish to expect them to become an ally of British communism. In 1926 came the British general strike, and for a few days hopes were rife in Moscow that the

At Hyde Park Corner, London, armored cars with machine guns stand ready to quell street rioting during the general strike of 1926.

situation would develop in a revolutionary direction. The Soviet trade unions transmitted what was for those days a considerable sum of money to the British strikers. Then the strike collapsed, and the Anglo-Soviet committee was dissolved in 1927. Trotsky blamed the whole sequence of events on Stalin: it was a mistake ever to have collaborated with the British Labourites.

While there was little logic behind blaming the regime for the collapse of the general strike and other untoward British developments, the opposition seemingly had a stronger case for blaming Stalin for the catastrophe that befell Chinese communism in 1926–27.

Here it is necessary to go back. The tactics of the Soviets' supporting "national liberation movements"—those revolutionary strivings in the Third World directed against Western rule or interests—were not an invention of Khrushchev in the 1950's. They spring from Lenin's thesis in his *Imperialism* and were in fact, though under a different name, pursued from the first days of the Communist regime. The most promising theater for these tactics in the 1920's was China. The overthrow of the Manchu monarchy in 1911 was followed by virtual anarchy, with rival governments and warlords carving out provinces of the vast country, intermittently warring and bargaining with each other and seeking favor with one or the other of the imperial powers who had business interests and concessions in China. In 1921 the Chinese Communist Party, still prevailingly composed of professors and young intellectuals, held its first congress.

But Soviet policies had to be attuned mainly to factors other than the still minuscule forces of Chinese communism. There was, first, the official government of China in Peking (whose effective authority extended only over the northern provinces minus Manchuria). It was with this government that the Soviet Union concluded a treaty in 1924. The treaty recognized, in effect, a Soviet protectorate over outer Mongolia and continued Russian ownership of the Chinese Eastern Railway. (Since the railway ran through territory controlled by the Manchurian warlord Chang Tso-lin, a special pact with him confirmed the latter provision.) Thus, for all the repudiation by the Soviet regime of the imperialist ways of prewar Russia, with its special concessions and spheres of interest in Oriental countries, the USSR held on to the heritage of the tsars in China, and in fact, its control of Mongolia became much more explicit.

The main thrust of Soviet policies in China in the early twenties was, however, associated with the Kuomintang. A nationalist organization with a base in southern China, headed by Dr. Sun Yat-sen, its declared aims were to unify the country and to free it from warlordism and foreign imperialism. As early as 1922 Comintern emissaries began to press Chinese Communists to enroll in the Kuomintang. In January 1923 came the Yoffe–Sun declaration. According to this agreement signed by Sun, then dominating the so-called Canton government, and the Soviet diplomat, Chinese Communists were to be admitted into the Kuomintang without giving up their separate party affiliations. Soviet help in arms and advisers was to be extended to Chinese nationalism.

In the next three years the power of the Communists within the Kuomintang grew rapidly, while the latter became a contender for power over all of China. After Sun's death in 1925 Chiang Kai-shek, who had had a period of training in Moscow, inherited the leadership of the Kuomintang; the Comintern's emissary, Mikhail Borodin, remained for the time being an influential adviser to the Chinese nationalists.

How far Chiang and the Kuomintang were to be trusted was a matter of some debate in Moscow throughout 1926, especially since, upon assuming the supreme political as well as military authority, the future Generalissimo took steps to limit the number of Communists holding important positions in the Kuomintang. But despite his future assertions to the contrary, even Trotsky continued to believe that for the moment the Kuomintang continued to be the best Soviet card in China. Chiang now embarked on his Northern Expedition, designed to expand his area of control. It was a spectacular success, and Chiang's rough handling of the Communists was being overlooked in Moscow in view of his prominence as the most successful leader of the nationalist and anti-(Western!) imperialist cause.

The Soviets were naturally hedging their bets. In October 1926, a left Kuomintang government which included two Communists was set up in Wuhan; it was hoped the Wuhan government would exert leverage upon Chiang and replace his regime should he openly break with the USSR and the Chinese Communists. The general Soviet attitude toward Chiang and the Kuomintang was well expressed in a confidential speech of Stalin to Moscow Party workers in the spring of 1927: "They have to be utilized to the end, squeezed out like a lemon, and then thrown away."

But simultaneously, the Chinese leader reached the same conclusion about the Communists. Having captured Shanghai, largely with their help, he proceeded to throw off his mask, and on April 12, 1927, his forces carried out a massacre of the local Communists and their supporters. He had recently been made an honorary member of the Executive Committee of the Comintern!

With the news of the Shanghai massacre, Chinese politics became the main battleground of Soviet politics. Trotsky, Zinoviev, and eighty-

Chiang Kai-shek at age 37, standing in formal photograph with Sun Yat-sen, founder of the Chinese Republican government.

one of their followers sent a letter to the Central Committee alleging that what was happening in China, as well as the setbacks of communism in other lands, was the fruit of the "petty bourgeois theory of 'Socialism in One Country.'" The revivified opposition claimed that world capitalism, emboldened by its success in the East, would now try to strike directly at Russia. Some superficial validity to these allegations was rendered by what was happening currently in Great Britain: Following a raid on the Soviet trade mission in London, which uncovered incriminating documents, the British broke off diplomatic relations with the USSR. (They had been established in 1924 by the short-lived Labour government.) Also at about the same time, the Soviet envoy to Poland was assassinated by a Russian émigré.

It is unlikely that any student of international affairs could in 1927 have agreed that there was any real possibility of the Western powers moving militarily against the USSR. The greatest danger that confronted the country was that of a diplomatic boycott: France had currently demanded the recall of the Soviet ambassador to Paris. But the alleged threat of war was neatly exploited by Stalin against the opposition. In July 1927, Stalin conceded that indeed there was "a real and material *threat* of a new war in general and a war against the USSR in particular." It was the British Conservative government, he went on, which was behind all the attacks and plots against the Soviet state, from the mishaps in China to Ambassador Voykov's murder in Warsaw. "These blows should not be regarded as accidental." Then, as he was to do so often in the future, he used this alleged foreign threat against his domestic enemies: "What can we say after all this of our wretched opposition and its new attacks on the Party in face of the threat of a new war? What can we say about the same opposition finding it timely when war threatens to strengthen their attacks upon the Party?"

The General Secretary skillfully fanned the war hysteria. Following the terrorist act in Warsaw, the GPU (the renamed Cheka—the initials stood for the innocent-sounding State Political Administration) rounded up and shot twenty people whose only sin was that they had belonged to the prerevolutionary nobility and upper bourgeoisie. With "the war threatening," the Trotsky-Zinoviev group was forbidden to publish their dissent. To discredit the substance of their attack, the Comintern now reversed its Chinese policy. After the Wuhan regime disintegrated, the Chinese Communists were unleashed against Chiang. A series of armed revolts in the countryside and attempted seizures of the urban centers was directed against the Kuomintang forces. But after some bloody fighting, especially severe in the southern metropolis of Canton, it was suppressed. Only scattered groups of Communist guerrillas, one of them led by Mao and Chu-Teh, remained in isolated rural locations.

The tempo of repression of the opposition was now stepped up. A joint plenum of the Central Committee and the Control Commission expelled Trotsky and Zinoviev from the former body. Now there was no more talk of mere "deviation." The charges against the former oligarchs came close to those of treason. Some of their partisans were already being expelled from the Party and imprisoned. On November 7, 1927, on the tenth anniversary of the Revolution, the oppositionists in their desperation took to the streets. In public demonstrations in Moscow and Leningrad, small groups of supporters of Zinoviev and Trotsky carried banners with subscriptions demanding the publication of Lenin's Testament and an end to indulging the kulaks and the NEP-men—a name for private traders and industrialists. Trotsky himself toured the capital, trying to address the workers. The regime early suppressed the demonstrations, which failed to invoke a wide response from the masses. On November 15, Trotsky and Zinoviev were expelled from the Party. At the Fifteenth Party Congress in December the Kamenev-Zinoviev wing of the opposition capitulated and begged to be readmitted. Trotsky and his followers spurned this act of self-abasement which in a few years would be exposed as futile. In January 1928, the ex-War Commissar, the comaker of the Revolution, was exiled to Central Asia; some thirty Party notables who had endorsed his position were likewise sent to distant locations; the five-year struggle, first for the leadership of the Party, then for preserving some vestiges of free discussion and the possibility of dissent within communism, had ended. Stalin stood supreme. The General Secretary was the leader, and he was now ready to launch the country and the Party on a social and economic experiment unprecedented both in its scale and in the human suffering it required.

Appraisal of the Era

The political destruction of much of the Bolshevik old guard, the effective end of the NEP, and Stalin's unmistakable emergence as the dictator make 1927–28 a major watershed in Soviet politics. Our attention has hitherto centered on intra-Party developments and on foreign policy of the Soviet state, and indeed the two of them provide the main key to Soviet history, not only between 1921 and 1928, but in general. In its main political characteristics the Soviet Union of 1928 was closer to Brezhnev's and Kosygin's Russia of 1974 than to Lenin's in the beginning of the NEP. In 1921, it was still not unthinkable that some political opposition would be allowed to challenge at least the Communist Party's policies, even if not its power. By 1928 there was no question of another party existing legally in the Soviet Union, and even within the Communist Party the official policies could no longer be discussed, as Bukharin and Rykov were soon to find out, without their critics' sharing the fate of Trotsky and Zinoviev. In 1921 there was still considerable uncertainty about the manner in which Communism would rule; one year later there was to be a brisk debate about constitution making, such details as the way in which the union republics should be represented in the Supreme Soviet causing a real controversy in which Lenin and Stalin found themselves on opposite sides. In 1928, just as in 1976, no one could argue that the formal legislative structure possessed any real importance: the Party monopolized not only policy making but all effective legislation, with the whole structure of soviets serving as a rubber stamp. The federative aspect of the constitution could also be seen as fiction, all the decisions affecting the union republics' political and economic, if not yet cultural, life being made in Moscow.

The most startling changes in these few short years had taken place within the Party. No one in 1921–22 could have foreseen that the Secretariat, then primarily an administrative organ, would grow into the dominant policy maker; that its head, then thought of as merely the chief clerk of the Party, would become the dictator, with the Politburo in effect an advisory organ, with the Central Committee consisting mainly of his nominees, and with the Party Congress, once thought of as the sovereign body of the Party, become mainly a platform where policies formulated by the Secretariat and discussed (if that much) by the Politburo would be announced and explained to the mass of membership. The control organs of the Party, conceived as a check on its leadership, had now become an extension of the Secretariat, an additional instrument for curbing dissent and weeding out the opponents of the General Secretary.

The use of political terror was, with the end of the Civil War, thought by many Communists to have lost most of its rationale. The renaming of the Cheka to GPU was thought symbolic of the change: the political police would from now on deal only with unreconstructed enemies of socialism rather than practice systematic terror as of old. By 1928 it was clear that, far from having been curbed or restricted, the secret police's functions, competence, and personnel had been enlarged and that terror, from having been an extraordinary way of dealing with an extraordinary situation in 1917–21, was well on its way to developing into a routine peacetime institution of the Soviet state, an instrument of suppressing not only any threat to the socialist state, but also any opposition to the ruling group, even if the opposition came from Communists.

A reader of Solzhenitsyn's *Gulag* does not have to be told that terror—arbitrary imprisonment, the death penalty, etc.—continued to be applied after 1922 as an instrument of social policy. The passive struggle pursued by the Russian Orthodox Church against the state's antireligious policies led to death sentences and imprisonments being meted out to a number of dignitaries of this church, and similar measures were applied to representatives of other religious cults.

Officially, the Communist doctrine proclaimed and the Soviet constitution acknowledged that, once the church and the state were separated, religious beliefs were a matter of individual conscience and choice. Yet communism also held that religious beliefs were socially harmful superstitions, and while the socialist state should eschew a brutal frontal attack on religion in view of its still considerable hold, especially among the peasants, antireligious education, especially of the young, held a high priority. But despite such cautions, terror and chicanery were often applied against the religious, and a modus vivendi between the Orthodox Church and the Communist state would not be reached until World War II.

Such classical devices of Stalinist terror as show trials, the use of agents provocateurs, and penal camps also made their appearance during the period under discussion.

In 1922 the Soviet government held a public trial of a number of Socialist Revolutionaries which in some of its features presaged the great Moscow trials of the thirties. Twenty-two of the accused were "really" tried while the rest were agents provocateurs and ex-SR's who had agreed to collaborate with the secret police and to accuse their old party of heinous crimes, such as that the Central Committee of SR's had authorized attempts on Lenin's life, collaborated with Denikin, etc. The genuine SR's, many of whom were already in jail when their alleged crimes were supposed to have taken place, vigorously denied the charges. Twelve were condemned to death, and their sentences were suspended and commuted to hard labor for life. The use of the secret police against troublesome Communist Party members was a novelty in 1921–22. Shlyapnikov and Kollontay complained at the Eleventh Congress that a GPU agent masquerading as an oppositionist approached them with a proposal to found a Fourth International and that their mail was being intercepted. But by 1928 such practices had become widespread. The twenties saw the inauguration of the penal camps, the Solovetsky Islands in the White Sea being the first sizable settlement of this kind.

Quantitatively, the precollectivization terror cannot, of course, be compared to what would transpire in the thirties. Yet foundations were already being laid not only for that state within the state which the secret police were to become in Stalin's heyday, but also for the broad philosophy of repression that was to be practiced by the despot. As perfected by him, not only would terror serve to protect the state from its internal and external enemies and the dictator from his actual and potential rivals, it would also have propaganda and educational significance (the intended lessons of the show trials) as well as an economic one (inmates of the camps' providing free labor for state enterprises).

The pattern of Soviet politics that emerged in 1921–28 would thus endure to our own days, even though the succeeding decades would bring vast economic and social changes, Stalinism, and, after 1953, de-Stalinization. The Party had grown into the state and absorbed not only complete political power but the direction of social and cultural policies as well. Within the Communist Party, the Party apparatus, headed by the Secretariat, had replaced its deliberative organs as the policy maker. To be sure, the Politburo was not yet completely dominated by Stalin, still remained a restraining factor on the power of the Secretariat, and would remain so until purged of the "right" oppositionists by the end of 1930. In the Politburo elected in 1927 after the Fifteenth Congress, Stalin's faction was represented among full members, in addition to himself, by the war commissar, Voroshilov; his principal aide in the Secretariat, Molotov; Kalinin; Kuybishev; and Rudzutak. His then allies soon transformed into the right opposition counted three members—Bukharin, Rykov, and Tomsky, the head of the Soviet trade unions; of the eight alternate members, seven were clearly in Stalin's faction. The other important body, the Organizational Bureau of the Central Committee (Orgburo), nominally a supervisor of the Secretariat, had in fact become its extension.

PARTY MEMBERSHIP

The shift in the power structure of the Communist Party was paralleled by changes in its membership. From a body of revolutionaries, which it had been before October and remained to a large extent during the Civil War, it became the ruling party, and toward the end of this period, one of the most important criteria for membership in good standing was loyalty to the ruling faction—that is, to Stalin. The practice of purges of the Party begun during the Civil War, having as its rationale the elimination of the careerist and corrupt element among the Communists, had, since 1921, been used to eject opponents of the ruling group, first unregenerate members of the Workers' Opposition, then Trotsky's and Zinoviev's followers. At the same time, successive mass enrollments of new members, such as the so-called Lenin levy, which, in commemoration of Lenin's death, brought into the Party 200,000 new members, still further weakened the old Bolshevik nucleus with its tradition of intellectual independence and sophistication. Between January 1924 and January 1928, membership grew from 472,000 to 1,304,471.[6] To most of those who entered after 1924, Stalin was the leader and Lenin's successor; his rivals, for all their now somewhat distant services to the Revolution, were people tainted with factionalism and intrigue. It is thus easy to understand how the purge or exile of such legendary figures of prerevolutionary and Civil War times as Trotsky and Zinoviev and

[6] Quoted in Leonard Schapiro, *The Communist Party of the Soviet Union*, New York, 1959, p. 309.

Kamenev could be met with, if not approval, then at least indifference by the mass of members.

In absolute numbers if not in proportion to the total population, the Communists were now a mass party. The most numerous element of the "vanguard of the proletariat" was now officials (38 percent) rather than industrial workers (35 percent). For a still predominantly agarian society, the percentage of Party members who were working peasants was still startlingly low (1.2 percent).[7] The Party still carefully scrutinized the social antecedents of candidates for membership, those with nonworker or nonpoor peasant backgrounds finding it more difficult to be admitted and having to undergo a longer probationary period. Such measures, designed to preserve proletarian purity of the ruling body, could not, of course, with the Revolution now more than ten years behind, guarantee the preservation of the ideological fervor or of the internationalist spirit that characterized the Bolsheviks on the eve of October. Domestic problems rather than foreign revolutionary adventures were bound to preoccupy the more recent adherents to communism. Again it becomes understandable why Trotsky's critique of Socialism in One Country found little echo. The successive waves of oppositionists attributed their failures to Stalin's administrative intrigues and to the Party's becoming increasingly bureaucratic in its composition. But there was in addition the undeniable fact that the average member craved normality and economic progress at home and could not be overly concerned with what was happening to Communists in Shanghai or Bulgaria.

The concentration on and popularity of domestic issues versus the old slogan of world revolution did not mean that the regime relented in its attention to and control over the Comintern and foreign Communists. Quite the contrary. The foreign Communist parties were purged of the followers of Trotsky and Zinoviev as thoroughly as had been the Russian one. How could Stalin impose his policies on those over whom, unlike the Communists at home, he could not exert direct controls? Part of the answer must be found in the conviction of foreign Communists that the Soviet Union was still a beleaguered fortress and that whoever exercised power there was entitled to absolute loyalty from the foreign comrades. There were also more practical reasons such as the dependence of many foreign Communists on the Soviet Union for financial help and shelter.

The Sixth Congress of the Comintern, held in July–August, 1928, though its main rapporteur was Bukharin, marked the sealing of Stalin's domination of international Communism. Greater emphasis was put on centralization: "International Communist discipline must be expressed in the subordination of local and particular interests and

[7] The figures are in Schapiro, *op. cit.*, pp. 312–13.

in the execution without reservation of all decisions of the central bodies. The Congress condemned emphatically Western socialist parties, and those of Germany and Austria were declared a particularly dangerous enemy of the proletariat, more dangerous than the avowed adherents of predatory social imperialism." Similarly, the Chinese Communists were now to fight resolutely for "the elimination of what has remained of the ideology of Sun Yat-sen." Until shortly before, the propaganda school for Asian Communists in the USSR bore the name of Sun Yat-sen University. Sharp reversals of the Comintern's tactics had not been unknown, but never had the directorate of the Comintern—by this time, in effect, Stalin, still assisted by Bukharin—presumed to lay down the precise policies that member parties were to pursue. Soon the Comintern was to order the American Communist Party to make one of its goals the erection of an independent Negro republic in the southern states, a policy that the American party, despite representations by some of its members that the focus of the Negro struggle for emancipation was the demand for equal rights, felt constrained to accept. There was obviously no limit anymore to foreign Communists' obedience to Moscow; those who objected to or criticized the Soviet Union's external or internal policies would be classified as Trotskyites (and soon Bukharinites) and ejected from their parties.

This summary appraisal of the era of the NEP—of Stalin's ascent to power—looks at it from the perspective of almost half a century. It is thus easy to recognize that it laid the foundations for what was to happen in the succeeding decades and that, even after the excrescences of Stalinism were removed, the edifice of one-party state perfected in those years stayed intact. But it is necessary to recognize that for an average Russian in 1928, looking retrospectively at what had been happening since the Revolution, the period since 1921 must have appeared in quite a different light. Compared with the sufferings and uncertainties of 1917–21, the NEP seemed a period of normality and hope. Except for the members of the prerevolutionary privileged classes and for those unalterably opposed to communism, what was soon to be seen as a breathing spell between two wars must have appeared as a period of social peace. Even among some émigrés and other opponents of Bolshevism the convictions grew that the realities of power had sobered up the Communists and that they had abandoned their millennarian plans in favor of a more rational attempt to cure Russia's social and economic ills; and, indeed, a superficial reading of the Socialism in One Country formula must have encouraged such impressions. A number of émigrés from the intelligentsia, including notable literary figures, returned home. Soviet administrative agencies, notably those in the economic field such as the Gosplan (the State Committee for Economic Planning and Statistics), were very largely staffed by non-Party specialists, many of whom had previous links with the Mensheviks.

The illusion of social peace was especially strong on the agricultural front. With the NEP in full swing, the peasant appeared to have been the chief beneficiary of the Revolution. It had given him more land, abolished his debts to the landlord and the state, and, after the burdensome interlude of war communism, left him in relative peace. Certainly, the peasant, especially in the beginning of the NEP, suffered from a scarcity of manufactured goods, even of the most primitive kind, and from exorbitant prices. (Thus the "scissors crisis" of 1923, when industrial prices soared relative to agricultural prices; their respective projections, noted Trotsky, were reminiscent of parted scissors.) But by 1925–26 the crisis in that respect had passed. Agricultural production approached that of the best years before the Revolution, and the average peasant probably ate better than prior to 1914. To a large extent, peasant life was still regulated by the old commune, now renamed the village assembly. Of course, even before 1928 there were portents of the coming storm. Even while rejecting the opposition's suggestions for extracting more from the peasant, Stalin intimated that the day would come when the Party would settle its accounts with the kulak. And as early as 1926, the regime took measures to squeeze the more prosperous villagers. But to the mass of the peasantry this might have appeared as yet another incident in the Communists' zigzag course in agricultural policy rather than a first salvo before a frontal attack. Stalin, it was remembered, had also declared that to deal with the peasant through forcible measures would lead to a new civil war. And Bukharin, then considered the chief theoretician of the regime, and such influential leaders as his future partners in the right opposition, Rykov and Tomsky, were known to be proponents of a cautious and gradual approach to the problem of socializing agriculture.

While the agrarian sector was to be dominated by the individual producer—some 24 million peasant households—the rest of the economy could be characterized as mixed in character. Heavy industry was in the hands of the state, the overall control exercised by the Vesenkha —from the Russian initials for the Supreme Soviet of National Economy—to which were subordinated industrial trusts, each in turn in charge of several factories and enterprises. Under this overcentralized and cumbersome arrangement Soviet industry and mining made their recovery from their nadir during the Civil War *almost* to the pre-World War I level by 1926.[8]

[8] Some figures for 1926 and 1913 respectively: coal, 29 million tons versus 27.6 million; steel, 3.1 million tons versus 4.2 million; cotton, 2,286 million meters versus 2,582 million. Alec Nove, *An Economic History of the USSR*, London, 1969, p. 94.

The small-scale and handicraft industry remained largely in private hands at the end of the NEP, the private sector still responsible for some 78 percent of this type of production as against 20 percent from cooperative and 3 percent from state enterprises. The NEP-men, small merchants and entrepreneurs, continued to remain an important element in retail trade, an essential link in furnishing goods to the villages, competitors of state and cooperative enterprises in the cities. Here again, it was easy to believe that the absorption of the trade and artisan sector by the state would be a long-drawn and gradual process and that the Communist regime would not, for all the official threats against the "speculators," risk the collapse of the whole consumer network by moving too precipitately against the private entrepreneur.

The industrial proletariat was in 1928 still very much of a minority in the "workers' state," where 80 percent of the population was peasant. The early postrevolutionary euphoria that had brought most of the politically conscious workers, even those with previously different party affiliations, to the side of the Soviet regime was a thing of the past. But so was the acute dissatisfaction with the realities of Soviet power which had drawn so many rank-and-file workers to the side of the Workers' Opposition in 1920–22. The revival of industry under the NEP arrested and then reversed the exodus of city workers to the villages. Real wages began to climb until, on the eve of the first Five-Year Plan, they probably surpassed the prewar level. The eight-hour work day and other social benefits conferred by Soviet legislation represented a partial fulfillment of the promises communism had offered to the working class. For all the growing bureaucratization of the Party, the rank-and-file worker was still an important element in the ruling body. The trade unions, while in no sense running the economy, as Shlyapnikov and Kollontay had once demanded, still retained a degree of autonomy from the state-Party apparatus. The right to strike had not yet atrophied. In most state-run factories the local trade union secretary still retained some influence on management policies. Such factories, subject to the directives from above, would often be run by a *troika* composed of the union man, the local Party secretary, and the (usually "bourgeois") specialist-director. The virtual ban on strikes, the director's complete authority, and drastic labor discipline —all those features of "mature" Stalinism—were still in the future. The NEP certainly did not usher in a workers' paradise for Russia, but again, judging by the recent past, it brought solid improvement in the wage earner's living standards and the hope, ephemeral as events would soon show, of better things in the future.

The NEP then, though it certainly cannot be viewed as the golden period of Soviet history, except in the unenviable context of what preceded and what followed it, was still, for the general mass of the population, a period of relaxation and of economic recovery. It is well, however, to retain a certain sense of proportion. When it comes to political or intellectual freedom, the years 1921–28 stand at a glaring disadvantage to the not very impressive record of tsarist Russia after 1905. Enough has already been said about the attrition of freedom of discussion even within the Communist Party. Culturally, one finds a degree of toleration of diverse literary and artistic strains that will not be again approximated in Soviet history, except perhaps for the 1956–64 period. It would be excessive to speak of full artistic freedom, but literature and the arts of the NEP were not as yet subjugated to the stifling uniformity of "socialist realism," nor was there as yet the official fear and disapproval of new and innovative artistic styles and techniques that survived Stalin's death. Under Lenin, a traditionalist in cultural matters, the Party itself restrained the attempts of some Communist writers and philosophers to impose an official revolutionary or proletarian standard on the arts (the so-called *proletkult* movement). During the NEP, while artistic and literary themes that clashed openly with communism remained impermissible, a certain degree of detachment from politics was still possible for an artist. Such luminaries of Russian literature as Pasternak, Akhmatova, and Mandelstam, subsequently silenced and, in the case of the last, destroyed by Stalinism, could still write freely. At the very end of the period Sholokhov's first version of *Quiet Don* presented a realistic picture of the Civil War, not unduly flattering to communism.

The regime's interest in and patronage of science, so natural for Marxists, was happily unaccompanied by the insistence that biologists or physicists should adhere to the Party line. To be sure, in philosophy and social sciences the Party could not afford such open-mindedness, and there official orthodoxy claimed and exacted its due throughout the NEP. It would have been impossible to expound a philosophy that clashed with materialism or to present any major features of Imperial Russia's politics or society in a favorable light. The teaching and writing of history was dominated by the school of Professor Pokrovsky, a talented but doctrinaire scholar with a severely negative view of Russia's prerevolutionary past—so much so that it was to be condemned by Stalin when he proceeded to glorify Russian nationalism in the thirties. Yet at the same time historians of the revolutionary movement could still deal fairly objectively with its non-Communist and even non-Marxist components. Only toward the very end of the period does one find the first attempts to fit the history of the Party itself into the framework of the rising Stalinist legend and cult.

In brief, the balance sheet of the NEP in cultural affairs must acknowledge that, for all the abundance of ideological restraints, the Party still did not seek to enforce a pattern of uniformity. In one respect, at least, official policies represented an advance over the tsarist period: Communism still encouraged a vigorous development of the cultures of the non-Russian nationalities of the Soviet Union; political centralization, which had rendered the federative aspect of the Soviet system a fiction, had not as yet been accompanied by a cultural one. There were, though, portents of things to come, such as the anti-Semitic motif in the political campaign against Trotsky and Zinoviev. But even the Georgian who was to make the evocation of Russian nationalism and cultural russification such a prominent feature of his despotism was as yet the advocate of untrammeled cultural development of non-Russian ethnic groups. The government's campaign to promote literacy led to the creation of local intelligentsia in areas like Central Asia, where, to weaken the association with the traditional Moslem culture, the local Turkic languages received the Latin alphabet in place of the old Arabic one. (In a few years, and characteristically, the Latin would be changed to the Cyrillic.) But the inherent paradox of this policy—cultural separatism cannot but promote claims to political autonomy—was already apparent during the latter phase of the NEP. The central regime grew watchful over the potential separatist threat in the largest of the non-Russian union republics: the Ukraine. The Ukrainian Communists in turn did not conceal their unhappiness over the fact that the head of their Party organization was not a native, but a russified Jew, Lazar Kaganovich. Although in 1928 the latter was recalled to the central Secretariat, where he was to be Stalin's right-hand man during the collectivization period, his successor was not a Ukrainian, but a man of Polish descent, Stanislaw Kossior.

The diverse strains of the NEP period were bound to lead, by 1927–28, to a new crisis within the leadership. All Communists could agree that the New Economic Policy had achieved its main aim: it had restored the economy shattered by seven years of foreign and civil wars. Most of the leading figures of the regime were also ready to acknowledge that the current situation of the country required, if not a change of policy, then a change of tactics. If the NEP brought Russia *almost* to the prewar economic level, then this, from the Communist viewpoint, could hardly be an occasion for self-congratulation. Wasn't prewar Russia in its social and economic as well as political aspects denounced by them as a backward and semi-barbarous country? And here in 1927 the dominant sector of the economy, agriculture, was in private hands more firmly than it had been in 1914, small-scale and inefficient production more entrenched than ever before. If the peasant produced almost as much as before the Revolution, then this was not reflected in the amount of grain the state was able to extract from him for feeding the cities and for export. In an unusually good prerevolutionary year, 1913, Russia exported 12 million tons of grain; in the best NEP years the amount never reached 3 million. This shortage in state marketing of grain, which reached the critical point in 1927–28, was connected not only with the further fragmentation of Russian agriculture since the Revolution, but also with the low price the government paid for grain. But to pay the kind of price that could scoop up sufficient grain from the countryside meant giving the peasant the decisive voice in regulating economic development, something that ran against the instincts of the most moderate Communists.

In view of the backward and inefficient performance of agriculture, *as it was seen by the regime,* industrialization obviously could not advance at a rapid pace. How could one build socialism without industrialization, how could one industrialize if, in view of the agricultural and food situation, Russia lacked sufficient capital and an adequate industrial working force? As it was, the lack of capital for industrial expansion was causing unemployment; at the end of the NEP the figure for the unemployed stood at approximately one and a half million—again, a fine state of affairs for a "workers' state" ten years after the Revolution.

And so the NEP policies had at least to be modified if the country was to embark upon building socialism. But how? One wing of the leadership, whose spokesman was Bukharin, believed in a gradual and orderly modification of the existing policies. The Party, through education and material incentives, would attempt to restructure agriculture. The peasant would be taught the advantages of collective as against individual farming. At the same time, the better-off peasant, the main producer of farm surpluses needed to feed the cities and for export, would be paid adequate prices for his produce. This would mean a slow but steady pace of both collectivization and industrialization but would avoid a dangerous social conflict which an outright attack on the kulak and the exploitation of the peasantry as a whole was bound to bring.

The other strategy of economic development was, it became clear by the middle of 1928, favored by Stalin. It involved, in the simplest terms, rapid industrialization financed by exploiting the broadest strata of the population, primarily the Soviet peasantry. When he threw off his mask in July 1928 at the meeting of the Central Committee, Stalin chose to speak with brutal frankness of how the peasant was and would continue to be squeezed. Where, he asked his fellow Committee members, were they going to get the resources for the ambitious schemes of industrialization that they had authorized the previous year? They were and would continue to get them out of the peasant: by taxing him heavily, by making him *overpay* for commercial articles he needed, by underpaying him for grain and other agricultural products. And he dotted the *i*: "Of course, this is an unpleasant business. But we would not be Bolsheviks if we tried to cover up this fact, if we shut our eyes to the truth that our country, our industry cannot do for a while without this extra exaction from the peasant."

With his sense of timing, Stalin did not choose to spell out his approach until the battle against the peasant and his protectors within the Party had already been joined. Until the end of 1927 he still basked in his reputation as a moderate on economic policies. In fact, the approach he was to announce was not different in principle from the policies he had denounced when advocated by such left oppositionists as Trotsky and Eugene Preobrazhensky—one of the best economic minds among the Communist notables of the twenties and an early opponent of Stalin—who argued that in the absence of a supply of foreign capital, industrialization would have to be financed from internal sources, which meant in effect exacting a tribute from the peasantry. (This was the celebrated theory of "primitive socialist accumulation," an echo of Marx's theory of primitive capitalist accumulation, according to which the early capitalist accumulated funds for industrial development by exploiting and in some cases squeezing out the small farmer and craftsman.) The difference was that Stalin was to apply the policy of squeezing out the sinews of industrialization with a speed and brutality that undoubtedly went beyond the wildest dreams of the earlier "get tough with the peasant" Communists.

The end of the NEP may thus be dated from the Fifteenth Party Congress in December 1927. The Congress authorized the first Five-Year Plan, an ambitious projection of industrial advance, with many of its goals, as it was to turn out, quite unrealistic. On the agricultural side, the directives for the plan called for a considerable increase in collectivization—some 12 to 15 percent of peasant households were to be contained in collectivized and state farms at the end of the plan, as against about 2 percent at its inception—yet it was assumed by everybody and stated by Stalin that collectivization would be entirely voluntary and that the end of the plan would still see individual household farming as the prevailing form of production in the countryside.

The very ambitious scope of the industrial goals had an eloquence of its own, and it is difficult to believe that Stalin did not already have an inkling of the agricultural revolution to which he was going to subject the country. The utter defeat of the left opposition now freed his hands to deal resolutely with those who believed in caution and gradualism in economic policy. The paradox of the NEP—the growing arbitrariness and centralization of political power against the background of moderate social and economic policies—and a similar paradox in Stalin's own position—acknowledged as *the* leader, he was still assumed to be an executor of policies devised by others—both were going to be resolved through a vast social and economic upheaval.

4.
The Third Revolution

Collectivization

The actual sequence of events that culminated in what is sometimes called the Third Russian Revolution began with the grain procurement crisis of 1927–28. In January 1928 state purchases of grain stood at 300 million *poods,* as against 428 million for the corresponding period the year before.[1] The reason for this deficit, which could fatally hurt the projected Five-Year Plan and bring food shortages in cities, lay not in a bad harvest but in government measures adopted one year before. In 1926 the government decided to cut grain prices by as much as 20 percent, an administrative fiat completely unrelated to the existing state of supply and demand. This was the first step in the offensive on the agricultural front. Simultaneously the regime took a number of steps against the kulak—the well-to-do farmer. Kulaks were to be banned from voting in the election for the soviets, and more important, since the soviets were now of but little importance, they were excluded from the village assemblies. Most crucial of all, in addition to the lower price he would now get for his grain, the better-off peasant was to be taxed more heavily. The sum total of these measures was to produce a powerful incentive for *all* peasants *not* to produce and sell grain. The middle peasant, if he increased his production and sales, ran the risk of passing into the kulak category,

[1] One *pood* equals 36 pounds.

with all the disadvantages and dangers it now portended. All peasants would have a strong stimulus to use more grain for cattle fodder, since meat prices stayed relatively high, or simply to withhold part of their surplus from the market in the reasonable expectation that the regime would see the light and raise prices.

But the regime, or, more properly, Stalin and his followers (since the advocates of moderation like Bukharin and Rykov were still part of the regime), took the procurement crisis as an indication that the kulaks had declared war upon Soviet power and decided to deal with this alleged challenge through other than economic measures. Stalin himself was one of a number of high officials who went on mission to the main grain-producing areas of the country to mobilize the Party in the struggle against the kulak and other recalcitrant elements in the villages. For three weeks beginning in January 1928 the General Secretary toured West Siberia and the Urals, addressing the local Party and state officials with the same message: The alleged shortage of grain was in fact the result of sabotage. The kulaks had plenty of grain hidden. Their hoards were to be seized and confiscated and the culprits were to be tried under the provisions of the law dealing with speculation, which provided up to three years' imprisonment and confiscation of the property of those found guilty of hoarding in order to cause an increase in prices. This was of course a revival of the exactions of war communism, which the NEP had presumably abolished forever. In his speeches Stalin went beyond the crisis of the hour and indicated that what was needed was a basic transformation of agriculture: "There will be sabotage of bread procurements as long as the kulak exists." And, forecasting methods he would soon use in fanning the class war in the countryside, Stalin directed that one-fourth of the grain confiscated from the kulaks was to be distributed to the village poor.

In the short run those coercive methods did work. By April the deficit in grain procurements was almost made up. But it was clear, if not to Stalin, then to the appalled moderates on the Politburo—Bukharin, Tomsky, and Rykov—that the forcible methods of grain procurement threatened agriculture and the country with disaster: one could force peasants to surrender the grain they had in their barns; one could not make them grow it beyond their own needs after they had had such a vivid demonstration of what could happen to the product of their labor. The pressure from the pro-NEP wing of the regime forced Stalin to make a partial retreat. At the April meeting of the Central Committee he allowed that forcible methods should be employed only in exceptional cases, and condemned "illegal confiscation of grain" and the use of police to bar peasants from selling to private traders. At the July meeting of the same body, his peasant policy now openly attacked by Bukharin, Stalin was constrained to agree to some emergency measures on the food front: state prices on grain would be raised, Russia would import some wheat. Yet, as we have seen, he coupled this concession with a plain warning that the burden of industrialization had to fall on the peasant's shoulders. But before spelling out the full meaning of this policy, he had to render powerless the Bukharin wing of the Party.

The next two years mark not only a complete dismantling of the NEP and the opening of the war on the peasantry, but also Stalin's ascent to a position of power where the term "dictator" becomes somewhat inadequate.

The two developments are closely connected. The social and economic revolution on which the regime embarked required a concentration of power and decision making going beyond the pattern in the last years of the NEP. And Stalin was eager to throw off the last constraints, such as the presence on the Politburo and in positions of authority of people who, though they acknowledged his primacy, still considered themselves his partners—even if junior—rather than servants.

The new or the right opposition, as Stalin dubbed it, was basically different from the ones he had encountered before. Bukharin and his partisans did not challenge Stalin's primacy or seek supreme power for themselves; they tried to reverse or at least modify his policies. And these policies, unlike those of the NEP which Stalin had defended against Trotsky and Zinoviev, were already by 1929–30 producing disastrous results. Furthermore, many of the right-wing leaders, especially Rykov and Tomsky, were people who enjoyed wide popularity within the Party. Why, then, did they not prevail and succeed in deflecting Stalin from what by 1930 seemed like suicidal policies, plunging the Party and the country into the worst crisis since the Revolution?

The answer must take several factors into account. In the first place, there was the combination of Stalin's political skill and his opponents' indecision and clumsiness. Throughout 1928 they could not bring themselves to break with him openly and heeded his pleas not to split the Party in its hour of trial. In fact, in November 1928, Bukharin and his friends subscribed to the condemnation by the Central Committee of the "danger of the right-wing deviation." The General Secretary could thus pick them off one by one, destroy the right-wingers' sources of support, and finally, when they were rendered politically impotent, present them to the Party as defenders of the kulak and enemies of the grandiose plan of industrialization on which the country had embarked. In 1928 Nicholas Uglanov, a sup-

Manual excavation work at Magnitka Hill in the City of Metallurgists. Photographed in 1929.

porter of Bukharin, was removed as the head of the Moscow Party organization. In 1929 the ruling faction struck at the one remaining mass organization that had preserved some shreds of autonomy from the Party apparatus: the trade unions. Tomsky was removed as their head and Stalin's henchmen, Kaganovich and Shvernik, installed as their managers. Now the dictator was ready to drop the other shoe: the Bukharinites opposed the Party line, he declared in the Politburo and soon in public: "Sad though it may be, we must face facts: a factional group has been established in our Party, composed of Bukharin,

Tomsky, and Rykov." Bukharin was "unmasked" as having schemed with the disgraced leader of the left opposition, Kamenev. On November 25, 1929, Bukharin, Rykov, and Tomsky publicly repudiated their views and supported Stalin's economic policies. The leaders of the right opposition, repeatedly assaulted and condemned, recanting their views, were finally all stripped of posts of any importance. It would be tedious to trace further details of their downfall. By the end of 1930, when Rykov was dismissed as chairman of the Council, they had sunk into political nullity. As yet they were not dealt with as harshly as the leaders of the left opposition: they were left in the Party and appointed to minor posts. But they were excluded from the Politburo, which was now one hundred percent Stalinist. There could be no doubt that the General Secretary was the master of the Party and the country. In 1930 his lieutenant Molotov became the chairman of the Council of Commissars. (Rykov's survival in that post for at least one year after he had lost all political influence is eloquent testimony to how little even the highest state offices counted against the power of the Secretariat.)

But the skill of Stalin and the ineptitude of his opponents are far from providing the total explanation for this victory over the moderates. While many in the Party shared, if silently, Bukharin's fears and reservations about the reckless plans for collectivization and industrialization, others, by the same token, became enthusiastic about the grandiose scope of the plan, about its goal of bringing Russia into the modern industrial age within five years, of doing away forever with the country's backwardness. To them, Stalin's campaign against the kulak seemed less of an economic folly than the fulfillment of the Communists' pledge to liquidate the remnants of capitalism in the countryside and to modernize Soviet agriculture. Many of the former followers of the left opposition who had chafed under what they considered the slow pace of the NEP now became convinced that the regime had converted to their viewpoint. In brief, along with the doubts and apprehensions of many Party members—perhaps the majority—there was enough enthusiasm and ideological fervor among others to provide support for Stalin as he led the regime in the war against the peasant.

He himself knew how to fan this class war and to appeal to fanaticism. His opponents, he said, believed in the "liquidation of class differences through the dying out of the class war and through capitalism evolving into socialism." His own formula—"exploiting classes can be liquidated only through the ruthless class war by the proletariat"—was well designed to appeal to that activism and passion for struggle on which totalitarian movements thrive. Again, as during the Revolution and the Civil War, the Party had tangible enemies to fight and conquer: the kulak and the NEP-man. The latter, the private trader and small entrepreneur, encouraged during the past six years, now overnight again became a class enemy, his enterprise confiscated, he himself imprisoned and consigned to a forced labor camp.

Simultaneously with the opening of this class war, the regime embarked on a series of investigations and show trials of engineers, economic officials, and other "bourgeois specialists." The wave of persecution of those people who for the most part had collaborated loyally with the regime and contributed to the economic recovery reflected to some extent the natural hysteria characteristic of revolutionary periods. But to a larger extent it was a deliberate policy which would be pursued by the regime during the next decade: to throw the blame for the deficiencies, shortages, and popular suffering resulting from its own economic policies on the "class enemy," who infiltrated the nation's economic institutions and enterprises in order to sabotage progress toward socialism. Thus in 1928, production difficulties and industrial accidents afflicted the Shakhty coal mines in the Donets Basin. While in fact those troubles were hardly out of the ordinary, granted the still low level of technical proficiency of Soviet industry, the difficulty of replacing worn-out machinery, etc., the secret police purported to have discovered "a major wrecking organization, having as its aims the disorganization and destruction of the coal industry . . . twenty percent of the engineers and technicians are engaged in diversionary activities." Speaking one month before the trial, Stalin showed remarkable foreknowledge of what it would establish: "Facts show that the Shakhty affair is an economic counterrevolution plotted by a number of bourgeois specialists . . . who received money for wrecking . . . from counterrevolutionary capitalists in the West." Needless to say, the trial of fifty-three wreckers established precisely that. As in the future trials, some of the accused were forced to make public confession of the most far-reaching plots of treason and sabotage. Though a few of the accused, including three German engineers, were acquitted, eleven of the convicted were sentenced to death, of whom five were executed. The charges, as those who approved the trial must have known, were fraudulent. But the regime, in view of the increasing economic troubles and deprivations, needed to impress the popular mind with this lesson: *All* bourgeois specialists as well as kulaks were potential enemies of the Soviet power; any breakdown of grain deliveries, every flooded mine *must* be the work of the wrecker, the class enemy. By 1930, the obliging GPU had uncovered several other rings of wreckers. Not surprisingly, one of the most extensive ones was in the food industry and it was financed by "foreign firms which had provided it with a million rubles for subversive work"; forty-six of the culprits were shot. The trail of treason and sabotage ran to the state planning agencies, whose officials, many of them former Mensheviks, acknowledged membership in a subversive organization, the Industrial and the Working Peasant Party, which schemed jointly to disrupt the Five-Year Plan and to support the kulak and the right-wing deviationists. The Central Committee's resolution on the uncovering of these heinous plots speaks for itself. "The more successfully the proletariat of the Soviet Union conducts its offensive, the more the counterrevolutionary elements within the country . . . placed their wagers on the attack of foreign imperialists against the USSR. The answer of workers and peasants . . . must be even a more resolute socialist offensive all along the front."

There was a crying need for saboteurs and villains, for things were going badly with the nation's economy. There was to be a considerable advance on the industrial front, but even so, targets as spelled out in April 1929 were to be far from fulfilled when the first *pyatiletka* (Five-Year Plan) was officially declared concluded three years later in 1932. The target for steel production was 10.4 million tons by 1932, raised from 4 million in 1927–28. The actual production in 1932 was below 6 million. The target for coal was to be 75 million tons, up from 35 million in 1928, and 64 million tons were actually produced; 22 billion kilowatt hours of electricity were to be generated, up from 500 million, but only 13 billion kilowatt hours were achieved; for chemical fertilizer the goal was 8 million tons, the 1928 output was 175 thousand tons, and the actual achievement only 1 million tons. And even so, the final official figures remain suspect.

But while the picture in industrial development, though unsatisfactory, still denoted progress, what was happening in agriculture was not only an economic but a human disaster of vast proportions. The April 1929 directive for increasing the socialist sector of agriculture provided that sovkhozes and kolkhozes (state and collective farms) were by 1932–33 to increase their share of total production from about 2 to 15 percent. It was also assumed that most of this growth would take place within the loosest form (hence the most acceptable to the peasant) of the collective farm, the so-called *toz*. (The collective farms were divided into three major types: the *toz*, where the peasants, retaining their individual holdings, banded together for the purpose of acquiring or renting the implements of cultivation or of jointly working some land; the *artel*, where the ownership and cultivation of *all* land (except for the individual peasant's small garden plot) were in common; and the *commune*, where private property was almost completely erased and the members worked and lived communally.)

In retrospect it is clear that Stalin and his principal lieutenants did not intend to be bound by any percentages and were simply biding their time until the moment when they could move toward a radical solution of the peasant problem. On August 12, 1929, the Central Committee's (i.e., its Secretariat's) Commissariat of Agriculture approved the plan for mass and rapid collectivization of whole regions. The means employed were to be partly voluntary, but coercion was masked under the term "intensification of the class struggle in the countryside." The kulak was to be struck hard through a high quota for grain deliveries; if unable to meet them, his property would be confiscated, he himself subject to exile or imprisonment. This "dekulakization" was in turn to have a coercive effect on the middle peasant. With the definition of kulak highly flexible, any recalcitrant peasant ran the danger of being classified as the village exploiter and of being dealt with accordingly.

In December Stalin turned the screws still tighter: from the policy of limiting the kulak's influence, the Party was now ready to proceed to the liquidation of the kulak as a class. The target level of collectivization set for 1933 had already been surpassed in several regions. But alongside these advances there were signs of mounting strife in the villages. Peasants, and not only the better-off ones, were responding to coercion with violence; Party members and officials enforcing collectivization were being assaulted in increasing numbers.

Undaunted, the regime proposed to proceed even faster. By the beginning of 1930, it was clear that Stalin and his henchmen counted on collectivization's being effectively completed within one year. On January 5, the Central Committee directive ordered a speed-up all along the line. The main form of the collective farm should be not the *toz* but the artel, "in which the main means of production are owned in common (live and mechanical inventory farm buildings and draft animals)." But here again the regime's official proclamations were being outdistanced by what in fact it was doing. In some regions peasants were chased into outright communes, even their tiny cottage plots and their dwellings being collectivized.

Rural Russia was thrown into an indescribable chaos as well as virtual civil war. In its haste the regime did not and could not specify how the collective farms were to be run, the basis for remuneration of their members, their working obligations, etc. Theoretically, such details, as well as the decision as to whether to join the collective farm, were being left to the village assembly. But as even the Soviet historians, beginning with 1953, have acknowledged, the actual means employed ranged from pressure through threats to physical compulsion: all recalcitrant peasants were threatened with being declared kulaks. And in dealing with real or alleged kulaks, the regime abandoned its last inhibitions: not only was their property to be confiscated, but for the "active counterrevolutionaries" among them was prescribed the "highest measure of punishment"—i.e., death by shooting, with their families being exiled to the "distant regions." The most leniently dealt with kulaks still lost their property and were subject to forced labor. Since the Party could not trust its peasant members to enforce this terror against their kin, a special levy of twenty-five thousand urban members was mobilized and sent into the countryside to run collectivization. Ignorant of conditions of rural life, taught to think of peasant Russia as the kingdom of darkness, these people frequently exceeded their instructions and evoked resistance even from the most submissive villagers. Often they would shut down the local church, strip it of its bells, and otherwise outrage the feelings of the people. Class differences among the peasants became almost obliterated as, except for their lowest stratum—the village riffraff—and the few genuine Communists among them, they fought the Party as if it were a foreign invader. In several regions GPU detachments had to be brought in to suppress peasant revolts. In some villages 15–20 percent of all peasants were branded as kulaks. If successful in its campaign of terror, the regime clearly intended to transform agriculture to the point where peasants were propertyless serfs. This was clear from the January 1930 Central Committee's directive, which commanded "the Commissariat of Agriculture . . . to work out in the shortest possible time a Model Charter of the artel form of the collective farm as a *transitional stage toward a full commune,* taking into consideration the impermissibility of admitting kulaks into it [my italics]."[2] Even in artels some of the more zealous managers of collectivization were forcing the peasants to surrender their cows and poultry to the collective.

On paper this mad venture of social engineering could be accounted a great success. On March 1, 1930, 55 percent of the total number of farm households had been collectivized. But along with the percentages grew the extent of the catastrophe. The peasants were slaughtering their livestock, consuming and giving it away rather than surrendering their animals to the kolkhoz. In 1928 the USSR had 32 million horses; in 1934 the figure stood at 15.5 million. For cattle the figures are 60 and 33.5 million head; for pigs, 22 and 11.5 million; for sheep, 97 and 32.9 million.[3] And by 1934 there was more livestock than in 1930–31.

It was at this point that Stalin called for a strategic retreat. On March 2 his famous article "Dizzy with Success" appeared in *Pravda.* He acknowledged widespread abuses and violations of the voluntary principle in the collectivization drive. These abuses were blamed on local officials who, in their zeal and ignorance, had allegedly exceeded

[2] The kulaks, in the broad sense of the term the directive meant, comprised something on the order of 5 percent of 120 million or so Soviet peasants on the eve of collectivization.

[3] Alec Nove, *Was Stalin Really Necessary?,* London, 1964, p. 28.

and distorted the regime's instructions. Stalin's brazen statement was echoed by the Central Committee. It urged that the voluntary principle be reemphasized, that middle peasants falsely classified as kulaks be rehabilitated, that collective farmers be allowed to retain their garden plots, nondraft animals, and poultry. To avoid a complete destruction of Soviet agriculture, it was felt necessary to permit those who so desired to leave collective farms. Millions of peasants hastened to avail themselves of this right. The figures for collectivized households fell from 57.6 percent on March 10 to 23.6 on June 1, 1930.

In any other, even totalitarian, regime a catastrophe of such proportions would have brought the downfall of its chief culprit. But Stalin's control of the state and Party apparatus was by now so complete, the success of the collectivization drive so bound up with the fate of the whole Communist regime, that not only did his power remain unscathed, but by the fall of 1930 the campaign to coerce the peasant was resumed. By the end of the next year most of the households were again collectivized, and by 1934 the process was virtually completed. The price continued to be heavy. Back in 1929 food rationing had been instituted. The city dweller suffered, though not so much as his peasant countryman. The former's consumption of meat, poultry, and fat fell from 47.5 kilograms per head in 1929 to 17 in 1932. In 1931–32 harvests were poor, and in the latter year there were already

A group of agricultural workers start for the fields from the Bejetzk Machine and Tractor Station, the central point for farm machinery in their district.

unmistakable portents of an approaching famine; yet the regime extracted 18 million tons from the peasants and exported 1.5 million. And so, in 1933, famine struck large areas of rural Russia. By conservative estimates, five million peasants starved to death during that year. The regime kept the news of starvation from spreading: in the most severely stricken regions, such as the Ukraine and North Caucasus, militia and GPU detachments barred people from leaving their villages. In Central Asia Kazakhstan lost 73 percent of its cattle and 88 percent of its horses during the collectivization. Since this was the main basis of the Kazakhstan nomadic economy, the region was hit by famine more severely than any other in the USSR; between one third and one half the Kazakhs died in the terrible year 1932–33.

The structure of agriculture as completed by about 1935–36, and as it was to remain with rather minor variations until the end of the Stalin era, was based on the artel form of kolkhoz. The state farm into which the regime hoped at one time eventually to transform the collective farm remained an important but quantitatively secondary form of agricultural organization; in the sovkhoz peasants were, like industrial workers, paid regular wages and, also in contrast to kolkhoz peasants, were entitled to old-age pensions and other forms of social security. The advantage of the kolkhoz from the point of view of the government lay in the fact that it enabled the government both to control and to exploit peasant labor. The collective farm's first obligation was to deliver a set quantity of produce to the state. Then the kolkhoz had to pay the local tractor station for the use of its machinery. (The MTS, as these stations were called, were more than agencies for mechanizing agriculture through providing farmers with tractors, trucks, etc. Each MTS, which served several collective farms, had a political department, members of which were selected with special care so that most of them had no local ties. Among the deputies of the political director, one was an agent of the GPU.) The residual share of the produce was then distributed among the members of the collective according to the classification and quantity of their work. Government exactions remained high and the price for commandeered grain and other produce low throughout the Stalin era. One may thus wonder how peasant Russia avoided further mass famines and how it could continue, even if inefficiently, to produce food. The answer is found in the one concession the peasantry won through its passive resistance in 1930: the retention of small garden plots by individual farmers. Though tiny—averaging about three-quarters of an acre—this remnant of private property in agriculture, along with the peasant's milk cow and poultry—also individually owned—provided a cushion against starvation in a bad harvest year. Since naturally the peasant lavished attention and work on his own rather than on communal plots and cattle, the tiny, privately owned sector of agriculture continued (and in some respects continues) to provide a disproportionately high percentage of the total production, especially of meat, milk, and eggs. By the same token, this nonsocialized segment of agriculture would be only grudgingly tolerated by the regime, with periodic attempts to curtail it, through limiting the size of the garden plot and the number of cows a peasant family could own, by taxing them more heavily, etc.

Economically, and quite apart from its human cost, collectivization was bound to be inefficient. As early as 1933 the regime recognized this fact by systematic and official falsification of crop statistics. Instead of, as before, reporting crop figures in terms of grain actually collected, the government began to give out statistics on the so-called biological yield—i.e., visual estimates of the crops standing in the fields. This resulted in overestimating harvests by 15 to 20 percent and thus concealing the fact that the overall Soviet agricultural performance continued to lag behind its precollectivization performance.

Yet from the regime's perspective, collectivization accomplished its main aims. In the first place, the regime could now commandeer food from the peasants at incredibly low prices and did not have to negotiate with them through the price mechanism. Then it acquired the additional working force for industrialization by scooping up excess rural labor—in place of some 25 million individual farm households there were now about 200,000 collective farms, and mechanization, especially after tractors began to be produced in quantity, released millions of rural youth for industries in the cities. In brief, the industrial "great leap forward" between 1929 and 1940 was financed and made possible primarily through the ruthless exploitation of the peasant population, and the collective system was the main instrument of this exploitation.

The Industrial and Social Impact of the Five-Year Plan

Since the targets of the first Five-Year Plan emphasized heavy industry (and this would remain the cardinal principle of Soviet economic planning until the 1960's) at the expense of consumer goods, the period involved suffering and deprivation not only for the peasants. By 1932 industrial workers' real wages fell by as much as one-fifth. The rapid expansion of urban population brought with it housing shortages, and here again the situation would not receive a decisive turn for the better until the 1960's (the industrial labor force almost doubled between 1928 and 1932; to the recent recruits into industry their strained and chaotic existence still must have appeared almost luxurious as compared to what was happening in the villages from which they came). The factories' competition for workers and the shortage of living quarters led in turn to a fantastic labor turnover. In its attempt to discourage wasteful wandering from one job to another, and also for police purposes, the regime instituted the internal passport—detailed identity papers listing one's national and social origins, employment record, and domicile. These were made compulsory for every Soviet citizen in 1932.

Whether in the factory or on the collective farm, the Russian worker was subject to draconian laws. A decree in 1932 prescribed the death penalty for stealing socialist and kolkhoz property, or if there were mitigating circumstances no less than ten years of forced labor. The law was used not only against thieves, but against peasants who withheld grain for state procurements. Under this law the father of Paul Morozov was shot for concealing grain, having been denounced to the authorities by his fourteen-year-old son; subsequently killed by enraged villagers, the boy was extolled by official propaganda as a martyr and example to Soviet youth. The industrial worker was not forgotten by the legislator: unauthorized abandonment of one's job, absenteeism, and lateness to work became subject to criminal sanctions. It is against this background that one must quote Stalin's words in 1933 from his reports about the results of the first Five-Year Plan: "We have undoubtedly reached the situation where the material conditions of workers and peasants have been growing better year after year."

If the period 1928–33 marks the travail of a whole nation—social coercion on a scale of which modern history can offer no other example—then one must not overlook the fact that it was also a period of enthusiasm exuded by many Communists in the pursuit of the goal of industrializing their backward country and laying the foundations of socialism. The theme that the grandiose effort and sacrifice were necessary if not only communism but Soviet Russia was to survive was expressed by Stalin in a famous speech in 1931. "To slow down the tempo [of industrialization] means to lag behind. And those who lag behind are beaten. The history of old Russia shows . . . that because of her backwardness she was constantly being defeated. . . . Beaten because of backwardness—military, cultural, political, industrial backwardness. . . . We are behind the leading countries by fifty-one hundred years. We must make up this distance in ten years. Either we do it or we go under." This sentiment found a responsive audience, especially among the younger generation of Party members, and explains their zeal in the task of remaking Russia and, at least partially, how the regime could survive the consequences of its economic follies and crimes.

But Stalin's speech quoted above contained also a new and clever rationalization of the cataclysmic social changes through which he was carrying the country. From the ideological argument for rapid industrialization—laying down the foundations of a socialist society—the emphasis now increasingly shifted to a nationalist one. Security of the Soviet Union as well as Russian *national* pride demanded that the country take its place among the leading industrial powers of the world. Once-backward Russia would "show" the world! Soon Stalin would proclaim the goal of "catching up and surpassing" the industrial giants of the West. He would praise explicitly the "American methods" of industrial organization and production. But no longer would Russia, as Lenin urged after the Revolution, merely seek to learn Western industrial techniques, she would, now that the foundations of modernization had been laid, soon surpass the capitalist world. "Relatively little is left for us to do: to learn technology, to master science. And when we accomplish that, we shall have rates of industrialization of which right now we do not even dare dream."

The unabashed appeal to nationalism (and not only Soviet but at times specifically Russian) was accompanied by other policies and propaganda themes that could be questioned by an ideological purist. Stalin's speech to industrial managers in 1931 gave the signal for a campaign against economic egalitarianism. Marxism, he said—correctly, though with more emphasis than any Communist leader had heretofore seen fit to use in making the point—does not prescribe equality of material rewards until the final stage of socialism, that of abundance, is reached. To talk of equality of wages under the current Soviet conditions was to follow petit bourgeois anarcho-syndicalism rather than Marxism. Industrialization required material incentives, and the wage structure in Soviet industry soon reflected this imperative, with a skilled worker getting three and four times the base pay of the common laborer. Furthermore, the campaign against the bourgeois specialist was now allowed to die down. (Many managers and engineers were of course to be victimized during the Great Purge of the middle and late thirties, but probably fewer proportionately than other segments of the Soviet hierarchy.) And so there began to grow up in the Soviet Union an elite of managers and "shock workers"—those who spectacularly exceeded their quota in production—who, in addition to high salaries and wage rates, would enjoy special privileges when it came to housing, automobiles, the right to purchase goods not available to the general public, etc. The old rule that a member of the Party, no matter what his government or managerial position, could not be paid in excess of the wages received by the average skilled worker was discarded. Against the economic distress of the population at large, this creation of a privileged class was a startling departure from the post-Revolution Communist mores. Yet such material incentives undoubtedly contributed to more efficient industrial management and administration, as well as strengthened the loyalty of the privileged elite to its creator—the dictator.

With the same abruptness, Stalin decreed and extolled single management of state enterprises and factories. The idea of workers' control had been left far behind. But the regime now commanded that managers and directors in good standing should be free of interference by labor unions and *lower* Party organs. Management by committee, until then a frequent Soviet practice, was abolished in favor of individual responsibility. And so if he fulfilled or exceeded his production quota, the Soviet manager would enjoy authority over his labor force and in general the management of his enterprise that could be envied by his capitalist counterpart.

It has been often observed that the requirements of industrialization made the Soviet regime adopt many social policies that had accompanied industrialization in Western Europe in the nineteenth century, as well as deliberately to discard many innovative features of the brave new world of postrevolutionary Russia. Until the early 1930's progressive education—reflecting partly John Dewey's ideas and partly Marx's—was the rule in Soviet schools. Grades and the authority of teachers were disparaged, and formal schooling was combined with labor training. Now traditionalist methods were restored, and progressive education condemned. Grades and strict school discipline were restored, as well as the more traditional type of curriculum. It may appear paradoxical that the Communist Party should have abandoned Marx's principle of combining study with production work, but it was thought unwise to introduce young people prematurely to the actual conditions of the industrial life of the period. At the same time, ideological indoctrination and the teaching of the Stalinist version of Party history were intensified.

Like many revolutions, the October one had a disruptive effect on the family. Some early Communist sociologists theorized about the eventual "withering away" of the family. For all of Lenin's rather traditionalist views in such matters, Soviet legislation had licensed wide latitude in morals; certainly in this respect the Soviet Union of the twenties was, as the term now goes, a permissive society. Divorce was easy to obtain, abortion was legalized, and criminal sanctions against sexually deviant behavior abolished. But such liberalism did not fit the new scale of values Stalin was now seeking to impose upon Soviet society. Sexual license is destructive of the wholehearted pursuit of production targets; stable family life, on the other hand, contributes to economic responsibility. And for obvious reasons the regime now needed a high birth rate. Divorce in Russia of the thirties became expensive to obtain, abortion made permissible only for medical reasons. And severe penalties were prescribed for the practice of homosexuality. This official imposition of Victorian standards reflected of course the economic needs of the hour, but also the incompatibility of any totalitarian system with an individualistic approach toward morals, and its inability to tolerate lack of norms and regulations in any social sphere.

The requirements of uniformity of the (Stalinist) Party line were extended into every sphere of culture and scholarship as well. It was natural that most of the previous writings on Party history should now be considered as reflecting right- or left-wing deviations, or as failing to stress Stalin's role as a cofounder of communism and Lenin's principal pupil and helper. But the regime, beginning with the thirties, laid down canons of what is correct and what subversive in fields like poetry, music, theoretical physics. The most extreme cases of enforcing arbitrary standards in the arts and science would come in the middle thirties and after World War II, but the gathering momentum in that direction can be observed as early as 1930. The dominant if not the only theme and style in the arts and literature was to be socialist realism—that is, positive representation of Soviet reality in a medium easily accessible, and understandable, to the mass of population. This of course meant not only political conformity but also the discarding of innovative and experimental artistic and literary techniques like atonal music, nonobjective painting and sculpture, blank verse, the individualistic and Freudian motifs in prose, etc. In contrast the artist was encouraged to create music that people could hum, the pop art kind of paintings of kolkhoz and factory life that could be reproduced as propaganda posters, poems and novels celebrating industrialization and collectivization and extolling Stalin's role in the Civil War. The artist who refused to conform (and requirements for conformity grew ever more detailed and oppressive; what was permitted in 1930 might by 1932 be deemed subversive) was effectively precluded from communicating his art to the public.

In science officially prescribed obscurantism and xenophobia, which were to become so prominent later on, especially during the Zhdanov period (1946–48), were already noticeable in the early thirties. The stress was on practical results: science was to help the Party and the government in their struggle to modernize Russia, hence a certain disparagement of pure science. The relativity theory, always suspect because of its alleged link with "idealist" philosophy—an anathema to Marxism—was denounced in philosophical journals, but for the moment physicists were left in peace. The stress on the practical was far from being an unmixed blessing for applied scientists: the government in general (and particularly Stalin, for whom this tendency was typical) was looking for scientific panaceas which with little expense would miraculously increase industrial and agricultural output, and this of course encouraged charlatans and quacks. Already in this period one encounters the name of Trofim Lysenko, the agronomist who, under the Party's sponsorship, was to become the dictator of Soviet biology and one of the outstanding charlatans in history.

The multifaceted network of terror, controls, and propaganda as well as the missionary zeal of a number of Communists provides a key to the ability of Stalin's regime to survive what, except for the years 1941–42, was its most precarious period.

The opposition within the Party lay shattered. Trotsky was forcibly exiled from the Soviet Union in 1929 and began the life of a wanderer through foreign lands that would end in Mexico in 1940 with a blow from a pickax by an agent of the GPU. Many of his former followers, having recanted, were readmitted into the Soviet administrative machinery though not in policy-making capacities. The same held true of the Bukharin wing of the opposition. Such former luminaries of Soviet politics as Bukharin himself, Rykov and Pyatakov now occupied subordinate government positions where their administrative, diplomatic, or publicistic talents could be used, but where their political influence was nil. (Pyatakov, for example, was mentioned in Lenin's Testament as the most promising of the Party's younger leaders; a former left oppositionist, Pyatakov in the early thirties served as an important economic administrator.) In a startling contrast to the Lenin era the very idea of *opposition* to the leadership was now impermissible and almost inconceivable. To question policies approved by the Leader, as Stalin was now called, meant no longer to incur the risk of being branded a "deviationist" but meant outright treason. Party congresses were becoming infrequent; instead of being convoked annually as they were until 1925, three years were allowed to elapse between the fifteenth (1927) and sixteenth (1930). And in a glaring violation of the Party statute which required a congress at least once every three years, the seventeenth would not meet until 1934. The very idea that Party congresses were forums where policies were decided or discussed now fell into abeyance. Their role became almost as decorative and devoid of political significance as that of state legislative organs. They served to extol the Leader, give a unanimous approval to policies formulated by him and his lieutenants, and to listen and applaud the regime's survey of domestic and international situations.

Of course, the trauma of forcible collectivization was found to give rise to wide and in most cases secret apprehension and revulsion even among the Party members. If there were zealots for whom the period represented an exhilarating adventure, there were also those who could not remain untouched by the suffering of millions or who simply feared that Communism would not survive such a foolhardy experiment. But Stalin now had no inhibitions about dealing with doubters and waverers, although not yet with the ferocity he would display in a few years. In one year, from January to December 1933, the Party was purged of more than one-fifth of its membership, the number of members and candidates decreasing from 3.5 million to 2.7. The slightest gesture of protest came to mean a plot. Thus in 1932 a group of rather obscure Party figures headed by one M. Riutin, once a borough Communist leader in Moscow, circulated a memorandum urging less draconian policies in the countryside and suggesting that Stalin be removed as general secretary. This was an action which a few years before would have led at most to the ejection of the signatories from the Party. Now in addition they were given prison terms, and there are grounds to believe that Stalin felt that this treatment was much too lenient. But already one hears of Communists' being sent to forced labor camps or, in at least one case, being executed for real or alleged contacts with Trotsky.

The survival of Stalin's rule requires some additional explanations. In the highest Party circles there was, in addition to fear, a realistic recognition that to overthrow the tyrant at this period of turmoil, to destroy the legend of his infallibility at the time when the Party's cohesion and decisiveness was its main weapon in the struggle against the majority of the nation would probably have led to the overthrow of the Communist regime. There are grounds to believe that several high Party officials were hoping that once the most hazardous phase of the country's economic transformation was over, Stalin's powers could be curbed and he himself would certainly not be killed or imprisoned (the regime's fate was too much bound up with his legend for that) but transferred to a position other than general secretary.

The Changing International Situation

Another reason why even those who might have considered desperate measures against Stalin felt compelled to stay their hand lay in the international situation. The period of the great internal upheaval in the USSR coincided with a drastic worsening of the world picture. Those were years of the great Depression which undermined the seeming stabilization of capitalism following the World War, and through mass unemployment in the leading industrial countries posed a threat not only to peace but to the democratic pattern of politics in the West.

The first phase of the world crisis could be watched by the Communists with equanimity. Traditionally, it was the economic and political stability of capitalism that they feared; depression, economic and social chaos within the Western countries were, it was held, propitious circumstances for the advance of communism. Thus the Locarno agreement of 1926 was viewed as a setback for Soviet diplomacy insofar as it promoted reconciliation between World War I enemies; the League of Nations was the kernel of a possible anti-Soviet coalition of capitalist powers.

But the growing fissures in the ramshackle international order soon began to have menacing implications even for the Soviet Union. At first danger appeared to be centered in the Far East. Chiang Kai-shek had severed Chinese-Soviet diplomatic relations in 1928. The Chinese Communists under Mao Tse-tung were still pursuing what at the moment appeared a hopeless struggle against Chiang's growing power. Between 1928 and 1934 their guerrilla activities were confined to the province of Kiangsi. Chiang's government situated in Nanking was, however, national only on paper. It ruled some provinces directly, but elsewhere its authority was maintained through very unstable agreements with the local warlords. One of the latter, who dominated Manchuria, was encouraged by Nanking to move against Soviet interests in the province. Soviet consulates were raided and later on the Chinese Eastern Railway, in which under the agreement of 1924 the USSR held joint ownership, was seized and its Russian officials chased out. For all his own weakness, Chiang undoubtedly hoped to profit by Russia's internal troubles. By the same token the Soviets were well aware of the danger of acquiescing in this act of force. The USSR government presented the Chinese authorities with an ultimatum; when it was disregarded, Soviet troops, under the future Marshal Blyukher, entered Manchuria. The Chinese troops, suited to clashes with the warlords but not to fighting an army equipped with tanks and planes, were easily routed. In December 1929 an agreement restored the status of the Chinese Eastern Railway as being under joint Russo-Chinese administration.

But it was a power much more formidable than Chiang's China that was to be the main cause of Soviet apprehensions during the next four years. The lesson of the ease with which the Soviets trounced the local troops was not lost on the Japanese. And Tokyo had reasons of its own for hostility to Chiang; until the Chinese Nationalists' agreement with the local boss, Manchuria had been a virtual protectorate of Japan's. And so in 1931 occurred the first of the major aggressions that were to lead to World War II: the Japanese occupied Manchuria and soon proclaimed its "independence." Directed as it was mainly at Chiang, this step had ominous implications for the USSR. The Soviet economic interests in Manchuria would now be threatened by a much more powerful state. Emboldened by their success and by the Soviet lack of reaction to it, the Japanese militants might now turn their attention to the Soviet Far Eastern territories, and to Moscow's virtual protectorate, Outer Mongolia.

And so Soviet policy makers had to hope that instead of attacking their country then, in the midst of a social and economic cataclysm, the Japanese would continue to nibble at China. And by the same token the USSR now had a stake in the survival and strengthening of the Chiang regime. Should Chiang give way to a pro-Japanese regime, or be forced to make a deal with Japan, Tokyo's hands would be free vis-à-vis the Russian Far East. How to avoid a Japanese attack would, from now until December 7, 1941, be one of the main preoccupations of Soviet diplomacy. One approach was to encourage Chiang in an anti-Japanese posture. Hence despite all that had gone on since 1926, the Soviet government in 1932 restored diplomatic relations with Nanking. Soon the USSR would help the Nationalist government with military supplies, and after the beginning of the full-fledged war between China and Japan in 1937, with military instructors.

While declaring their readiness to parry any military attacks in the Far East, Soviet foreign policy sought at the same time to appease Japan. Following the setting up of the Japanese puppet, Manchukuo, Moscow offered to sell its interest in the Manchurian Railway to the latter. (The sale was finally concluded, the Soviets obtaining but a fraction of their holdings' real worth, in 1935.) Also, Moscow offered to negotiate a nonaggression treaty with Japan. But for all the resources of Soviet diplomacy as well as the considerable strengthening of the Soviet Far Eastern forces, which were put in a position to maintain military operations without immediate help from European Russia, the Japanese threat continued to weigh heavily on the consciousness of the Soviet leaders. Unlike the alleged threats of "capitalist intervention" evoked by the regime in the 1920's for propaganda and political purposes, the danger from Japan was real and imminent, and it added poignancy to Stalin's warning that rapid industrialization was imperative for national security.

The rise of fascism in Europe appeared at first to pose no danger to the Soviet Union comparable to that in Asia. Soviet relations with Mussolini's Italy had in general been correct and the international implications of the phenomenon of fascism were to become clear only with Hitler's coming to power in 1933. The preceding three years, which marked a gradual collapse of the Weimar Republic and a spectacular accession of strength to the National Socialists, were viewed by both the Kremlin and the German Communists with equanimity if not satisfaction. A collapse of democracy in Germany could not but profit the cause of the Soviet Union and communism. Even if Hitler did come to power, he obviously could not cope with the problems of unemployment and general economic collapse—his rule would be but a short interval before the masses would turn to the Communists as the only party capable of dealing with their economic distress. And though Hitler exuded anti-Communist sentiments, his quarrel, it was believed in Moscow, was mainly with the victors of World War I. The middle-class German parties were, on the contrary, committed to the policy of reconciliation with France and Britain. And so the German Communists rejected resolutely any and all proposals by the Social Democrats for a joint front against Nazism and for the preservation of the Weimar Republic. Official pronouncements of the Comintern continued to brand socialists everywhere as "social fascists." For all this blindness, Soviet foreign policy in the early thirties was taking note of the heating up of the international situation. In 1932, when such treaties were still thought to possess considerable importance, Soviet diplomats sought and obtained nonaggression treaties with France, Poland, and the Baltic states. The treaty with France was a sign that Stalin was hedging his bets and opening up the possibility of seeking a rapprochement with the West should Germany, whether under a Nazi regime or a coalition of right-wing parties (in 1932 still thought the more likely eventuality), turn against the USSR. The agreements with Poland, then under the semiauthoritarian regime of Marshal Pilsudski, and the Baltic states had the same rationale. Any actual military operation against the Soviet Union could be launched only through these states.

The coming to power of Hitler did not, at first, lead Moscow to alter its course. The Kremlin still did not believe that National Socialism had staying powers. And militarily Germany could not as yet be considered a threat comparable to that posed by Japan. Though Germany from the time of the treaty began to evade the military provisions of Versailles, in 1933 it still appeared to be years away from reaching military equality with, let alone superiority over, France. But within a few months of Hitler's appointment as chancellor on January 30, 1933, there were clear portents of things to come. First, Nazism was clearly not a transitory phenomenon which in time would give way to a German October. The Communist as well as other parties were brutally suppressed and, outside of the Reichswehr and the unruly elements within the National Socialist movement itself, no one remained who could challenge Hitler's growing power. Only a blind man could fail to perceive that the German "masses," not to speak of the middle class, far from wishing for a revolutionary upheaval, were increasingly under the spell of the Führer's nationalistic oratory. In

Molotov, Stalin, and Litvinov inside the Kremlin.

the second place, Hitler, far from abandoning his inflammatory anti-Communist rhetoric, now employed it not only for internal purposes, but also in order to convince the conservative circles in the West that National Socialist Germany was their natural and staunchest ally against communism. A decisive reorientation of the Soviet attitude toward Germany and hence toward the West was not to come until 1934. There were still influential circles in both countries desirous of continuing the collaboration begun by the Rapallo agreements. But late in 1933 the long-term collaboration between the Reichswehr and the Red Army came to an end. The German instructors who for more than a decade had clandestinely helped the Soviet military departed, the German training installations on Soviet soil were disbanded. Germany was now rearming openly and needed no subterfuges, and in view of Hitler's increasing threats it would have been folly to let

German military personnel move freely throughout the Soviet military establishment.

This summary view of Soviet Russia's international situation in the early thirties makes it clear how much Stalin was the beneficiary of the external dangers that confronted the country. Even the most resolute enemy of the dictator had to grant logic to his dictum that the country had to make up its industrial backwardness within a few years or go under.

Like everything else in the Soviet Union, the general lines of foreign policy had been laid down first by Lenin and then, incomparably more so, by Stalin with the advice of the Politburo. Yet since the attention of the top leaders was usually riveted on pressing domestic problems, the actual management of diplomacy was, more than in other branches of Soviet administration, left to the given minister. Neither Georgi Chicherin, who skillfully conducted Soviet foreign relations in the twenties, nor his successor, Maxim Litvinov, who took over the Foreign Commissariat in 1930 (although, in view of Chicherin's illness, he had in fact assumed charge some years before), was of first-rank political importance. They were executors rather than makers of policies, and thus there is no doubt that Chicherin had very little to do with the policy toward China in the mid-twenties or Litvinov with the Comintern's instructions to the German Communists, which contributed to the collapse of the Weimar Republic. Yet by the same token both of them and especially Litvinov contributed a great deal to the general style of Soviet diplomacy. Being men of wide culture and with extensive experience in the West, both Chicherin and Litvinov were able to minimize and mollify foreign complaints about the nexus between the USSR and international communism, and to gain for Russia a gradual acceptance into the European concert of nations, in a way that probably none of Stalin's then principal lieutenants could have done. It is still unclear to what an extent Stalin sought, and if he did whether he paid heed to, Litvinov's advice on the general lines of his foreign policy. But the success of the new pattern of Soviet policy that began to emerge in 1932–33 was very largely due to the Foreign Commissar's expertise and personality. It is he who in 1933 personally conducted the negotiations that concluded with the establishment of formal diplomatic relations between the United States and the Soviet Union. The new Democratic administration in Washington was more receptive than its predecessor to the normalization of relations with the USSR, and the common apprehension of both states at the growing power and aggressiveness of Japan was a forceful argument in favor of a diplomatic rapprochement. The two obstacles to the recognition on the American side had traditionally been the eternal question of the prerevolutionary

Russian debts, and of course the Comintern. As to the first, it was agreed to postpone the discussion until *after* the recognition and, to be sure, the issue was eventually allowed to expire with the passage of time. As to the Comintern, Litvinov sought to satisfy the American craving for legalistic assurances by formally pledging the Soviet government "to refrain, and to restrain all persons in government service and all organizations of the government, or under its direct or indirect control . . . from any act overt or covert liable in any way whatsoever to injure the tranquillity, prosperity, order or security of any part of the United States, its territories or possessions."

Recognition by the United States[4] completed the circle of great powers that had normal relations with the Communist state, which had thus gained the prescriptive right to conduct its own relations with the capitalist world in what was, by pre-1914 standards of diplomatic life, an unorthodox way, being simultaneously a "normal" state and the center of an international political movement. As to the more substantive benefits the Russians expected from the agreement, they were bound to be disappointed: in an isolationist mood and coping with the Depression, the United States was not going to pursue a very active policy in the Far East, nor would it hold out the prospect even of economic aid to the USSR should the Soviet Union be attacked by Japan.

At the end of this period the rulers of the USSR, confronting the ineluctable facts of the rapidly worsening international situation, realized that to meet the dangers Soviet foreign policy must become more than ever free from ideological preconceptions. And so there was little ideological rhetoric but a great deal of somber realism in Litvinov's survey of international relations delivered in December 1933. The danger spots were clearly identified: "(A) revolution . . . brought a new party to power in Germany preaching the most extreme anti-Soviet ideas, . . . Japanese policy is now the darkest cloud on the horizon." The current and future Soviet tactics were equally clearly spelled out: to seek friendlier relations with the West, but without giving up the hope of coming to an agreement with the would-be aggressors. As to the former, "Any state, even the most imperialist, may at one time or another become profoundly pacifist." But he was almost pleading in his references to Germany and Japan. The Soviet Union was not unduly disturbed over Hitler's repression of the German Communists: "We as Marxists are the last who can be reproached with allowing sentiment to prevail over reason." So wouldn't Hitler promise not to attack Russia, not only now but also

[4] The formal relations begun in a glow of amity soon developed dissonances. The first American envoy, William Bullitt, long a proponent of Russo-American rapprochement, became through his experience in Moscow bitterly anti-Soviet.

"when Germany will have greater forces to put those aggressive ideas into effect"? He reminded the Tokyo government that when its Manchurian coup led to the discussion of joint action against Japan, the USSR resolutely refrained from any participation. "We declined to take part in the international action taken and prepared at the time, firstly because we did not believe in the sincerity and the firmness of purpose of the states which did take part, but chiefly because we did not and we do not now seek an armed conflict with Japan."

The forthcoming changes in Soviet foreign policy were thus in no sense as unanticipated or abrupt as they are sometimes presented. Beginning in 1934 the connection between Soviet domestic politics and the international situation became much closer than it had been at any time since 1921, and foreign danger would be both a partial cause of and the rationalization for unprecedented terror at home.

5. Foreign Threats and Domestic Terror

A Conciliatory Mood

The Seventeenth Party Congress, which assembled on January 26, 1934, could and did celebrate the regime's victory on the collectivization front. Through its system of procurements at low prices, the state now exacted even higher tribute from the peasantry than in the tragic years of 1928–32.[1] With the foundations laid for a rapid growth of heavy industry, it was now felt that the regime could and had to do something for the long-suffering Soviet consumer. The second Five-Year Plan, which began officially in 1933 but was modified through a resolution of the Congress, still proposed tempos for industrial growth, but allowed for a considerable increase in consumer goods. (However, the foreign danger was by 1936 to shift the emphasis again to heavy industry, and the targets for both heavy and light industry were to be adversely affected through the dislocation caused by the massive purges and terror.) The dictator and his associates could feel that, for all the darkening international situation, they had emerged not only unscathed but more powerful from a desperate domestic crisis.

The Seventeenth Party Congress thus took place against the back-

[1] The average figure for state procurements for 1933–37 would be 27.5 million tons of grain, or 37.7 percent of the total crop, as against 18.2 million and 24.7 percent for 1928–32. Lazar Volin, *A Century of Russian Agriculture*, Cambridge, Mass., 1970, p. 232.

ground of a certain relaxation, and of the hope, fatuous as events were to demonstrate, that the worst was behind. The occasion marked a virtual deification of Stalin. Every speech at the congress began and ended with a fulsome tribute to the leader. Former oppositionists like Bukharin, Zinoviev, and Kamenev were allowed to address the gathering once again to denigrate themselves and to pay tribute to the "leader of the working classes everywhere . . . of progressive mankind . . . the outstanding genius of the era." The secretary of the Leningrad Party, Kirov, declared that it would be useless to discuss in detail the general line of the Party: "It will be more correct and more useful for the work at hand to accept as Party law all the proposals and corroborations of Comrade Stalin's speech." And his proposal, like all the congress' resolutions, passed unanimously.

Yet, the official Party documents in the Khrushchev era hinted, this worship and eulogizing of the tyrant partook of something in the nature of a plot. Some of Stalin's lieutenants, while realizing that it would be impossible to get rid of him, evidently tried to persuade him to abandon day-to-day operations of the Party affairs, to assume a government position and leave the post of general secretary. The name mentioned most frequently in this connection was that of Sergei Kirov. Thus it was evidently hoped that, while extolling Stalin and appeasing his megalomania, his powers could be curbed, and the Party and the nation could be protected from sudden shifts, such as the one on collectivization in 1929–30. There are also indications (the whole subject still remains obscure) that, whether genuinely convinced or deeming it polite to appear so, Stalin at the moment appeared to be willing to go along with the plan. In the announcement of elections to the highest Party organs following the congress, the list of the Central Committee secretaries listed Stalin as merely one of them rather than, as hitherto, *general* secretary. And Kirov was one of the two newcomers to the Secretariat. In addition to Stalin and Kirov, Kaganovich and Andrei Zhdanov were elected.

If indeed there was such a plot, then it bears a striking resemblance to what was to happen in the 1960's within the Chinese Communist Party, when some members of the hierarchy evidently tried to elevate Mao into a combination of tutelary divinity and elder statesman while undercutting his real powers. In China Mao was to respond by unleashing the "Cultural Revolution." In the Soviet Union, this plot by adulation, as it might be called, was to contribute perhaps to the savage repression of the 1930's. After terror was unleashed in 1936, participants in the Seventeenth Congress were to be among its main victims. Of 1,966 delegates to this "Congress of Victors," as it was called at the time, 1,108 were purged, arrested, or worse. Of the 139 members and alternates of the Central Committee elected upon the occasion, 98 were to be executed.

For most of 1934, such horrors were still hidden in the future. The mood of the Party and the country, while in no sense reflecting Stalin's extravagant and oft-quoted statement "Life has become better, comrades, life has become gayer," was still one of relief. One could find some elements of comfort even in the international situation. The war with Japan had not come, though the Japanese and their Manchurian puppets were subjecting the Soviet-owned Manchurian railroad to increasing chicaneries. If the German threat was becoming clearer, then it was hoped by many that it might have some beneficial effects at home. It was reasonable to expect more liberal domestic policies now that public opinion in Britain and France was being courted by Russia, and Litvinov was so eloquently presenting the USSR as a peace-loving, law-abiding state, so different from Germany with its open threats and its *publicized* concentration camps.

And indeed in 1934 the Soviet attitude toward the outside world appeared to be undergoing a wholesale reassessment. The USSR entered the League of Nations, once characterized in Communist parlance as the "league of the imperialist robbers." Soviet accession (the USSR was granted a permanent seat on the League Council, thus emphasizing its status as a great power) was unaccompanied by an illusion, still current in the West and especially in Britain, as to the League's efficacy in stopping aggression. But it laid foundations for a closer rapprochement and perhaps an alliance with the West, now clearly alarmed over the open character and quick pace of German rearmament. Hitler was still courting the West and presenting himself as the champion of European civilization against the threat of communism, but Germany had left the League, while the USSR by entering it vouchsafed its commitment to collective security and the preservation of peace. The contrast was telling.

It is not surprising that a parallel shift was taking place in the policies of the Comintern. The posture of uncompromising hostility toward socialist and other left-wing parties decreed by the Sixth Comintern Congress in 1928 was now seen as having contributed to Hitler's coming to power. If persisted in, it might result in victories of the right in countries like France, with nefarious results for any prospects for further rapprochement between the USSR and the West. And so Moscow, without any inhibitions or apologies for past errors and miscalculations, now authorized and indeed urged Communist parties everywhere to reverse their stance and to seek an alliance with the socialists and democratic forces in general to mount a common front against fascism. This was to become known as the policy of the Popular Front. (Prior to 1934–35 foreign Communists pursued the tactics of "the Popular Front from below"—i.e., wooed the rank and file of the socialist parties, seeking to make them repudiate their leadership. The new policy, on the contrary, meant that the Communists would abandon their radical phraseology and seek agreements and electoral alliances with the leaders of other parties of the left.)

The convictions both that Hitler had the staying power and that *for the moment* it was fruitless to seek an accommodation with him ripened in Moscow after June 30, 1934. This was the date of the famous "Night of Long Knives" when the Führer slaughtered the high command of his private army, the SA, throwing in for good measure a few inconvenient politicians and generals. He thus got rid of potentially dangerous elements within his own movement and cemented the alliance with the Reichswehr. Unchallenged master of Germany, his hands were now free for foreign adventure, once the country's rearmament reached an advanced state.

Internally the developments of 1934 seemed at first to justify the hope that in response to the danger of war, the regime would become less repressive and exacting. It could be taken as a reassuring sign that the dreaded GPU was now renamed the Commissariat of Internal Affairs (with the Russian initials NKVD), even though the secret police remained under its previous officials, the chief of them Henryk Yagoda. A long-time high official of the Cheka and GPU, Yagoda had gained special renown as manager of great public works projects built with convict labor, such as the White Sea canal. A more substantive ground for satisfaction was provided by the Central Committee's decision in November to end the rationing of bread and flour. The special political departments of the Machine Tractor Stations, which functioned as instruments of control and aggression in the countryside, were abolished. From now on the director of each station would have a political deputy subject to the *local* Party organs. This could be taken as a sign of normalization on the peasant front.

But these reassuring signs were followed by an event that racked the Party and country. On December 1 Sergei Kirov, secretary of the Central Committee and head of the Leningrad organization, was assassinated in the local Party headquarters. This was the first major political assassination within Russia since the Civil War.

More than forty years after the deed the full circumstances of the murder still remain a mystery. In the great Moscow trials of 1936–38 the crime was laid at the door of (and in varying degrees "confessed" by) the whole galaxy of past opponents and erstwhile allies of Stalin's, beginning with Zinoviev and Kamenev (inspired, of course, by Trotsky) and including, as "revealed" in the last trial, none other than Yagoda himself! The post-Stalin versions as presented by Khrushchev in 1956 and 1961 by implication absolved those notables (all executed in the 1930's) and hinted broadly though vaguely at Stalin's complicity. As elaborated by some other writers (including a current Soviet dissenter, Roy Medvedev), Stalin, envious of Kirov's alleged popularity in the Party and seeking a pretext for the liquidation of the Bolshevik Old Guard, ordered the secret police not to interfere with the designs of the actual assassin, one Nikolayev.

All that can be said with some assurance is that the murder was committed by Nikolayev, a Party member and former minor Leningrad official. He and some alleged accomplices, all one-time members of the Komsomol in Leningrad when Zinoviev was its boss, were tried *in camera* and executed within days of the crime.

Whatever the truth about Stalin's role (and there is no solid evidence backing his involvement), he responded by unleashing terror. The very day of the murder an official decree ordered all investigations of terroristic acts to be completed within ten days; the judicial organs were not to hold up execution of death sentences for such acts or attempts since no appeals would be considered. Further, even more drastic laws followed. And to show that the law was not a mere threat, newspapers on December 6 announced the execution of several dozen people, entirely unconnected with the Leningrad murder. Political assassination is a highly contagious business and the dictator was taking no chances. Mass deportation, again of people who could not even be remotely connected with Nikolayev and of former oppositionists, took place in Leningrad. Some accounts speak of as many as 250,000 being exiled from the northern metropolis, many of them to labor camps. In January 1935 Zinoviev, Kamenev, and some of their former associates were tried for moral complicity in the murder. All were sentenced, Zinoviev to ten years, Kamenev to five. A precedent was set for branding former Communist greats as inspirers of treason and murder; Trotsky had already been officially identified as the man who from abroad provided funds for the Leningrad murder ring.

The full unleashing of terror was still not to take place for a year and a half, when, from being possible, a European war became probable, and Stalin decided to liquidate all those who might threaten his rule once enemy troops penetrated the Russian border. But even before the terrible years 1936–38 there were indications that the dictator and his lieutenants (some of whom were to be among his victims) were no longer thinking of terror exclusively as a means of crushing opposition, whether actual or potential. Systematic repression was to become an administrative technique. The initials NKVD acquired a connotation even more sinister than those of its predecessors, Cheka and GPU; "wrecking" and sabotage became standard explanations for any major industrial accident, any case of nonfulfillment of a planned target. Closeness to the dictator was no longer a guarantee against an abrupt arrest and horrendous charges. Thus in 1935 Abel Yenukidze, secretary of the Presidium of the Executive Committee of the Supreme Soviet, was summarily dismissed, ejected from the Party, and arrested. And Yenukidze was one of the oldest of Stalin's personal as well as political friends. (He was shot, without a trial, in 1937.)

Incongruously, while the machinery of terror was gathering momentum, on the international scene the USSR was aligning itself with European democracies. The German danger was already clear if not imminent. Hitler's endeavor to gain an understanding, if not actual assistance, in the West was not making any headway; but in addition to the rapidly growing German military might, he could boast of some diplomatic successes. The League of Nations' half-hearted attempts to restrain Italian aggression in Ethiopia alienated Mussolini from France and Britain and started the sequence of events that culminated in the Rome-Berlin Axis. Italy was being taken seriously as a great power. And Hitler's nonaggression treaty with Poland opened up the possibility of Polish collusion in Germany's anti-Soviet designs.

And so 1935 saw two major steps in the Soviet–West rapprochement. On May 2, 1935, the Franco-Russian treaty of mutual assistance was signed. Each country was pledged to come to the other's aid "in the case of an unprovoked attack on the part of a European state." It is not too much to say that both sides hoped that the mere fact of this alliance would discourage aggression, rather than thought seriously of the treaty's becoming operative in the case of an actual war. In any case, no detailed discussions or conventions between the two general staffs about the implementation of the treaty were to take place until the summer of 1939. Also unlike the case of the pre-World War I alliance between France and Imperial Russia, it was difficult to see how if Germany attacked France, the Soviet army could render effective help to the latter unless Poland authorized the passage of Soviet troops through her territory (something which in 1935 appeared more than problematic). Still it was an undoubted and important success for the USSR. Hitler could no longer count on French and hence presumably British neutrality if Germany (with Poland's collusion) should launch an attack upon the Soviet Union. In order to avoid war on two fronts, something his generals, with their memories of 1914–18, dreaded, he would have to detach France from her alliance or make a deal with Stalin. (In the very same year, in the course of Russian-German commercial negotiations, Soviet diplomats probed discreetly whether Hitler would be interested in political discussions with the USSR. At the time he was not.)

The enhanced international standing of the Soviet Union was emphasized by the visit to Moscow of the French foreign minister, Pierre Laval, later of Vichy notoriety. For internal political reasons, the Frenchman sought a declaration from the highest authority of communism that the defense policy of his government was supported in Moscow. Stalin obliged in a public statement which, at the time, created much stir in Europe, since it involved a right-wing politician invoking Soviet interference in the internal politics of his country: "Comrade Stalin expressed complete understanding and approval of the national defense policy pursued by France with the object of maintaining its armed forces at a level consistent with its security requirements."

The French Communists were more than ready to take the hint. For a year they had pursued the Popular Front tactics, and their plea for collaboration with the Socialist and Radical Socialist parties (the latter, the great party of the Third Republic, neither socialist nor very radical, but championing republicanism and anticlericalism) included an avowal that, because of the German danger and the fascist one at home, their party would now support French rearmament. The position of the French Communists, which crystallized after a visit to Moscow by their leader, Maurice Thorez, was but a forerunner of the general line adopted by the Comintern in the summer of 1935.

The struggle against fascism was the leitmotiv of the Seventh (and last) Congress of the Comintern, held in Moscow July–August 1935. Ernst Thälmann, the leader of the German party, then languishing in a Nazi concentration camp, was elected honorary chairman of this world assembly of communism. George Dimitrov, the Bulgarian Communist, who not long before had taunted Nazi dignitaries at the Reichstag fire trial, was a prominent figure and was elected general secretary of the Comintern. Most speeches breathed defiance of Germany and of Japanese militarism. But neither the congress nor the Popular Front line laid down by Moscow represented, as it was sometimes thought in the West, an abandonment of the traditional Communist policy and a new, clear-cut stance in favor of an alliance with the forces of democracy. The Soviet and hence international communism's aim was to erect a barrier against a further spread of fascism to prevent an attack on the Soviet Union, but *not* to enhance the strength of Britain and France to enable them to dominate European politics as they had done between Versailles and 1933. Implicit in this qualified friendship gesture toward the West was the belief that Britain and France still had the upper hand militarily and that it was not in the interest of the USSR to strengthen them unduly vis-à-vis Germany. Thus the French Communists, though they would now vote for the French military budget, would still oppose the extension of military service to two years. The current Soviet-Communist line was far from being a clarion call for a crusade against fascism in all its varieties. In Europe the Soviet objective was a balance of forces between fascism and the "camps of imperialists," as the West was still called in the congress' resolutions. It was hoped that such balance would render an attack upon the USSR unlikely and might in due time make even Hitler realize the need for an accommodation with the USSR. (It is unreasonable to assume that Stalin already foresaw or worked for a deal with Hitler such as he was eventually to conclude in 1939. The dictator sought, as any Soviet Communist in his place would have, to have several options open to him in the growing international crisis, and to avoid either Russia's isolation or an overcommitment to either side.) The Communist Party of China was "to extend the front of the struggle for national liberation and to draw into it all the national forces that are ready to repulse the robber campaign of the Japanese." In other words, the Chinese Communists were to seek an alliance with the Nationalist government, thus to strengthen the Kuomintang's somewhat faltering resolution to stand up to Japan. With a renewal of hostilities in China, Tokyo would hardly think of attacking the Soviet Far East.

The subtlety of the Soviet position escaped notice in the West. To much of the liberal opinion in Britain, France, and the United States, the USSR was taking an initiative in fighting fascism while their own governments foundered in indecision about rearming or appeasing the dictators or, like the United States, sought refuge in isolationism.

The image of progressive and quasi-democratic Russia was to gain in 1936. This was the year in which the new "Stalin" constitution came into effect in the Soviet Union. On paper it was (and is) advertised as "the most democratic constitution in the world." Elections were to be free, equal, and secret. Disenfranchised members of the former exploiting classes were now allowed to vote; the weighting of votes in favor of the urban as against rural population was abolished. The previous cumbersome pyramidal system of soviets was changed in favor of the Western pattern of two parliamentary chambers: the Soviet of the Union elected in equal electoral districts and the Soviet of Nationalities according to the federal principle—twenty-five deputies from each union republic, eleven from each autonomous republic, etc. To the list of individual rights found elsewhere, the Soviet document proudly added the right of every individual to demand that his government provide him with employment. It could not escape attention in the West that at the time Hitler preached his racist doctrine the Soviet constitution proclaimed: ". . . any advocacy of social or national exclusiveness or hatred or contempt, [is] punishable by law." And those without closer knowledge of the realities of Soviet politics had to be equally impressed with provisions such as "citizens of the USSR are guaranteed inviolability of the person"; "judges are independent and subject only to the law"; "the right freely to secede from the USSR is reserved to every Union Republic." Even people sophisticated about conditions in the USSR, such as some Russian political exiles, were tempted to view the new law as laying down the foundations of at least possible development in the direction of democracy.

It would be oversimplified to view the new constitution as designed merely for propaganda effect in the West. To a considerable extent it was also intended to impress the Soviet citizen with the idea that the great task of social engineering undertaken under the leadership of Stalin had been successfully concluded and that the USSR was now a new type of society. Exploiting classes, declared Stalin solemnly, had now disappeared, and in the brave new Soviet world there were just two friendly classes: workers and collective peasantry. The intelligentsia, Stalin elaborated, was not a separate class, for, unlike its prerevolutionary predecessor, it was predominantly recruited from workers and peasants and had no separate class interest distinct from the workers'. Thus the USSR had entered the era of socialism. But lest the naïve draw wrong conclusions, the Communist Party was specifically mentioned, as it had not been in the previous Soviet constitution, as "the vanguard of the working people in their struggle to build a communist society . . . the leading core of all organizations of the working people, both social and state." If one is asked to assess the real rather than rhetorical significance of the 1936 constitution, one is left with a rather slim residue: it marked the end of *legal* discrimination against the former exploiting classes with respect to voting and other rights; thus priests, etc., were no longer barred from the polls.

The Great Purge

Ironically, the year of the constitution was to see the beginning of that great terror which did illustrate the equality of all citizens: for the next three years terror was to claim victims among all strata of the population. Except for one man, no one, from Politburo member down to the humblest worker, was to feel secure from sudden and arbitrary imprisonment or execution. The complete catalogue of reasons that impelled the Stalin regime to unleash terror still eludes us, but the international situation was one potent factor. In 1936 the apparent equilibrium in Europe that had been reached through the Franco-Soviet alliance collapsed and the threat to the USSR became not only clear but imminent.

The international situation was transformed first of all by the entrance of German troops into the Rhineland on March 7. This was a violation not only of the Versailles Treaty but also of the voluntary German pledge under the Locarno agreement to keep this area demilitarized. At the same time the collective security system under the League of Nations was exposed as an illusion when Italy conquered

Ethiopia. Italy now drew close to Germany, and their dictators became partners in international blackmail that was to lead to war.

With German troops in the Rhineland, the Franco-Soviet alliance lost much of its original value as a brake on potential German aggression, at least insofar as the USSR was concerned. As long as the Rhineland was demilitarized, this part of Germany lay at the mercy of France in case of war. But now it was reasonable to foresee such a situation as was actually to arise in 1939–40: If Germany were to make an aggressive move in the east, France, even if it chose to meet its treaty obligations, would be unable to come speedily to the aid of an eastern ally, be it the USSR or, as the case actually was in 1939, Poland. Whatever the eventual outcome of a European war, the USSR, as had Imperial Russia between 1914 and 1917, might then suffer crippling defeats and territorial losses. Those defeats were a potent factor in the collapse of Imperial Russia. But Stalin's Russia might find itself in an even worse predicament should the Germans invade Soviet territory while conducting a war in the West. After all, the Soviet government had just subjected millions of peasants to untold suffering and imposed upon them a social and economic system they still resented. Within the Communist Party also there were many who suffered and were disgraced because of their opposition to the regime. For the moment they were silenced and acquiesced, or pretended to, in Stalin's leadership. But would they remain loyal and obedient in the case of war, especially a war that began with defeats and in the course of which a large part of the population might, as was very likely, refuse support to their tyrannical government? And it had to be assumed as probable that the Soviet Union, despite all the progress in industrialization, would still find itself unable at the outset to match German technology and armed might, and war would be fought on Russian territory.

Thus massive terror directed this time at the Communist Party itself was, if we follow the above hypothesis, a prophylactic measure intended to wipe out everybody who *might* oppose the regime if war broke out. From Stalin's point of view, it was especially important to destroy those Party figures who, though reduced by him to political insignificance, had at one time been close to Lenin and high in the Party councils. People like Bukharin and Tomsky presumably still had secret followers within the Party and in case of war they, either collectively or individually, could appear to many as a desirable alternative to Stalin's leadership. Since by now opposition to the dictator was held as equivalent to disloyalty to communism and the Soviet state, it was easy to push this association one step further and to assert that Stalin's erstwhile rivals and potential future opponents were by this very fact at least potential traitors. The arch oppositionist Trotsky, exiled from Russia in 1929, had for some time been branded by official propaganda as a fascist agent. (The charge was paradoxical as well as false, since Trotsky had warned about the danger of Hitler and urged Communists to join a coalition against him before this became the official Soviet position.) Both treason and instigations of murder were alleged and "proved" in the first trial of Zinoviev and Kamenev.

The focal point of the great purge was the three Moscow show trials—the one of 1936, with Zinoviev and Kamenev as the main figures; the 1937 one, with Pyatakov and the brilliant Communist publicist Karl Radek in star roles; and finally the most notorious one, in 1938, when a galaxy of former oligarchs such as Rykov, Bukharin, and Yagoda, as well as an assortment of lesser figures, was made to plead guilty to a variety of fantastic charges and, like most of the previously accused, sentenced to death and executed. The motif that opposition to Stalin was intrinsically linked with crime and treason runs through all the trials. As Zinoviev was made to say in the first of these spectacles: "My defective bolshevism became transformed into antibolshevism and through Trotskyism I arrived at fascism." And Kamenev: "Is it an accident that alongside of myself and Zinoviev . . . are sitting emissaries of foreign secret police departments, people with false passports, with dubious biographies and undoubted connections with the Gestapo? No, it is not an accident."

This intended propaganda lesson was accompanied by another one. Much of the past suffering incidental to collectivization, the lowered standard of living in the early thirties, etc., were now explained as having been caused by sabotage and wrecking carried on by both the left and the right opposition in order to discredit the regime and to topple Stalin. And if in the first trial the connection between all these crimes and horrors and foreign powers was but hinted at, in the final one of 1938 the wholesale treason was spelled out in all its fantastic detail: the accused were charged with, and for the most part confessed to, working on the direct orders of the German, Japanese, and, for good measure, Polish and British intelligence services.

As well as acknowledging sabotage and treason, the victims were branded with all sorts of other heinous crimes. It was "proved" that the most prominent of the fallen leaders were involved in the murder of Kirov, as well as in assassination plots and attempts against Stalin and his current lieutenants. The 1938 trial prominently featured medical murders; distinguished Soviet doctors confessed that on the orders of Yagoda they disposed, through "wrecking" medical treatment, of such notables as Politburo member Valerian Kuibyshev (he died in fact of a heart ailment) and Maxim Gorky, the celebrated Soviet writer and long-time fellow traveler (though occasionally opponent) of bolshevism.

The trials compounded this gothic tale of horrors with the drama of the courtroom, where the accused blandly confessed to the assorted absurdities of the indictment, where the prosecutor Andrei Vyshinsky bullied the victims and concluded his case: "Shoot them like mad dogs!" (One, N. Krestinsky, repudiated his confession in open court, but next day was again brought in line. Bukharin, though admitting some charges, still denied the most opprobrious ones.) With the trials still going on, mass meetings of workers would pass resolutions demanding death penalties, and the courts almost superfluous to say, obliged. Only a few of the accused, notably Radek, received jail sentences, but of those none was to emerge alive from prison.

The story of the preparation and management of the Moscow trials must be a high point of both human depravity and irrationality. The post-Stalin regime acknowledged by implication that the charges were entirely false, and confessions extracted from the victims by torture (for the most part psychological rather than physical) and threats against their families. Yet there has been no formal public nullification of the verdicts. The subject, like much else that went on under Stalin, remains, in the opinion of the present rulers, too painful and dangerous to be dealt with by a public inquest or debate.

As to the rationale of the gruesome spectacle, it would be unreasonable to argue that the regime's hopes were disappointed about the lesson it hoped the people would draw. The constant barrage of propaganda, the recollections of the recent economic chaos and privations, fear of the foreign invader, plus the fact that the accused in open court confirmed the charges—all of these in the eyes of the Soviet man in the street gave at least some plausibility to the charges. After all, there were at the time many abroad, and by no means all of them Communists or fellow travelers, who came to believe that no regime would have accused people so high in its past councils without at least some real guilt on their part. Superficially it might seem that it was hardly clever propaganda to present Lenin's closest collaborators, people who had ruled the Soviet Union and world communism for years, as men who degenerated into murderers and traitors. But again there was a reason to this apparent madness. The trials and the great purge in general were designed to instill in the masses the conviction that there was only one man who stood above any suspicion and on whom the safety of the country and its future depended. And so any attempt to question the leadership of the tyrant, any attempt to moderate the fearful bloodletting to which he subjected the country would now in itself serve as a presumptive proof of treason. By associating the regime's and the country's survival with his personal power, Stalin believed he was purchasing security against being overthrown, whether through a palace coup or through a popular uprising. And that his calculations were not unreasonable was to be vividly demonstrated in the first days of the German invasion in 1941. Due to his derelictions, the country was unprepared for war, the Red Army was dealt catastrophic defeats; but though suffering from nervous shock and unable to function for a week, the tyrant was still not overthrown. In a way, his very crimes had rendered him indispensable!

To what degree did the instigators of the trials, notably Stalin himself, believe in the tales of horror the former potentates were made to confess? This is the most difficult question of all. But it is at least probable, strange as it must seem to somebody who has not immersed himself in the atmosphere of the period, that the dictator and those of his servants who stage-managed the purges simply lost the distinction between potential and actual treason, that, to use a term from the idiom of ideology, they came to believe that "objectively" the defendants were guilty, even if in their more sober moments they acknowledged that it was sheer fiction to picture Trotsky as an agent of the German general staff or to assert that Bukharin at the behest of the British intelligence service was plotting to detach central Asia from the USSR.

The process of involving the regime as well as the whole society in mass hysteria, though rapid, was still gradual. The first trial dealt with the former left opposition, but the network of treason was to be broadened by implicating others, including the former right oppositionists. And so Kamenev confessed that Bukharin, Rykov, and Tomsky were privy to his designs. As a good prosecutor should, Vyshinsky then announced that investigation was begun as to the activities of those gentlemen. But in three weeks it was announced that the proceedings against the three rightists were dropped because of lack of evidence. It is clear that at this point there was some opposition within the Politburo as well as perhaps the secret police to Stalin's plans for a wholesale slaughter. For the moment he conceded. But on September 25, 1936, he demanded and obtained Yagoda's dismissal as commissar of internal affairs. His successor, Nikolai Yezhov, was a recent favorite of the tyrant's, and indeed he was to prove a more pliable instrument of terror, so much so that the most intense period of horrors—1937–38—was to pass into history and the popular parlance as *Yezhovshchina* (the times of Yezhov—a rather undeserved slight to Stalin; Yezhov, though undoubtedly a monster, was a mere executor of orders, and eventually, his task accomplished, he was himself removed and liquidated).

The execution of Lenin's closest collaborators as well as the circumstances of their trials might well have led to a shock abroad as well as a renunciation of Russia's current image as a constitutional state, ready to take its place beside democracies in the struggle against totalitarianism. But though there were some expressions of incredulity and horror, attention in the West became riveted on the new development in Europe's slide toward the world war. The Spanish Civil War erupted on July 28, 1936. Fascism was taking the offensive. Another sign that a war was now almost inevitable was the Anti-Comintern Pact between Japan and Germany. For all the pious language of the treaty, which pledged the two powers to cooperate in opposing the *spread* of communism, it had to be taken as a portent of an attack on the USSR from both East and West. And so all those tales of treason and international plots featured in the Moscow trials no longer seemed so fantastic. The Spanish Civil War was to make "fifth column" a familiar term. Wasn't Stalin right in liquidating the potential fifth column in his country, even if in the process he was laying it on too thick?

The Spanish events thus helped to obscure the negative impression of the purge. More than that, they clearly helped the new image of the Soviet Union as one power that was doing something to stop the march of fascism. Italy and Germany, though they had signed the fatuous nonintervention agreement proposed by Britain and France, publicized their help to the insurgent forces of General Franco. The USSR also signed the ineffective agreement, but to the edification of liberal and progressive forces throughout the world, hastened to assert its support of the legitimate Spanish government. On October 7, 1936, Stalin, in his public telegram to the secretary general of the Spanish Communists, expressed support for the cause of the embattled republic.

While gathering moral credit for its stance, the USSR was cautious in its support of the anti-Franco forces. Italy and Germany sent sizable contingents of their troops and air force to fight on the Nationalist side. The USSR channeled its help mainly through the Comintern. International brigades were recruited all over the world, but not in Russia. There were battalions on the Republican side bearing the names of Thälmann and Abraham Lincoln, but none named after Lenin or Stalin. The USSR did not spare military and technical advisers, and sent munitions and other supplies to the Republican side. Among Soviet emissaries were officers of the secret police. At various periods, with the collaboration of the Spanish Communists, they carried out a campaign of assassination of Trotskyites and of declared anti-Communists among the anarchists (always strong in the Spanish left), creating at times a virtual civil war within the Republican camp. Characteristically, many of the Soviet personnel attached to the Republicans were themselves to fall victims of the Russian purge. (An amazingly large number of victims of the post-World War II purges in the Communist countries of eastern Europe were also veterans of the international brigades.) The Soviet involvement in the Spanish imbroglio was thus of a qualified and cautious nature, and while it brought the USSR considerable propaganda dividends, it avoided a head-on collision with the German and Italian forces fighting in the war, as well as a share of the blame for the eventual collapse of the republic.

In the Far East the Japanese kept probing Soviet resolve and preparedness through a series of border incidents. The Soviet response was a mixture of firmness and appeasement. Under the latter, one must include the sale to the Japanese satellite state of Manchukuo of the East China Railway for a fraction of its worth. At the same time the Soviet government left Tokyo in no uncertainty as to its response in the case of a Japanese attack upon Soviet or Mongolian territory and accentuated its friendly attitude toward Chiang.

The key design of Soviet policy in the Far East had been for some time to make the Nationalist government of China take a more active anti-Japanese stance. This in turn depended on Chiang Kai-shek's giving up his resolve to liquidate the Communist forces within his country before grappling with the Japanese danger. In December 1936 Chiang was planning yet another campaign against the Chinese Communists, to be spearheaded by troops commanded by the former boss of Manchuria, Chiang Hsueh-ling. But the latter refused to fight his fellow countrymen, and when Chiang Kai-shek flew to the mutinous general's headquarters in Sian, he was arrested. There followed negotiations with the participation of the Communist emissary, Chou En-lai. Eventually the Generalissimo was released, but only after he pledged to end the fratricidal war and to take a strong anti-Japanese line. And so now there ensued further negotiations on the details of collaboration between the Chinese Nationalists and the Communists. (Most recent Soviet sources are explicit in revealing that the Comintern at the time *ordered* the Chinese Communists to seek a joint anti-Japanese front with Chiang. They maintain that at the time Mao was opposed to the Comintern's directive and sought to sabotage an accommodation with Chiang.)

The Sian episode was a fateful turning point in modern history. Quite likely it saved the Chinese Communists from destruction at the hands of the superior Nationalist forces (even though Chiang's previous "anti-bandit" campaigns, as he called them, had failed to achieve this aim). Quite possibly it averted a Japanese blow against the Soviet Far East. For with the negotiations going on between Chiang and the Communists, Tokyo decided to strike the Chinese first. On July 7, 1937, the Japanese attacked the Kuomintang forces and within a short time brought most of the maritime areas under their occupation. But no more than any other foreign power in modern times could they hope to conquer all of China. For obvious reasons, Tokyo's getting stuck in the Chinese quagmire had to be a source of relief and satisfaction to the Kremlin. In August, the Chinese and USSR governments signed a treaty of nonaggression and friendship. Soviet munitions and credits and military instructors began again to flow to Kuomintang China. The Chinese Communists, for their own part, declared on September 22 that in the interests of national unity they repudiated their revolutionary progress and placed their armed forces under the government of the Chinese Republic. The alliance was to prove most precarious and was marred by intermittent fighting between the two Chinese factions, but formally at least the agreement endured through World War II.

The threat of Japanese aggression against Russia was substantially diminished but it could not be entirely discounted. World War II was to demonstrate that the Japanese were more than capable of operating militarily in other theaters besides China. And in Europe the danger of war was growing. German rearmament was proceeding rapidly, that of France and Britain sluggishly. The coming to power of the Popular Front in France after the May 1936 elections, in which the Communists entered into an electoral compact with the Socialists and Radicals, could superficially be accounted as a dazzling success of the Comintern's new tactics: the new government headed by Socialist Léon Blum (which the Communists supported though they refused to participate in it) was pledged to carry on and solidify the Franco-Soviet alliance. The Communist vote was significantly increased. But the victory of the left and the wave of sit-down strikes that followed it polarized even further the country's political life and, as the events of 1940 were to show, contributed both to France's military unpreparedness and to the growth of defeatism on the right. War could be avoided only through a rapid increase in the West's military might combined with the resolve to stand up to Hitler's blackmail, and on both counts the picture was not encouraging.

For all the undoubted successes of Soviet diplomacy and the Comintern tactics, the international position of the USSR was unenviable. Again it must be stressed that at this stage of the international game chances of a Soviet-Nazi deal of the kind reached in 1939 looked extremely slim; Hitler was simply impervious to any hints in that direction. On the contrary, his public pronouncement continued the hard anti-Soviet line, such as the celebrated mention that Germany needed *Lebensraum* for her expanding population, and that the Ukraine was the logical area. Poland, which would be the logical path for invasion, appeared at the time quite close to Germany. Nor could Stalin take the alliance with France as a safeguard against war, or, in case it came, as an iron-clad guarantee of French help. No Communist could be convinced that, when it came to the crunch, a capitalist country, even one with a leftist government, would rush in to save the Communist state. And Stalin had to fear that even an initial defeat and partial occupation of the territory of the USSR might spell the end of his regime.

Russia's general vulnerability and the special vulnerability of Stalin's personal power were at least partial reasons for the crescendo of terror. The connection between the foreign danger and the domestic horrors comes out well in the second great purge trial in January 1937. One of the accused was made to recite the following alleged instructions from Trotsky: ". . . the question of power will become a practical issue . . . only as a result of the defeat of the USSR in war . . . since the principal condition for the Trotskyites coming into power, if they fail to achieve this by means of terrorism, would be the defeat of the USSR, it is necessary as much as possible to hasten the clash between the USSR and Germany."

The moral and physical destruction of former Communist greats was now deemed by the tyrant to be insufficient. The purge was to extend throughout the whole Party, and then other areas of Soviet life. Terror now claimed victims within Stalin's closest entourage, even those who had been his coadjutors in the rise to power. In February 1937 newspapers announced the sudden death by heart attack of Gregory "Sergo" Ordzhonikidze, commissar of heavy industry, an old friend and faithful political ally of the dictator. Only in 1956 was it officially revealed that Ordzhonikidze, hounded by the secret police and with members of his family imprisoned and tortured by the police, in fact had committed suicide. Undaunted, at the meeting of the Central Committee, which began in the same month, the General Secretary gave the signal for a wholesale holocaust. The Party officials were upbraided for their "carelessness, indifference, and naïveté in unmasking the wreckers, spies and murderers." Facts have established, said Stalin, that "the wrecking and spying activity of foreign agents in

Reviewing the 1937 May Day Parade. Left to right: Shvernik; Khrushchev; Dimitrov, head of Comintern; Stalin; Molotov; Mikoyan; and Chubar.

which the Trotskyites played a sizable role hurt to a lesser or greater degree all or almost all our institutions—economic, Party, administrative. Second: foreign agents, among them Trotskyites, have infiltrated not only lower ranks but also some leading posts." The very success of communism was increasing the internal danger, said Stalin, formulating his famous and sinister contribution to Marxism: The closer you get to socialism the sharper becomes the character of the class war! Look beyond the mere appearances: "A real wrecker will from time to time do good work, because it is the only way for him to gain confidence and to continue wrecking." Always practical, Stalin urged a hurried-up training of new cadres: they were needed to replace the officials who had been, were being, or were about to be liquidated. The dictator rode roughshod over some mild protests. This is when Bukharin, Rykov, et al., were turned over to the NKVD. The purge was now in full swing.

During the next year and a half terror became an everyday feature of life. Stalin aimed to remake entirely the instruments of power: the Party, the army and the security forces, as well as the country's intellectual and artistic elite. By 1939 some 850,000 Party members had been purged—one-third of the 1937 membership[2]—and it is more than likely that the great majority of those purged suffered more than just the loss of their Party card.

The purge was deliberately planned. The security organs at least in some cases had definite quotas of "enemies of the people" they had to apprehend. But of course a purge of such dimensions could not be conducted in an entirely cool and deliberate way. Spy mania and denunciations flourished. People would be arrested because of real or alleged transgressions of their relatives or friends, or because of some trivial or suspicious incident in their dossier which might have taken place before the Revolution. Readers of Solzhenitsyn's *Gulag Archipelago* don't have to be told how those arrested were dealt with: interrogation sometimes accompanied by physical torture or threats against the prisoner's family, all designed to make him confess to sometimes grotesque charges, as well as to implicate others. "Who recruited you" and "Whom have you recruited" were the standard questions. Sentences were dealt out in a wholesale fashion, usually by a three-man collegium of the NKVD sitting *in camera* which might spend ten or fifteen minutes on each case. The exact number of victims probably will never be known. Loose estimates speak of some 500,000 executed between 1937 and 1939. Estimates of the number of those incarcerated in the vast network of forced labor camps, often under conditions where mortality was high, range from a very con-

[2] L. Schapiro, *The Communist Party of the Soviet Union* (New York 1960), p. 436.

servative three million to twelve million, which appears fantastic but not impossible. That physical torture was used on many of those who were not produced in open court is clearly established by the directive to the NKVD of January 20, 1939 (when the most intensive terror was supposed to be over): "the Central Committee considers that physical pressure should be used obligatorily as an exception applicable to known and obstinate enemies of the people as a method both justifiable and appropriate."

Abroad, even the most inveterate enemies of the Soviet system could hardly suspect the true dimensions of the purges. It was assumed, correctly, that they struck mainly at the elite, but most foreigners failed to perceive how pervasive the process was. What caused most reverberations abroad was the purge of the Red Army's high command. It unfolded with a lightning speed following the announcement of June 11 that eight top Soviet military commanders, including former Assistant War Commissar Marshal Tukhachevsky and commanders of the two most important military districts, were found guilty of treason by a military court and sentenced to death. There ensued a veritable decimation of the officers' corps: three of the first five marshals of the Soviet Union, three of four full generals; all twelve lieutenant generals; sixty of sixty-seven corps commanders.[3] Within the next two years 136 of 199 divisional commanders were to be liquidated. The holocaust among the naval commanders was even worse, and in the lower officer grades the loss was also considerable, though not on the same scale. Some of the officers, including Tukhachevsky, were victims of a provocation arranged by the German intelligence service, but in the main the purge reflected a deliberate decision of the regime (though undoubtedly compounded by hysteria and spy mania; some victims, like the future Marshal Rokossovsky, were released on the eve of the war and served with distinction) to do to the army what was being done to other branches of the Soviet officialdom. Unlike the political leaders, *all* of the executed Soviet military leaders were rehabilitated in the post-Stalin era, charges against them declared entirely false.

Abroad the effect of the military purge was telling. Of how much worth as an ally, how dangerous as an enemy could be an army in which treason was so rampant and in which more than half of the officer corps has been liquidated? And current Soviet sources put much of the responsibility for the disastrous Russian military reverses during the first two years of the war on this wanton destruction of the old officer corps, and their replacement by people who in many cases were incompetent and for the most part inexperienced.

[3] The rank of marshal was restored in 1935. The title "general" is given here for the assimilated rank; officially it was not restored until 1940.

The great purge also dealt a nearly fatal blow to the country's military preparedness in other areas. Industrial expansion had come almost to a stop during the terrible years 1937–39. The country's leading scientists, industrial managers, planners, as well as simple workers were also caught in the vast network of terror. Some perished or went to the camps. The luckier ones among those "people's enemies" were allowed to carry on their work in the jail institutes described so vividly in Solzhenitsyn's *First Circle*. Some leading Soviet aircraft designers and engineers, headed by Andrei Tupolev, imprisoned on absurd charges of having sold blueprints to the Germans, were inmates of one such laboratory run by the NKVD. But even those who escaped suspicion and remained free must have worked under conditions that, to put it mildly, were not conducive to efficiency and high production tempos. An officer who drew attention to the advanced state of German military or air technology would be denounced and arrested as a fifth columnist propagating defeatism. A technician or scientist who objected to bureaucratic interference with his work would seldom escape the label of "wrecker" and its fearful consequences.

One might well pose the question how the society as a whole, not to mention the regime, could survive the fearful strain of those years. First of all, the fear of war was real. Terror had not stifled the patriotic response. And the regime struggled more strenuously than ever before to make Russia's cause its own. The ideological motif became attenuated in favor of the nationalistic one. Great figures of Russia's prerevolutionary past were not only rehabilitated but glorified. The Soviet moviegoer was treated to such historical sagas as the victory of Prince Alexander Nevsky over the Teutonic Order in the thirteenth century, to the drama of the modernization of Russia undertaken by Peter the Great at the same time that he was repulsing and then conquering the foreign foe. The patriotic theme ran through much of contemporary literature and historiography. Russia's great cultural past was now freed from ideological taboos and reservations and proclaimed a legitimate heritage of the Communist state, which, like the state, was endangered by the would-be Nazi invader, for whom the Slavs were a lower race. Other ethnic groups were not neglected in this patriotic propaganda, but the Russian motif was clearly dominant. In brief, all the vast resources of the totalitarian regime were employed to convince the people that national survival and greatness were inextricably bound up with the regime and the man who epitomized it.

One must also acknowledge that this period of suffering and fear for many was for some also a time of opportunity. The turnover in the leading positions, whether in the Party, the army, government, or industry, bordered on the fantastic (it was not unusual for three or four successive heads of a Party organization or ministry to be unmasked within one year as "enemies of the people"). The ones who survived this lottery of terror and opportunity often found themselves at or near the top at a very early age. There was a deliberate policy on Stalin's part to create a new Soviet elite, people who because of their age could not have had any connection or sympathies with the fallen greats of communism, who had grown up when he was already the acknowledged leader of his country and world communism. Many of the present leaders of the USSR are graduates of this "Stalin class" —people like Kosygin, who in his early thirties advanced to be the head of an industrial enterprise, then within a year became mayor of Leningrad, and after another year, a USSR minister. Members of this new elite were loaded with honors and material perquisites, the earlier egalitarian inhibitions now clearly a thing of the past. Nor were special privileges and emoluments confined only to the managerial class. A parallel development among the workers started in 1935, when coal miner Alexei Stakhanov set a new production record in extracting coal. After that production records were kept, often under suspicious circumstances, in various branches of industry and agriculture. These records, as a rule, were then used to set up new and higher norms of productivity per worker, a speed-up technique called Taylorism in the capitalist countries, and long opposed or banned by the trade unions. The shock workers, or Stakhanovites, as they became known, grew into the veritable aristocracy of Soviet labor, with special rates of pay, bonuses for surpassing the norm, and various civic honors and decorations.

Unusual incentives as well as unparalleled coercion characterize Soviet society in those fateful years. Ambition as well as fear provide an explanation of the regime's ability to endure the consequences of both its follies and its crimes.

By the beginning of 1938, terror had reached dimensions that, in the opinion of its author, threatened to plunge the administrative and economic machinery into chaos. When a similar situation obtained in 1930 in agriculture, Stalin had called for a temporary halt and thrown the blame for the excesses on his subordinates. These tactics were now repeated. The Central Committee resolution of January 1938 spoke of the abuses and blamed them on "careerists trying to gain merit by throwing people out of the Party, trying to gain security for themselves through mass repressions against the rank and file."

The regime did not mean to give up terror any more than in 1930 it had been ready to jettison collectivization. All that Stalin proposed to do was to use repression more selectively. In fact, following the Central Committee's directive, there unfolded the drama of the most spectacular of the purge trials, the one featuring the array of former leaders headed by Bukharin and Rykov (Tomsky had anticipated the inevitable by committing suicide in 1936), and for good measure a few directors and minor figures. An exercise in surrealist fantasy, the trial stands unsurpassed even in the history of Soviet terror. The indictment asserted that the veteran makers of communism indulged in a variety of crimes, including proposed dismemberment of the Soviet Union (at the behest of the British, German, and Polish intelligence services), forced or cajoled some leading figures of Soviet medicine to kill through "wrecking" medical treatment such luminaries of Soviet life as Valerian Kuibyshev, and the writer Maxim Gorky and sought to ruin the economy of the USSR. In addition to destroying his former rivals and collaborators both physically and morally, Stalin sought to throw on them the blame for all his own past errors and crimes. Thus the former minister of agriculture, during the worst period of collectivization, duly recited how, at Rykov's instruction, he had attempted "to incense the middle peasants by extending to them the repressive measures which the government laid down for the kulaks," how he was "to take special account of the national feelings of the Ukrainian population and to explain . . . that these (abuses) were a result of the policy of Moscow . . . to rouse the peasants against the Soviet government. . . ." Crop failures in the early 1930's and the widespread mortality of cattle were exhibited as the result of wrecking. Thus the regime provided, as if in a distorted mirror, the record of its own failures and loaded them on the hapless accused. One can also see in the accusations a catalogue of the dictator's fears: nationalism and their recent sufferings would drive the Ukrainian and Byelorussian peasants to opt for the foreign invader, and similar reasons would stir up separatism among the Turkic peoples of Central Asia. Indeed were this not also a testimony to human villainy, self-debasement, and suffering, the trial would have produced a comical effect, so disingenuous and palpably false were both the indictments and confessions. (Yagoda, while confessing to some horrendous crimes, still insisted he had not been a spy. The long-time chief of the Soviet security apparatus made a very telling point: "If I had been a spy, dozens of countries could have closed down their intelligence services—there would have been no need for them to maintain such a mass of spies as have now been caught in the Soviet Union.")

Whether he felt that Yezhov had laid it on too thick, or that the monstrous man had let enthusiasm for repression run beyond his instructions, Stalin now decided to get rid of him. An old-time confidant of the dictator's and a fellow Georgian, Lavrenti Beria, was brought from the Caucasus in July 1938 to become Yezhov's deputy. After a few months of this on-the-job training Beria advanced to become commissar. Yezhov lingered on for a few weeks as commissar of water transport. Then he disappeared, at least insofar as the public was concerned. We now know that he got a taste of his own medicine: arrest, forced confession, etc., and then was shot. There now followed, as after the removal of Yagoda, a purge of the purgers, most high officials of the NKVD sharing the fate of their late boss. Repression slackened and became more discreet. But we do know that Beria's initial tenure of office saw the arrest and "investigation" of some very important figures. Thus in 1938–39 perished such important Party leaders, and up to the moment of their demotion and disappearance assumed-to-be-exemplary Stalinists, as former members of the Politburo Stanislaw Kossior (formerly first secretary of the Ukrainian Party), Vlas Chubar, and many others. A prominent army casualty was Marshal Blyukher, of legendary exploits in China in the twenties when he guided the Kuomintang armies, and later commander-in-chief in the Far East. Having just beaten off a Japanese incursion over the Soviet frontiers in the summer of 1938, Blyukher was summoned to Moscow and some weeks later arrested on charges of being a Japanese agent. Blyukher, also a hero of the Civil War, died under torture.

The landscape of Soviet officialdom at the end of 1938 was one of desolation. Thus several layers of leadership of the Ukrainian Party had been destroyed and a Russian, Nikita Khrushchev, was dispatched to take over as first secretary in Kiev. Even those bigwigs who remained in good standing often had their relatives imprisoned or worse. The wife of the president of the USSR, Mikhail Kalinin, was sent to a camp and remained there for years while her husband continued appearing at Stalin's side. In years to come similar fates were to strike Kaganovich's brother (Mikhail Kaganovich, a Jew, was accused of being a German agent and committed suicide), Molotov's wife, and Mikoyan's son. At one point no single admiral remained in the Russian navy, and a captain had to be made its commissar.

The purges brought to the fore new men who would be Stalin's lieutenants for the next fifteen years and some of whom would dispute the succession, such as Khrushchev; Andrei Zhdanov, boss of the Leningrad Party and probably closest to Stalin in the prewar years; and Georgi Malenkov, who, as the head of the cadres (personnel) section of the Party Secretariat, supervised the purge. They as well as the handful of veterans who survived, such as Molotov, War Commissar Voroshilov, and Mikoyan, constituted the inner circle around Stalin. Zhdanov and Khrushchev were elected full members of the Politburo in 1939, Beria and Malenkov not till 1946.

If the tempo of repression slackened in 1938 and no further major purge trials were to take place after the Bukharin-Rykov-Yagoda one, this perhaps also reflected the realization that the European war was much closer than had been expected.

The German Threat

In March 1938 Hitler seized Austria. Almost immediately Germany began to pressure and threaten Czechoslovakia, alleging persecution of the German citizens of the little republic. Czechoslovakia was bound by an alliance with France and, conditional on France's honoring her obligations, also with Russia. The Soviet government's first reaction to the German threats was to reassert its determination to stand by its pledge. On March 17 Moscow announced its readiness to consult with other interested states for the purpose of "checking the further development of aggression and of eliminating the increased dangers of a world massacre." But the British declined the Soviet initiative. There began the sequence of events that was to lead in September to the Munich meeting of the heads of the British and French governments with Hitler and Mussolini, the meeting at which it was decided that the Sudeten area of Czechoslovakia should be detached and go to Germany. Abandoned by its allies, the Czechoslovakian government saw no alternative to capitulation. Subsequently the dismembered republic had to grant territory to Hungary and Poland, and autonomy to Slovakia and the Carpatho-Ukraine. It is difficult to decide what would have been the position of the USSR had France, with British backing, decided to stand up to Germany and had war ensued. The Soviet Union at the time had no common frontier either with Czechoslovakia or with Germany. The Munich agreement excluded the Soviet Union from the councils of Europe and provided an ominous augury for the future. The value of the French alliance was now, at most, problematic. The British government under Chamberlain seemed bent upon exploring further the possibilities of appeasement. Poland virtually seconded German pressure on Czechoslovakia. For all purposes the Soviet Union seemed isolated on the European scene. And to add to the woeful picture, Japan in 1938–39, for all her involvement in China, provoked border incidents with the USSR and Mongolia, some of those "incidents" involving units of corps size.

The bleak outlook was drastically changed by Hitler's new, as yet diplomatic offensive. Impatient for new conquests, the Führer now began to pressure Poland as well as to plan for complete absorption of the rump of Czechoslovakia. Had he waited to digest his conquests, had he allowed Czechoslovakia, now virtually a conglomerate of German satellites, to continue its shadow existence, Hitler might well have succeeded in obtaining a free hand in the east, the principal aim of his foreign policy since 1933. Now through his greed and impatience he was to convince influential circles in the West that appeasement had been a mistake—Germany's territorial appetite was insatiable. And if war was still to be avoided, and in case it broke out, France and Britain needed Russia.

Until Hitler showed his hand, Russia's position following Munich was unenviable. To be sure, while the West was still in the dark about it, the Soviet government must have had an inkling about Hitler's design on Poland. In November Germany had approached Warsaw with the proposal to "settle" Polish-German differences. As communicated to Polish Foreign Minister Beck, this involved German absorption of the Free City of Danzig and an extraterritorial road linking East Prussia with the rest of Germany and running through the so-called Polish Corridor. The Polish government, well realizing that the German demands were but the first step in blackmail, was not to reveal them until April. But Poland now sought to improve its relations with the USSR, and on November 26 the two countries issued a declaration reaffirming their nonaggression treaty of 1932, which was to run until 1945. The Soviets, however, could not be absolutely sure that the Poles would withstand the German pressure and that the whole affair would not turn into another Munich. And if so and if Poland became a German satellite, then the nightmare of the Kremlin, a foreign aggressor in immediate proximity to the Soviet Ukraine and Byelorussia, would become a reality.

As it was, the Soviets were already warned by the Carpatho-Ukraine. This minuscule creation, officially an autonomous part of the living corpse of Czechoslovakia, had only 700,000 inhabitants. But with discreet German encouragement, it became the center of nationalist Ukrainian propaganda, directed at the Ukrainians in the USSR and in Poland. Officially the Soviet position was one of unconcern: How, asked Stalin rhetorically, could the "gnat"—i.e., the Carpatho-Ukraine—absorb the "elephant"—i.e., the Ukrainian SSR—with its more than thirty million inhabitants? But in fact the gnat and its broader implications were the object of deep apprehension.

The Eighteenth Party Congress, the first after the unprecedented interval of five years, met in March 1939. It took place against the background of three years of unprecedented terror and in the shadow of the most pressing foreign danger. Stalin was at some pains to assure the people, whom he might soon have to ask to fight for his regime, that the horrors of the past would not return and that they had not been willed by himself: "There is no doubt that we will not use again the method of the mass purge." And this lame excuse: "One cannot say that the purge was conducted without serious mistakes. Unfortunately, more mistakes were committed than one could have foreseen." Rather disingenuously he sought to deny what must have been on the minds of his listeners: that the purges had fatally weakened the country. He deplored the lies of the foreign press about "the weakness of the Soviet army . . . the decomposition of the Soviet air force . . . unrest in the Soviet Union." All such lies, the dictator declared, were designed to prod Hitler: "You just start a war with the Bolsheviks and everything will go easy." In fact the purges, for all the mistakes and abuses, strengthened the Soviet Union and national unity.

On foreign policy Stalin's speech at the congress bore a somewhat Pythian character. It was to be claimed after the Nazi-Soviet Pact that back then in March he had given signals to Hitler—thus his famous statement that the USSR would not go to war "to pull somebody else's chestnuts out of the fire." But at the time Stalin still could not know that Hitler would need a pact with the USSR. He would not need it unless faced with the certainty of having to fight on two fronts if war came—that is, if, unlike the year before, Britain and France stood up to him. Hence Stalin spoke flatteringly of the Western powers, regretting only their lack of resolution in standing up to the blackmail and offering Russia's help if they did: "peaceful, democratic states, taken together, are without doubt stronger than the fascist countries . . . we support the nations which have fallen prey to aggression, and which fight for the independence of their country."

But at this point Hitler helped end Russia's diplomatic resolution. On March 15 Germany swallowed Bohemia and Moravia. Moravia became a satellite of Germany and the Carpatho-Ukraine was allowed by Berlin to be occupied by Hungary. This dealt a death blow to the policy of appeasement. Britain belatedly took the lead in trying to erect a barrier to further German aggression. The Polish government having now acknowledged the German pressure, Prime Minister Chamberlain announced in the House of Commons on March 31 that Britain and France would come to Poland's help in the case of a German attack.

France and Britain began negotiations with the USSR, looking toward a joint front vis-à-vis Germany. Soviet diplomacy responded, but the actual negotiations dragged on: the USSR wanted military guarantees for all eastern European states between the Baltic and the Black seas. On the Western side there was still considerable reluctance about entering into a binding military agreement with the USSR—the British and French hoped that the mere fact of their guarantees to Poland plus their negotiations with Russia would make Hitler abandon or moderate his designs. On the Soviet side there was a corresponding hope that the British and French overtures would make Hitler see the light and seek through an agreement with the USSR to secure its neutrality. On May 3 Litvinov, as a Jew not particularly suitable for negotiations with the Nazis, was replaced as foreign commissar by Molotov. (A Soviet diplomat sought out the German reaction to this shift but received a noncommittal response.)

Not until July 27 did a breakthrough occur in Soviet-German relations. Two second-rank Soviet diplomats in Berlin on commercial negotiations had a secret conference with a German representative. Both sides expressed interest in improving their relations. The Soviet representatives queried the German as to what would happen to the eastern part of Poland (i.e., that inhabited mainly by the Ukrainians and Byelorussians) in the case this state disappeared from the map. They received an encouraging answer: Germany understood the interest of the USSR in this question, as well as Russia's similar interest in the Baltic states and parts of Rumania.

Secret negotiations with Germany as well as public ones with Britain and France dragged out for another month. Now that the Germans had swallowed the bait, Stalin had every reason to be careful and wary: he had to make sure that a German-Soviet agreement was going to be followed by a war in which Britain and France would fight on Poland's side. Were such an agreement followed by a Munich over Poland, the USSR would find itself in a more precarious position than before.[4] And by the same token Hitler was in a hurry to spring his coup of Soviet-German agreement: confronted by it, he believed, Britain and France would be scared off from helping Poland, which they would not be able to help anyway, so he had to have his agreement before he struck at Poland.

Pressed by Hitler, Stalin gave way, much as he would have preferred to delay the pact until the war had already started and France and Britain had committed themselves. On August 23 German Foreign Minister Ribbentrop arrived in Moscow. One day's negotiations produced the fateful agreement. Publicly the two powers signed a treaty of nonaggression. A secret additional protocol provided for the distribution of the prospective loot. Russia was to be handsomely rewarded for facilitating Hitler's task. Should a "territorial and political rearrangement" take place with respect to Poland, as the protocol delicately phrased it, the USSR would receive the Ukrainian and Byelo-

[4] This argument runs counter to the Soviet official explanation that the USSR signed with Hitler only because of the Western powers' procrastination and obvious bad will. Yet it is clear that the agreement made sense from the Soviet point of view only if it was followed by a prolonged and difficult war. Should there be another Munich and should Poland share the fate of Czechoslovakia, Germany would be in immediate proximity to the Soviet Ukraine and Byelorussia, and the USSR, treaty or no treaty, would be the next logical object of Hitler's aggression. Britain and France, having been tricked by Stalin, would be most unlikely to come to Russia's help.

Conclusion of the Soviet-German Nonagression Treaty. Left to right: Gaus, von Ribbentrop, Stalin, and Molotov.

russian portions of the deceased state as well as a slice of ethnic Poland. Russia was to have a free hand in Estonia, Latvia, and Finland; Germany, in Lithuania. The USSR also declared its "interest" in Rumania's Bessarabia; Germany took note of it.

Ever since August 12 a Franco-British military mission had been in Moscow, engaged in tortuous negotiations on eventual military collaboration in the case of war. Now the Western negotiators were dismissed by Marshal Voroshilov with the explanation that Poland's refusal to allow Soviet troops to pass through its territory in case of war made further negotiations useless.

The Molotov-Ribbentrop agreement, as it became known in history, produced a shock in the West. But its immediate consequences served to justify Stalin's gamble and disappointed Hitler's hopes. Britain and France reaffirmed their pledge to Poland. On September 1 Hitler attacked. On the third, the Western powers declared war. Russia remained at peace. There was an additional dividend for the USSR in the Far East. The Japanese, disheartened by this sudden shift of their partner in the Anti-Comintern Pact, relaxed their pressure on the Soviet Far East; the fighting between the troops of the two powers, which had been going on for some time, stopped, and on September 15 they pledged to solve border questions through negotiations.

If one leaves moral considerations aside, the Stalin-Hitler deal must be described as the logical one from the Soviet point of view. It is unlikely that any other Communist ruler of Russia would, under the circumstances, have chosen a different path. Ideologically, it could hardly be described as a betrayal any more than was the Treaty of Brest Litovsk—from the point of view that the differences between Nazism and the Western capitalism were not fundamental but only of degree. A prolonged European war was likely to leave all the capitalist powers weakened and create new opportunities for communism. But the dominant considerations were undoubtedly of a very practical nature. After the travails of collectivization and terror, Russia needed a breathing spell rather than a war whose outcome for the regime and the country would be at best uncertain and more likely—especially for the former—disastrous. The Soviet-German pact offered Stalin what had been the objective not only of Soviet but of Russian policies for centuries: the unification of all Ukrainians and Byelorussians within the Russian state. It promised to make good the territorial losses of the First World War: the Baltic states, Bessarabia, as well as other enticing opportunities in regard to southeastern Europe. Inherent in Stalin's rationale there was, however, a huge miscalculation, but one that at the time was shared by practically everybody else, including the German General Staff: He did not realize how strong Germany was, and conversely how weak militarily France was. Hence when military operations actually came in the West there would not be a long-drawn-out conflict on the model of 1914–18, which would bleed both sides and leave Russia the arbiter of Europe, but a German *blitzkrieg,* which would put the USSR in mortal danger.

6.
The War Years

The Prelude, 1939–41

In August 1939 the Soviet Union stood as the arbiter of the fate of Europe. A few weeks later the situation was drastically changed and Stalin, for all the real estate that it brought him, might well have had second thoughts about his bargain with Hitler. The reason lay in the speed of the German conquest of Poland and in the military inactivity on the Western front, both unwelcome surprises from the Soviet point of view. Outnumbered and technologically backward, the Polish army was destroyed within a few days. Even worse, the French army remained inactive behind the Maginot line. For the moment the Soviets' fond hope of the Reichswehr's being bloodied in extensive fighting on both fronts was disappointed.

As early as September 6 the Germans generously proposed to the Russians that they could now go ahead with their part of the bargain —i.e., move into "their" part of the dying state. The Soviets were militarily unprepared and they were obviously afraid that Hitler would doublecross them: The USSR might find itself at war with Poland and hence England and France, while Germany would stage another version of Munich; or even worse, what if the Reichswehr kept marching beyond the Soviet-German demarcation line and farther— beyond the Polish-Soviet border? Before the German ambassador, Count von der Schulenburg, Stalin could not conceal his anxiety: "Stalin said somewhat suddenly that on the Soviet note there were certain doubts as to whether the German high command . . . would stand by the Moscow agreement and would withdraw to the line that had been agreed upon."

On September 10, the government ordered partial mobilization even though the forthcoming operation in Poland, with the Polish army shattered, would seem to require only the regular Red Army units. On September 17 the Soviets finally moved to claim their allotted share of Poland. The official communiqué, needless to say, did not refer to the Soviet-German protocol: the Soviets were moving in because, with the Polish state in collapse, they had to protect the Ukrainian and Byelorussian populations there.

To Moscow's relief the division of spoils went on as agreed, and the Western powers gave every sign of their continued resolve to carry on with the war. But the display of the German might had a sobering effect on Stalin. Now he would have to eschew any appearance of playing a double game. Ribbentrop's second visit to Moscow on September 27–29 brought modifications of the original agreement. The Soviets were now eager to get rid of the slice of ethnic Poland that was theirs under the stipulation of the secret protocol: Germany could take it over but in exchange the USSR could help itself to most of Lithuania. Stalin had to abandon any appearance of neutrality: a joint Russo-German declaration claimed that with the disappearance of Poland—"an ugly offspring of the Versailles Treaty," as Molotov characterized it in a speech to the Supreme Soviet—there was no further reason for France and Britain to continue with the war, and if they did the USSR and Germany pledged to "engage in mutual consultations in regard to necessary measures." This sounded like not so veiled a threat of Russia's joining the war on Hitler's side. The Russians also entered into an extensive commercial agreement with Germany, designed to help the latter's war economy. They would be compensated with industrial equipment but the trade was obviously not equal: the USSR would furnish badly needed raw materials, but the Germans in return would often send obsolete matériel. A Soviet naval base near Murmansk was placed at the disposal of German submarines.

In addition to these formal (and secret) concessions, the USSR felt constrained to take another important step bound to help Hitler. The news of the Molotov-Ribbentrop agreement had fallen like a thunderbolt upon foreign Communist parties, till then in the forefront of the anti-Nazi movements in their countries. Still, when the war began the French Communists pledged solidarity with the rest of the French nation in the struggle against Hitlerism; Communist recruits answered the call to the colors. But at the end of September this policy was drastically reversed: the Communists declared against the war and

RUSSIA
September 1, 1939
MILES
0
300
600
0
300
600
KILOMETERS
Arctic Ocean
GREAT BRITAIN
London
FRANCE
Paris
BELGIUM
Brussels
Amsterdam
THE NETHERLANDS
LUX
DENMARK
NORWAY
Oslo
SWEDEN
Copenhagen
Stockholm
FINLAND
Helsinki
KAREL-FINN
Petrozavodsk
Leningrad
EST
Tallin
LAT
Riga
LIT
Kaunas
GERMANY
Berlin
AUSTRIA
Vienna
HUNGARY
Budapest
Warsaw
POLAND
Minsk
WHITE RUSSIA
Smolensk
Moscow
ROMANIA
Bucharest
Kiev
Dnieper
UKRAINE
Black Sea
Volga
Stalingrad
TURKEY
GEORGIA
Tbilisi
ARMENIA
Yerevan
AZERBAIJAN
Baku
Caspian
Sea
SYRIA
IRAQ
Baghdad
Teheran
IRAN
KUWAIT
SAUDI ARABIA
KAZAKH
Aral Sea
TURKMEN
Ashkhabad
UZBEK
Tashkent
Stalinabad
TADZHIK
Frunze
KIRGIZ
Alma Ata
Lake Balkhash
AFGHANISTAN
Kabul
PAK
INDIA
R U S S I A
Ob
Yenisey
Novosibirsk
Lena
Lake Baikal
Ulan Bator
MONGOLIA
CHINA
Peking
Sea of Okhotsk
Sea of Japan
KOREA
Seoul
JAPAN
Tokyo
Pacific
Ocean

started a defeatist campaign, their leaders deserting from the army (Thorez was to surface in Moscow). All the Communist parties now declared against the French-British position in the war and agitated for a negotiated peace. Quite clearly Stalin felt that Hitler could not be convinced of his good faith so long as foreign Communists remained anti-German. Publicly the Soviet dictator had to appear to be working for what privately he must have dreaded most: a peace on German terms!

Officially the Soviet regime could and did congratulate itself on achieving the aim that for centuries had eluded the tsars: the vast majority of Ukrainians and Byelorussians had been united with Soviet Russians in one state. The first move into eastern Poland encountered but little resistance; the Red Army incurred only 2,500 casualties. The new territories were integrated with the USSR in a hurry. There were Soviet-style elections to assemblies of Western Ukraine and Western Byelorussia, as those temporary creations were styled. These assemblies in turn petitioned that Western Ukraine and Western Byelorussia be allowed to join the corresponding Soviet republics. There was a considerable Polish minority in the newly acquired territory (the larger cities were predominantly Polish) and Ukrainian nationalism, both anti-Polish and anti-Russian, was strong, especially in what had been Eastern Galicia. But this difficulty was solved in the Stalinist fashion through mass deportations, which for obvious reasons were to reach their peak in the summer of 1940. The Polish, Jewish, and Ukrainian intelligentsia and professional people were sent to camps in Central Asia.

From its allotted share the USSR ceded to Lithuania the city and district of Vilna, a gesture eloquent of its firm belief in the country's eventual and full absorption into the USSR. Vilna, the ancient capital of the Grand Duchy of Lithuania—and eventually to become the capital of the Lithuanian Soviet Socialist Republic—was in 1939 predominantly Polish and Jewish in its population, the surrounding countryside mostly Byelorussian. For the moment Lithuania and its sister Baltic republics, Latvia and Estonia, were compelled to agree to have Soviet military bases and troops quartered on their territories. The governments of these small countries had no illusions what this portended for their independence but, warned by Germany to accede to Soviet demands, they had no choice but to comply.

Territorially the gains to the Soviet Union were dazzling: from Poland more than 76,000 square miles, with a population of thirteen million; the Baltic states, in October 1939 already as good as money in the bank, would bring the USSR 65,000 square miles and more than five million new citizens. As against these satisfying statistics, there was the melancholy fact that the USSR now had an extensive frontier with Nazi Germany.

On the surface the relations between the two dictatorships were most amicable and indeed it is not too much to describe them as an alliance. But seldom has an alliance been accompanied by so much mutual fear and distrust, and the conviction that it was bound to end in war. Most alliances are based on a community of interests and the fear of a third power. This paradoxical alliance was based on Hitler's grudging realization that, with the French and British facing him in the West, he could not indulge his main desires of further eastern expansion and of destroying communism and on Stalin's faltering hope that the West would engage Germany in a long and inconclusive war which would enable Russia to prepare for future contingencies. The only link of common interest lay in the two powers' desire to consolidate their territorial gains. Thus by the September 29 agreement both were pledged to suppress any Polish agitation in their territories and to synchronize police movements for that purpose. The Germans' brutal repression of Poles and Hitler's avowed intention of not countenancing any Polish state must have been a source of secret comfort in Moscow. The Polish government-in-exile was now on French soil, and Britain and France would find it impossible to begin negotiations with Hitler short of Germany's agreement to restore Poland in some form. On the other hand, the fact that there was virtually no war in the West—this was the period of the so-called phony war—must have been bad for the Russians' nerves.

Tied as he was for the moment to Hitler's victorious chariot, Stalin could not afford any gesture that might arouse his terrible partner's suspicion. Russian supplies to Germany went on schedule, while the Germans were often late with theirs or supplied the USSR with junk rather than up-to-date industrial and military equipment. Diplomatic relations with Germany's enemies were reduced to the most formal contacts, while the Soviet press's tone about Britain and France was uniformly scathing. At the same time, the Kremlin still had to be apprehensive that Germany might try to inveigle the USSR into war with the West.

This fear affected the timetable of further Soviet moves to collect the loot stipulated by the Molotov-Ribbentrop agreement. This agreement also gave Russia a free hand in Bessarabia, a logical objective of further Soviet territorial ambitions both on account of its largely Ukrainian population and because it had been part of the Russian Empire. But the current possessor of Bessarabia, Rumania, had been given an Anglo-French guarantee in the spring of 1939. Following Poland's fall, the Western powers could not be expected to rush to Rumania's help were she threatened—whether by Germany or by Russia—and indeed they so notified the hapless government of King Carol. But one could never be sure, and anyway Rumania was not Estonia. Soviet hints that Rumania should sign a mutual assistance pact with the USSR, on the model of those entered into by the Baltic states, remained ineffectual. Equally fruitless were Soviet efforts to arrive at an agreement, this time on a more equal basis, with Turkey. For the moment all thought of territorial and diplomatic advance in the south had to be given up.

Stymied in that direction, the USSR sought added security in the north. Negotiations with Finland began in October, but they took a different turn than those with the other small Baltic neighbors of the USSR. The Russians demanded that the frontier on the Karelian Isthmus be moved farther from Leningrad. They offered Finland in return a large though desolate area of Soviet territory. The Finns were agreeable to the territorial exchange, but they would not countenance the other demand—for Soviet naval bases on Finnish soil. The Soviet leadership's usual caution gave way to irritation at the way this country of fewer than four million people was resisting its demands. At the end of November the Soviet Union resorted to armed action and, at the same time, decided to deal with the Finnish problem once and for all. On December 1, the USSR recognized and signed a treaty with the government of the Democratic Republic of Finland—i.e., with a handful of Finnish Communists domiciled in the USSR and headed by a veteran of the Comintern, Otto Kuusinen.

The Kremlin's impatience led to a costly and, as events were to show, almost fatal error. Considering that the war lasted only about three months and that it was carried out against a small and weak nation, Soviet casualties were huge; by Moscow's own acknowledgment more than 200,000, including 50,000 killed. The command was incompetent, field officers lacked experience and initiative, coordination between the various branches of the armed forces was chaotic. Soviet expectations that the whole affair would be over in ten or twelve days were crudely disappointed.

Even more disturbing were the wider implications and reverberations of what seemed a Soviet debacle. The previous and slighting estimates of Soviet military strength, the conviction that the purge had irretrievably weakened the Red Army appeared to be confirmed. The attack on Finland and the hard time the Soviets were having at it brought a wave of indignation in the democracies, and barely concealed amusement and satisfaction in Germany. The attack produced a wave of resentment in the United States not only because of the David-Goliath aspect of the affair but also because of Finland's punctilious payment of its debts to the United States while all other European powers defaulted during the Depression. Sympathy for Finland and bitterness at the Soviet "betrayal" of the previous summer led the British and French governments to indulge in more foolishness of their own. The French prepared to send fifty thousand volunteers and a bomber force to help the Finns; the British, an air force contingent. The Western command in the Near East toyed with the idea of bombing the oil centers in the Caucasus.

It is possible that Soviet intelligence got hold of the Anglo-French plans; in any case, Stalin, unlike Hitler, was prompt to extricate himself from the consequences of his blunders (at least in the international field). By March the vast preponderance of Soviet manpower began to tell. With one million troops thrown against them, the Finns were forced back and the little country could be expected to fall. But the international situation was menacing. And so the Kuusinen "government" was told to disband, and on March 12, 1940, the USSR concluded a relatively lenient peace with Finland. The frontier was pushed away from Leningrad and the USSR obtained naval and military bases. But Finland was to keep her independence both a few months later when the other Baltic countries were absorbed and, rather miraculously, after the end of World War II. Perhaps it was the recollection of the international reverberations of the Winter War, as the Finnish affair was known, as well as of the fierce resistance by the Finns that was to stay the Soviet government's hand when eastern Europe lay at its mercy.

In one respect the consequences of the Finnish war were salutary: it led to some badly needed reforms in the Red Army. Stalin's crony, Marshal Voroshilov, was made to surrender the War Commissariat to a younger man, Semyon Timoshenko. Some other commissars unfit for modern warfare were let go. And a few military victims of the purges were rehabilitated and rejoined the army. New means were adopted to restore military discipline, self-respect, and preparedness. The rank of general, so redolent of tsarist times that it had not been restored even when that of marshal was created, was now reintroduced; soldiers were henceforth to salute officers. But as 1941–42 was to show, these belated steps were far from undoing the vast harm of the previous purges and chicaneries.

The Finnish experience could not embolden Stalin in his dealings with Germany. This was well demonstrated in the Soviet reaction to the German invasion of Denmark and Norway in April 1940. Apprised of the news by Schulenburg, Molotov wished Germany "complete success in her defensive measures" and begged rather than demanded that Germany not undertake similar "defensive measures" in respect to Sweden and Finland!

On May 10 Schulenburg informed the Foreign Commissar of the German attack on the Low Countries and France. This was a crucial test of Stalin's premises in striking his bargain with Hitler. If the war developed into a prolonged stalemate à la World War I, his decision would be vindicated; if not, it was a fatal mistake.

Within two weeks the Anglo-French armies were either destroyed or compelled to retreat. The Soviets, in the vain hope of slowing down the German juggernaut, concentrated substantial forces on the Soviet-German frontier. This presumably would make Hitler detach some forces to the east, and at least slow down the German advance in France. But by the time this became known to the High Command of the Wehrmacht, the game was over in the West. The news reached Hitler's headquarters on June 20; on the twenty-third, France capitulated. Having now an additional proof of Soviet perfidy, Hitler reverted to his long total aim. On July 31 he intimated to his military chiefs that Russia must be smashed in the course of 1941. (He also announced that the war with Britain would be over in a matter of weeks.)

Hitler's unexpected success prompted the USSR to cash in the dividend from the Molotov-Ribbentrop agreement. In June the Soviet Union annexed the three small Baltic states. Then it was Rumania's turn, but here the Soviet demands went beyond the 1939 stipulations. Now the Soviet ultimatum to Bucharest demanded not only Bessarabia but also northern Bukovina, with a largely Ukrainian population but never previously part of the Russian state. After ineffectually pleading with Germany for help, the Rumanians were forced to acquiesce. But the USSR's expectations that the rump of Rumania would become a Soviet satellite were disappointed. Germany now took over the "protection" of Rumania. In practical terms this meant further partition of the unhappy country, Germany awarding parts of it to its other satellites, Bulgaria and Hungary. And to preclude any further Soviet games the German army moved in, thus effectively extending the German-Soviet frontier to the Black Sea.

In the generally bleak outlook there remained one bright spot: Great Britain, now under Churchill, refused to negotiate with Hitler, and the expected German invasion of the British Isles did not come off. This in turn led to a certain stiffening of the Russian attitude toward Berlin. When in September Germany signed a tripartite treaty with Italy (which had joined the war against Britain and France) and Japan, Molotov expostulated with the German ambassador, demanding to see the secret clauses of the treaty and expressing disbelief when told that there weren't any.

Though the German plans for a campaign against the USSR were already in an advanced state, there were still figures in Hitler's entourage who appreciated the incalculable risk of a war against Russia, with England still unconquered and the United States getting ever closer to an actual involvement. In November Ribbentrop prevailed on Hitler to invite Molotov to visit Berlin and to compose the differences marring the friendship of the two powers. But the visit of the Soviet Union's second man served only to fortify Hitler's resolve to deal with the problem in a straightforward manner. During his discussions with the Foreign Commissar, the Führer sought to beguile him by indicating that, with the fall of the British Empire imminent, the USSR should "move" in the direction of the Indian Ocean. This, and correctly, was bound to be interpreted by the Russians as yet another attempt to inveigle them into the war. Conversely Soviet complaints about the growing German influence and troop movements in Rumania and Finland were brusquely rejected. On Molotov's return Stalin tried further appeasement: the USSR was willing to join the Tripartite Pact and participate in the disposal of the British riches *provided* German troops were withdrawn from Finland and Rumania, while Russia was allowed to "negotiate" for military and naval bases in Bulgaria and Finland. This request never received a formal German answer, unless it was the curt communication to Molotov in February that Bulgaria had acceded to the Tripartite Pact and that German troops were being sent there! But all this diplomatic sparring was now very largely meaningless. On December 18 Hitler signed the directive for Operation Barbarossa: The invasion was to begin on May 15, 1941; "the German Wehrmacht must be prepared to crush Soviet Russia in a quick campaign."

That the Germans would attack sometime in 1941 was virtually a public secret. Overflights of Soviet territory by German aircraft became a frequent occurrence, beginning in March. Having been apprised by the Polish underground of German troop movements toward the east, the British conveyed this information to the Soviets. But Moscow did not need foreign warnings: its own intelligence network was sending in the same information.

Yet in the face of all such warnings the highest Soviet leadership remained incredulous. The preparedness measures, though considerable, still fell far short of what was needed to meet the onslaught of Germany, now master of the continent. There were several reasons for the Soviet leaders' uncharacteristic blindness in the face of foreign danger. First, while Stalin could be under no illusions as to Hitler's feelings concerning Russia and communism, he could not bring himself to believe that war, while inevitable, was imminent. It was logical to expect that Hitler, repulsed in 1940 by the RAF, would make another major effort to crush Britain, whether again through massive air offensive or by actual invasion. The rumors about the forthcoming invasion of Russia and the German concentration near the Soviet borders were evidently believed to be the means of pressuring Moscow psychologically. These premises, which in 1939 had led to the Soviet-German pact, still argued for a hope against hope that the Soviet Union, with its fresh scars from the collectivization and purges, would not be exposed to the supreme test. Further appeasement at worst promised to gain badly needed time. Then, too, the Soviet regime felt that it was damned if it did, as well as if it did not: a too obvious preparation for war might provoke Hitler. Evidently Stalin believed that Hitler and especially Ribbentrop (whose influence on German policies he vastly overestimated) tended toward peace, or at least a postponement of the conflict, while some German generals and conservative circles were staunchly anti-Soviet.

It is this involved calculus of hopes and fears that explains the rather inconsistent Soviet policies on the eve of war. At times Stalin seemed to realize that too appeasing a policy toward Germany could encourage those who thought that the Wehrmacht might have as easy a time in Russia as it had had in France. Thus when a coup d'etat in Yugoslavia on March 25 overthrew a pro-German government of Prince Regent Paul, the USSR not only hastened to recognize the new regime but in April signed a treaty of nonaggression and friendship with Yugoslavia, obviously in the hope that it would bolster the new regime's independent stance vis-à-vis Berlin. But this was yet another miscalculation. The very same day Germany struck, and within a short time both Yugoslavia and Greece were subdued by the Wehrmacht. (Germany had to rescue her partner Italy, which for some time had been conducting an unsuccessful military campaign against the Greeks, launched for no other reason than Mussolini's ambition to emulate Germany's feats of arms.) This in turn brought yet another humiliating appeasement gesture by Moscow. In May the USSR withdrew its recognition from the Yugoslav government-in-exile, and similar steps were taken in regard to two other countries swallowed by Germany: Belgium and Norway.

Amidst those fears and humiliations Soviet diplomacy could boast of one very important success. This was the signing on April 13 of the Soviet-Japanese Neutrality Pact. Japan's foreign minister Matsuoka was given a most flattering reception in Moscow, Stalin himself taking the lead in negotiations. The treaty provided for neutrality between the two parties in the case of aggression by a third party and for the inviolability of the two powers' satellites, Manchukuo and Outer Mongolia. Though the value of such pacts had been and would again and again be exposed, the Soviets could have reasonable assurance that this one would be observed, at least in the immediate future: their intelligence sources reported that the anti-American party within the Japanese military was gaining an upper hand over those who would prefer war against Russia. But the treaty also contributed to a further miscalculation: if Hitler had acquiesced in Japan's treaty with Russia (Matsuoka had visited Berlin prior to signing the pact) then this certainly did not suggest that an attack on the USSR was imminent.

On the eve of the great war the Soviet regime represented the epitome of one-man dictatorship. Khrushchev in his memoirs tells us that he, then a member of the Politburo, was entirely ignorant of the Soviet-German negotiations until the very day of Ribbentrop's first visit to Moscow. Most crucial decisions in foreign as well as domestic affairs were being made by Stalin alone, and even the circle of those who were called on for advice probably did not extend beyond three or four men: Molotov, Zhdanov, Malenkov, and Beria, the boss of the security apparatus with all its vast ramifications.[1] Another echelon of control and information gathering was through Stalin's personal secretariat, headed by A. Poskrebyshev. In terms of efficient operation even of a tyrannical system, such centralization was clearly counterproductive: Stalin himself had to make decisions on highly technical matters (what thickness of armor and what kind of guns should be carried by the new model tanks) and only four or five men had a clear idea of the general line of Soviet foreign policy. Thus up to the very day of the German invasion the Soviet general staff had to operate without any contingency provisions for structure of command or operational plan in case of war. The standing army orders made no dispositions for a defense in depth, the traditional Russian strategy against the invader, the refusal to do so undoubtedly reflecting Stalin's belief that any war fought *on Soviet soil* would be disastrous—if not for the Red Army, then for his personal power.

Similar constraints handicapped the regime in the efforts to solidify the domestic front for the coming cataclysm. Mass terror was abandoned as an instrument of social policy, or as a prophylactic technique for weeding out the unreliable and potentially treasonous among the population at large, though the purge of the elite continued through 1941, even if not on the 1938–39 scale. But the government could not afford to seek popularity through relaxing social discipline or favoring the consumer. On the contrary, the danger of war urged even more ruthless mobilization of human resources and more stringent economic policies.

In some cases the regime persisted with unpopular policies for ideological rather than preparedness reasons. Such was the case in agriculture: the Eighteenth Party Congress legislated a limitation on the peasants' private plots and raised their obligation to the collective

[1] The NKVD through its forced labor camps supervised a sizable portion of the Soviet labor force and played a considerable economic role. Many imprisoned scientists and technicians worked in special jail institutes and laboratories, some of the outstanding designs for Soviet planes, tanks, etc., having been devised under the "sponsorship" of the police ministry. The long arm of the security organization extended even into the foreign service, several diplomats having been recruited from Beria's men (such as P. Dekanozov, ambassador to Germany 1940–41, to be shot with his boss in 1953).

farms. More understandable, if equally likely to breed resentment, was the tightening up of industrial discipline. For all the existing controls and sanctions, Soviet industry was still suffering from a high labor turnover and absenteeism. A law of 1938 provided for a labor passport listing every worker's employment record and performance. A series of decrees in 1940 did for the urban worker what was already in force in regard to his rural counterpart: tied him to his place of employment by forbidding him to leave his job without permission. Absenteeism, lateness to work by as much as twenty minutes, if repeated, subjected the offender to a jail sentence. Skilled workers could be transferred by a governmental fiat. The working week was lengthened from forty to forty-eight hours.

Party life, like everything else during this interval, was being affected by the lengthening shadow of the European war. One would have thought that the national emergency would prompt the regime to rehabilitate a number of purge victims from among the old Bolsheviks who were still alive and in prison or camps. But while this was true of some military figures, insofar as his former Party rivals or subordinates were concerned, the danger of war only enhanced Stalin's savagery. Several of the imprisoned former bigwigs were liquidated, most of them in the summer of 1940, the measure reflecting the regime's apprehensions following the fall of France: should war come and with it the almost inevitable initial defeat, Stalin did not want to have any potential pretenders to power emerging from his camps and jails. During this time death by shooting came to several former members of the Politburo who once had assisted Stalin in his rise to power. And the long hand of the NKVD reached out several thousand miles from Russia to strike down the arch enemy who, even though abroad, might in the case of war cause major trouble: on August 20, 1940, a Communist fanatic near Mexico City assassinated Leon Trotsky. (Wholesale liquidation of potential troublemakers was to be repeated during the most precarious moments of the war: thus the Soviet military reverses of June–July 1941 and in the summer of 1942 led to the shooting of several notables who previously had been sentenced only to jail terms.)

But even the unquestionably loyal were dealt with severely if found wanting in performance. At the Eighteenth Party Conference in February 1941, a special warning was given that even those closest to the highest men in the state would suffer for administrative derelictions: Pauline Molotov, a former commissar, was removed as candidate member of the Central Committee. Lazar Kaganovich's brother Mikhail, previously removed as commissar of the aviation industry, was given a severe reprimand. While thus obliquely warning his closest collaborators, Stalin at the same time was promoting new leaders, people who had always known him as the Boss—the appellation given to him in the inner Party circles—rather than as an erstwhile colleague, as had Molotov and Kaganovich. Most prominent of this new generation of Stalinists were Georgi Malenkov and Nikolai Voznesensky, who, still in his thirties, emerged as the chief economic administrator. Their careers epitomize the other side of the purges: by destroying the old Party governmental managerial elite, they thrust into prominence new people, unconnected with old Bolsheviks and the past Party disputes, brought up in worship of their leader and benefactor. These developments within the elite paralleled what was happening in the Party at large: between the Eighteenth Congress in 1939, which signified the end of mass purges, and February 1941 1.5 million were added to the membership rolls to make the total almost 4 million. For most of the newcomers the fate of Communists and of Russia must have seemed inextricably bound up with the man who since 1925 had been the arbiter of their destinies.

On May 6 Stalin became chairman of the Council of Commissars, replacing Molotov, who continued as foreign minister. The new office, the first *governmental* position he chose to assume since 1922, could not of course mean any increase in his already absolute power. But he was leaving nothing to chance: if war came it just might be important who had the *formal* right to negotiate, issue decrees, sign a peace, etc. But to the last—despite all the repeated warnings and intelligence reports, such as that since April the Soviet air space had been breached by more than 180 German unauthorized flights—Stalin remained hopeful that the war could be postponed. On June 14 the Soviet press agency published a communiqué emphatically denying "rumors spread by forces hostile to the Soviet Union and Germany" that a conflict between the two powers was imminent.

On June 21 the Soviet general staff, with clear-cut evidence in its hands that a German attack was imminent, obtained Stalin's permission to put the frontier troops on the alert. But the order could not fully be put into effect. On June 22, just before dawn, the German armies struck along the entire frontier from the Baltic to the Black Sea.

The Struggle for Survival

The original German plan envisaged the invasion as beginning some time after May 15. Due partly to unfavorable weather conditions, but mostly to Hitler's decision in April to deal decisively with the troublesome Yugoslavs and Greeks, the date had to be moved, something that undoubtedly saved the Red Army from even more disastrous defeats than it was to suffer in the first months of the war. As it was, the Germans managed to achieve almost complete tactical surprise. On paper Soviet forces at the beginning of the war were formidable. The official figure for the army was 4.2 million, and this was not counting the sizable frontier and NKVD troops or reserves in paramilitary organizations. Even with a considerable force guarding against the Japanese in the Far East, this should have provided a solid defense against some 3 million troops that Germany and her satellites launched on June 22. But the actual disposition of the Soviet troops was ideal from the point of view of the invader. Massed near the frontier but in several echelons, they could not withstand the initial surprise attack nor regroup for a counterattack. Planes were massed wing-to-wing on airfields within easy reach of the Luftwaffe. Nine hours after the attack—by midday on June 22—twelve hundred Soviet planes had been destroyed, eight hundred on the ground.[2] By June 24 the Germans were 100 miles and more inside Soviet territory.

Though preparedness for war had been the uppermost consideration of the regime and the official rationale of all the privations and sufferings imposed upon the population for more than ten years, civilian as well as military leadership was thrown into chaos and near panic by the invasion. For nine hours after it began, the Soviet radio still carried its routine programs; only at noon were the Soviet people told the dire news and then not by the dictator but by Molotov. We now know from Soviet sources that for several days Stalin was unable to function, suffering from nervous prostration. When the High Command of the forces was set up on June 23, Marshal Timoshenko was designated as its head and supreme commander, with Stalin just a member of the council, and apparently he was unable even to attend its meetings during the first seven days of the war. Civilian leadership lapsed into the hands of Molotov. It was he who negotiated with the British mission headed by Ambassador Sir Stafford Cripps, which reached Moscow on June 28, the provisional form of alliance between the two powers. The dictator's incapacity and the undeniable fact that his blindness in the face of repeated warnings had contributed to the magnitude of the disaster might well have led to his deposition. But the purges had removed most of those who could have challenged Stalin's leadership under precisely those circumstances. Those members of the Politburo who had to run Russia during the first desperate week of the war might well have realized that the emergency was so dire that to remove the man who in the eyes of the people and the whole world had become synonymous with the regime would have

[2] The figure given in a Soviet source, *The History of the Great Fatherland War,* II, Moscow, 1963, p. 16.

brought uncontrollable panic and irretrievable collapse. And so other members of the Politburo pleaded with Stalin to take hold of himself and to resume the reins of power. He must have recovered by June 30, for on that day was instituted the State Defense Committee, "uniting in its hands the plenitude of powers"; it was headed by Stalin, with Molotov as vice-chairman, and Voroshilov, Beria, and Malenkov as its other members. Once himself again, the dictator was eager to grasp all the levers of power and supervision of the war effort. In mid-July he became commissar of defense, and on August 7 he assumed the title and duties of supreme commander-in-chief. Marshal Timoshenko in the meantime was relegated to a field command.

Stalin's address on the radio on July 3 was the first occasion on which the Soviet people could learn the magnitude of the military disaster that had already overwhelmed the country. As against the previous official communiqués which had sought to conceal it (the Soviet loss in planes on the first day of the war had been given as seventy-six!), Stalin admitted that the enemy had already seized Lithuania, Latvia, Western Byelorussia, and large parts of Western Ukraine, and was still advancing. He welcomed Churchill's statement that Britain stood by Russia in her hour of need, and the American government's assurance that the United States would send material aid. Though the listeners could not but notice the speaker's heavy breathing and tired voice, the dictator had recovered enough self-confidence to address his countrymen as "brothers, sisters, I turn to you, my friends," and to urge them "to unite around the party of Lenin and Stalin." He pictured the struggle as desperate, called for a scorched earth policy in the areas to be evacuated and for partisan warfare in the enemy's rear.

Militarily the situation continued to deteriorate. The ablest Soviet commanders had been liquidated during the purge, and those who had to step into their shoes were simply not qualified for the task. Thus the three main army groups ("fronts" in the Russian usage) were entrusted to Voroshilov, Marshal Budenny of Civil War cavalry fame, and Timoshenko. The first two were completely unfit for command under modern warfare conditions and had to be replaced. And this situation was paralleled at the army and division levels, their commanders—hastily promoted in the 1937–39 period—lacking experience and training. At first the High Command would not countenance any retreats, thus causing huge Soviet losses in encirclements. The morale of the army suffered not only due to defeats. After the German breakthrough on the central (Byelorussian) front its commander and his principal aides were shot as traitors. Officers and soldiers who broke out of an enemy encirclement and reached the Soviet lines were often

Soviet dead, World War II.

disarmed and imprisoned. Soviet equipment in the first months of the war could not match the German, perhaps another consequence of the period when so many industrial designers and managers had worked under abnormal conditions. Planes, tanks, field guns were generally of poor quality, and such up-to-date weapons as the T-34 medium tank, which was to prove more than a match for anything the Wehrmacht had to offer, only began to come off the assembly line when the war started.

Civilian morale was not in much better shape. Up to the very day of invasion, official propaganda had assured the people that war was unlikely and if it came it would be fought on enemy territory. Now the legend of the regime's and Stalin's infallibility stood exposed. In many places, and not only in the territories acquired since 1939, the invaders were greeted by the civilian population as liberators. It took exposure to German brutality and the first Soviet victories to transform this attitude and to turn the struggle into what it is officially known in the Soviet sources: the Great Patriotic War.

Foreign help in any form became a crying necessity. In the hour of supreme danger no ideological or traditional compunctions were allowed to get in the way of this goal. From the very beginning Soviet pleas for help, both direct and material, were insistent. On

July 18 Stalin, in a letter to Churchill, demanded an immediate opening of a second front in France and/or British air and naval collaboration with the Soviet army in the "north"—i.e., in Finland and Norway. (Finland had entered the war on Germany's side and Leningrad was already threatened with an encirclement.) In late July President Roosevelt's emissary, Harry Hopkins, reached Moscow to ascertain Soviet needs in munitions. At the time Stalin's demeanor was calm: there seemed to be a prospect of stabilizing the front line some distance from Moscow, Kiev, and Leningrad. In fact this was a lull before a new storm. German supply lines had been overextended; also the Germans were undecided whether to aim the next major blow in the direction of Moscow or Kiev. By August–September the German offensive was again gaining momentum; the Wehrmacht had trapped huge Russian forces near Kiev, and Stalin's communications to Churchill became almost panicky: ". . . without help the Soviet Union will either suffer defeat or be weakened to such an extent that it will lose for a long time any capacity to render assistance to its allies." Only something close to despair could explain the suspicious dictator's pleading for a British army to be sent to fight alongside the Russians: Great Britain should land twenty-five or thirty divisions in Archangel or transport them to a southern Russian front! At the end of September the Soviets were buoyed up by the promise of substantial Western help—to be sure, in supplies rather than troops. A British-American mission headed by Beaverbrook and Averell Harriman brought a list of proposed shipments which, though far from satisfying Russia's desperate needs, still were a welcome assurance that Britain and the United States were in earnest about helping to stem the German advance. But even in the hour of extreme peril, the Soviet government would not tie its hands in regard to postwar arrangements. On July 30 the Soviet Union signed a treaty with the Polish government-in-exile which abrogated the Molotov-Ribbentrop agreement. But the Polish attempt to have the Russians commit themselves to the restoration of the pre-September 1939 frontier with Poland—to disgorge their territorial gains—encountered Soviet refusal. The Russians promised to release over a million Polish citizens who had been deported to the Soviet Union following their 1939 annexations, and to allow the formation of a Polish army on Soviet soil.

But Allied supplies, which would be forthcoming through vast distances—through the submarine-infested approaches to Russia's northern ports and through Iran, jointly occupied by the Soviets and the British in August 1941—could not immediately affect the outcome of the struggle. Hitler's plans called for German occupation by the winter of 1941 of most of European Russia, up to the line running from Archangel along the Volga down to Astrakhan. The German armies were running behind the timetable but even so, by late October, they had occupied a vast area with a population of some sixty million, comprising all of the Ukraine, Byelorussia, and the Baltic region, as well as parts of Russia proper. The lost territory had produced most of the USSR's steel, coal, and iron, and the Ukraine, of course, was the major agricultural area. It was fortunate for the Soviets that much of the industrial expansion of the thirties had taken place in the eastern regions, but even so, important industrial centers such as Kharkov were lost or, like Leningrad, virtually surrounded and seemingly bound to fall to the enemy within a matter of weeks. (In fact the city was to withstand two and a half years of blockade, the only land channel of communications for much of the time being a road across the ice of Lake Ladoga. Some million Leningraders were to die during the city's heroic resistance.) On October 15, German armor effected a breach in the Soviet lines not far from Moscow, and for a few days the capital and nerve center of the Communist state lay virtually defenseless. (The Germans apparently failed to realize this.) The very same day the city was ordered evacuated of state and Party apparatus and defense plants. Most state agencies shifted to Kuibyshev (old Samara) on the Volga. Though it was never announced officially, it is almost certain that Stalin himself left Moscow on the sixteenth and did not return until three days later, when it became clear that the Germans would not exploit the breakthrough. But during these days panic and chaos gripped the capital; civil and military authority virtually disappeared. Many Communists who could not get away were tearing up their Party cards since the Germans were known to deal especially cruelly with those who were identified as members. On Stalin's return on the nineteenth the city was put under martial law. The defense of Moscow was put into the hands of (then) General Georgi Zhukov. Zhukov had gained distinction in the border war with the Japanese. Chief of staff during the first months of the war, he had the courage to resign when Stalin would not authorize a tactical withdrawal that would have saved the Soviet armies around Kiev.

Mid-October represented the height of the Soviet military danger. The German offensive was then slowed down largely because of the fall rains, which mired roads and hampered the German Panzer and motor transport. On the eve of the celebration of the anniversary of the Revolution, November 6, Stalin delivered a speech that reflected the regime's increased confidence, and promised a radical turn in the war. His listeners must have been shocked by the figure of the Soviet casualties: 1.7 million—and yet it was a million and a half short of the true one. The Wehrmacht by now had lost about 750,000 men, though to cheer up his people Stalin claimed that the German casualties were 4.5 million! Next day, speaking in Red Square, Stalin found a more inspirational theme: "The war you are fighting is a war of liberation, a just war," and, abandoning the ideological motif, he evoked famous figures from Russia's past, going back to the medieval prince Alexander Nevsky, who in the thirteenth century defeated the Teutonic Order and concluding with Suvorov and Kutuzov, the Russian generals who fought Napoleon. From now on until the end of the struggle the patriotic theme would push aside the class one; it would be a war for the survival and glory of the Soviet state and more specifically of Russia rather than for communism.

Like Napoleon before him, Hitler was not prepared for the Russian winter, or rather had been confident that most of his strategic objectives would be achieved before it set in. And so, though on December 3 a German patrol was to reach the suburbs of Moscow, the Nazi offensive, which had resumed in mid-November, ground to a halt by the end of the month. On December 6 Soviet armies led by Zhukov counterattacked and within six weeks threw the Wehrmacht back from 60 to 200 miles. Moscow would never be threatened again.

Militarily the Soviets were unable to exploit the victory and to deal a decisive blow or to recover much territory, except in front of the capital. But politically the victory made a tremendous difference: the legend of German invincibility was broken, the memory of the regime's unpreparedness and panic partly effaced. With the United States now in the war, the question became *when* rather than *how* the war would end. Though the Red Army would still suffer cruel defeats, to it would now belong the undeniable credit of being the first land force to stop the Wehrmacht. And, perhaps undeservedly, the chief beneficiary of the victory was Stalin himself. To the people in Allied countries he no longer appeared as a cynical despot, who after signing with Hitler fell victim of his own perfidy, but as a great national leader. And equally undeservedly, the fate of the regime, which might well have collapsed had the enemy taken Moscow, now was for most Russians bound up with the struggle for national survival. Prior to December, partisan activity in the German rear had been sparse; now, with faith in an eventual victory restored, the underground and guerrilla groups in the occupied territory became a formidable force harassing the German communication lines and sabotaging their exploitative economy.

While Hitler's dream of mastering Russia was shattered before Moscow in the winter of 1941–42, it is equally probable that a wiser military and especially political strategy would have enabled him to exploit his previous victories and to prevent or at least postpone the future Russian ones. With the defeat, he dismissed the commander-in-chief, Field Marshal Brauchitsch, and personally assumed the command of the German armies. While his first major decision to stand up to the Russian counterattack was undoubtedly justified—to retreat substantially under the winter conditions would have turned the defeat into a rout—his future strategy would duplicate Stalin's errors of 1941. Rather than authorizing tactical withdrawals in the face of superior Soviet forces, the Führer would insist on the German armies' fighting to the last and thus incurring huge casualties, the classical example being that of the battle of Stalingrad.

The military mistakes of the Russian campaign pale, however, against the political ones. Nazi ideology prevented an effective exploitation of the vast reservoir of discontent which years of Stalin's tyranny had built up among the Soviet people. In the eyes of the Nazi fanatics, Hitler included, Russians—as other Slavs—were "subhumans" who were to be ruled by force and denied even a pretense of self-government. Until it was much too late, there was but little attempt on the German part to appeal to the anti-Communist feelings among the conquered population by the kind of treatment and policies that would compare favorably with those they had experienced under their own rulers. A logical step in enlisting the sympathy of the peasant masses would have been to abolish or modify the collective farm system. But though some promises were made in this direction, and belatedly some laws promulgated, the Germans found the Soviet agricultural system convenient administratively for extracting food from the peasants, and refused to scuttle it. (Soviet propaganda propagated rumors that after the German defeat collective farms would be modified or even abolished.) More fundamental in reversing the original and sizable sentiment for collaboration with the invader was the sheer savagery of the German rule, which after a while, incredible though it seems, dimmed the recollections of the horrors of collectivization and purges. Soviet prisoners of war were treated in a way that had no precedent in the annals of modern warfare: interned often even in winter in open air camps, barely fed (starvation was widespread, cannibalism not unknown), the tales of their fate provided the best pro-Soviet propaganda among both the Soviet soldiers and the populations of the occupied areas. In the latter the military rule was invariably harsh but it paled in comparison with what happened when the front line moved forward and the German "civilians" accompanied by the notorious SS special detachments took over. It went without saying that the Jews, those who could be identified as Party members, and the intelligentsia were indiscriminately massacred. But for the most part even the bulk of the population was treated in an inhuman and degrading manner. As the war went on and German manpower needs grew, desperate millions of civilians would be snatched for compulsory labor in the Reich.

There were Nazi officials who realized and deplored, if not the inhumanity, then the political imbecility of the official occupation policy. The official German overlord of the whole occupied area, Alfred Rosenberg, a Baltic German, had been born and bred in prerevolutionary Russia. He urged more realistic policies and advocated especially that an appeal should be made to separatist and nationalist feelings among the non-Russian nationalities, such as the Ukrainians. But Rosenberg, an ideologue, was held in contempt by the tougher breed of Nazis such as the police chief, Heinrich Himmler, and Rosenberg's nominal subordinate Erich Koch, the Reich commissar for the Ukraine. The Ukrainian nationalists' attempt to erect a rudimentary political structure of their own following the German conquest was brutally repressed, many of their leaders with undeniable anti-Soviet credentials being arrested and executed. Within a few months of their conquests the Germans made it clear that, even in the non-Russian areas, they did not desire eventual junior partners or even satellite states but only ruthless exploitation of human and economic resources. Hitler's own statement during a conference on the administration of the occupied territories may stand as the epitaph of German occupation policies: "Naturally this giant area would have to be pacified. The best solution was to shoot anybody who looked askance."

Yet against this background the fact remains that collaboration with the enemy in the occupied area was widespread, and during the first year of the war probably more prominent than open or passive resistance to the invader. Reasons for it were complex. In non-Slavic areas, such as the Baltic states, or the northern Caucasus during its brief occupation in 1942, the German rule, especially when it was exercised by the military rather than civil authorities, was considerably more lenient than elsewhere. Occasionally a German administrator would display untypical humanity or intelligence and succeed in obtaining cooperation from the local population. Though not all, as the Soviet propaganda would make us believe, but some collaborators came from the strata dealt with especially cruelly during the twenties and thirties: the prerevolutionary middle class, the real and alleged kulaks and their families. Among hundreds of thousands of Soviet prisoners of war who volunteered for service with the Germans, either as soldiers or members of the labor units, the prevailing motive was undoubtedly the desire to escape starvation and other horrors of the camps, as well as the knowledge that having been prisoners would always brand them in the eyes of the Soviet authorities.[3] Finally,

[3] The mere fact of having been taken prisoner unless heavily wounded carried the presumption of desertion or even treason. Many ex-prisoners of war repatriated after 1945 were to be tried and sentenced to hard labor. The discussion of the tragic dilemma of the Soviet prisoner of war is one of the high points of Solzhenitsyn's *Gulag Archipelago*.

there was a not negligible element of collaboration that had an ideological motivation, even if unconnected with any sympathy for Nazism as such. The latter was the case of General Andrei Vlasov. One of the outstanding Soviet field commanders in the battle for Moscow in the summer of 1942, he fell into German hands. With some encouragement from the Wehrmacht authorities, Vlasov proposed to launch a Russian political movement of liberation. Strongly nationalist, Vlasov resisted the role of a simple agent of the Germans, and the ideology of his "movement," while anti-Stalinist, was far from repudiating the heritage of the Revolution. But it was not until the eve of the German military collapse, in 1944, that Vlasov and his collaborators were allowed to establish the Committee for the Liberation of the Peoples of Russia and to organize an armed force. (It was this force that, turning against the Germans, was to liberate France in May 1945. Vlasov and some fellow officers of his were then to seek refuge in the American zone of Germany. In 1946, after having been turned over to the Soviet government, they were executed by hanging.)

But whatever one's evaluation of Vlasov, and of similar movements among the Ukrainians and Byelorussians, their story underlines the fact that because of its inhuman philosophy Nazi Germany was utterly incapable of political exploitation of its military successes. In contrast, as we have already seen, Stalin's regime proved incomparably more flexible. In its struggle for survival it put aside its ideology: it tried and did persuade the great majority of the people (of course, with powerful help from Hitler) that they were fighting not for Marxism-Leninism but for their national existence. No source of support was scorned. Antireligious propaganda was discontinued. In fact the regime made gestures of reconciliation toward the Orthodox Church: Stalin received a delegation of clerics, and a church synod was allowed to elect the patriarch, an office that had remained vacant since 1925. The official antireligious organization, the League of the Godless, already curbed in the thirties, was dissolved in 1941. No effort would be spared during the war to persuade the people that the regime had had a change of heart: the bad old days of the thirties would not return, victory would bring a new era, if not of freedom in the Western sense of the word, then of social peace.

In 1942, however, few had the leisure or incentive to think of the postwar world. The Grand Alliance of the USSR, Britain, and the United States was to remain on the defensive till the end of the year. The Japanese were completing the conquest of Southeast Asia, and the American counteroffensive in the Pacific was not to begin till the summer. Britain's principal theater of war in the Near East was to be the scene of dazzling successes of Rommel's Afrika Korps, and the situation would not be drastically altered till the battle of El Alamein in October. But the most crucial of the fronts remained in Russia. It was here that the bulk of Germany's forces were concentrated. The Soviet winter counteroffensive, while saving Moscow, failed to dent the German lines, and the Red Army's casualties had been much greater than those of the Wehrmacht. The Soviet High Command could now, in view of Japan's involvement in the Pacific, transfer to the European theater the bulk of the troops from the Far East. (In fact this shift had begun in 1941, the Soviet espionage network in Tokyo having obtained information about the forthcoming Japanese attack on Pearl Harbor.) But the manpower situation still remained precarious. The enormous territorial and hence economic losses had a telling effect on the Russian war effort, even though Allied supplies had started coming in, and the Soviets performed veritable miracles in evacuating and restarting industrial plants from the occupied territories.

Under those circumstances, with time running out on him, it was natural to expect Hitler to make yet another supreme effort to destroy the Russian armies. And again the German offensive was to be facilitated by Soviet tactical errors and the High Command's (principally Stalin's) disregard of warning from intelligence sources as to the timing and direction of the German blow. Convinced that the Wehrmacht would once more aim at Moscow, Stalin ordered a diverting attack by the forces of the southern front, commanded by Timoshenko. This spring offensive turned into a disaster: two whole Russian armies were destroyed in an encirclement. After that Timoshenko was in no position to resist when in late June the Germans opened their major drive.

Though the enemy, unlike the preceding summer, was attacking mainly in the south rather than all along the front, the pace of the Soviet defeat appeared as catastrophic as in 1941. Within three weeks the Soviet armies were thrown back 250 miles. The Donets Basin, with its mineral deposits, was lost. By the end of July the Wehrmacht had overrun the northern Caucasus; it seemed inevitable that Transcaucasia would be cut off and then overrun by the invader. This would deprive the Soviet Union of her oil resources and sever the line of British and American supplies through Iran. The northern prong of the enemy offensive was reaching toward Stalingrad, threatening to paralyze the Volga waterway.

Stalin's order of the day of July 28 epitomized the desperateness of the moment: "Not a single step backward . . . you have to fight to your last drop of blood to defend every position, every foot of Soviet territory." The regime took some belated steps to improve the morale and efficiency of its armed forces. Zhukov, the victor of Moscow, was

Stalingrad on February 2, 1943. The 163 days' German siege reduced the city to ruins.

appointed deputy supreme commander; another general trusted by the officer corps, Vasilevsky, became chief of staff. The institution of political commissars, who previously could and did interfere with command decisions, was abolished; they now became political deputies of military commanders.[4]

Few hackneyed historical judgments are more justified than the one that holds the battle of Stalingrad to have been the turning point of the Russian campaign and World War II. It was perhaps the fascination with the city's name that made Hitler neglect the Caucasus, the original major aim of his offensive, and throw his largest army to seize the city of Stalin. Confronted with desperate Soviet defense, the Germans in August decided to take Stalingrad by a frontal assault, another major error, for in street fighting the German superiority in planes and tanks was bound to be at a discount, the Soviet infantryman's tenacity at its highest. Heroically defended by the Soviet 62d

[4] The history of this institution epitomizes the government's attitude toward the officer corps: political commissars were introduced in 1937 at the beginning of the Red Army purges, abolished after the lessons of the Finnish campaign in 1940, restored at the moment of the regime's greatest panic about the reliability of the army in June 1941. The subordination of the Party representatives at the field level did not mean that the highest commanders remained free of political supervision. Every front and army continued to have a council, composed of the commander, his chief of staff, and the political member, the last often an important Party figure. Thus the front commander at Stalingrad, Yeremenko, had Khrushchev as his political counterpart. In addition, crucial fronts were inspected by members of the State Defense Committee, especially Malenkov and Beria.

army under the future Marshal Chuikov, the city was turned into a sea of rubble with the Germans in occupation of most of the ruins, but the Russians for three months holding on to the mile-and-a-half-deep strip along the Volga. By November it was clear that the Wehrmacht would not succeed, and yet Hitler refused to sanction a withdrawal of what remained of his sixth army. On November 19 came the Soviet counteroffensive aimed at the weak flank of the German army group between the Volga and the Don. Within a week the German forces in and around Stalingrad were encircled. Still Hitler would not permit an attempted breakthrough: if his soldiers were not to win they were to lay down their lives rather than to escape or surrender. And to make sure that nothing would mar this inspirational sacrifice, the Führer elevated the local German commander, Paulus, to field marshal. No German officer of this rank had ever allowed himself to be taken captive. But the final Soviet drive in January 1943 overwhelmed the half-starving, unsupplied, and exhausted remnants of what had been Germany's proudest army. Paulus and his bedraggled troops surrendered. The catch included, in addition to the marshal, twenty-four generals and upward of 100,000 officers and soldiers.

Moscow had saved the Red Army and the will to resist. Stalingrad inspired people with confidence in victory and a sense of Russia's greatness. There would still be military setbacks, and an appalling toll of casualties, but the faith in eventual victory would not recede. Prior to January 1943 the Soviet leaders had to concentrate on the military aspect of the war, with political considerations, while present in their minds, taking, of necessity, a secondary place. Now for the Soviets the war would become increasingly political, even the military strategy influenced by considerations concerning Russia's role and power in the postwar world.

Stalin was quick to appropriate a considerable part of his country's new military glory and symbolism. He made himself a marshal of the Soviet Union and to the end of his days he would wear a marshal's uniform, which replaced his previously proletarian accoutrements. To his title of supreme commander would be added a redundant one of generalissimo. Shoulder tabs and epaulets evocative of the tsarist times were introduced for officers. There was a profusion of new decorations—Orders of Suvorov and Kutuzov and the highest one, of Victory, set in diamonds, two of which the dictator bestowed on himself. (Others receiving it were Zhukov and Vasilevsky and, among the Allied commanders, Eisenhower and Montgomery.) As if to compensate the officer corps for the sufferings and humiliations it underwent in 1937–39, outstanding soldiers were loaded with benefits: many commanders were raised to the rank of marshal, their exploits were celebrated in the Orders of the Day, and those who fell on the battlefield were honored with statues in their native cities, their families receiving generous pensions.

For all this display of military glory and self-confidence, the regime could not but remain apprehensive about the postwar situation in which the USSR was bound to find itself. The enormous losses the country had already suffered and would continue to incur would leave Russia weak in everything but military prestige. The vast production effort that was already gathering momentum in the United States was the portent of future American economic domination. There was considerable apprehension in Stalin's mind whether this predominance of economic and hence general power on the Anglo-American side would not be increased by a conscious policy of his Western allies to let the Red Army carry on the burden of land fighting while they concentrated on Japan and on the sea and air struggle against Germany. Such a policy would delay the reconquest of Russia's lost territories and would also postpone if not altogether prevent the Red Army's reaching Central Europe and there staking Soviet claims for a share in the fruits of victory. (The British and Americans might invade Europe when the Wehrmacht was definitely defeated but still away from German soil.)

The primary aims of Soviet diplomacy were thus to be the opening of a second front as soon as possible and, connected with it, a recognition on the part of her allies that Russia's sacrifices and new status entitled her not only to the territorial gains she had secured during her alliance with Germany, but at least a sphere of influence in eastern and southeastern Europe.

The Grand Alliance

The diplomatic struggle for these objectives began well before Stalingrad. In the spring of 1942 Molotov visited London and Washington. In the former he tried to obtain the British government's agreement (to be contained, of course, in a secret protocol) to Russia's recovering what she had gained in 1939–40, in return for which the Soviets would be willing to have the British secure bases in France, the Low Countries, and Scandinavia. At the time, the Americans objected to any binding territorial arrangements for the postwar world, and thus the treaty of alliance signed on May 26 between the USSR and Britain contained no such sinful and/or secret provisions. The outstanding fear of the Soviets in dealing with the Western powers had to be that the latter's policy would be formulated by Churchill, whose anti-Communist views, though in abeyance for the war period, were well known and bound to be revived once the common enemy was disposed of. On this count Molotov's visit to Washington must have been reassuring. President Roosevelt was eager to prove to the Russians that he and Churchill were not going to gang up on them, and he could not have left any doubt in Molotov's mind that there were considerable differences of opinion between him and his British friend and that Allied policy and strategy were not going to be determined in London.

Reassuring though such a report must have been, the Soviets' primary objective—a second front *in Europe* in 1942—was not to materialize. It fell to Churchill during his first visit to Moscow, which unfortunately coincided with the summer of 1942 crisis, to inform Stalin that the Anglo-American forces would invade North Africa, from the Soviet viewpoint something that could but feebly affect the desperate struggle that was to unfold on the Stalingrad front. There followed one of the few moments when Stalin lost control of himself in front of a foreign visitor: Were British soldiers afraid to fight the Germans? he insultingly asked. But later on the dictator managed to recover his self-composure and even to charm his guest.

After Stalingrad the Russians no longer needed to appear as mere supplicants. The western and eastern theaters of war remained largely uncoordinated in operation. Operations in the former were guided by the British and American combined chiefs of staff, ultimately by Roosevelt and Churchill; in the latter, of course, exclusively by the Soviet High Command. But what the Russians, now victorious, desired weighed heavily on the minds of the West's policy makers. And public opinion in Britain and America, already affected by the Moscow battle, now became vociferously pro-Soviet, with several voices seconding the Soviet pleas for a second front. To some extent this was the result of skillful Soviet propaganda: the image of totalitarian society gave way to an oversimplified vision of a people united in the struggle for freedom; of the Soviet regime, if not a democracy in a Western sense, still a form of government warmly approved by the nations of the USSR, its head not a tyrant, but a father figure to his people—"Uncle Joe," as he became known in the West. But the best propaganda for Russia was the mere fact of the Soviet losses and sacrifices, and a certain guilt feeling that the British and certainly Americans were far from matching Soviet sacrifices. Even such astute politicians as Roosevelt brought themselves to believe that the war had wrought fundamental changes in communism and that if trust was shown toward the Soviets they were bound to reciprocate by loyally collaborating in building a better postwar world. Those on the Allied side who, like Churchill, felt that for all the comradeship at arms, the task of evolving a viable postwar community required not only mutual trust but tough bargaining with the Soviets found themselves at a disadvantage in trying to impress this idea on their colleagues in the councils of war.

Russia's heightened status within the Grand Alliance offered it more freedom for diplomatic maneuver. By the spring of 1943 the Soviet government availed itself of these new opportunities in its moves on the Polish issue.

The Polish government-in-exile—the "London Poles" in wartime parlance—had for some time had strained relations with the Kremlin. The main bone of contention was the future fate of those Polish territories annexed by the USSR in 1939. If before Stalingrad the Kremlin would have considered some compromise on this issue, after it there was no chance that, short of very strong pressure by Britain and especially the United States, it would relinquish its claims that Western Byelorussia and Western Ukraine should after their reconquest be united with the Communist state. The London Poles just as stubbornly refused to concede any territory that had been Poland's before September 1939.

In the spring of 1943 the Germans announced that they had uncovered in the Katyn Forest near Smolensk a mass grave of Polish officers. It was claimed by the Germans, and despite the source of these claims they have been supported since then by all impartial evidence, that these were corpses of *some* of 15,000 Polish officers who had been in Soviet camps until April 1940 (captured in the Soviet move into Poland in 1939) and about whose subsequent fate the Soviets had professed ignorance. The Polish government requested that the International Red Cross investigate the charges. This gave Moscow an opportunity to put on a show of indignation, blame the murders on the Germans, and break relations with the London Poles. Thus the issue was joined and to the end of the war the Polish question would remain as the greatest challenge to intra-Allied unity.

Though the enemy was still deep in Soviet territory the Kremlin was already taking steps to secure some assets for the forthcoming debate about the fate of postwar Europe. In March the Union of Polish Patriots emerged in Moscow, clearly designed to offset the London Poles, perhaps to become the nucleus of the pro-Soviet government in that country. In July came another hedge against the future: the Free German Committee was set up, including a few German Communists, but also with some aristocratic German officers and even generals captured in the war. Both steps portended Soviet moves in central and eastern Europe, but it is unreasonable to read into them any already existing Soviet blueprint to impose Communist regimes on Poland and Germany. For the moment these organizations were but counters in the game Soviet diplomacy would have to play once the war reached its final stage.

Other counters were represented by the partisan and underground Communist resistance forces that sprang up all over German-occupied Europe after June 22, 1941. It was natural that with their long training in working under illegal conditions, the Communists should assume a prominent, sometimes leading role in the resistance movements. The initial Soviet concern had to be that those Communist resistance forces should *not* be demonstratively ideological, or indeed even pro-Soviet, in their programs and pronouncements; the defeat of Germany still had the first priority, and at this stage Moscow did not desire to feed its allies' apprehensions about its postwar aims. Thus the partisan movement in Yugoslavia, headed by Tito, was reprimanded for its open hostility to the proroyalist Serbian resistance forces of General Mikhailovich. In March 1942 Tito's headquarters received this curt communication from the Russian commander: "Is it really so that besides the Communists and their followers there are no other Yugoslav patriots along-side of whom you could fight against the enemy?" In fact the Soviet military mission to the partisans' headquarters did not arrive till February 1944, the British mission having been there since 1942.

The desire to allay Western suspicions was also instrumental in the dissolution of the Comintern, announced on May 15, 1943. This would put to rest the last lingering allegations about an international Communist conspiracy centered in Moscow. And Stalin was confident—and the future was to confirm, at least until the defiance by Tito and then by Mao—that the psychological and organizational ties between international communism and the USSR were strong enough to assure Soviet domination even without the existence of the formal machinery of the Comintern.

The military course of the war in 1943 justified the Soviet perception that political considerations were now foremost. In July came the last German attempt at a large-scale offensive on the Russian front, and it ended with the Soviet victory in the battle of Kursk. From now on the Germans would be in an almost continuous retreat, ending in the streets of Berlin. Their allies' military effort could not, however, be considered by the Russians with equanimity. They invaded Italy, a secondary front, rather than France, and this carried a suggestion that the British and Americans, especially the former, were eager to put the Anglo-American armies in the Balkans and central Europe before the Red Army could get there.

The November 1943 meeting of the heads of the three great Allied Powers was probably the most important diplomatic event of the war, certainly from the Soviet point of view. For it was at this meeting in Teheran (then jointly occupied by the Russians and the British) that Stalin was able to score a decisive political breakthrough on the most important postwar problem; Yalta and Potsdam for the most part only confirmed the general agreement reached in the Persian capital.

On the crucial Polish question, the head of the Soviet government could, after Teheran, feel confident that the USSR would have its way. Both Churchill and Roosevelt acquiesced (as yet without a formal agreement to this effect) that Russia would retain the territories she had seized in 1939. The nature of the postwar Polish regime was not specifically discussed, but again a strong impression emerged that Britain and the United States would not strenuously oppose Stalin's goal of replacing the London Poles by a body more subservient to Russia. The Polish problem spilled inevitably into the German one. It was Churchill himself who actually proposed what the Soviets had previously merely insinuated: Poland should be compensated with German territory up to the Oder River. This would dissipate another Soviet fear: that his Western allies would after the war hasten to rebuild German power as a barrier to Soviet domination of central and eastern Europe.

On the matter of the second front, Soviet insistence brought this time definite promise of the Anglo-American landings in France in the spring of 1944. And beyond any promises and concessions the most gratifying result of Teheran must have been the realization that President Roosevelt was eager to meet Russian demands and aspirations as much as possible, and that the United States was not likely to join in any British (that is, Churchillian) scheme to deny the Russians what they considered legitimate fruits of the forthcoming victory.

Though the deliberations of Teheran remained secret, many, including some east European politicians, saw the writing on the wall. In December 1943 President Benes of the Czechoslovak government-in-exile traveled to Moscow to secure a treaty of friendship and alliance. He got what he came for, but in the course of his visit his hosts suggested that Russia might need a modification of Czechoslovakia's northeastern frontier when the Red Army got there (thus in 1945 the Carpatho-Ukraine would be ceded to the USSR). And in compliance with his hosts' hints, Benes broadened his government to include Communists and other pro-Soviet politicians.

The year 1944 was one of uninterrupted Soviet victories. By its end all of the territory lost since the beginning of the war was liberated; Russian armies had thrust deep into ethnic Poland and the Balkans, and entered Germany proper in East Prussia. The Allied landings in Normandy in June sealed the fate of Nazi Germany and for the moment dissipated any fears on the Soviets' part that the Western powers might still engage in a double game or even seek a separate peace with Germany.

The Anglo-American opening of a "real" second front brought one of the few public Soviet expressions of gratitude and admiration of the Allies' war effort. Stalin generously called the crossing of the Channel by Eisenhower's armada a military feat without precedent in history. And uniquely during the war, not to mention after it, the Soviet people were given an inkling of the magnitude of the material help they were receiving from the West. On June 11 *Pravda* quoted some of the figures of American Lend-Lease deliveries the USSR had received as of that date: "6,430 aircraft and in addition 2,442 aircraft received from the U.S. on account of British obligation; 3,734 tanks . . . 206,771 trucks . . . 3,168 antiaircraft guns . . . 5,500,000 pairs of army boots . . . food deliveries of 2,199,000 tons." Figures of the supplies received from Britain and Canada were also quoted and, in proportion to those countries' resources, they were at least as impressive. This wide publicity given to the help from the "capitalists" reflected genuine gratitude and relief, but there was also an undoubted element of calculation. With the war entering its final stage and with the demonstration of the enormous power of the United States—outproducing the rest of the world industrially and barely bloodied in the war as compared with Russia—the Soviet government was eager to show to its allies that it appreciated their efforts.

An incident during the summer underlined how precarious and easily strained were the links of the Grand Alliance. When the Soviet armies reached the Vistula line, the Polish government in London ordered its underground forces in Warsaw to stage an uprising. This would prove to the world, and especially to Washington and London, that the exile government enjoyed, despite Soviet insinuations to the contrary, a wide support among its people; it would preclude the Russians from imposing a regime after conquering Poland's capital. The first part of this premise proved correct: the ability of the Polish underground to engage several German divisions equipped with tanks and artillery and to fight them for sixty-two days was a convincing proof of the extent of support the exile government had in Poland. But the assumption that the Soviets would not dare to outrage world public opinion by letting its armies sit on the other side of the Vistula while the Germans suppressed the uprising proved false. It is possible that the crossing of the river in August when the drama of Warsaw began was not in the plans of the Soviet High Command. But the Soviets refused to lend any help or, at first, even to allow British and American planes to supply the insurgents (they were eventually allowed to fly in, but from bases in Italy). Stalin made no secret about his eventual plans for Poland: in reply to Churchill's and Roosevelt's pleas to help the Poles, he wrote: "Sooner or later the truth about the group of criminals [i.e., the London Poles] who have unleashed the Warsaw adventure will become known to everybody." Warsaw now was almost totally destroyed; when its ruins were finally occupied by the Soviet army in January 1945, the Russian-sponsored Polish group would be installed there.

This group, to which the Soviets were already turning over the administration of conquered ethnic Poland, was the Committee of National Liberation, installed provisionally in Lublin and headed by a Communist, Boleslaw Bierut. The Polish issue was no longer confined to territorial readjustment: the Soviet goal was obviously to convince and cajole Britain and the United States to withdraw their recognition from the hapless London Poles and to acknowledge the Soviet-sponsored group as the legitimate government. The Western powers were as yet not ready to do that, but it must have been obvious to the Kremlin that its insistence and especially the Soviet army's presence in the disputed area were steadily eroding Washington's and London's resistance.

It was clear that the Soviet military strategy was already attuned to Stalin's political goals. After the great successes of the spring and summer offensives, the most logical and shortest route to the heart of Germany lay through Poland. But the Soviets were eager to step into the Balkans, Hungary, and Austria before the British could get there from Italy. So two entire army groups were diverted into the Balkans and Hungary. In Rumania King Michael ousted his pro-German regime and brought his government and army over to the Soviet side. Germany's satellites and allies were now dropping out of the war. Finland quit in September and, judged by the usual standard, the Soviet conditions were quite lenient: no occupation and territorial acquisitions limited to what the USSR had obtained in 1940. Again, this was done with an eye to Western public opinion: the Soviets had not forgotten America's concern over and admiration of the little country's stand in the Winter War in 1940. It was prudent to be moderate with the Finns if one was after bigger game: Poland, Bulgaria, Rumania, etc.

On the Western side Churchill, despairing of checking Soviet imperial ambitions altogether, hoped to moderate them. In October 1944 the Prime Minister on another Moscow visit tried to interest Stalin in a division of eastern Europe into spheres of interest, the relative influence of Britain and the USSR to be expressed by percentages: thus Yugoslavia was to be fifty-fifty; Greece 90 percent British, 10 percent Russian, Rumania vice versa, etc. Stalin was noncommittal: he knew that the United States was opposed to such a sinful imperialistic bargain, and through the Red Army and local Communists he hoped to get much more than his ingenious British friend proposed. (The legend has grown since then that an actual bargain was struck in Moscow. In fact when Churchill presented him with the paper listing the famous percentages, all Stalin did was to make "a rather large tick upon it," as Churchill testifies.)

The Russian aim to dominate eastern Europe could not be checked or delimited by a piece of paper. The controlling factor was to be the presence of the Red Army. Once there, it installed as local regimes those elements who could be counted on as pro-Soviet, whether they had popular support or not. Many politicians, not all of the left persuasion, were ready to recognize that Soviet influence was going to be dominant and were ready to trim their sails accordingly. Some hoped, and the Soviets at the time encouraged these hopes, that the Kremlin would be satisfied with a pro-Soviet regime and would not insist on one entirely Communist. Hence a variety of "popular," "national," etc., "fronts"—i.e., political coalitions in which the local Communists played varying roles—were being installed in power by Soviet military authorities. By the same token, parties and personalities who refused to be amenable were denounced as German collaborators and dealt with by imprisonment, exile, or worse. In Yugoslavia, which the Soviet troops reached in the fall, local communism was strong enough to make an immediate bid for complete power. Marshal Tito, a life-long Communist, and his Partisan forces now took over the country and would soon shed the monarchy and other appurtenances of the old Yugoslav state. Elsewhere the process was to be more protracted, and occasionally the Soviets had to curb the more hotheaded of the local Communists.

This seeming moderation proceeded not only from the realization that the Communist popular following was often minuscule (only in Czechoslovakia was a free election to give the Communists a plurality of votes) and that time and nondoctrinaire policies were needed to repress the anti-Communist sentiments of the majority. For all the tangible assets in his hands—i.e., the Red Army's presence on the spot —Stalin could not risk a head-on clash with Roosevelt and the United States.

The problem of securing U.S. acquiescence to what went against the grain of both American politicians and public opinion—replacement of German by Russian domination of eastern Europe—became, during the last phase of the war, the principal goal of Soviet diplomacy. (At this point Washington's voice was clearly the dominant one on the Western side of the alliance. Britain was bound to follow along despite Churchill's much more realistic evaluation of Soviet goals.) Toward this objective, Soviet diplomacy had several assets in addition to the still warm recognition in the West of Russia's sacrifices and services in the common struggle. One was America's hope and expectation that, following the conclusion of the European conflict, the Red Army was going to assist the Americans in what was still expected to be the long and arduous task of bringing Japan to its knees. Another was American statemen's desire to bring the USSR into a world organization, which with the war's end would secure peace and international security. Discussions as to the organization of the future United Nations and the general outline of the postwar world began during the summer of 1944. Haunted by memories and fears of isolationism, President Roosevelt and his advisers believed that such an organization could be approved and wholeheartedly embraced by their people only if it included all the great powers and thus promised to do what the League of Nations had failed in. In their eyes the erection of a stable framework of postwar collaboration and peace took precedence over any territorial settlements and issues.

Well realizing the premium put on it by the American policy makers, the Russians proved hard and *almost* intractable negotiators about the shape and powers of the proposed new organization. Thus they demanded that the future permanent members of the Security Council have the right to veto not only on substantive, but also on procedural questions before the United Nations. The Soviets at first demanded that all sixteen of the Soviet union republics, as well as the USSR itself, should have seats in the Assembly, etc. To a large extent these objections were raised only to be dropped at a point when the Americans would be so grateful for Russian concessions as not to quibble unduly about Bulgaria or Poland.

On the latter Soviet diplomacy felt it timely to turn the screws more tightly. The Lublin committee having declared itself the provisional government of Poland, the Soviets—despite Roosevelt's pleas at least to delay this step—recognized it in January 1945, the same month in which a great Soviet offensive cleared the rest of the country of the Germans. By February the Red Army had cut deeply into the enemy's land.

Thus by the time the Big Three, Roosevelt, Churchill, and Stalin, met in the Crimean resort of Yalta on February 7, one of the most crucial problems of postwar Europe was largely resolved through unilateral Soviet action. And with the Russian armies now 50 miles away from Berlin, it would have taken most tenacious bargaining by the West to reverse the drift toward complete Soviet domination of Poland, which in turn was to affect more than symbolically the fate of other countries liberated from the Nazi yoke, and in fact the very central issue: the future status of Germany itself.

The Yalta decisions spelled out the end of any lingering doubts concerning the future fate of central and eastern Europe. Poland's eastern frontiers would in general follow the line of the Molotov-Ribbentrop agreement. In the west, though this decision was more tentative and to be sealed only at Potsdam, Poland would absorb a

At Yalta, February, 1945. Seated: Churchill, Roosevelt, Stalin. Standing: Eden, Stettinius, Molotov, Harriman.

sizable chunk of ethnic Germany up to the Oder-Neisse line, a shift that would mean the displacement of seven million Germans. Even more important was the decision as to the country's future government: the Western powers would drop the London Poles, and the Soviet protégé, the Provisional Government of Poland, was to be the nucleus of the future regime, with some additional politicians to be added to it subject to the Soviet veto. Germany, thus deprived of much of her agricultural land and the rich industrial area of Silesia, would be divided into zones of occupation by the Big Three and France. So much for the British hopes of preserving a balance of power on the Continent by re-creating a united and economically viable Germany. In return for these enormous concessions, which would seal Soviet domination of eastern Europe for generations, the Russians proved quite amenable on the United Nations: they would not insist on the great powers being able to veto procedural matters; and instead of sixteen Assembly seats, they would settle for just three. (Thus the Ukraine and Byelorussia in addition to the USSR have seats in the Assembly.) President Roosevelt greeted these concessions as "a great step forward which would be welcomed by all peoples in the world."

The Soviet Union met yet another desire of the United States by promising to enter the war against Japan shortly after the conclusion of the European conflict. But here the Soviets set explicit conditions: they would have to get southern Sakhalin and the Kurile Islands. Since these were Japanese property, this request presented no difficulty; but the Americans felt a bit more constrained about promising Stalin what after Japan's defeat should logically have reverted to China: the Manchurian Railway complex, Port Arthur, and Dairen. President Roosevelt promised to assist Soviet diplomacy in making the government of Chiang Kai-shek see the need for these concessions, which would lay a firm foundation for Sino-Soviet friendship.

Thus on almost every issue the Western powers conceded to Stalin what he wanted, a tribute not only to the exploits of the Red Army, but to Soviet diplomacy. The effect of the decisions on Germany and Poland has already been stated. In the Far East the Soviet entrance into the war would have a decisive influence on the future successes of the Chinese Communists, certainly on the division of Korea. Though the Yalta agreements remained for the time being secret, they had an immediate result in speeding up the tempo of Soviet encroachments in eastern Europe. In Rumania King Michael was coerced into appointing a Communist-dominated government. And the Czech ambassador in Moscow, a thoroughgoing fellow traveler, was appointed the head of the Czechoslovak government.

The Soviet haste in cashing in their gains under Yalta led to a potentially dangerous dispute with Washington. President Roosevelt's policy of meeting Stalin's demands considerably more than half way was based on a genuine though fatuous belief that he could convince the dictator of his allies' good faith and make him adhere to his agreements. But trust in his fellow humans was not an outstanding characteristic of Stalin's, and he insisted on putting his own interpretations on any agreements the USSR had undertaken. Thus on the Polish question he would not agree on a genuine reconstruction of "his" Polish government, but at most on some cosmetic changes that would leave the Communists and their allies in the dominant position. The Western expostulation this time brought a tentative cancellation of Molotov's proposed trip to the founding meeting of the United Nations scheduled for April 25, a veiled threat that Russia might not enter this organization unless the Americans stopped bothering about Poland and other east European problems. And the news that the Germans were negotiating for a surrender of their forces in northern Italy evoked the despot's old fear: His allies might still make a separate treaty with Germany! Correspondence on both of these problems between Washington and Moscow grew acrimonious and might well have led to a change in Roosevelt's attitude toward Stalin personally and about the general trustworthiness of Soviet pledges and motives. But on April 12 the President died. The sad event served to smooth over the tensions that had arisen, and Stalin was persuaded that the north Italian business involved only a local capitulation.

Berlin fell to the Russian armies on May 2. On May 8 came the German capitulation, and for the Russians the real end of World War II. The war against Japan, would, compared to the one they had just concluded, be for them a minor affair, with none of the emotional and political meaning of the struggle against the invader who had caused devastation all the way to the Volga and to the suburbs of Moscow and Leningrad.

To the world at large the most impressive lesson of the war was the awesome military might of the USSR. With the Soviet flag over the Reich chancellery in Berlin and Soviet troops soon in Manchuria, Soviet manpower appeared limitless, and the USSR, should it so decide, capable of further military and territorial expansion. In fact the legend of Russia's overwhelming power, of her armies' being capable of a rapid thrust to the English Channel and being restrained only by America's monopoly of the atom bomb, was to become one of the decisive factors of world politics, not only at the war's end but for several years afterward. Yet we now know and common sense should have argued at the time that Russia, though victorious, emerged from the war in almost as weakened a state as Germany or Japan. The number of people lost, never given out officially, must be estimated as around twenty million. Far from Soviet manpower's being limitless, the USSR at the time of the German capitulation had fewer men under arms than did the United States. As to the sinews of modern warfare: the USSR was desperately weak in industry and food; how could it be otherwise? In 1940 the country produced over 20 million tons of steel, in 1945, 10.6. The total harvest was also under half of the prewar figure. In the course of war the enemy had destroyed more than 30,000 factories; 65,000 kilometers of railway lines (out of a total of 122,000—more than half the rail length); 1.2 million dwellings in Soviet towns; 3.5 million rural dwellings. Agriculture, which in 1939–40 had just made up the losses incurred during collectivization, was so much affected that to restore it to the prewar level would take, a Soviet author estimated in 1947, an increase of 70 percent in grain production, 50 percent in cattle; production of hogs would have to be quadrupled, that of horses more than doubled.[5] The total material damage, which could hardly be given with any precision, was estimated by the same source at $357 billion (at the 1947 value).

The economic and hence military weakness of the USSR at the end of the war was paralleled by sociopolitical vulnerabilities. The latter part of the war was accompanied by a patriotic upsurge on the part of the majority of the population; for most Soviet citizens, especially the Russians, it was the Great Patriotic War. But inherent in this sentiment was a widespread expectation that life would become easier

[5] N. A. Voznesensky, *Soviet Economy during the Second World War*, New York, 1949, p. 135.

after the cruel test was over, and certainly that the horrors of the prewar decade would not return. While no one expected a basic alteration of the Communist regime, it was certainly hoped by many that some of the freer and more relaxed ways of Russia's allies would rub off on her own society. Conscious of the danger inherent in such aspirations, the regime, as the war drew toward the end, shifted its propaganda line: the ideological motif returned. The war had been a successful test not only of national unity but of Russia's social and political system. The cult of personality, to use a later expression, returned with a vengeance; Russia's victories, the brilliant leadership of the military effort, were increasingly attributed to Stalin personally and to the Communist Party, which he had inspired. At the war's end, during the famous celebration of Victory Day on May 18, Stalin hinted to his entourage that he, now sixty-five, was seriously thinking of retiring; if so, this mood soon passed and the tyrant reemerged from behind the national leader. As the Soviet armies reconquered Russia's soil, those guilty of even the slightest collaboration with the invader were dealt with mercilessly. Mass repression returned as a prophylactic measure. Whole nationality groups were made to suffer for the disloyalty of some of their members. Thus several national districts were officially dissolved and their populations—as in the case of the Crimean Tatars, Volga Germans, Chechen, Ingush, and others—transported wholesale and dispersed far away from their homelands. Hundreds of thousands of ex-prisoners of war and forced labor victims, whether they returned voluntarily or were turned over forcibly by the Western authorities to the Soviets, found themselves exchanging German camps for Soviet ones. In brief, the regime realized that if the old system was to be reimposed, if the enormous task of making the USSR what it was already believed to be abroad—a superpower—was to be accomplished, political leadership had to appear and again to be resolute and ruthless. Similar considerations were to weigh on Stalin's foreign policy in the immediate postwar period. Were the West to realize the enormous weaknesses and vulnerabilities behind the facade of military greatness, were the Kremlin to prove unduly tractable in the negotiations about the postwar settlement, then not only the fruits of victory but the Soviet system itself might become endangered.[6]

It has sometimes been asserted that had the West—and primarily

[6] This psychological insight was undoubtedly the main reason why the USSR did not pursue the idea of a large loan from the United States. At one time Russian officials intimated that they would like, once Lend-Lease ended, credits on the order of $6 billion. Then it became apparent that the Americans might attach political conditions to the negotiations about long-term credits, and the Soviets dropped the idea, despite their desperate need for economic assistance. The Soviets were, however, along with the rest of liberated Europe, to be helped by supplies distributed by UNRRA.

the United States—followed different policies toward the USSR after the war, the postwar history would have been different: shown some trust, Stalin's regime would have been more cooperative; perhaps the Cold War would have been avoided. What has been said before casts considerable doubt on such constructions. Even for purely domestic reasons Stalin's Russia needed, with the war's end, a period of isolation to enable it to reconstruct the political system in its full rigidity, to lay at rest any illusions that had sprung up during the period of cooperation with the democratic states. Continued amity and hence economic and cultural intercourse with the West could have led to ideological coexistence that even Brezhnev's Russia, so much more powerful, prosperous, and self-assured than was Stalin's in 1945–46, feels it cannot afford. The secrecy, the menacing air the USSR was to cultivate in its dealings with the external world were also intended to conceal the country's weakness and to persuade the capitalists that it was both hopeless and dangerous to try to make the USSR abandon or loosen its grip on eastern Europe. And it worked!

7. The End of the Stalin Era and the Beginning of the Cold War, 1945-1953

World War II Ends

Viewed from the Kremlin, the international situation at the end of the war with Germany offered both dazzling opportunities and considerable danger. The Soviet armies had overrun eastern Europe and thus it appeared more than probable that all those small and medium powers that in the interwar Europe served as a *cordon sanitaire* or, in the Soviet parlance, as part of the capitalist encirclement around the USSR, would now be in the Soviet sphere of interest, with the decision being up to Moscow whether and to what extent they should become Communist as well. At the same time, the Soviet government adhered to a joint declaration of the Big Three at Yalta which proclaimed that the nations liberated from the Nazi yoke should be free to determine their own form of government and policies. Neither the British nor even the American government had many illusions what this free choice would mean with the Red Army actually occupying those countries, but a too drastic defiance by the Soviets of the libertarian and democratic rhetoric in which the Grand Alliance had couched its postwar aims might well have led to a head-on collision with the Western powers. The Kremlin might well have been aware of Churchill's proposal, as communicated to the U.S. government, that the Anglo-American armies, which as of May 8 were in occupation of a considerable German territory rescheduled to be in the Soviet zone, refuse to surrender it to the Soviet troops until and unless the Russians demonstrated their goodwill and observed their pledges concerning Poland and other east European countries.

A sober calculation of risks of a premature rupture with America and Britain determined also the Soviet attitude toward Communist parties in the West. There, and especially in France and Italy, they emerged from the underground with a considerable popular following and conceivably might have made a bid for power upon the ejection of the Germans. But the Soviet advice to the Western Communists was that they should continue on their nondoctrinaire nationalist course and eschew any appearance of revolutionary activities. The French and Italian Communists disarmed their partisan detachments and continued their partnership in the coalition governments.

Insofar as the Far East was concerned, the Soviets were sensitive to the American determination to dominate the peace settlement after they had borne the burden of the Pacific war. Stalin hoped to receive a reward for helping the Americans bring this war to a conclusion. The Soviets had gone to considerable lengths in trying to persuade the Americans that the Chinese Communists, still in an uneasy alliance with Chiang Kai-shek, were an indigenous movement over which Moscow had no influence. And at the time (1945), and for some time afterward, it must have seemed unrealistic to assume that Mao's forces were capable of conquering *all* of China, or that the United States would let them do so in view of Washington's almost proprietary interest in the Kuomintang regime. (Only near the end of the war did the American attitude toward Chiang's government begin to change, in view of the Chinese Nationalists' military ineptitude and the stories of the regime's corruption and repressive policies.)

The main factor in the configuration of forces in postwar Europe was the fate of Germany. But at least one of the keys to that problem lay in the disposition of the Polish issue, and on this score Soviet persistence and diplomatic skill were finally to carry the day. To clear the table for the forthcoming meeting of the Big Three, President Truman dispatched Harry Hopkins to Moscow in late May. The subsequent negotiations led to a "solution" of the Polish problem, insofar as the nature of the future government of the unhappy country was concerned. The Soviet-sponsored government of Poland was to be diluted somewhat by the inclusion of a few non-Communist politicians, notably the erstwhile premier of the London government, Mikolajczyk; thereupon Washington and London would officially recognize this government and break off relations with the London Poles. (The newcomers were subsequently shuffled off to unimportant posts, Mikolajczyk receiving the largely nominal post of deputy prime minister. Positions of real importance remained in the hands of the Communists and their allies.)

Having achieved what had been one of his main postwar goals, Stalin now proved tractable on other issues that agitated the Americans. He withdrew the Soviet reservation concerning the voting procedure in the Security Council. He reaffirmed the Soviet pledge to enter the war against Japan once Soviet preparations for it were completed. (The original understanding was that the Soviet entry would come about three months after the capitulation of Germany, and it did almost to the day. The Soviets have a legitimate grievance against those who see their declaration of war as having been prompted by Hiroshima. Another point often made, that the United States in view of its atomic bomb, did not need Soviet assistance may well be true, but at the time American military leaders, including General MacArthur, were almost unanimous in insisting that the Soviet entry was necessary to speed up the collapse of Japan and to save American lives.) But he insisted on the conditions stipulated at Yalta and appeared to add another one, "The Marshal [Stalin] expects that Russia will share in the actual occupation of Japan and wants an agreement with the British and us as to occupation zones," reported Hopkins. His American interlocutor was impressed by Stalin's handsome acknowledgment that the United States would have to play the dominant role in the postwar Far East; on China he was complimentary about Chiang and disparaging about the Chinese Communists: "No Communist leader was strong enough to unify China."

The agenda for the last meeting of the Big Three, which opened in Potsdam in the middle of July, repeated in the main those of Teheran in 1943 and of Yalta a few months before. On the main problem, that of Germany, the victors of World War II were determined, and wisely, not to repeat the mistake of their predecessors in World War I: then a peace settlement was imposed on the defeated party shortly after the war's end with passions and enmity still running high. But of course circumstances were to make this wise restraint lead ultimately to perverse and dangerous consequences: no formal peace treaty would be signed with Germany and for a generation the problem of this key country would remain a sore on the body of Europe and a danger to world peace.[1]

The main Soviet objective had to be to prevent in any foreseeable future the renascence of Germany as a great industrial and military power. To introduce communism into all or part of Germany was, at the time, at most a very secondary consideration. The results of Potsdam went far to meet the Soviet main goal: as agreed before, Ger-

[1] The series of agreements signed between 1969 and 1972 involving the four victorious powers of World War II (the Big Three and France), the Federal Republic of Germany, the German Democratic Republic, and Poland may be taken in their sum as constituting a *de facto* peace treaty on the German problem.

At the Potsdam Conference in July, 1945, Clement Atlee and Harry S. Truman now represented Great Britain and the United States.

many would be provisionally divided into four spheres of occupation. Should Germany be reunited—and even Stalin at the time could not suspect that Germany's case would demonstrate the truth of the dictum: nothing endures like the provisional—the Soviet zone could be bargained against the neutralization and prohibition of rearmament of the country as a whole. But in addition Germany would be permanently weakened by having her eastern parts detached, part of East Prussia going to the USSR, the rest, as well as Silesia and Pomerania, to Poland. Since this amputation was to be accompanied by expulsion of some six to seven million ethnic Germans, they would presumably settle in the Western powers' occupation zones. The Soviets could confidently hope that the latter would be thrown for years into economic and social turmoil and would remain a source of weakness rather than strength for the West. The Russians insisted and finally won the day on this point, that Poland should get a larger slice of Germany than Britain and America thought they had agreed on. (It had been assumed at Yalta that the Polish-German frontier would run along the Oder-Neisse line. But there turned out to be *two* Neisse rivers, and the line as agreed at Potsdam was to run along the Oder-*Western* Neisse, thus adding to the Polish gains valuable mining and agrarian areas.) To be sure, the West won a hollow concession: the "final determination" of Poland's western frontier was left to the peace conference, but in the meantime (and a long meantime it turned out to be) the German territories were to be left under Polish administration.

On some other much less momentous issues Soviet desires were stymied. Thus the Western powers rejected Stalin's plan that the USSR should have a naval base on Turkish territory to secure its entrance and egress from the Black Sea[2] and should be awarded trusteeship of part of Italy's colonial empire. Britain and America also rejected the demand that they should break diplomatic relations with Franco's Spain. The Soviets had the strongest claim on the issue of German reparations for the devastation caused in Russia by the war; it was agreed that these should come from current production. (The Soviets as a matter of fact dismantled and transported home much of the industrial equipment they found in their own zone.)

The atmosphere of Potsdam, though friendly, still carried the portents of the forthcoming Cold War. The Western powers', and especially Britain's, expostulations that Soviet actions in eastern Europe bore little resemblance to the Declaration on Liberated Europe agreed upon at Yalta, which pledged the Big Three to abide by the free verdict and free elections in the nations liberated from the Nazi yoke, met with Soviet refusals even to debate the issue or counteraccusations that the British were suppressing democracy in Greece. (Upon the liberation of Greece, the British had suppressed a Communist uprising, evidently unauthorized by the Soviets, and were currently, and for the next two years, to provide support to the monarchical government.) The British, especially Churchill, who, as a result of the British elections, was replaced in the course of the conference by the new prime minister, Clement Attlee, could not conceal their bitterness at the new configuration of world politics in which the USSR, now dominant in east and southeast Europe, was clearly replacing Great Britain as the second superpower. President Truman obviously did not share his predecessor's belief that, if shown trust, the Soviets would reciprocate and abide by their agreements.

On the day the conference opened, July 16, the first atomic bomb was exploded in New Mexico. The news about the existence of this new and frightful weapon was, with some diffidence, communicated by Truman to Stalin: what if the dictator asked for a sample or to be allowed to dispatch Soviet observers to Los Alamos! But Stalin merely expressed his satisfaction and hope that the bomb would be used

[2] This would also have been the means of pressure on the Turks to return those parts of Transcaucasia Turkey had kept since 1918 and the recovery of which would remain on the agenda of Soviet diplomacy until Stalin's death.

WESTERN RUSSIA
1914
Sept. 1, 1939
Today
NORWAY
SWEDEN
FINLAND
RUSSIA
Oslo
Stockholm
Helsinki
Leningrad
Tallin
ESTONIA
LATVIA
Riga
Moscow
DENMARK
Copenhagen
LITHUANIA
Vilnius
Smolensk
Minsk
WHITE RUSSIA
THE NETHERLANDS
GERMANY
Berlin
EAST
Bonn
Warsaw
POLAND
LUXEMBURGH
WEST
Prague
Kiev
UKRAINE
CZECHOSLOVAKIA
Vienna
Bern
SWITZERLAND
AUSTRIA
Budapest
HUNGARY
MOLDAVIA
Kishinev
ROMANIA
Bucharest
Belgrade
YUGOSLAVIA
Black Sea
ITALY
Sofia
BULGARIA
Rome
TURKEY
Ankara
Tirana
ALBANIA
GREECE
0 MILES 300
0 KILOMETERS 300

against Japan. We know from Soviet sources that research on nuclear weapons began in the USSR in June 1942, at first on a modest scale but gaining momentum after January 1945, when intelligence reports indicated that the Americans were making rapid progress. Stalin thus could not have been entirely ignorant of the matter, though it is unlikely that he, any more than many American military leaders, could have, prior to Hiroshima, realized that a new era had dawned with the explosion in the New Mexico desert.

The Potsdam Conference sealed Soviet mastery of eastern Europe. And though at the time it was commonly assumed that a peace settlement with Germany would be forthcoming in two to four years, the decision on zones of occupation presaged the current picture. To the conferees, the Russians included, zones of occupation did not preclude a central direction of German affairs: the Central Council of the four Allied commanders was to act as the supreme body for all of Germany, and presumably in due time a central German government would be erected to negotiate the peace treaty. But this arrangement assumed a continuation of the alliance between the USSR and the West, and when it broke down, giving way to conflict and the Cold War, it became almost inevitable that two German governments would emerge, one Communist, one democratic. An additional and infinite amount of trouble was to be the consequence of another decision: Berlin, deep in the Soviet zone, was itself to remain divided into four areas governed by the four victorious powers. A similar overall arrangement was provided for Austria. But the little country was allowed to have its own central government, and because of its relative unimportance in the general configuration of European politics, Austria in 1955 was to be freed of foreign occupation and allowed to preserve national unity.

Soviet planning for war against Japan began long before the end of the German war and had been meticulous. Hiroshima came on August 6. On August 9, having formally declared war, Soviet armies struck into Manchuria and China. Soviet superiority over the enemy was overwhelming, two to one in men and planes, to five to one in tanks. Units of the Chinese Communist armies opened their own offensive on August 10, and it dovetailed with the Soviet moves. Mindful of America's dominant military and political role in the Far East, the Soviets hastened to stake out their claims to prevent possible contention about areas scheduled to come under their occupation. Soviet armies and those of Mongolia surged into Manchuria and northern Korea and effected a linkage with the Chinese Communist forces (something that would be of enormous importance for the future course of the Chinese civil war). The announcement of Japanese capitulation on August 14 did not stop Soviet military operations. Although some Japanese units were still fighting, the decision had obviously been reached, and it would have spared Soviet as well as Japanese lives to withhold further offensive action and to await the local Japanese commander's surrender. But the Soviets were obviously nervous that, with the bomb's having brought about a "premature" Japanese capitulation, the Americans might renege on some of their promises unless the Soviet troops were on the spot. Thus Stalin reacted frantically to General MacArthur's order of August 15, which did *not* include the Kurile Islands in the regions the Japanese were to surrender to the Russians. In his telegram to Truman, Stalin reminded the President that according to Yalta the Kuriles were to go to the USSR. And for good measure he wanted some additional loot: Part of the Japanese homeland, half of the northernmost island of Hokkaido, should be occupied by the USSR. "Russian public opinion would be seriously insulted if the Russian armies were not to receive an occupation zone in some part of Japan proper. I earnestly hope that my modest wishes as expounded here will meet no opposition." But on Japan, unlike Germany and eastern Europe, the Americans were to prove tough and obdurate. The Kuriles, as promised, were delivered, but Truman would not hear of a Soviet occupation zone in Japan, where America proposed to be the exclusive boss. And thus Japan escaped the fate of Germany and Korea. The Soviets would be represented on the Allied Control Council in Japan under the imperious MacArthur, but the Soviet representative there would have as much power as an American or British delegate to a similar body in Bulgaria or Hungary.

But if denied a share of Japan, the USSR and communism were to obtain a far more fabulous prize in the Far East. And in due time this success of Soviet-Communist policies was to become the source of the greatest perplexity and potential danger to the rulers of the USSR. This fantastic—from the perspective of 1945—sequence of events began August 14, 1945, with the signing of the Treaty of Friendship and Alliance between the Republic of China (Chiang Kai-shek's government) and Russia. Ostensibly this treaty constituted a partial payment for Russia's entrance into the war as stipulated at Yalta between Stalin and Roosevelt. The treaty contained provisions painful to Chinese national pride, such as the acquiescence in the loss of Outer Mongolia (though this was but a recognition of *status quo* as it had existed for a long time), the Soviets' acquisition of Port Arthur as a naval base, and their sharing in the port facilities of Dairen. (Thus the Soviet Union was claiming and receiving special rights and bases in the classical manner of pre-1914 European imperialism, while simultaneously the Western powers were surrendering their extraterritorial rights and turning the international settlement in Shanghai over to the Chinese.)

But the most important provision was the one that stipulated that the Soviets would again share the ownership of the Manchurian Railway, and since the Japanese had built the line into a vast business and multi-industrial enterprise, its ownership would give Russia a powerful influence in the economy and politics of China's richest province.

Chiang Kai-shek undoubtedly thought that these concessions were more than compensated for by the Soviet pledges not to deal with any Chinese faction except the official government of the republic and speedily to withdraw Soviet troops from Manchuria after the end of military operations against Japan. The Chinese dictator believed that by appeasing his Soviet counterpart he could induce the latter to withdraw or at least to limit severely Soviet help to the Chinese Communists under Mao, and that the mere fact of the treaty would be a blow to the prestige and expectations of his rivals.

But while the Soviets neither expected nor perhaps even wished a complete Communist victory in the world's most populous country, they had an obvious interest in strengthening Mao's position. It was reasonable to assume that the civil war between the Kuomintang and the Communists would erupt again now that the Japanese defeat had removed the only reason for their uneasy accommodation. (Between 1941 and 1945 both the Nationalists and the Communists had dragged their feet in fighting Japan, husbanding their forces for the forthcoming internal conflict. But Chiang's reluctance to pursue the fight against the invader wholeheartedly could not but be noticed and resented by American observers, and this contributed to the decline of his prestige with the Americans.) If by some miracle American arbitration was to stave off the conflict, Moscow's interest lay in having the Communists in a strong position in a coalition regime, thus to offset American influence with the Nationalists. If, as was more likely, an armed conflict could not be avoided, Soviet interests would be well served by two Chinas, the Communist one including the rich province of Manchuria.

The situation in China was to prove even more favorable to communism than the Soviets expected. Chiang's regime had been weakened by the war and internal corruption; in the areas recovered from Japanese occupation the Nationalists behaved like foreign invaders rather than liberators. Inflation was rampant. The Americans, while helping the Nationalists and transporting their troops to prevent Communist take-overs of liberated areas, grew increasingly exasperated with their protégés. It was thus difficult for Washington to take notice of the Soviets' violation of their pledges both to Chiang and to the Americans. Soviet troops were not to withdraw from Manchuria until May 1946, and until then would not let the Nationalists obtain effective control of the area. What is more, the very considerable stocks of captured Japanese arms were turned over by the Soviet command to the Communist partisans. Before the Soviet entrance the Communist forces in Manchuria numbered 10,000; by November 1945 they had grown to 215,000. After the Soviet evacuation, Chiang was at first successful in reconquering Manchuria; but he wasted his best forces in the process, thereby ensuring his eventual and catastrophic defeat in 1948–49. For good measure, before their withdrawal the Soviets looted Manchuria of most of its industrial equipment, their depredations being on the order of $2 billion.

Thus 1945 marked the emergence of the Soviet Union as one of the world's two superpowers. The British Empire, for more than a century an object of Russia's emulation and the rival first of Imperial, then of Soviet, Russia in the Orient, would now be in a state of progressive dissolution. Economically and politically, Great Britain would never recover the position it held before 1939. The same was true of France, which in addition to pressing economic problems would be, like Great Britain, preoccupied with international and domestic problems arising out of the dissolution of its empire. Russia's traditional rivals, Germany in Europe, Japan in the Far East, lay prostrate and under foreign occupation. In addition to the enormous power that the outside world assumed Russia wielded, communism all over the globe increased dramatically in strength, reflecting both the new prestige of the fatherland of socialism, and the leading role many Communist parties played in the struggle against the Axis of the fascist powers. Communism's successes in eastern and southern Europe would reflect, of course, the presence or proximity of the Red Army rather than (with the partial exception of Czechoslovakia and Yugoslavia) its local strength. But in the two great Western countries, France and Italy, the Communists now were mass parties. With something like one-fourth to one-third of the electorate likely to follow them and their allies and with their control over the trade unions and considerable influence among the intellectual elite, the French and Italian Communists appeared in a fair way to bid for power. In Asia the Communists were powerful not only in its largest country: the inevitable demise of the Western colonial system would make local communism a factor of crucial and at times decisive importance in areas like French Indo-China, Burma, the Dutch East Indies, not to speak of Korea, where as in eastern Europe Soviet occupation would beget a Communist state, and of northern Iran, where a similar situation appeared to suggest similar developments. And in 1945–46 one could still have high hopes concerning the fortunes of communism in Japan and India.

Where, as in the Near East and Black Africa, communism as yet was insignificant, the Kremlin expected to achieve eventual influence because of its traditional anticolonial stand. The policy of supporting "bourgeois nationalism" when directed against Western imperial domination and influence, which the weak and economically backward USSR had tried with indifferent success in the 1920's, now could be renewed with more confidence in view of Russia's new status and the correspondingly weaker position of the imperial powers. In the eyes of the emerging nations of what was now to be called the Third World, the USSR would appear as the natural ally in the struggle against the decaying imperialism of the West.

As against those vast assets and the dazzling prospects of expanding Soviet power and influence to all corners of the globe, the USSR as it emerged from the war displayed countervailing elements of weakness. The basic one lay in the devastated state of the Soviet economy. Those abroad who spoke fearfully of the Soviet armies being capable of sweeping rapidly to the English Channel were forgetting that in modern times no military machine could be stronger than the economy behind it. The vision of unlimited Soviet manpower beguiled Western observers for several years after the war, while in fact Soviet demobilization proceeded as rapidly as American: from over 11 million troops under arms the Soviet forces were by 1948 reduced to 2.8 million—men were badly needed in the factories and on the farms. Quite apart from such factors as America's monopoly of nuclear weapons, the USSR, well into the 1950's, would be incapable of pursuing policies that, in the opinion of its rulers, could incur a high risk of war. Yet at this period, and especially during the Berlin blockade (1948), many Western statesmen assumed that only the fear of America's nuclear weapons acted as a brake upon the Kremlin's aggressive intentions.

This basic economic weakness had of course social and political consequences within the country. Even before the end of the war the regime had given clear indications that more liberal policies at home, which so many Soviet citizens expected as a reward for victory and their sacrifice, would not be forthcoming. On the contrary. The approach of and the actual arrival of the hour of victory was accompanied by a new wave of repressions. We spoke already of massive evacuations and other punishments administered to those national groups that in the eyes of the government had behaved disloyally. Thousands of ex-prisoners of war were sent to forced labor camps. The regime was now in a hurry to undo any untoward effects of wartime collaboration with democratic states, to make clear that, to use a later term, ideological coexistence would be no more tolerated than it had been prior to 1941. The nationalistic motif had not been jettisoned, but again it was increasingly accompanied by the ideological one. As Stalin said in his speech of February 6, 1946, "Our victory means above all that our *social* system has won . . . our *political* system has won."

In the same speech the dictator went on to dissipate any still remaining illusions about the character of the policies he was prepared to pursue. Collectivization, he emphasized, was the cornerstone of the Soviet system. His speech left little doubt that rapid industrialization would remain, as before, the supreme goal, that its main burden would be borne by the peasantry, and that, though peace had come, everyone had to work almost as hard as during the struggle for survival. Reviving the theme that had been in abeyance since June 22, 1941, Stalin stressed that the USSR could never be secure so long as capitalism and with it imperialism remained. And to gain even relative security one had to push industrial development to new heights; the Soviet Union must achieve as soon as possible annual production of 60 million tons of steel, 500 million of coal, and 60 million of oil. "Only then will our country be guaranteed against all kind of eventualities."[3]

The economic burden imposed upon the Soviet people in the wake of their wartime sufferings was breathtaking. And only the most repressive totalitarian system could get away with demanding and exacting such sacrifices in peacetime. It has been estimated that in 1947 real wages of the Soviet worker stood at about one half of their level for 1940. As in every other country, the war had led to a huge increase of the amount of money in circulation and hence to inflation. But only the Soviet system could deal with the problem by wiping out the bulk of the population's savings. The currency reform decree of December 14, 1947, ordered that old rubles had to be exchanged for new ones at the ratio of ten to one; savings banks' holdings were exchanged at one to one, up to 3,000 rubles, with lower ratios for higher deposits. State bonds were depreciated by two-thirds and would pay a lower rate of interest.[4] In no other country, it is fair to say, could such an act of spoliation be carried out without provoking a revolution. As in the past, the blow fell hardest on the peasants, who tended to keep their savings in cash. In addition to the measures already described, the regime imposed higher taxes on production from private plots and individually owned cattle. The system of state procurements and prices was so arranged that for some of their crops collective farmers were paid much less than the costs of production. This was the case, for example, with potatoes. As Khrushchev in 1958 was to describe the effects of the postwar agricultural policies: "Under such conditions the more the given kolkhoz produced potatoes, the more it fell in ruin, because not only was it not compensated for its production, but the price was insufficient to cover the cost of its transportation [to the government collection center], and the loss had

[3] Stalin specified those figures as the target for 1960; actually Soviet production then was to surpass those targets by a substantial margin.

[4] Nove, *An Economic History of the U.S.S.R.*, p. 308.

to be made up from other crops." And in addition to other forms of exploitation, the peasants, most of their cash gone after the reform of 1947, were assessed an unrealistically high quota of subscriptions to the "voluntary" state loans!

Stalin's personal dictatorship continued unabated and the end of the war found the despot no more willing to share or to limit his power than before. One would have thought at various times between 1943 and 1945 that, with the Soviet armies now covered with glory, their senior officers would aspire to and would be allowed to play at least modest political roles. But in fact the official propaganda now even more than before stressed that the main credit for planning and execution of the victorious campaigns lay with the supreme commander-in-chief and the Communist Party. Official accounts of the victories of Moscow and Stalingrad minimized the role of Zhukov, their chief architect and Russia's most prestigious military leader, and Zhukov himself, after a brief tenure as the Soviet commander in Germany, was consigned to the obscurity of provincial command. The army's subordinate status was unpleasantly emphasized by having such political figures and henchmen of the dictator's as Beria and Bulganin accorded the rank of marshal of the Soviet Union.

Of Stalin's manner of ruling postwar Russia, the poet Tvardovsky was to write in 1960: ". . . Though alive yet cut off from life by the Kremlin Wall, he stood over us like a dread spirit." And indeed the government continued not only to be repressive, but in a sense it became even more distant from and mysterious to the average citizen than it had been before the war. The dictator spoke but infrequently and eschewed public appearances except upon a few festive occasions like the anniversary of the Revolution when he, along with the oligarchs, could be seen on the top of the Lenin Tomb. According to Khrushchev's subsequent revelations, the operation of the highest Party organs had come to a virtual standstill, most of the crucial decisions being made by Stalin and a handful of whoever happened to be his close advisers at the given time. No Party Congress was to meet until a few months before Stalin's death, in 1952. We have only two authenticated cases of the Central Committee's assembling during that period, and even the Politburo met but seldom, Stalin at times banning some of its regular members from its sessions!

The Byzantine atmosphere of the Kremlin was enhanced by the dictator's advancing age and his growing inability to keep himself informed and in control as hitherto of all the main aspects of policy and administration. Hence even more than before, he shifted his main lieutenants around and played them against each other. Lavrenti Beria preserved the overall control of the security apparatus, which was now split into two ministries: the MGB (the ministry of internal security) and the MVD (of internal affairs). But at the same time, a Central Committee secretary, Alexei Kuznetsov, was charged with the supervision of security matters on behalf of the Party, a clear indication that Beria, despite his advancement in 1947 to full membership in the Politburo, was not invulnerable or fully trusted by the despot. A similar, though temporary, reduction in status was the fate of another favorite. Malenkov was also named to the Politburo in 1946, but was superseded as Stalin's deputy in Party affairs by Zhdanov.

The latter, the boss of the Leningrad district ever since Kirov's assassination in 1934, had spent the war years in his city directing its heroic defense. He now recovered his position as Stalin's right-hand man. Until his death in 1948 his name was synonymous with domestic repression, especially directed against intellectuals and artists who allegedly imbibed too much foreign influence during Russia's wartime collaboration with the democracies. Assuredly, the term the "Zhdanov times" (*Zhdanovshchima*), as was the case with the "Yezhov times" (1936–38), commemorates somewhat unfairly the executor rather than the real initiator and designer of repressive policies, who of course in both cases was Stalin.

The campaign for intellectual and artistic conformity was intended to suppress the aftereffects of the relaxation that had developed in Soviet intellectual life during the war. As before, socialist realism was to be the rule in literature and the arts, imitation or emulation of foreign models was to be forsworn. Nationalism thus merged with the renewed stress on ideological purity. In Zhdanov's words: "Does it become us, representatives of advanced Russian culture, Soviet patriots, to play the role of worshipers of bourgeois culture, or the role of pupils. . . . Where do you find people and country like ours?" As an example of harmful decadent influences in literature, Zhdanov cited a talented writer, Mikhail Zoshchenko, and the great poet Anna Akhmatova. This was not a matter, as it was to become in the sixties and seventies, of attacking or curbing literary and intellectual dissent, because such dissent simply could not be expressed in Stalin's Russia. Both writers were attacked simply for being apolitical, for their "individualistic, non-Party" approach to literature. The campaign then reached into other spheres: a Party official, Georgi Alexandrov, was attacked for a very unexceptional history of Western philosophy, simply because he spoke too favorably about some non-Marxist philosophers and displayed a latitude of views that was highly recommended between 1941 and 1945, but that by 1947–1949 had become highly suspect if not indeed subversive. The campaign turned into obscurantist reviling of everything that was not Russian and Marxist in approach; among its targets were "followers of Einstein," existentialism as propagated by Jean-Paul Sartre, nonobjective art as exemplified by Picasso (even though the latter was a member of the French Communist Party), etc. The theater, movies, music, painting were in turn subjected to scrutiny by the Party and found wanting. Modern music, said Zhdanov, reminded him of the whirring of the dentist's drill. While the consequences of the cultural pogrom were not as sinister as in the Yezhov times—culprits for the most part were simply forbidden to publish, exhibit their paintings, or perform their music rather than imprisoned or worse—the accompanying hysteria was reminiscent of the real purge. The sinners were expected to, and for most part did, repudiate their scandalous work; artists, scientists, and writers joined in signing manifestos denouncing their unfortunate colleagues.

Two aspects of this cultural offensive were to have broader implications. One of the main targets was "cosmopolitanism"—allegedly worship of foreign models and lack of reverence for Russia's own cultural tradition and achievements. Many of the purveyors of this cosmopolitanism were found to be Jews, and the cultural campaign, especially after the establishment of the state of Israel, took on an unmistakably anti-Semitic tinge. The euphemism employed for Jewish transgressors was "rootless cosmopolites." After a while some attacks spoke openly of noxious "Zionist" influences, and the Jewish artists and critics who were being attacked and who had Russian-sounding names were not infrequently identified by adding their previous, unmistakably Jewish names in parentheses.

The most dramatic aspect of the cultural purge in science was the enthronement of Trofim Lysenko as the veritable Stalin of Soviet biology. The renowned charlatan and faker of experiments succeeded in suppressing any opposition to his fraudulent theories. The Party banned teaching and experimentation in genetics and in other branches of biology tainted by "bourgeois" and "idealistic" influences. And some of his opponents not only found themselves stripped of professorships and research appointments, but also suffered the traditional fate of real or alleged political dissenters.

If not in terms of actual victims, then in general atmosphere of fear and isolation, the Russia of 1947–48 began to be reminiscent of that of 1936–39. As before, the main rationalization for domestic repression was foreign danger. But whereas in the years preceding the war the threat from Germany and Japan was real and imminent and felt as such by the regime, nothing indicates that in the postwar period Stalin and his associates were seriously worried that the USSR might soon have to fight for its survival.

Many historians, including some in the West, have attributed the beginning of the Cold War to Russia's nervousness over America's possession and monopoly of the atomic bomb. But everything points to the fact that the Soviets perceived correctly that public opinion in the West would not tolerate any policies that might bring a renewal of a world crisis only a few years after the end of the most devastating war of all times. And the figures for Soviet demobilization, like the American ones are eloquent in this respect. Everything points to the fact that Russia's domestic repression and ominous isolation, belying the quite recent hopes of people like Roosevelt that the Soviet Union, through its partnership in the war, had committed itself to friendly coexistence, had an essentially internal rationale: Stalin and his associates' determination to restore in full the totalitarian rigor of their society.

Foreign Relations East and West

In foreign affairs Soviet apprehensions were of an indirect and long-range nature. Stalin did not fear war; he feared, however, that in due time the United States might challenge his plans, that the Americans might eventually seek to restore and rearm Germany and Japan and, through this new balance of power, seek to wrest from the USSR its hegemony in eastern Europe. A "tough" stand vis-à-vis the United States was designed to persuade the Americans that they could not stop the expansion of Communist power in countries like Poland, Czechoslovakia, etc., without risking a real shooting war. At the same time, whenever U.S. policies hardened and its reaction to some Soviet move seemed to portend the kind of change in the American attitude that the Soviets were afraid of, the USSR would back down. Prior to 1946 the Soviets gave every indication that they planned to retain troops in Iran, where under their aegis two puppet regimes had been established in the northern part of the country and where the central government had been under Soviet pressure to grant the USSR all sorts of concessions. In brief there seemed to be every indication that the east European pattern would be repeated in Persia. The United States and Britain protested Soviet actions both in the UN and directly. Such protests might have been no more effective than those about Poland, Bulgaria, etc. But in March 1946, former Prime Minister Churchill delivered his famous speech in Fulton, Missouri, where he spoke of the iron curtain that had descended on eastern Europe and urged resolute action and collaboration by the United States and Britain to prevent similar developments in the rest of the world. The coincidence of the Iranian crisis and Churchill's Fulton appeal was awkward: public opinion in the West might congeal in an anti-Soviet mood. On March 26 the Soviets pledged to withdraw their troops from Iran and in six weeks did so. The pro-Soviet regimes in the north were easily liquidated.

From the Western perspective the Soviet withdrawal in Iran was but one and an uncharacteristic incident in what was now going to become known as the Cold War. On the great majority of issues the Soviet Union, far from withdrawing, was pursuing, if not warlike, then expansionist policies. Between 1945 and 1948 the Communist parties in eastern Europe, with Russian help and encouragement, liquidated the last remaining traces of democracy and opposition in their countries. In 1947 Mikolajczyk, his Peasant Party subject to government repression and chicanery, was forced to flee from Poland. The final blow to the hope that the Soviets would tolerate a genuine multiparty system within their sphere of interest was to come in Czechoslovakia in February 1948, when those non-Communist ministers who challenged the increasing sovietization of their country were forced to resign, and communism, as everywhere else (with the exception of Finland), was to rule supreme, though most of the "people's democracies" were to preserve some vestigial forms of parliamentarian and coalition government. The Soviet decision to impose outright communism on its satellites, rather than to tolerate subservient though not Communist governments there as in Finland, undoubtedly reflected the conclusion reached in 1946–47 that *at that time* the process could not be effectively opposed by the West and hence had to be carried out as rapidly as possible. A similar decision was reached in relation to the Soviet zone of Germany. Though the outward structure of joint Allied control was to persist until 1948, Moscow had begun to impose a satellite status upon "its" Germany practically from the moment of occupation. As in other satellites the weak popular appeal of local communism was overcome by forcing the Socialist Party to merge with the Communist one. The product of this merger, the Socialist Unity Party, was run by old-line Communists, headed by Walther Ulbricht; using traditional methods, it succeeded in repressing all political opposition.

While turning the screws tighter in what they could claim was the sphere of influence accorded to them by the war, the Soviets at the same time sought to expand communism around its periphery. The Greek civil war flared up again in the summer of 1946. The Communists' partisan warfare was considerably helped by the sanctuaries and supplies the insurgents received in the neighboring Communist countries of Yugoslavia, Albania, and Bulgaria. At the same time the USSR did not abate its propaganda war against Turkey, its violence seeming to presage military intervention.

To repeat, there can be but little question that the USSR neither wanted nor expected a new major war. From the Kremlin's point of view, its foreign policies followed the traditional pattern of those of a major power: the USSR was merely solidifying its grip on its sphere of influence, the area the Western powers had, by implication, surrendered in agreements from Teheran to Potsdam, and it was unreasonable for Washington and London to expect that the Soviet Union, having liberated eastern Europe, would tolerate there governments and parties actually or potentially hostile to Russia and communism. And outside its allotted sphere the USSR, again in the traditional pattern of great powers, was seeking to expand, probing for weaknesses and political vacuums.

By the same token, in Western—especially American—eyes Soviet activities added up not only to a violation of solemn promises the USSR had given at Teheran, Yalta, etc., but also to a deliberate design to gain hegemony on the European continent. Apart from the actual area of Communist control and, as in Greece and Turkey, of Communist challenges, the Soviet menace was present in the West in France and Italy, whose Communist parties, while for the moment utilizing parliamentary means, might conceivably revert to the methods of their Greek comrades.

Western hopes of relieving tension and containing Soviet expansion through diplomacy were meeting with but little success. Formally the joint machinery for consultation and negotiation set up during the war was still functioning, but both in the Allied Control Council for Germany and in the periodic meetings of the Big Four's foreign ministers, the Soviets were proving obdurate and could not be swayed from what appeared as a collision course. Predictably the UN, in which much great hope was put, was proving equally impotent in making the Soviets "behave." The USSR was uninhibited in exercising its veto power and thus in rendering nugatory any resolutions, would-be investigations, censures, etc., of Soviet policies. Apart from the burning issues of European policy, the United States was particularly frustrated by the Soviet refusal even to consider the American plan for control of atomic energy. This so-called Baruch Plan envisaged the formation of an International Atomic Development Authority, which would acquire a virtual monopoly on all forms of atomic production, and which would be endowed with the power to impose sanctions on any state violating the agreement and its regulations. The United States was willing to surrender its then monopoly of nuclear technology *provided* that sanctions on a violator of the authority's rules would be imposed by a majority vote. Thus the right of veto reserved to each of the five great powers on other types of violations of international agreements would be removed. On this crucial issue, the Soviets stoutly refused to contemplate any agreement that weakened, not to mention removed, their right of veto or granted an international authority the right to inspect Soviet atomic facilities. (This position was yet another refutation of the thesis that the Soviets were seriously apprehensive about the American monopoly of the atom bomb—that is, fearful that the United States would use it against Russia. In 1946, three years before the first Soviet nuclear tests, it would have been in their interest to temporize, to sign an agreement on the principle of atomic development, and to delay the whole issue as long as possible, rather than to reject the American proposal brusquely and unconditionally.)

The American policy makers were puzzled as to the means of obtaining a handle on the Soviet problem. By 1947 public opinion in the United States had crystallized in an anti-Soviet and anti-Communist mood, and the point of view espoused by former Vice President Henry A. Wallace that the breakdown of the wartime alliance was at least as much America's fault as Russia's enjoyed but scant support. But any forceful policy that might bring about war was repugnant to the vast majority of people in the United States and the West. The policy makers for their part were hypnotized by the myth of Russia's vast standing army; to use traditional crisis methods of diplomacy—breaking off diplomatic relations, issuing ultimatums—they believed, might provoke the USSR to direct military action. And then the Soviet armies would sweep to the English Channel, and the United States, for all its atom bombs (not so many at the time), would not be able to do anything about it!

Faced with this frustrating dilemma, the United States decided to cope with the problem indirectly: America would help countries fighting Communist insurgency or threatened by it. It would embark on a vast program of economic help designed to restore social and economic stability to Europe and thus presumably make countries like France and Italy immune to Communist take-over. The United States assumed the burden of furnishing supplies and military instructors to Greece and Turkey. In announcing the doctrine that bears his name, President Truman on March 12, 1947, clothed it in high rhetoric: "It must be the policy of the United States to support free peoples which are resisting subjugation by armed minorities or outside pressures." Despite the uncomplimentary references to communism in the President's speech (communism, he asserted, was "based upon the will of a minority forcibly imposed upon the majority. It relies upon terror and oppression, a controlled press and radio, fixed elections, and the suppression of personal freedom"), the Truman Doctrine did not seem to have disturbed the Kremlin unduly. It committed the United States to intervene whenever the local Communist movement, with or without Soviet orders or encouragement, posed a challenge to the constituted authority. And at least in Stalin's lifetime, it would have been inconceivable, except in China and later on in the special case of Yugoslavia, that a Communist party or regime would disobey Soviet instructions. At the same time, by implication, the Truman Doctrine did not propose to turn history back in the areas where the USSR was already dominant (a conclusion that was amply borne out by what was to happen in Czechoslovakia in 1948), nor did it threaten the Soviet Union with any consequences for actions of its protégés.

Ironically, it was the next great initiative of American policy, on its surface purely economic in its thrust, that was to arouse the Kremlin's deepest suspicions. This was the Marshall Plan, proposed by the United States in the same summer. Secretary of State George Marshall proposed a comprehensive plan for European economic recovery, funded mostly by the United States and open for participation to all European states. The USSR at first gave signs of being willing to participate in the program, and Molotov met on June 27 with the British and French foreign ministers to consider actual ways of supplementing American proposals. Seemingly, the USSR had nothing to lose by joining in the plan. Were it to be approved by the Congress, the Soviet Union would get an infusion of desperately needed economic assistance; on the other hand, alarmed by the prospect that the plan, which was to stem the tide of communism, was actually going to help the Communist power, the Americans might draw away in horror from the whole idea, thus perpetuating economic chaos in the West. But participation in a joint undertaking with the West would have required at least external changes in Soviet foreign policy; it would have led to partial return to wartime intimacy and to the greater realization in the West of how weak and backward the Soviet economy still was, how unrealistic in many ways were fears about Russia's military might. And so on July 2, Molotov was ordered to break off the negotiations, on the pretext that the Marshall Plan would infringe on the European states' sovereignty. Subsequently the Soviets forbade Czechoslovakia and Poland, which at first, and understandably, showed enthusiasm at the idea, to join in this capitalist design for the enslavement of Europe.

The basic idea of the Marshall Plan, even granting its political implications, must still have been puzzling to the Soviets, since it clashed with the basic Marxist-Leninist premises about the behavior of capitalist states. Since when did capitalists give away billions to restore the economy of their commercial rivals? It was therefore not surprising that to the original suspicions there succeeded a firm belief that, far from being an essentially defensive measure and an attempt to contain communism and to diminish its appeal by re-creating a stable and prosperous European economy, the European Recovery Program was part of an *offensive* design to "roll back" (to use a term subsequently employed by Secretary John Foster Dulles) the Soviet sphere of influence. How would this work? In the Kremlin scenario the primary aim of the Marshall Plan was to restore the economic strength of western Europe, not for its own sake but to enable the West to mount a sizable military establishment. The British and Americans, who had already merged their zones in Germany in December 1946, were obviously going to allow West Germany to rearm. A rearmed and emancipated West Germany would act as a magnet on the Soviet-occupied zone. There would be revolts there as well as in other east European satellites. Such "wars of liberation," again to use a later term, might then be helped by the West.

The Soviets' apprehensions were enhanced by a certain distrust of the leadership of the Communist parties, both in the East and the West. In order to establish tighter control over them, in 1947 the Kremlin created the Cominform. The new organization, officially the Communist Information Bureau, did not have the worldwide scope of the old Comintern: participatory parties were those of the USSR, Poland, Czechoslovakia, Yugoslavia, Rumania, Hungary, Bulgaria, and of the nongoverning parties, the Italian and French.[5] The Cominform could not really increase the given parties' dependence and/or subservience to Moscow, but it was expected to provide an internationalist gloss to Soviet-prescribed policies and decisions. Thus the founding conference approved Zhdanov's "two camps" analysis of the world situation: a statement that collaboration between the USSR, and hence world communism, and the West was definitely a thing of the past, and that Western policies, like those embodied in the Marshall Plan, were part of the new offensive against the camp of socialism. The French and Italian parties chimed in with dutiful attacks on the European Recovery Program and pledges to do everything possible to disrupt its operations. (The French and Italians bowed to Moscow's desires on this score rather unhappily; public attacks on America's help to their countries were bound to end their hopes of coming to power constitutionally, i.e., by securing a majority at the polls.)

The Cominform was intended to serve as the means for the ruling Communist parties to synchronize their policies in a way that would cover up the centralized direction of foreign communism by the Soviet Union. It was evidently also hoped that the new organization, like the Cominterm of yore, could be used to rap the knuckles of a dissident member party, the rebuke or sanctions coming ostensibly not from the Kremlin but from the collective body. Within one year of its

[5] Logically the list should have included two other satellites, Albania and East Germany. But at the time, Albania was, so to speak, a subsatellite, being in a state of dependence on Yugoslavia, and East Germany officially was not yet a state but a zone of occupation.

formation the Cominform was thus employed in the case of a sudden and unprecedented crisis which shook international communism.

Yugoslavia, hitherto thought of as an exemplary Soviet satellite, was read out of the family of Communist nations by the USSR and the Cominform. Marshal Tito, the most prestigious east European Communist leader thrown up by the war, and his colleagues in the leadership found themselves—and would remain for the next five years—targets of a strenuous Soviet campaign of subversion and vilification. The immediate reasons for this momentous event, presaging a new era in communism, must be sought mainly in the morbid suspiciousness and intolerance that Stalin, especially in his last phase, exhibited in dealing with his subordinates at home and abroad. But the ability of the Yugoslav regime to withstand the propaganda onslaught and to survive in this unprecedented situation—as a Communist regime excommunicated by Moscow—must be ascribed to a new phenomenon in world politics. It was now demonstrated how foreign Communists, even if, like Tito and his group, loyal servants of Moscow *when out of power,* would, once masters of their own country, develop their own point of view and national pride which would enable them to resist Soviet dictates when those dictates threatened the independence of their country or their own power. Moscow, for some time suspicious of Tito's ambitions to become a sort of Balkan Stalin—i.e., to preside over a federation of states that would include, to begin with, not only Albania but also Bulgaria—vetoed in March 1948 the plan for the Balkan union to which previously it had given its blessing; and simultaneously it authorized subversive activities designed to bring down the imperious Yugoslav dictator and his closest associates and to replace them by more pliable Communists. When this campaign fizzled and Moscow's agents were unmasked and imprisoned, the Kremlin disingenuously demanded in a series of written communications that the Yugoslav leadership acknowledge its "incorrect" internal and external policies and dismiss a number of high officials as alleged imperialist agents—in short, perform the ritual of recantation and self-abasement that would prepare the ground for Tito's removal. The Yugoslavs stood their ground, published the Soviet accusations so as to acquaint the rank and file of their party and their people both with the absurdity of most charges (some, to be sure, were true, but rather piquant when coming from Stalin and Company—e.g., that the Yugoslav party was being run undemocratically) and with the incredibly insolent tone in which they, rulers of an independent state, were being addressed by their ideological comrades. The Cominform, which ironically enough had hitherto had its headquarters in Belgrade, moved to Bucharest, where it expelled the Yugoslav party from its midst. But the great majority of the

Yugoslav Communists supported their leaders and the Yugoslav secret police dealt efficiently with those who did not. Many Yugoslavs opposed to communism now rallied around Tito as the defender of their country's independence.

Apart from its long-run significance, the Soviet-Yugoslav imbroglio had two immediate consequences. By 1949 Yugoslavia would no longer serve as the sanctuary for the Greek Communist rebels. Weakened also by the purge of alleged Titoists in their midst, the Greek Communists increasingly gave way to the government forces and by the end of 1949 their rebellion subsided.

The other effect of the Yugoslav defiance was to speed up the process of sovietization of other people's democracies. Moscow now demanded social and economic measures that hitherto the local Communists had eschewed or pursued but gradually, such as rapid collectivization of agriculture, a frontal assault on organized religion, especially the Catholic Church, and the final extirpation of political forces and movements not under Communist control. In view of the hunt for real and potential Titoists, it was natural to expect that east European Communist parties would themselves be thoroughly purged, and indeed the atmosphere in the satellites between Tito's defection and the death of Stalin grew reminiscent of that in the Soviet Union in 1936–39. Those Communist leaders who in the past had given the slightest hint of independence or of opposition to the Soviet exploitation of their countries now fell victims of terror, some undergoing the traditional ritual of arrest, public trial where they would confess to a variety of crimes, including treasonous contacts with the Yugoslav and Western powers' intelligence services, and execution. Such was the route traveled, to mention only the most prominent of the victims, by Bulgaria's Traicho Kostov, Hungary's Laszlo Rajk, and Czechoslovakia's Rudolf Slansky, all of them at one time at or near the top of their countries' power structure. Poland's Gomulka, though purged and arrested, escaped with his life. Reflecting the growing anti-Semitism within the Soviet Union of the period, some charges depicted the fallen potentates as being in the service not only of Wall Street and Tito but also of their ally international Zionism. And many victims, such as Rudolf Slansky and most of his codefendants—perhaps the term should be coconfessants—in the great Prague trial of 1952 were themselves Jewish.

There is no question that most of the victims of the terror had been (as was the case with Tito himself prior to 1948) innocent of any anti-Soviet feelings, not to speak of the opprobrious charges under which they were sent to death or to prison. Also, had they even wanted to they would have been incapable of "Titoism"—that is, of successful defiance of the USSR. None of them approached Tito's stature as the unchallenged master of his country's political and military establishment, nor could they count on as wide an emotional following among their nations' Communists. Furthermore, in most satellites the intrinsic appeal and power of communism was weak, the local regimes relying if not on the actual presence of Soviet troops then on the general assumption that a popular revolt would bring about Soviet military intervention. It would have been thus virtually impossible for, say, the Polish or Hungarian Communists to defy Moscow and yet to retain control over their own people (we shall see how the situation had changed by 1956). In any case, policies and politics of the satellite states would, between 1948 and 1953, be controlled by the Russians much more directly and tyrannically than had been the case before.

While the situation in eastern Europe was both a result and a symptom of the Cold War, another Soviet move of 1948, potentially much graver in its consequences, brought about a confrontation between the USSR and the Western powers. The Soviet squeeze on West Berlin began in the spring. The three Western powers' determination to organize a West German state, heralded by the decision to establish a joint currency for the western zone, had become very clear, and with it Soviet determination to go very far to block such a step. The underbelly, so to speak, of the Western position in Germany was Berlin, deep in the Soviet zone. And it was here that the Soviets struck by announcing the suspension of all passenger and freight traffic, and thus opening up the prospect of this outpost of Western influence's being literally starved into submission.

The blockade of Berlin was a departure from the hitherto rather prudent pattern of Soviet diplomacy. This was a *direct* challenge to the U.S. might. This rather considerable risk was taken—then and in the subsequent Berlin crises—not to force the Western powers out of the city, but because of much larger considerations. The blockade was undertaken to prevent the setting up of the West German state with its logical corollary (though many in Washington, London, and especially Paris did not see it as yet) of German rearmament. What would the Soviets have done had the Americans and British chosen to challenge the blockade directly? Undoubtedly backed down. The Kremlin left itself some avenues of—albeit less than gracious—retreat. Stalin took pains to receive Western diplomats and to assure them that the Soviets did not intend to swallow Berlin, broadly hinting that if the idea of the West German state were abandoned, the whole matter could be solved most amicably and expeditiously: "we are still allies."

There were people in the West, such as the American commander in Germany, General Clay, who wanted to call the Soviet bluff through an armed forcing of the blockade. But could one be abso-

A night scene at Berlin's Templehof Airport in July, 1948, as food for the blockaded Western sector of Berlin is unloaded from U.S. transports.

lutely sure it was a bluff? As the Soviets were well aware, 1948 was the year of presidential elections in the United States. What did happen was something that prior to the blockade nobody would have thought possible: the Anglo-American airlift managed to provide West Berlin with bare essentials for almost a year. By the time the blockade was lifted in May 1949 (following confidential negotiations between American and Soviet representatives), the outcome of the whole crisis could be adjudged a draw. The Soviets' aims had not been achieved: the West German state was coming into being, and on April 4, 1949, the North Atlantic Treaty was signed in Washington. The Soviet move had crystallized the West's resolve to stand up to an actual Soviet aggression. On the other hand, the West received no pledges on the access to Berlin—America's tenacity in standing by its rights was balanced by a demonstration of unwillingness to risk a direct confrontation with the USSR, a lesson that would not be lost on Stalin and his successors and would produce new crises until 1962.

The Berlin crisis focused the attention of the two superpowers on Europe and thus may have contributed to the timing of the momentous developments in China, if not to their eventual outcome. A full-fledged civil war had raged there ever since January 1947, when the

Communists broke off their negotiations with the Nationalists. The year of decision was 1948. The Nationalists' position in Manchuria and northern China now became untenable, and the Communists, shifting from partisan warfare, engaged in a series of pitched battles in which they were almost invariably victorious. By the end of 1948 it looked probable for the first time that the Chinese Communists would not only win Manchuria and the north, but would come to dominate the whole mainland.

As stated above, it is unlikely that a *completely* Communist China had been either expected or wished for by the Soviets. But by late 1948, when this for the first time appeared as a practical possibility, the USSR and the United States were locked in a sharp conflict over Germany and chances looked very strong that in a few years a revived German army, backstopped by the U.S. Strategic Air Command, might threaten Soviet acquisitions in central and eastern Europe. This was then hardly the moment to interfere with the triumphant progress of Mao's forces: whatever the hypothetical dangers of Titoism in China, the victory of communism in the world's most populous country would inevitably create a lot of trouble for the United States in Asia and would make the Americans less prone to stir up anti-Soviet mischief in Europe.

Even so, the Soviets did not hurry to recognize the Chinese Communist regime. When in April 1949 the Communists occupied Nanking, most of the foreign ambassadors, including the American one, remained in the former capital; but the Soviet ambassador followed the fleeing Kuomintang regime to Canton. For his own part, Mao, as if fearful to the last that some sort of Soviet intervention might still snatch the full victory away from him, chose repeatedly to assert his solidarity with the "Elder Brother," the current Chinese Communist term for the USSR. On April 3, the Chinese Communists issued a declaration condemning the North Atlantic Treaty and reaffirming their loyalty to their "ally, the Soviet Union." In July Mao himself said, "We must lean to one side . . . not only in China, but throughout the world, one must lean either to imperialism or to socialism."

Such professions notwithstanding, Stalin's Russia continued to treat the Chinese Communists in a way that could not but be hurtful to their national pride and which undoubtedly contributed to the future bitter conflicts between the two Communist powers. In July, with Mao's regime still not officially recognized, a delegation from the Manchurian region headed by its local boss, Kao Kang, went to Moscow and there concluded a trade agreement between *Manchuria* and the USSR. This seemed to portend that the USSR would continue to insist on special rights in those regions of China traditionally within the Russian sphere of interest and that the Mao regime would not be treated by Stalin with any more consideration than he displayed vis-à-vis, say, Bulgaria. But once in full control of the mainland, the Chinese leader was to demonstrate to his Soviet counterpart that things were going to be different.

The proclamation of the Chinese People's Republic took place on October 3, 1949, and on the same day the Soviet Union extended diplomatic recognition to the new regime while withdrawing it from the Kuomintang. On December 16 Mao arrived in Moscow, but Stalin did not deign to meet him at the station. The negotiations that followed were long—not until February 17 was Mao to leave for his country—and must have been spirited. In the end the Soviets had to concede Communist China, if not equality, then the status of a junior partner rather than a satellite. This must be the interpretation of the Sino-Soviet Treaty of Alliance of February 14, 1950. The Soviet Union had to renounce the special rights on Chinese soil it had extracted from Chiang in 1945: by 1952 at the latest the Manchurian Railway complex, Port Arthur, and Soviet rights in Dairen were to revert to China. As against these concessions, pleasing to Chinese national pride, there was the fact that the military alliance signed between the two Communist powers was one-sided. It provided for mutual assistance against aggression by Japan and any other state that united with Japan, thus hardly giving an automatic pledge of help by the USSR to China should aggression be launched from Taiwan, where the Chiang regime now resided. Underlining the still inferior status of China were the trade agreements. Soviet economic exploitation of its fellow members of the socialist bloc took two main forms, which were to continue till some years after Stalin's death. One was that terms of trade would often be unequal—e.g., Polish coal would be sold to the USSR at well below the world market price. The favorite form of economic exploitation was the notorious joint companies, used to run many branches of industry in the satellites. The Soviets provided little beyond the managerial and technical personnel and extracted 50 percent of the profits. The Sino-Soviet agreements provided for joint companies for the exploitation of Sinkiang and Manchuria and for air transportation between the two countries.

Stopped in Europe, communism was apparently on the threshold of triumphant expansion in Asia. In the wake of decolonization a strong Communist movement sprang up in what was now Indonesia, in the Philippines, and even in India. And in 1950 both the USSR and China recognized officially Ho Chi Minh's insurrectionary regime in Vietnam, though it was still far from wresting even the northern part of the country from the French.

But these dazzling successes and prospects of Asian communism carried for Russia some disquieting implications. Communist China, just barely emerging from forty years of political chaos and civil war, economically backward, could and did insist on the Soviet Union's abandoning its outposts on Chinese soil. Russia's own experience suggested that once the Communist regime consolidated its grip over the vast country, it would embark on an ambitious program of industrialization, and in the process would demand and expect economic help from the Elder Brother.[6] It did not take much imagination to foresee that the unifying power of Marxism and Leninism would not be sufficient to keep China, especially when it had advanced industrially and militarily, even in that partial state of dependence on the USSR that the 1950 agreement expressed; and as time passed one had to expect outright clashes and China's challenge to Russian domination of world communism. And there was also the troublesome fact that large parts of the Asian USSR had at one time or another been under Chinese sovereignty and that Mao, in every way as much the heir of Imperial China as Stalin was of Imperial Russia, was not likely to forget that Russian territorial expansion at his country's expense continued even after the Revolution: Mongolia, *legally* as late as 1945 part of China, was a Soviet satellite.

Trouble with China could be prevented or at least indefinitely postponed if one or both of the following developments were to take place: if another large Asian country like Japan became Communist, and/or if the Chinese regime was to find itself in a direct conflict with the United States. Under the former, the Soviet Union could play off one Asian Communist nation against the other. And if at some form of war with the United States, Peking would need Soviet help.

It was undoubtedly such considerations that played a major part in the Soviets' authorizing, if not indeed ordering, their North Korean protégés to attack South Korea on June 25, 1950. From the Soviet point of view this must have appeared as much less of a gamble than the Berlin blockade. The USSR was not directly involved. The American officials' public announcements had not included South Korea (unlike the Philippines) among those countries the United States would feel compelled to defend, and if the United States had acquiesced in China's defection from the "free world," would it now react violently to the Communist take-over of a small and, on the face of it, unimportant country? Should the Americans stand on the sidelines and let the North Korean Communist armies, equipped with the most modern Soviet weapons, sweep through the south, the Japanese Communists would receive a powerful psychological impetus. The United States then might agree to withdraw its armed forces from Japan, in which case its fall to the already very active Communist movement

[6] Mao demanded Soviet economic help in 1950 and got a mere pittance; the USSR *loaned* China $300 million spread over five years!

could be just a question of time, or alternatively the Americans might strengthen their military presence in Japan and take steps to prevent the Chinese Communists from completing their conquest by occupying Taiwan, to whose eventual fall the United States had appeared quite resigned prior to June 25. This would have, from the Kremlin's perspective, two highly desirable corollaries: American resources and armies would be deflected from Europe; threatened by the United States, the Chinese Communists would become more docile toward the USSR.

As with the Berlin blockade, so now Soviet assumptions proved only partly correct. The United States did intervene militarily to save the South Korean regime of Syngman Rhee from what would have otherwise been a complete and rapid defeat, followed by a united Communist Korea. The American intervention, furthermore, was sanctioned by the UN Security Council. (The Soviets could not veto the Council's resolution because ever since January 1950 they had boycotted its meetings on the ground that its Chinese seat should go to Peking rather than continue with the Chiang regime in Taiwan.) By September, the American forces under MacArthur effected a dramatic turnabout in the Korean War, freeing the Communist-occupied area. In October, they launched a drive into the Communist north. For the first time, it appeared that the process of Communist expansion was going to be reversed and a Communist regime liquidated.

But the other part of Stalin's calculations was to be largely vindicated. The Korean venture led to a military confrontation between the United States and Communist China, and even after that confrontation ended the two powers remained in a sharp conflict which was to have, for nearly a generation, momentous consequences for world politics.

President Truman's decision to intervene in Korea was coupled with his order to the U.S. Navy to prevent any Communist attack on Taiwan as well as any attempt by Chiang to move in the opposite direction—thus making America a party in what was still the Chinese civil war. But the U.S.–Peking conflict was further escalated when General MacArthur's forces pursued the defeated North Korean armies, thus giving every indication that they would conquer the North and reach the Chinese and Soviet borders by the end of 1951. From Peking's point of view, this was highly unfair: the Americans in a sense were punishing the Chinese for something they were not even indirectly responsible for. (There is no indication that the Chinese Communists participated in the decision to attack South Korea. Nor is there even any clear evidence that they had prior knowledge of the attack. Certainly from their point of view, with Taiwan still unconquered, it could not have come at a more inconvenient moment.) It was also highly dangerous: a complete UN (i.e., American) victory in Korea would have been a palpable demonstration of how easy it was to push back and undo the victories of Asian communism. It was therefore natural to warn that if the American drive continued, Peking would intervene. The Chinese Communist forces entered the conflict in late October, but then on November 7 they broke off action and, insofar as the American command was concerned, vanished. But when the Americans did not heed even this warning and continued their offensive, the Chinese troops entered action, this time *en masse,* on November 26. It was the beginning of a new war which, between November and January 1951, led to American defeats and precipitous withdrawals not only from the North but once more from part of the South.

The Chinese intervention and its sequel must have been highly pleasing to the Kremlin. It was China that had to pay the cost of Soviet miscalculation. Though the Chinese forces fighting in Korea were officially proclaimed to be volunteer, Peking could not be sure that this transparent fiction would save it from an American attack upon China proper, perhaps in conjunction with the Chinese Nationalists. Indeed, there were voices in the United States calling for the use of nuclear weapons. Peking became the lightning rod for America's wrath and frustration, while the Soviet Union played the role of a sympathetic bystander. Soviet exploitation of its ally was carried very far: the "volunteers" fighting in Korea were equipped with modern Soviet weapons, but the Chinese had to pay Russia for the arms used in what was essentially Russia's war. In the spring of 1951 the Americans counterattacked, and the front line moved up to what had been the border between the North and the South. Fighting was to continue while truce negotiations (proposed by the USSR but to which the Soviet Union, of course, was not a party!) were to drag out for two more years. Only after Stalin's death (and this was not a coincidence) was a truce arranged which in effect restored the precarious status quo as before June 1950. In the meantime the United States had become much more committed in Asia: it had assumed partial support of the French struggle in Indo-China, increased its aid to Taiwan and the Philippines, etc.

But if in the short run Soviet diplomacy (and American clumsiness) succeeded in turning around what might have been the catastrophic consequences of Soviet miscalculations, then in the long run the effect of the Korean affair was to damage irreparably the Soviet influence on China. The war contributed to the psychological emancipation of the Chinese Communists: the regime could and did mobilize resources of Chinese nationalism behind it. Its ability to inflict first a defeat, then a stalemate upon the American armies illustrated dramatically the emergence of a new world power. And by the same token Mao and his colleagues had come to see in a clearer perspective the cautious duplicity of Soviet policies and must have contrasted it with what they felt was their own forthright resolve to meet the imperialists' challenge, no matter what the risks.

The narrative in this chapter has centered around foreign policy, reflecting the fact that the Soviet rulers in the postwar period saw it as their central task to mask the country's real weaknesses, the results of wartime devastation and economic backwardness, by forceful external policies. A Russia collaborating with the West and "behaving" in the international sphere would have been, they believed, much more subject to external pressures, much less feared. In years to come America's statesmen would speak of negotiating with the USSR from a position of strength. Yet never again would the U.S. position vis-à-vis its protagonist be as powerful as it was in the years 1945–50.

By 1950 the Soviet economy had managed to make up most of the wartime losses, a prodigious achievement for which the Soviet consumer and worker paid a stupendous price. If we compare production in some crucial branches of heavy industry in the last prewar year with production in the year of Stalin's death (1953), we get the following picture: the output of steel grew 210 per cent, of coal 193, oil 169, electricity 280.[7] Allowing for a degree of exaggeration typical of Soviet economic statistics in Stalin's time, the progress must still have been impressive. Certainly, agriculture lagged far behind other branches of the Soviet economy, and the Soviet consumer, if an urban dweller, would by 1950–53 barely have recovered his prewar standard of living and, if a peasant, would still fall short of it. And Soviet industrial production was as yet far behind that of the United States.

Soviet self-assurance vis-à-vis its rival grew not only as the consequence of rapid industrial growth. In the fall of 1949 the USSR exploded its first atom bomb. In purely military terms, this hardly added to Soviet security; in fact, during the next few years American nuclear research and development combined with the enormous American superiority in the means of delivery in the pre-Sputnik period would make the U.S. nuclear superiority even more devastating than before. But psychologically even a few atom bombs in the hands of a totalitarian regime tend to offset a large stockpile of such weapons when held by a democracy. Soviet propaganda unerringly exploited this motif. The peace movement launched by the Soviet Union, which reached its most intense stage in 1949–50, was designed to impress on world public opinion that it was America's *possession* of atomic weapons rather than Soviet *policies* that constituted a threat to peace.

[7] Figures from V. T. Chuntulov, *History of the National Economy of the USSR*, Kiev, 1962, p. 268 (in Russian).

The high point in this campaign was the Stockholm Appeal of 1950, which called for the ban on the atom bomb and which was to be signed allegedly by 500 million people! No such campaign was mounted at the height of the war danger between 1936 and 1939: Hitler and the Japanese were not likely to be inhibited by millions of signatures on any peace appeal.

Changes in the Political Situation and the Death of Stalin

The story of Soviet internal politics during this period of international strain and, as many Western statesmen and the Soviet man in the street must have believed, of an imminent danger of war remains largely obscure. For all the subsequent revelations under Khrushchev, we still lack a clear picture of Stalin's aims and of his lieutenants' maneuvers during this last period of the tyrant's life. There must be, however, a strong impression that old age and growing physical debility strengthened Stalin's always inordinate suspiciousness and, though definite evidence on this point is still lacking, led to some clearly psychopathic behavior on his part. With Zhdanov's death in 1948, Malenkov again became the dictator's right-hand man. The old Stalinist guard, those who had been closest to him in the thirties and during the war, suffered a partial eclipse in 1949; they were stripped of their ministries—power bases—while being retained as deputy prime ministers and Politburo members. Thus Molotov surrendered the Foreign Ministry to Vishinsky of purge trials notoriety; Bulganin surrendered Defense to a professional soldier, Marshal Vasilevsky; and Mikoyan, Trade to Mikhail Menshikov. Other sources hint strongly that these stalwarts, along with such other Stalinist veterans as Beria and Voroshilov, fell increasingly under suspicion. (Molotov's wife was exiled in 1948, one of Mikoyan's sons imprisoned.) But if they were slated for an eventual retirement, then much more abrupt and horrifying was the fall of some recent favorites of the dictator's. The head of Soviet economic planning, Politburo member N. Voznesensky, was stripped of his office in 1949 and one year later executed. Sharing his fate were numerous high Party officials, all of them previous associates of the late Andrei Zhdanov, including Alexei Kuznetsov, a secretary of the Central Committee, and Mikhail Rodionov, prime minister of the Russian Soviet Republic. This so-called Leningrad affair, from Zhdanov's and the others' longtime association with Leningrad's Party organization, still remains one of the most obscure incidents of recent Soviet history, even though all of its victims were to be rehabilitated in Khrushchev's time and its main impresario, the then minister of state security, Victor Abakumov, sentenced to death and executed in December 1954 for his part in the purge.

Such mysterious and horrifying goings-on were probably connected with maneuverings for eventual succession to Stalin and the dictator's possibly not unfounded suspicions that some of his associates were plotting to turn him into a figurehead while gathering real power in their own hands.

It is even more difficult to discern whether, apart from personality clashes, there were at the highest level real differences on policies. If there were, then few such conflicts ever surfaced in public and even so one cannot be sure that they were not contrived affairs. Thus in 1950 Andrei Andreyev, the Politburo member charged with the supervision of agricultural matters, was publicly criticized for advocating a looser organization of labor on the collective farms. Andreyev had long stressed the advantage of working in small units, the so-called links. His critics called for stress on brigades, teams of about fifty to one hundred workers. His main critic, Nikita Khrushchev, just transferred from the Ukraine to the Central Secretariat, demanded the consolidation of collective farms into larger entities. Within a year, Andreyev having recanted his previous views and endorsed the brigades, the number of the kolkhozes was reduced by one half. But then it was Khrushchev's turn to be rebuked and repudiated: not content with amalgamation into fewer units, he wanted the whole collective farm system to be replaced by "agricultural cities," where the peasants would live in apartments rather than their traditional cottages, and private plots would be merged into common holdings. It would have been difficult to propound a more chimerical idea, mainly because of the vast amount of labor, investment, and materials that would have to be used in the peasants' apartment buildings, and one that would arouse more desperate resistance among the peasants—inevitably it would have led to the disappearance of the private plot. After well-publicized attacks on Khrushchev's proposals by some Party officials, the whole notion of rural cities was dropped. But did all those initiatives and retreats on the agricultural front represent genuine differences of opinion on how to deal with the Achilles heel of the Soviet economy, or simply Stalin's moods and trial balloons?

We are equally at a loss for the reason that made Stalin and his lieutenants convoke the Nineteenth Party Congress in October 1952, after a thirteen-year hiatus. The seventy-three-year-old dictator was no longer equal to delivering the several-hours-long report of the Central Committee, which was given instead by Malenkov. (Perhaps to offset the impression of his physical decline, Stalin on the eve of the congress published a pamphlet on *The Economic Problems of So-*

Stalin photographed with Malenkov in 1951 at a commemoration of the 27th anniversary of the death of Lenin.

cialism in the USSR, a heavy and unoriginal work which, of course, was immediately acclaimed as the finest flowering of Marxism-Leninism. At the congress itself, he spoke but a few minutes in a special address to foreign Communists.) The proceedings of the congress gave but little indication of the future course of Soviet policies, the only noteworthy changes being those in the name of the Party and some of its organs. The All-Union Communist Party (b) now became and remains the Communist Party of the Soviet Union. The Politburo was renamed Presidium and the Orgburo abolished. There was no satisfactory explanation of these changes in the nomenclature.

If proceedings of the congress were in themselves unenlightening, then some somber and far-reaching conclusions could be arrived at from changes in the membership of the highest Party organs as elected by the gathering. The Central Committee was almost doubled in size. But the most important was the new appearance of the Politburo-Presidium and the Secretariat. The pre-1952 Politburo usually had fourteen to seventeen members. The new Presidium had twenty-five full members and eleven alternates. The Secretariat increased from five to ten members. One of the new secretaries and alternate Politboro members was Leonid Brezhnev. Though but few of the old Politburo members were dropped or demoted—notably Andreyev and

Kosygin reduced to alternates—this influx of new men boded no good for the Stalinist old guard. And we do know that at the first meetings of the new Central Committee Stalin launched a verbal attack upon Molotov and Mikoyan. And so chances were very strong that the tyrant was planning a new purge, and that the newcomers to the Presidium would, after a period of training on the job, replace such people as those whom Stalin had reviled, and also Beria, whose star had evidently been setting for quite some time.

This construction must be reinforced by the weird and ominous developments in the wake of the congress. In January 1953, an official announcement apprised the Soviet public of the "unmasking" of a group of criminal doctors, most of them employed by the Kremlin Medical Service, which catered to high Soviet officials, Stalin included. They were charged with a phantasmagoric variety of crimes, including the medical murder of A. Zhdanov and similar unprofessional conduct in relation to a number of high military officials, "all in order to undermine the health of leading Soviet military personnel . . . to weaken the defense of the country." Seven of the nine culprits were Jewish, and it was stated that they were connected with the "international Jewish bourgeois organization 'Joint' established by American intelligence [which] . . . conducts extensive espionage, terrorist, and other subversive work in . . . the Soviet Union."

The anti-Semitic (masked as an anti-Zionist) campaign had been going on in the USSR for some time and indeed had already led to the execution of several writers of Jewish origin. But this announcement was taken, and probably correctly, as the first step in a new wave of terror. Quite possibly it would have affected the Jewish population as a whole; but almost without doubt the new purge would have struck at the highest circles of the Party and government. The criminal doctors were alleged to have carried on merrily since at least 1945, not a hopeful sign for Beria, long the supervisor of the Soviet security apparatus. The anti-Semitic implications of the announcement could have had ominous consequences for those of Stalin's pals who, like Molotov and Andreyev, had Jewish wives, and whom he was eager to get rid of. What the intended scope of the purge was, whether in these last months Stalin finally crossed the line that separates morbid suspiciousness from clearly psychopathic behavior are questions for which we may never know the answer. For on March 4, it was announced that on the night of March 1–2 the dictator had suffered a paralytic stroke. On March 5 Joseph Stalin died.

Within a month of his departure the "doctors' plot" was officially recognized as having been a criminal fraud, and the surviving doctors —one evidently had succumbed, possibly under torture, during the investigation—were fully rehabilitated. The alleged instigator of the ghoulish affair, Mikhail Ryumin, then deputy minister of security, was duly denounced himself and, after a secret trial in July 1954, shot.

Stalin's death removed the man who not only had been for more than a generation his country's dictator but whose name for much of that period was virtually synonymous with the USSR and communism. The awe he had inspired at home and abroad, his skill (and luck) at practicing despotism made him not only the most powerful tyrant in history, dwarfing in that respect even Hitler at the height of his successes, but obscured and masked many of the country's domestic and foreign problems. No other regime or man would be able again to submit the Soviet people, and especially the peasants, to so much suffering and privation and yet be able to get away with it, nor to survive such colossal miscalculations and errors as those of Stalin, which brought about the horrors of the famine of the thirties and the catastrophic defeats in the first year of World War II. Nor would one man and the Soviet Union ever again be able to dominate world communism in the same manner, make foreign Communist tools not only of Soviet policies but of the despot's whims. Signs of the portending changes could already be seen in Stalin's last years: Tito's defiance, Mao's ability to exact some concessions from the Soviets. But even the Chinese Communists were awed by Stalin's authority: They remonstrated with Stalin; to his successors they would address demands. Yet had Stalin lived a few more years, the clash with China might well have come sooner and in a more violent form than under Khrushchev. Both in domestic and foreign policies, the legacy of the Stalin era still weighs heavily on the USSR and the world.

8. Transition and the Khrushchev Era

Reorganization of the Power Structure

Though tearful in public, most of the associates of the tyrant could not but privately congratulate themselves on the event of March 5. Yet the death was bound to throw the Party and government apparatus into confusion and a sense of vulnerability. With rare candor, the communique of March 7 announcing government and Party changes spoke of the need for "the greatest unity of leadership and prevention of any kind of disorder and panic." As to that unity, brisk bargaining about the allocation of power and offices began even with Stalin dying. Its immediate outcome as announced on March 7 spelled the undoing of the Nineteenth Congress, dilution of the membership in the highest Party organs. Most of the then newcomers were now ejected from the Presidium, this body being reduced to ten full members and four alternates. There was, in other words, a reassertion of the power of the old Stalinist guard and a demotion (or worse) for their putative successors. The old oligarchs were eager to snatch back those bases of power that in the last few years had slipped from their group. Beria recovered direction of the reunified agencies of security and police; Molotov went back to the Ministry Foreign Affairs, Bulganin to the Ministry of Defense, Mikoyan to Trade.

No single man could have or would have been allowed, even if he could, to succeed to Stalin's full panoply of power. Insofar as the nation and the world could discern, the bulk of power was lodged in the *troika* of Malenkov, Beria, and Molotov. Malenkov appeared as the principal successor, inheriting Stalin's job as prime minister. But a significant straw in the wind was provided one week later when Malenkov was made to abandon his position on the Secretariat and Nikita Khrushchev became for all purposes (though as yet without the formal title) the principal Party secretary. For reasons which still remain obscure, the title of general secretary had not been used by Stalin since 1934. Beria would enjoy the enormous power associated with the security apparatus, and there was undoubtedly some betting that he would not remain number two for long. Molotov, though his sphere—the Foreign Ministry—hardly provided a power base comparable to Malenkov's or Beria's, was number three in virtue of his seniority and long association with the dead tyrant. In a transitional situation even the office of the figurehead president of the USSR could assume importance, hence it was lifted from Nikolai Shvernik, who had been chairman of the Presidium of the Supreme Soviet ever since Kalinin had died in 1946, and assigned to Marshal Voroshilov, in view of his age (seventy-two) not a likely candidate for supreme power.

The new rulers obviously did not feel too secure either vis-à-vis each other or collectively. This comes out in several instances. Following March 5, the center of Moscow was for several days ringed with security troops. Marshal Zhukov, in disgrace and obscurity during Stalin's last years, was promptly brought back into the limelight and appointed deputy minister of defense. Even more revealingly, on March 10 *Pravda* published a picture of Stalin, Mao, and Malenkov, thus suggesting that the new premier was not only in apostolic succession to the late boss but also had the blessing of the head of the world's largest nation. The picture was a crude composograph made from a photograph taken at the signing of the Sino-Soviet alliance in 1950, when the three gentlemen were indeed present but both in company of and separated by a number of other Soviet and Chinese dignitaries.

Stalin was buried with barbaric splendor on March 9, his mummy placed alongside Lenin's in what until 1961 would be the Lenin-Stalin Mausoleum. Funeral speeches delivered by the triumvirs praised the deceased in terms almost as extravagant as was the custom in his lifetime: "Our Party, the Soviet people, and all mankind have suffered a most grievous, irreparable loss." The other motif was "our Party . . . is closing its ranks still more closely . . . it is united, and unshakable."

Yet for all this rhetoric, the process of de-Stalinization began almost immediately, as if the successors were convinced of their inability to maintain the full extent of tyranny associated with "Comrade Stalin whom we all have loved so much and who will live in our hearts for-

Stalin's funeral procession passes through Red Square. Right to left: Khrushchev, Beria, Chou En-lai, Malenkov, Voroshilov, Kaganovich, Bulganin, and Molotov.

ever." And equally the events of the next few weeks were to expose the alleged "unshakable unity" of the Party and its leadership.

Amnesties in Russia or elsewhere have traditionally been proclaimed on festive occasions, such as the tsar's coronation prior to 1917, or since then on major anniversaries of the Revolution. And so the amnesty of March 27 was rather unique in its timing. Its provisions throw a grim light on what had constituted criminal offense prior to Stalin's death. The law canceled forthwith all investigations and proceedings concerning a large number "of malfeasance and economic as well . . . as military crimes"; these included lateness to work, inefficiency in production, desertion as *proved by having been a prisoner of war,* etc. The Ministry of Justice was also to revise the criminal code concerning the above crimes *within one month*—thirty days to abrogate the entire system of laws and penalties in the shadow of which every Soviet citizen had lived for so many years. The vast "archipelago" of forced labor camps began to disgorge its victims. Another category now pardoned was that of the people exiled without "deprivation of freedom"—i.e., those confined to some Siberian town or village, or barred from the main cities, etc. Among those who now could rejoin their families were relatives of the highest personages in Soviet Russia: Molotov's wife, Mikoyan's son, Maxim Litvinov's widow.

The abrupt termination of the Kremlin doctors' case followed in April, and it was accompanied by the toppling of another important official. Ignatiev, the minister of internal security when the unfortunate doctors had been "investigated" and who as recently as March 14 had advanced to become one of the five secretaries of the Central Committee, was dismissed on April 7 for having displayed in his previous job "political blindness and heedlessness." (It was not "heedlessness" but what might be described as the fear of headlessness that had prompted Ignatiev. As Khrushchev was to reveal later, when Ignatiev expostulated with Stalin, the latter informed him that he had to obtain the doctors' confessions otherwise he would be "shortened by a head.")

This process of liberalization or the "thaw," as it became known in the Soviet Union, evidently had the support, though in varying degrees, of all the members of the leadership. But it soon became clear that the main credit for it was sought by Beria. Rather paradoxically, the man who for so long had been the principal executor of Stalinist terror now became an aroused advocate of "socialist legality." Equally significantly, Beria took the lead in denouncing the excessive russification of Stalin's last years, and in insisting that important jobs in non-Russian union republics should go to their natives. He combined this campaign for popularity with the purge of the security apparatus, replacing with his own creatures those officials who were placed there during his decline in Stalin's favor.

We cannot be sure whether all these moves by Beria added up to a bid for supreme power or an attempt to reform the Soviet system. (There are also unsubstantiated stories of Beria's contemplating far-reaching changes in foreign policy, including concessions to the West.) In any case, his colleagues had enough. On July 10 it was announced that the hitherto number-two man of the Soviet Union was arrested. In December Beria, along with a number of his associates, went to his death. The official charges against him stressed that he had tried to sow discord among the fraternal nations of the USSR and, rather disingenuously, that he had been a foreign agent. From then until Khrushchev in 1956 dropped the other shoe and denounced Stalin himself, Beria was to be the convenient scapegoat for all of the real and alleged crimes of the pre-March 5 era. His fall also signified a definite decline in the political influence of the security organs. From now on they would be firmly controlled by the Party, rather than being, as between 1937 and 1953, a veritable state within the state. In

1954 the Ministry of Internal Security was again split into one of Internal Affairs and the Committee of State Security (KGB). And a number of trials were to take place between 1953 and 1956 in which former perpetrators of terror were arraigned on charges of having violated "socialist legality," of the "use of impermissible methods of investigations," etc., yet it is certain that only a small proportion of the perpetrators of terror had been tried and punished. Those who had not been associated too closely with Beria or his henchmen were quietly pensioned off or simply continued their careers with the KGB.

Apart from lopping off such excrescences of Stalinism as mass terror, the leaders hastened to improve the standard of the population. Whether because of common sense or fear of an explosion of pent-up popular discontent now that the man who had hovered "over us like a dread spirit" was no longer there, they saw the need for economic improvements. The consumer's needs could no longer be neglected as against industrial growth, the peasant could not be as mercilessly exploited as he had been ever since 1929. As early as April 1 the government announced sizable reductions in the price of food. More boons followed—in August Malenkov announced a reduction in the agricultural tax, and in what was in reality another form of taxation, the allegedly voluntary subscription to the state loans. But it fell to Nikita Khrushchev at the September 1953 Plenum of the Central Committee to sketch out the details of the new agricultural policy. The Plenum marked Khrushchev's ascent to the position of number two vacated by Beria. The fifty-nine-year-old leader was now formally named the Party's first secretary, the office that would enable him in a year and a half to reach the very top and to oust his younger rival.

Khrushchev revealed what Malenkov had already hinted at: agriculture was a mess, and the collective peasant was being skinned alive. (He would provide more details in 1958 after Malenkov, Molotov, and others allegedly responsible for agricultural policy before 1953 had bit the dust. "Allegedly" because Khrushchev himself had had a hand in those policies.) He exposed the fraudulent statistical practice of overestimating the grain crop through the use of the "biological yield." He called for and the Party legislated an immediate rise in the procurement prices paid by the government to the peasant. The price for the meat quotas was increased more than five and a half times, doubled for milk and butter, increased two and a half times for potatoes, etc.[1] Payments for products commandeered from kolkhozes increased by more than 100 percent. The government promised to increase substantially the amount of investment going to the rural sector of the economy.

[1] Lazar Volin, *A Century of Russian Agriculture*, Cambridge, Mass., 1970, p. 379.

Without as yet directly repudiating Stalin, his successors hastened to remove or to alter the main features of the system of oppression and exploitation synonymous with his name. That their fear of internal disturbances was not entirely unrealistic was proved by a mass strike and then revolt in the labor camps in Vorkuta in Russia. But the new leaders were still Stalin's pupils: the revolt, never publicly acknowledged, was mercilessly suppressed.

International Relations in a Transitional Era

There was an equally harried attempt to relieve international tension. Stalin, his successors felt, had pushed the confrontation with the West to the danger point. His death coincided with the installation of the new Republican administration in Washington. Its secretary of state, John Foster Dulles, spoke of replacing the policy of "containment" of the USSR with one of the "rollback" of the Soviet sphere in Europe. There were hints that the United States, frustrated by interminable delays in reaching an armistice in Korea, might consider the use of atomic weapons there. For this and other reasons the Chinese Communists, already incensed by having had to pull Soviet chestnuts out of the Korean fire, were growing increasingly anti-Soviet. The satellites, their Communist parties thrown into chaos due to purges, their populations restive, were so many powder kegs. In one of them, East Germany, an actual explosion took place; driven to despair by increased work norms and poverty, sensing a degree of confusion and uncertainty among their masters following Stalin's death, the workers in East Berlin and other cities rose in spontaneous revolt. Soviet armor had to be brought in to suppress what threatened to become a revolution. This was a preview of what might happen in Poland, Czechoslovakia, and elsewhere.

Malenkov's speech on August 8 represented a Soviet bid for the lessening of world tension. The USSR had relinquished its territorial claims on Turkey, one of the main Soviet threats that had led to the Truman Doctrine. It extended its friendship to Iran. Diplomatic relations with Israel, broken off since the "discovery" of the "doctors' plot," were to be restored. Ambassadors were now exchanged with heretical Yugoslavia and with Greece. There was a much friendlier tone about the United States, though Malenkov gently chided its government for encouraging subversion abroad.

When it came to other Communist countries, the new Soviet policy went beyond gestures. First of all China had to be appeased; at a time of upheaval it was imperative that the West did not get the slightest inkling of any trouble and discord between the two Commu-

RUSSIA
Today
MILES
0 300 600
0 300 600
KILOMETERS
Arctic Ocean
GREAT BRITAIN
London
FRANCE
Paris
BELGIUM
Brussels
Amsterdam
THE NETHERLANDS
DENMARK
Copenhagen
NORWAY
Oslo
SWEDEN
Stockholm
FINLAND
Helsinki
LUX
Bonn
GERMANY
W
E
Berlin
Prague
AUSTRIA
Vienna
CZECH
POLAND
Warsaw
HUNGARY
Budapest
LIT
LAT
EST
Vilnius
Riga
Tallin
Leningrad
Minsk
WHITE RUSSIA
Smolensk
Moscow
ROMANIA
Bucharest
Kiev
Kishinev
MOLDAVIA
Dnieper
UKRAINE
Black Sea
Volga
Volgograd
TURKEY
GEORGIA
Tbilisi
ARMENIA
Yerevan
SYRIA
AZERBAIJAN
Baku
Caspian
Sea
IRAQ
Baghdad
Teheran
IRAN
KUWAIT
SAUDI ARABIA
TURKMEN
Ashkhabad
UZBEK
Aral Sea
KAZAKH
Lake Balkhash
Tashkent
Alma Ata
Frunze
KIRGIZ
Dushanbe
TADZHIK
AFGHANISTAN
Kabul
PAK
INDIA
R U S S I A
Ob
Yenisey
Lena
Novosibirsk
Lake Baikal
Ulan Bator
MONGOLIA
CHINA
Peking
Sea of Okhotsk
Sea of Japan
JAPAN
Tokyo
N
KOREA
S
Pyongyang
Seoul
Pacific
Ocean

nist giants. On his return from Stalin's funeral, Chou En-lai expressed his willingness to end the deadlock in the Korean negotiations, and it was resolved by an armistice in July. (The fact that Mao himself did not deign to head the Chinese delegation to the obsequies of the number-one Communist was already a portent of future troubles.) A trade and commercial agreement signed with China on March 26 provided for new credits and considerable Soviet technological and scientific help toward China's economic development. The North Koreans received a free grant, a thing unheard of in Stalin's time, of one billion rubles.

Some of the thaw spread to the European satellites. The USSR began to curtail its economic exploitation and had forgone further reparations from East Germany. The satellite governments were advised, indeed commanded, to liberalize their internal policies. Purges for the most part were stopped; the inveterate Stalinists among the satellite leaders were demoted or told to share their power within collective leadership, as was the current fashion in the USSR itself.

The lowered temperature of international relations was demonstrated by the 1954 Geneva meeting of foreign ministers of what was still referred to as the Big Four plus China. This marked the entrance of Peking, still of course unrecognized by the United States, upon the arena of world diplomacy—a development certainly not welcome to Washington and unlikely to create much enthusiasm in Moscow. The conference arrived at a Solomon-like judgment about Indo-China, where the Vietminh had just scored a victory over the French at Dienbienphu. The unhappy country was, in the manner of Germany and Korea, divided into two parts, with Ho Chi Minh's regime obtaining the northern section, another indirect success for Chinese diplomacy but also a portent of future troubles.

The changed nature of relations between the USSR and China was underlined in September of the same year when a prestigious Soviet delegation headed by Khrushchev went to Peking. No more summons to Mao or Chou to come to Moscow! Despite the official expressions of cordiality and "unshakable unity" of the two Communist states, this was in fact a melancholy occasion for the Soviet policy makers. Port Arthur and Dairen were to have come under Peking's exclusive sovereignty in 1952, but the Soviet departure had then been postponed, allegedly at the request of the Chinese. Now their last bases on Chinese soil were to revert to China. Another result of the negotiations was to liquidate the joint Sino-Soviet companies for the exploitation of Sinkiang, etc., and to turn their assets to China. Only much later was it to be revealed that Mao took the occasion to demand that Mongolia should also come back under Chinese sovereignty. Thus far the Soviets were not ready to go. Another outcome of the trip was the beginning of the intense personal hostility between Khrushchev and Mao that was to affect Sino-Soviet relations so much for the next ten years.

The fact that it was the First Secretary rather than the Prime Minister who headed this important mission was already a sign that Malenkov's star was setting, Khrushchev's rising. Increasingly the latter was seizing the initiative in domestic and foreign policy. His ebullience, earthy humor, and talent for improvisation assured him of widespread support in intra-Party circles. In contrast, Malenkov suffered by his too close connection with Stalin in his last years, and from his incapacity to adjust to the new style of political leadership and intrigue on the Soviet Olympus. Malenkov tried to offset Khrushchev's growing authority among the officialdom by espousing the policy of providing more consumer goods at the expense of slowing down the rate of industrial growth. This gambit was turned against him. In February 1955 Malenkov was replaced, but in a more civilized way than had hitherto been the case in replacing Soviet potentates. He was made to surrender the chairmanship to Bulganin but remained a minister and Politburo member. Khrushchev was now number one.

For the next nine years the irrepressible new leader was to inject color and confusion into Soviet policies and politics. Far from being, in the manner of Stalin, "cut off from life by the Kremlin Wall," he established the patterns subsequently emulated by his successors, as well as statesmen like Kissinger, of being always on the move. He traveled widely abroad and throughout the Soviet Union, negotiating, haranguing crowds, firing local secretaries and ambassadors on the spot, issuing threats intermittently with appeals for coexistence. In many ways he epitomized the change in Soviet politics from the times of the suspicious tyrant who in his last years abhorred and avoided public appearances.

Khrushchev's manner was to tackle problems head on. To paraphrase an American political slogan, he proposed to "get the USSR moving." To cure the chronic ailment of the Soviet economy, in 1954 he sponsored and for the next five years energetically promoted the plan of expanding the area under cultivation. This was the celebrated virgin lands campaign, bringing into production vast new territories, hitherto uncultivated steppe lying mostly in Siberia and Kazakhstan. This eventually meant expanding the spring wheat production area from 75 million acres in 1953 to 120–25 million by 1962.[2] There were voices raised in protest, some agricultural experts as well as Khrushchev colleagues claiming that because of soil and climatic conditions much of the new land was unsuitable for long-run cultivation, that for

[2] Volin, *op. cit.*, p. 485.

all the huge investment in resources and labor one would end up with vast dust bowls. This prophecy was to come largely true in the early sixties, but for the first years of the plan it was a dazzling success. By 1958 there was a spectacular rise in agricultural output. The campaign was carried out in a spirit of ideological fervor, recalling the pioneering days of rapid industrialization: hundreds of thousands of Komsomol members were mobilized or volunteered to go from central Russia to the distant regions, there to live and work, often under the most primitive conditions. And by the time the whole plan was shown to have been less than a success, Nikita Sergeevich was ready with new improvisations—or, as his successors were to characterize them rather uncharitably, "harebrained ideas."

Similar (perhaps even greater) rashness characterized Khrushchev's foreign ventures. Ever since 1953 Soviet-Yugoslav relations had been improving. But the slow pace of the process was not to the First Secretary's liking. In what was to be the most startling diplomatic visit at least until Henry Kissinger stepped out in Peking in 1971, one May day in 1955 Khrushchev and Bulganin descended on Belgrade to visit the man to whom, until 1953, they along with other Soviet dignitaries referred as the "agent of imperialists and Zionists." Tito by this time had established close ties with the West, had received substantial American help, was not going to be reduced overnight into an unconditional return to the "camp of socialism." Still, despite Khrushchev's brazen declaration that all the past troubles beween the two fraternal Communist nations had been due to those traitors Beria and Abakumov and despite his social boorishness (partial to strong spirits though evidently not as much as his traveling companion, Bulganin, Khrushchev passed out at an official reception and had to be carried out), the visit was a moderate success: Tito and the Yugoslav Communists were flattered by this gesture of penance. They also appreciated that now they could have the best of both worlds. In one year the Yugoslav dictator would make a triumphant tour of the Soviet Union and would have the satisfaction of seeing the Cominform, the organization the Russians had employed to try to subvert his regime, dissolved.

Other 1955 trips by Khrushchev and Bulganin, though not nearly as spectacular as the Belgrade one, were to delineate the shifting lines of Soviet foreign policy. In the fall they were to tour India, Burma, and Afghanistan. This portended that the USSR would much more than hitherto pay attention to the developments in the Third World, and try to gain influence there not primarily through the local Communist parties but by developing friendly relations with the governments of those, for the most part, new states. The demise of colonialism and the growing political weakness of Britain and France were opening new opportunities for Soviet diplomacy. And by the same token, the USSR would exploit the lingering anti-imperialism and anti-Westernism in the new lands in its competition with the United States, and its superior economic and political power in the already beginning contest with the new claimant for primacy in Asia, Communist China.

While sharply competitive with the West (and in a sense enlarging the area of that competition), Soviet foreign policy under Khrushchev would also seek what later on would be called détente and what in his time was dubbed peaceful coexistence with the United States. The key problem in the Soviet-West relations remained, as in Stalin's time, Germany. The original Soviet objective of preventing the rearmament of West Germany by 1955 had to be acknowledged a failure—the Federal Republic in that year joined NATO. But even so, the Russians would strive to curb German rearmament and especially, the most imperative necessity in Soviet eyes, to deny Bonn nuclear weapons. (The problem of nuclear weapons was increased several times in magnitude and frightfulness in 1954, when both the United States and the USSR exploded their first hydrogen devices.) The pursuit of this goal would carry Khrushchev to extremes: he would be close to offering the United States a virtual alliance at one time, at another he would force a confrontation that seemed to bring the world to the brink of war.

In 1955 the "coexistence" mood of the Soviets was signaled by the USSR's agreeing to the Austrian peace treaty, thus freeing the fortunate little country from foreign occupation, and providing the rather novel precedent of Soviet troops in Europe withdrawing from an area they had held since 1945. Of course, the Russians had to be paid off: Austrian goods were to compensate them for the properties they had seized in their zone. But primarily the Austrian gambit was to serve as a come-on with regard to Germany; in return for their withdrawal, the Soviets obtained permanent neutralization of Austria. At about the same time the USSR also surrendered its bases on Finnish soil.

But of course the German problem was hugely more complex than the Austrian. The Federal Republic was a member of NATO and in the process of acquiring a military establishment (though the treaty still banned nuclear arms for Bonn). The Soviet creature, the German Democratic Republic, would soon join what might be called anti-NATO: The Warsaw Pact organization was set up to synchronize military forces of the USSR and its satellites. On the surface the new organization, which came into being in 1955, did not add anything to the Soviet military potential; satellite armed forces had been under Soviet control from the beginning. But the Warsaw organization was to serve two purposes: It was a diplomatic tool—the Soviets would repeatedly offer to dissolve it in return for the disbandment of NATO and it was a convenient cover for Soviet military intervention in the satellites—Budapest in 1956, Prague in 1968.

The German question provided the main agenda at the new-style summit in July 1955 in Geneva. Khrushchev and Bulganin, accompanied by a delegation that included Molotov and the new defense minister, Marshal Zhukov, joined the West's leaders in a fruitless discussion of outstanding international issues. Yet this new "summitry" was not without tangible gains for the USSR. The sense of danger that had given impetus to NATO and other drives toward Western unity was now replaced by a certain complacency: The Soviets obviously were not going to march their armies across Europe. Neutralism began to gain adherents in the West, and also especially in the Third World. The new flexibility of Soviet policy was also evident in separate approaches to various Western powers. Chancellor Adenauer was invited to Moscow, but the doughty German statesman would not be detached from the United States; the visit produced only diplomatic recognition by the USSR of the Bonn republic and the Soviet pledge to return the German war prisoners still in Russia.

For all the successes of the "new look" of Soviet foreign policy, 1956 was to bring a severe crisis in the Soviet empire. The year opened with the Twentieth Party Congress held in February. It was there that Khrushchev delivered in a closed session his famous speech containing a startling critique of the Stalin era. Heard by thousands of people, the speech of course could not remain secret and soon its contents made the rounds of the world. For the first time the country and the world heard from the lips of the highest Soviet official an official confirmation of *some* of the most horrendous details of Stalin's tyranny, of his personal megalomania and suspiciousness, of the violation by him of the Party rules, etc. What Soviet propaganda had branded as slander and fabrication was now confirmed in the presence of delegates from all over Russia and from foreign Communist parties: innocent people, including most of the makers of the Revolution, were sent to their death on imaginary charges, torture was used to extract confessions, had Stalin lived a while longer most of the current Party leadership would have shared the fate of Bukharin and Zinoviev. Khrushchev's attack was not unqualified: he drew a sharp distinction between Stalin's activity before 1934—most of it positive—and his increasingly tyrannical and psychopathic behavior afterwards. Thus by implication Stalin's collectivization policy was defended, as were his seizure of absolute power and his political if not physical liquidation of such famous Bolsheviks as Trotsky, Kamenev, Bukharin, and others.[3]

[3] Verdicts of the infamous Moscow trials of the 1930's have never up to this day been annulled.

Khrushchev's denunciation of Stalin, though it must have been approved by the collective leadership (i.e., the majority of the Presidium), undoubtedly represented his own initiative, a bid to identify himself with the process of liberalization and to push against the wall those members of the oligarchy who, like Molotov, Kaganovich, and Malenkov, were associated in the public mind with the horrors of the past. And, as the latter must have warned, there was an undoubted psychological danger in such frankness. There was bound to be a wave of revulsion at home and abroad, not only against Stalinism but communism as a whole.

To be sure no untoward (from the point of view of the Communist hierarchy) developments were to take place within the USSR. But in the Soviet satellites the story was to be different. Their leaders were virtually cast adrift. How far and in what direction were they to de-Stalinize? The more ambitious leaders were bound to think of the example of Tito, the more timid ones (a great majority) of how they could contain their ambitious colleagues, not to mention their people, without firm Soviet support. Ghosts from the recent past arose to challenge the current Soviet satraps. They were supposed, if not indeed ordered, by Moscow, to rehabilitate some of the victims of terror. But this was bound to send a shock throughout their nations. Communism in the USSR had successfully merged with Russian nationalism, but in Poland or Hungary the explosive force of nationalism was bound to be set off by the public acknowledgment of past crimes, and other signs of weakness of the current masters.

Thus a popular explosion took place in the Polish city of Poznan. A workers' demonstration about their grievances developed into a clash with the police: more than one hundred demonstrators were killed. A severe crisis now seized the Polish Communist Party. Its current leaders sought to appease discontent by inviting Gomulka, disgraced as a Titoist in 1948–49, to rejoin the Party councils. But the rising wrath of the masses now communicated itself to the Party membership. It was not enough to rehabilitate Gomulka; most of the Central Committee members wanted to install him as the first secretary, and they met for this purpose on October 19. This brought Khrushchev, accompanied by some other Soviet potentates, including Molotov, to Warsaw, while Soviet military units from East Germany and Silesia drew closer to the capital. But after a tempestuous interview (on seeing Gomulka at the airport, Khrushchev allegedly exclaimed, "What is this agent of Zionists and Wall Street doing here?"), the Soviet leaders realized that Gomulka had the great majority of the Party and nation behind him and that he was a loyal Communist who would not lead Poland out of the Soviet bloc. And so in an atmosphere of general enthusiasm the erstwhile "Titoist" was installed as the leader of the Party and state. Other Soviet concessions followed: the USSR was to extend credits and Soviet Marshal Rokossovsky, who since 1949 had headed Poland's army, was sent back to Russia.

The Polish October episode raised hopes throughout eastern Europe. The Soviets proceeded to make a virtue out of necessity and to use the Polish arrangement as the model for agreements with other people's democracies. The USSR would provide loans and cancel outstanding debts, thus compensating partially for the years of economic exploitation. Stationing of Soviet troops was linked to the Warsaw Treaty, thus removing the stigma of occupation and likening the arrangements to NATO's. For a while it seemed that an entirely new pattern of relations was to develop between the USSR and other Communist countries. But within days the Hungarian developments were to dash these hopes.

In Poland Gomulka's popularity and resoluteness had kept the revolt against the former regime from developing into a full-scale popular revolt against communism. But in Hungary the wave of popular discontent could not be contained. Riots in October brought into power the once-disgraced Communists Imre Nagy as prime minister and Janos Kadar as first secretary, while the erstwhile Stalinist bosses Gerö and Rakosi left hurriedly for the USSR. But the momentum of the revolt could not be contained. Nagy was forced to ask for the removal of Soviet troops and to announce that Hungary would cease to be a one-party state and would leave the Warsaw Pact.

This was more than the Soviets could tolerate. After some hesitation Moscow decided upon military repression. Soviet troops poured into the country and on November 4 began an attack upon Budapest and other cities. In the meantime Kadar was persuaded or compelled to make himself an accomplice of Soviet intervention; he denounced Nagy and announced the formation of a new government. Within a few days the Soviet tanks crushed poorly armed Hungarian workers' militia and military units, and the revolt was suppressed. Nagy and his closest associates, who left the asylum of the Yugoslav embassy after receiving a safe conduct, were promptly arrested by the Soviet military authorities. On June 16, 1958, it was announced in Moscow and Budapest that the erstwhile premier and three of his colleagues had been condemned and executed.

The Hungarian crisis—massive strikes and other forms of resistance continued throughout the winter of 1956–57 and some 200,000 Hungarians fled to the West—demonstrated that the Kremlin, while allowing its satellites a degree of internal autonomy unimaginable in Stalin's time, would not tolerate any true independence or threat to the Communist regime.

Equally eloquent was the fact that for all the expressions of admiration for the Hungarians and of horror at the Soviet coup forthcoming from the West, its actions were confined to solemn declarations in the United Nations and appeals to "world public opinion." As it happened, the Hungarian revolt coincided, most fortunately from the Soviet point of view, unluckily for the Hungarians and the West, with the Suez crisis.

The latter represented a fantastic compounding of errors by the Western powers and its main consequence was to give the USSR a foothold in the Near East, and thus to make this already explosive area the number-one danger spot to world peace. Ever since the overthrow of monarchy in Egypt, Colonel Nasser's regime had been a thorn in the side not only of Israel but also of Britain and France. Egypt had openly supported the Algerian rebellion, which was to bring down the Fourth Republic in France. And with the nationalization of the Suez Company in July 1956, both France and Britain decided that their remaining interests in the area, indeed their status as great powers, could be preserved only by bringing down the militantly nationalist regime. The United States was not consulted or informed. Israel attacked across the Sinai desert on October 29 and the Anglo-French intervention, first in the form of bombing, then of actual landings in the Suez area, followed within days.

The scenario for the Anglo-French-Israeli operation could have been written in Moscow. It diverted the world's attention, at least partly, from the Soviet troubles and repression in eastern Europe, it gave the USSR a wonderful opportunity to score propaganda points with the Arab world, and it marked the final demise of British and French influence in the Near East, though the French were to hang on to Algeria for a few more years. It also brought a welcome discord within the Western alliance. The United States disapproved and Prime Minister Anthony Eden, forcefully warned by President Eisenhower, announced the scuttling of the operation on November 6, with the UN Security Council also demanding an immediate cease-fire. But though it was America's action that was decisive in Britain and France's desisting from their foolish enterprise, it was Russia's extravagant threats that struck a responding chord in the Arab world. On November 5 Bulganin, in a note to Paris and London as well as to Israel, warned these powers to cease and desist and reminded the helpless British and French that they no longer could lord it over subject peoples—the USSR was determined to crush the aggressors and they should know that the Soviets possessed intercontinental missiles capable of carrying nuclear weapons (actually the USSR was just developing them). Bulganin wrote to Eisenhower proposing that the two superpowers should jointly put down this outrageous aggression. What would happen to the UN should this armed interference in the affairs of an independent state go unchecked and unpunished?

With the armistice in the canal zone, the Soviets still went on with their posturing—it was announced that the USSR was ready to send volunteers to help Egypt and that thousands of Soviet citizens were volunteering for the task!

Khrushchev's Consolidation of Power

The Suez crisis, the split and other troubles in the Western world (there was the ominous precedent of the Arab countries' declaring, though at the time quite ineffectively, an oil boycott of Britain and France; Prime Minister Eden had to resign) had obscured for the time the very serious convulsions within the Soviet bloc. The success of the brazen Soviet tactics and atomic diplomacy in 1956 may well have spurred Khrushchev to try them again, and so he would until they brought him grief in 1962. But for the moment Nikita Sergeevich was in deep trouble. The close call in Poland and Hungary provided ammunition for his enemies on the Presidium, who all along had held that the too fast pace of de-Stalinization and immoderate courting of Tito were bound to end in disaster. Soviet relations with Yugoslavia now became more reserved and criticisms of Stalin slackened. With Khrushchev's position undermined, it appeared that it was only a question of time before he would be removed. At the December meeting of the Central Committee the First Secretary did not give an address, an indication that he was on the skids, and somebody else, possibly the chief *rapporteur* at the session, Mikhail Pervukhin, was being groomed to take his place. But Khrushchev fought back—in February 1957 he presented a plan for reorganizing the economy through establishing a system of regional economic councils (*sovnarkhozy*) which would replace most of the existing economic ministries. The new arrangement conferred additional power on the local Party secretaries, and thus in addition to introducing a degree of decentralization of the economic administration, it was undoubtedly a bid by Khrushchev for support within the Central Committee, as against the growing opposition to him within the Presidium.

The plot against the Soviet First Secretary was led by Molotov who had been dismissed as foreign minister in 1956. (He was replaced first by Khrushchev's *then* favorite Dmitri Shepilov, then by Gromyko. In early 1957 Shepilov became a party secretary.) The erstwhile right-hand man of Stalin enlisted the majority of the Presidium. On June 19, 1957, on a return from one of his trips, Khrushchev hardly got back to the Kremlin when the majority of the Presidium informed him that he was fired. But to the consternation of his colleagues the

First Secretary refused to submit. He enlisted the help of Marshal Zhukov, who provided planes to bring Central Committee members posthaste from all over Russia. There followed the tragicomic spectacle of Khrushchev's partisans literally beating on the doors of the Presidium demanding a reversal of the decision. Supported by Zhukov and three full members of the Presidium, Khrushchev got the Central Committee behind him and turned the tables on the plotters: Molotov, Kaganovich, Malenkov, and the ungrateful Shepilov were expelled from the Presidium and dubbed the "anti-Party group." In accordance with the Soviet habit of secrecy, the full dimensions of the plot were not publicly revealed at the time. It was only in the next two years, as they were being dropped from the Presidium and otherwise disgraced, that it was given out that Khrushchev's traveling companion, Bulganin, the two economic administrators, Pervukhin and Saburov, and even the aged Marshal Voroshilov had all conspired against the First Secretary. "Conspired" is not the right word since undoubtedly members of the Presidium had, by the Party statutes, every right to *propose* dismissal of Khrushchev to the Central Committee. Zhukov was now among those of Khrushchev's supporters who were advanced to full membership in the Presidium. But, alas, there is no gratitude in politics. A man who combined military renown, popularity, and a high Party office was obviously a potential threat to the First Secretary. And so within a few months the ax fell on Zhukov. Upon his return from a diplomatic trip, he was discharged from his government and state offices and denounced rather unconvincingly for having "Bonapartist" ambitions. Marshal Malinovsky became minister of defense; an old pal of Khrushchev's of no standing within the Party, he would not make any trouble. Political purges in the USSR were now becoming more civilized: the disgraced oligarchs were simply given unimportant jobs. Molotov was sent to Mongolia as ambassador and he soon disappeared from the public eye. Zhukov went into retirement to write his memoirs.

This lenient treatment of his enemies, as compared with the past practices, was to prove one of the factors limiting Khrushchev's power, and eventually it contributed to his downfall. It is difficult to curtail opposition and political intrigue in a system like the Soviet one, unless those who are tempted to gamble know that if they lose they will pay the supreme penalty. Khrushchev's triumph enabled him to dominate Soviet policies domestic and foreign for the next four years; in 1958 he would combine premiership with his Party post. But it should have been clear that even during that period he was far from being an absolute dictator, not to mention another Stalin. And in the last two years of his tenure of office his position was to be quite precarious.

The main factor in the constraints on his power was that the majority of the leaders in the Presidium as well as in the Central Committee still had reservations about the character and pace of his reforms, especially de-Stalinization. They were willing to go along with Nikita Sergeevich as long as his policies appeared to be successful. Once there was trouble on the domestic front, as in the early sixties, and a spectacular failure in foreign policy as in 1962, Khrushchev's days were numbered.

For the time being, Khrushchev, his ebullience unimpaired by his close shave, dominated the Soviet and much of the world scene. Though de-Stalinization was now pursued more circumspectly (at least until 1961–62), there was clearly a new atmosphere in society at large. By 1956 extreme isolationism was abandoned; foreign travel and cultural exchanges with the West were encouraged, if closely measured and carefully watched. The First Secretary did not want his country to be shut off from the West; he wanted the USSR to compete successfully with it, whether in industrial production, sports, or even cultural influence among the newly born states of the Third World. Old requirements of ideological orthodoxy and correctness in the arts, literature, and sciences, if not abandoned, were certainly relaxed. Thus, following 1953, Trofim Lysenko was dethroned as the Stalin of Soviet biology, and one could again teach or research in genetics. Unfortunately the enterprising charlatan still retained Khrushchev's trust insofar as agronomy was concerned and thus remained a person of consequence until 1964. The struggle against the cult of personality (the general euphemism for Stalinism) led to a relaxation of controls in historiography as well. One could write more objectively about the postrevolutionary as well as the imperial period, even though the Soviet historian would no more than Khrushchev himself be allowed to tell all or even most about such tragic periods as the times of forcible collectivization and mass terror. Nor would, Khrushchev, any more than Brezhnev after him, tolerate what was to become known as ideological coexistence—i.e., a complete removal of Party controls over intellectual and artistic life, or completely free intellectual intercourse with the West. But to the more conservative element of the Soviet establishment, liberalization had already gone too far: publicity about Stalin's crimes complicated the life of the Party apparatus. In their view, especially those in the secret police and the youth organizations, foreign visitors, foreign travel by Soviet citizens, films from abroad, etc., were spreading undesirable influences. Foreign art and films carried with them the moral decline and indiscipline of the young. Foreign travel, now accessible to more than just a handful of officials as under Stalin, could and occasionally did bring new discoveries and a revulsion against the stereotypes of Soviet propaganda, a craving for greater freedom at home. A Party official spoke for a sizable proportion of the bureaucracy when he decried "individual, immature writers, artists, and composers—from the youth as a rule . . . [who] suffer from such illnesses as pseudo-innovationism and formalism in art. True they are a paltry few, but if an illness is not nipped in the bud it can become dangerous." And even Khrushchev would occasionally break out with violent abuse if he felt an artist, writer, or moviemaker had departed too far from the straight and narrow path. Thus violent abuse was showered on Boris Pasternak when the great poet's *Doctor Zhivago* appeared abroad. The novel, though really apolitical, still carried an implied critique of the Soviet experiment. It could not be published in the USSR and Pasternak was forced to renounce the Nobel Prize.

A partial rationale of the liberalizing policies pursued by the First Secretary and his partisans was a genuine belief in the vitality of Communist ideology once it was freed from the paralyzing dogmatism and terror in which it had been clothed during the preceding era. The downgrading of Stalin was accompanied by the intensification of the cult of Lenin. There was an obvious effort to recharge the Communist Party with new dynamism and a sense of purpose. Its congresses were now assembled at intervals prescribed by the Party statutes. The Central Committee, moribund in Stalin's last years, now was convoked more often, and occasionally its minutes were made public. The proponents of the new course did not, needless to say, propose to dispense with repression, but they obviously believed that it should be used moderately and judiciously, that the new freer ways would of themselves assure the loyalty of the bulk of Soviet citizens while at the same time releasing and enhancing creative forces within the Party and the nation.

Changes were taking place in other areas of policy. The intense russification process and the merciless suppression of whatever gave the slightest appearance of, say, Ukrainian or Uzbek nationalism, be it in the most innocuous cultural sphere, became a thing of the past. The Soviet regime continued to be predominantly Russian and the primacy of the most numerous nationality of the USSR remained the reality, whether in political or cultural matters. At the same time native personnel were allowed to assume a more important role in running the Party and government agencies in the non-Russian areas. The traditional pattern in the non-Russian republics (with the exception of the Caucasian ones) had been that the first secretary of the local Party organization was a native while the second in command was a Russian. In the Asian and Baltic areas the top officials of the security apparatus also tended to be Russians or Ukrainians. This pattern began to change with Beria's ascent to the top, and the process continued even after his fall.

It would be difficult to assess the total effect of these changes which are summarized under the heading "the thaw." Structurally, the regime preserved its totalitarian appearance and essence, and the weapon of repression would be unleashed unhesitatingly against anything smacking of political opposition to the regime. Yet while the Khrushchev era did not bring with it political or intellectual freedom, it certainly dissipated the atmosphere of fear in which the average Soviet citizen had lived for a whole generation before 1953, the feeling that, no matter what one's station in life or attitude toward the regime, one might for some mysterious reason fall victim of terror.

It does not detract from Khrushchev's achievement to say that he was motivated not only by humanitarian reasons but also by those of political calculation, and that in addition to strengthening the Soviet system he expected the thaw to bring dividends in terms of enhancing his own powers. Though himself a high official under Stalin, he attempted and to a large extent succeeded in dissociating himself from the horrors of the previous system, and to brand (not always justifiably) those who opposed this or that policy of his as unregenerate Stalinists. The objective of his campaign was not so much to gain him acceptance in the nation at large, though he was genuinely a man of the people as against the bureaucrat epitomized by a Malenkov or a Molotov, but support within the Party hierarchy. By abolishing capricious terror and providing a degree of personal security, he undoubtedly enlisted, for a time, the sympathy of the majority of Party officials; by adding to their power and prestige as against the central bureaucracy he secured the support of the local Party secretaries, numerically the predominant element on the Central Committee.

Insofar as the economy was concerned, the Khrushchev regime was a beneficiary of the prodigious effort and sacrifices that went into the rebuilding of the Soviet economy in the immediate postwar years. By the middle fifties the USSR thus could continue on what was a spectacular industrial growth while showing some as yet modest improvement insofar as the consumer was concerned. In 1956 came the introduction of the minimum wage, which substantially raised the remuneration of the lowest-paid workers. Old age and disability pensions were also increased, while the normal working week was being reduced, eventually to be set at forty-two hours, and fewer in especially hazardous and strenuous occupations. Malenkov's demotion in 1955 was the occasion for the reiteration of the priority of heavy industry over consumers' goods. Now the second industrial power in the world, the USSR was set on the course of "catching up and overcoming" the first one, and epitomizing this ambition was the rapid growth in the production of steel, which by 1960 would surpass Stalin's goal for that year (thought unrealistically high when proclaimed in 1946) of 60 million tons. Similarly spectacular increases were being registered in such indices, as well as sinews, of industrialization as electricity, extraction of coal and oil, etc.

To be sure this impressive growth, as well as the achievement of Soviet technology marked by the launching of the first earth satellite, Sputnik, in 1957, masked the still considerable inefficiencies and backwardness of the Soviet economy. The vast material and human resources of Soviet society could be harnessed to effect a rapid quantitative growth, especially in those basic commodities like steel which bore directly on the country's industrial and military potential. But the productivity of the Soviet worker still remained low as compared with that in the most advanced Western countries. The cumbersome, overcentralized structure of Soviet industrial organization and decision making discouraged innovation and managerial responsibility and efficiency. Khrushchev's constant reorganization of and improvisations in industrial and agricultural administration, while failing to eliminate bureaucratic rigidity in economic planning and management, served to increase confusion as to lines of authority. There was no real incentive for the factory director or engineer to concentrate on the quality of the product or even on reduction of costs; from the point of view both of his position and of the bonus he would receive, his main objective had to be to meet and if possible to overfulfill the assigned quota; "more" had an absolute priority over "better" or "more cheaply."

The main dilemma of the Soviet economy, which could be summarized as control versus efficiency, was even more pronounced in agriculture. In industry it took the form of alternating periods of de- and re-centralization; but with a bureaucracy—be it in Moscow or at the seat of the given regional economic council (*sovnarkhoz*)—always in the saddle, any initiative or improvement at the production level was impeded. In agriculture there were parallel zigzags (and the resulting red tape and confusion) between the policy of giving the collective farmers more leeway and material incentives and conversely of trying to limit and tax more heavily their private plots and livestock and of merging collectives in larger units. Thus in 1958 the government ordered the liquidation of the Machine Tractor Stations and the sale of their equipment to kolkhozes. This was meant to give the collective peasantry more control over their economic activities. But at the same time Khrushchev, who because of his peasant background fancied himself as an agricultural expert, continued to issue fiats as to what crops should be emphasized, how they should be grown, etc. As early as 1955 he convinced himself that the success of American agriculture was due largely to the widespread use of corn. For the next few years his enthusiasm for this crop was to know no bounds: corn acreage was hugely expanded, even in areas that were climatically unsuitable for it. Soviet agronomists were dispatched to the United States to study this miracle crop in Iowa, etc. The First Secretary became popularly known as Nikita the Corn Grower.

Nor was the Khrushchev who in 1950 had proposed the agrocities entirely dead. There was further amalgamation of kolkhozes into larger units, and pressure to turn them into state farms. In 1958 he revived and then again dropped the idea of housing peasants in apartment houses. The main reason behind all these alarums and excursions was the regime's goal to limit and eventually to abolish the private plot, which for Khrushchev, as for Stalin, was the main reason why the peasant did not work harder and more efficiently on the communal land and livestock. The net result of all this interference and confusion was to perpetuate the discrepancy between the industrial and rural work force, in terms of both its productivity and its material well-being. It was estimated in the late fifties that the collective peasant's real income was still below 60 percent of the industrial worker's. (The peasant on the state farm did somewhat better. He was also entitled to old-age pensions and other social benefits not enjoyed by the collective farmer.) And as late as 1972 official Soviet statistics were to give the productivity of the American industrial worker as about twice that of the Soviet one, while in agriculture the proportion was allegedly just more than four to one.[4]

Khrushchev's Adventures in Foreign Policy

In the field of foreign relations Soviet policy of the Khrushchev era appeared to pursue the same erratic and inconsistent course as in agriculture. Yet underlying the First Secretary's pyrotechnics, such as attempted nuclear intimidation of the West intermittent with his plea for a virtual alliance with the United States, were some abiding concerns of the USSR leadership. These tended to concentrate on Germany and Communist China. Most plainly the Soviet government would seek to prevent both Bonn and Peking from acquiring an arsenal of nuclear weapons. In pursuing these objectives the Kremlin could not afford to be direct and fully reveal its aims: widespread knowledge of Soviet fears, and especially of the Soviet apprehensions

[4] *The National Economy of the USSR in 1972*, Moscow, 1973, pp. 798–99. In fact the disproportion is much greater: on the order of six or seven to one.

about their fellow Communists in Peking, would provide valuable bargaining counters to the United States—protestations of the "unshakable friendship" between the USSR and the People's Republic were being taken in the West at face value until at least 1960. Hence the course of Soviet diplomacy had to be more subtle.

On Germany, the USSR strove for a German peace treaty that, while preserving the division of the country, would prohibit any future manufacture or possession of nuclear bombs by the Federal Republic. But for the time being neither Washington nor Bonn would hear of a peace treaty that would legitimize Communist East Germany. The Soviets at times sought to outflank, so to speak, this objection. Thus in 1957–58 Poland's Foreign Minister Rapacki "proposed"—it is a safe bet that the proposal was really authored in the USSR—the creation of a "de-nuclearized zone in Central Europe." This zone would comprise Poland, Czechoslovakia, the German Democratic Republic, and the German Federal Republic. Under the treaty nuclear weapons would be neither manufactured nor stockpiled in this area and no installations for their servicing would be allowed. But the Americans, without fully realizing the real meaning of the proposal, rejected it, believing it would confer special advantages on the USSR. (At the time it was believed, largely on account of Sputnik and Khrushchev's bravado, that the Soviet Union was much more advanced in the development of the long-range ballistic missile than it actually was.)

Even more circuitous were the Soviet tactics concerning the other goal, that of preventing the Chinese People's Republic from becoming a nuclear power. For all the growing tension between the two great Communist powers, both Peking and Moscow realized that to reveal it to the world would be to strengthen immeasurably the position of the West. The recurrent crises of 1956–58, whether of the Communist bloc, in the Near East, or even within the Soviet leadership itself, made it imperative for the USSR to preserve the appearance of complete unity between Russia and China. But the Soviet Union had to pay for this support. In addition to enhanced economic aid, Moscow agreed in October 1957 to provide China with nuclear know-how and at a point in the future with a sample atomic bomb. This agreement assured the Soviets of Chinese backing in the series of crises that were to erupt within the next two years, but at the same time sowed the seeds of the violent dispute that was eventually to break out between the two Communist states.

In 1958 the USSR became more active in the Near East. It pledged to finance the construction of the huge Aswan Dam, and emerged now as the protector not only of Egyptian but of Arab nationalism. The next development was a coup d'etat that overthrew the pro-Western

Mao Tse-tung and Nikita Khrushchev in China prior to open Sino-Soviet conflict.

regime in Iraq and installed General Kassem. To prevent the loss of their remaining clients in the area, the Western powers acted with speed. The Americans landed marines in Lebanon, the British parachutists in Jordan. This brought out the essential Khrushchev: in a letter to Eisenhower and to British Prime Minister Macmillan, he reminded them that the USSR had "atom and hydrogen bombs, aircraft and navy plus ballistic missiles of all kinds including intercontinental ones." He demanded an immediate meeting of the Security Council. "Time is precious, as the guns are already beginning to fire" exclaimed the incorrigible bluffer. But his playing with fire and especially the call to negotiate within the context of the Security Council—of which *Nationalist* China was still a member—brought a strong reaction from Peking. And so on July 31 Khrushchev had to go to Peking to assuage Mao.

The Near Eastern crisis cooled off but was succeeded by a Far Eastern one. As if to test the extent of Soviet support, the Chinese Communists began in August to shell the coastal islands of Matsu and Quemoy, which, though a few miles from the mainland, were occupied by Chiang's forces. President Eisenhower reiterated the American pledge to defend Chiang, thus warning Peking that an invasion of the tiny islands would not be tolerated by the United States. This in turn triggered off Khrushchev's warning to Eisenhower that an "attack on the Chinese People's Republic which is a great friend, ally and neighbor of our country is an attack on the Soviet Union."

We now know that the Chinese Communists' move led to considerable apprehension and irritation in Moscow. Eventually this crisis passed too. But both Communist powers realized that they would not be able to preserve the illusion of their "unshakable unity" for long. Nineteen fifty-eight was the year when the Mao regime initiated "the Great Leap Forward," a hasty and ill-conceived attempt to industrialize China through its own resources. The main motivation was undoubtedly the desire to reduce economic dependence on the USSR and to prepare for the contingency of Soviet industrial help's being cut off.

The Soviets for their part were eager to squeeze the last ounce of benefit from their fast-waning alliance with China. In November the USSR precipitated another Berlin crisis, which in a changing form was to be a feature of world politics for the next four years.

As in the previous Berlin trouble of 1948–49, the real Soviet aim, though this was not fully understood in the West, was not to push the Western powers out of Berlin but to use its vulnerable position to pry out of the West the kind of German peace settlement the USSR desired.

The Russian note to the three Western powers demanded a general German settlement. Should there be no such agreement within six months, the USSR would turn over East Berlin to the East Germans and sign an agreement with them renouncing any vestiges of occupation. It would then be up to East Germany to regulate the Western powers' access to West Berlin, with the full right to ban their communications across its territory. In brief, the West was told to sign a treaty and recognize Communist Germany or be ready to get out of Berlin. And Khrushchev implied that this time a land blockade would be supplemented by an air one. Should the United States and its allies attempt to break the blockade by armed means, the USSR would consider an attack on East Germany as an attack on itself.

The Chinese on December 21 hastened to associate themselves with the Soviet position. But again this did not come free. On February 9, 1959, the Soviets announced the most extensive credits yet to China. Five billion rubles' worth of Soviet services and goods, mostly in heavy industry, were to be provided within the next seven years.

The two conflicts, an open one with the West and the clandestine one with China, increasingly absorbed the energies of Soviet leadership. In addition to the complicated design of Soviet fears and hopes, one gets the impression of clashing tendencies with the Khrushchev regime which did not allow him a completely free hand either in foreign or domestic affairs. The special Twenty-first Party Congress, summoned with great fanfare for January 1959, failed to make any domestic decisions, and one must suspect that some of the First Secretary's scenario for the congress had to be abandoned or modified because of a division within the Presidium. But in his speech Khrushchev did give a hint that he still hoped somehow to prevent China from acquiring nuclear weapons. "One can and must construct in the Far East and the whole Pacific Ocean a zone of peace and first of all a zone free of atomic weapons." (We now know from the subsequent Chinese revelations that Khrushchev wanted Peking to authorize him to say to the West that Communist China would not manufacture atomic weapons if the West made a similar pledge in regard to West Germany. But the Chinese, after at first seeming to go along with the Russian idea, were then to reject it out of hand.)

The elaborate skein of Soviet design began to unravel during 1959. The West remained obdurate on the German issue. Thus Khrushchev had to postpone (the first of several such postponements) the execution of his threat of the preceding November, i.e., of signing a separate peace treaty with East Germany. However, in exchange he extracted an invitation to the United States. But this visit in turn was bound to worsen relations with China. Peking already began to suspect that for all their promises and credits, the Soviets were in effect working for a deal with the United States that would make the two superpowers joint arbiters of world politics, one of the main foundations of such an understanding being their common fear of China. Insofar as Khrushchev's own position was concerned, they were not too far wrong!

But the visit itself, for all of its theatrical aspects, failed to produce any tangible results. Of course, it was sensational in itself that for the first time Russia's leader—and a Communist one to boot—should set foot on American soil. It was a pleasing recognition of Russia's status as a superpower and undoubtedly, though only very briefly, a boost to Khrushchev's status at home. For two weeks the American press and television followed the antics of the First Secretary, who was in his most "coexistential" mood and whose trip was undoubtedly prompted, quite apart from his designs, by the desire to learn about and see as much of America as possible, not only the White House and the American capitalists, but also Disneyland and a model Iowa farm. But though it was a high point in the career of the erstwhile peasant boy and despite the friendly tone of official communiqués—one issued after the conference between Eisenhower and Khrushchev in the President's rural retreat gave rise to the short-lived "spirit of Camp David"—it failed to move forward the Berlin-Germany issue. And so this fundamental problem of East-West relations was to be taken up at the Big Four summit meeting in the spring.

Even so, in Peking the trip aroused the darkest suspicions, if not indeed conviction of Soviet treachery. Relations between the two Communist powers were building up toward an open break. In June 1959 the Soviets in effect repudiated their nuclear agreement with China by refusing to turn over to the latter a sample atomic bomb. An added source of Chinese irritation was the fact that when in September 1959 a frontier dispute erupted between India and the People's Republic, the Soviet official stance was far from one of wholehearted support for Peking. And so almost immediately upon his return from America Khrushchev had to set out on a much less congenial trip to Communist China. The atmosphere of his negotiations with Mao was, as we now know, tempestuous, but for a few months a public break was postponed.

In the course of 1960 two elements of Khrushchev's juggling act came crashing to the ground. The Soviet Union's now intense conflict with China became public knowledge, first in the Communist world and then in the West. Coincidental with this but not unconnected came the collapse of the summit meeting and of any hope of solving the German issue through negotiations.

On April 16 a Peking journal published an article, evidently written by Mao himself. Under its involved semantics and esoteric allusions, the article conveyed a warning that if the Russians pushed détente with the West one step further, Peking would denounce them as revisionists. And both in the article and in their other public pronouncements around this time the Chinese made it clear that they would not agree to "any international disarmament agreement and any other international agreements which are arrived at without the formal participation of the Chinese People's Republic." Thus the Soviets would not be able to trade off a prohibition of nuclear weapons for China in return for a similar limitation on West Germany. And it became increasingly clear that the United States was not ready for one-sided concessions on Germany.

The celebrated U-2 episode afforded Khrushchev an opportunity to wreck the Four Powers' summit, which in view of American and Chinese attitudes would undoubtedly have been both fruitless and embarrassing. American overflights of Soviet territory, with a view of ascertaining Soviet missile capabilities, had been going on for some time. But on May 1 the Soviets finally managed to bring down an American spy plane and to capture its pilot, Gary Powers. This unleashed Khrushchev's pent-up frustrations. He now became as abusive about the Americans and President Eisenhower personally as he had been, at least in public, cordial and hopeful ever since his U.S. visit. When the heads of the four powers assembled in Paris on May 14, Khrushchev continued his theatricalities and demanded that the President apologize publicly. The conference was aborted and the Soviets withdrew their invitation to Eisenhower to visit Russia.

The next few months were to be a bad period for the First Secretary. The collapse of the "spirit of Camp David" was followed by that of the "unshakable unity of the Soviet and Chinese peoples." The two conferences of world Communist leaders, first in Rumania in June and then in Moscow in the fall, revealed to the world the extent of the Sino-Soviet split. In 1963 the Chinese Communists were to characterize the Soviet behavior at those meetings as follows: "It is a plain lie for . . . the Central Committee of the CPSU to describe that meeting as 'comradely assistance' to the Chinese Communist Party. . . . Khrushchev took the lead in organizing a great converging attack on the Chinese Communist Party. . . . He vilifies [its leaders] . . . as 'madmen,' 'waiting to unleash war,' . . . 'dogmatic,' . . . 'left adventurists.'" During the summer of 1960 the Soviet Union had recalled all her industrial, technical, and scientific experts and advisers from China. The Sino-Soviet conflict led to the Soviet-Albanian one. This tiny satellite, whose Communist leaders had for long been apprehensive about Soviet courtship of Yugoslavia, now took the Chinese side. The pro-Soviet elements within the Albanian Communist party were purged, and the Soviet navy had to evacuate its Albanian base in the Adriatic.

There intervened a humorous episode. Frustrated in its main foreign objectives, the USSR was now exploiting to the hilt all the troubles

Nikita Khrushchev with a shoe at the ready on his desk at the United Nations October 12, 1960. Seated next to Khrushchev is Soviet Foreign Minister Gromyko.

and conflicts consequent upon the breakdown of the imperial system and the rise of the new states in the Third World. Nineteen sixty was the year of the Congo. The internal troubles in that African country following its emancipation from Belgium provided the USSR with yet another opportunity to blame the West for its "imperialism" and to accuse the UN, which was trying to smooth the transition in the Congo (now Zaire), of being a tool of U.S. policy. This gave Khrushchev a pretext to travel again to New York, but *not* to the country whose President he had publicly insulted, but to the international territory of the UN! Again little transpired during that visit, except the uninhibited antics of the First Secretary: he banged his shoe on the table during a UN debate, he visited another bête noire of the United States, Castro, in his hotel in Harlem, and in general the expression "like a bull in a china shop" seemed to have been devised specifically to describe Khrushchev's behavior on this occasion.

This was also the year of a profound crisis with the Communist world. The Sino-Soviet dispute now became public knowledge—though it was still not realized in the West how pervasive it was and how deeply it affected the overall posture of Soviet foreign policy—and quite apart from their dispute, both major Communist powers experienced internal troubles. The disastrous consequences of the Great Leap Forward were now revealed. China's industrial output went down, and the drive to transform collective farms into communes had brought a severe crisis in agriculture which would lead to widespread famine in 1961–62. Probably not unconnected with these was the crisis within the leadership, a portent of the Cultural Revolution which would come in a few years. In 1959 Mao had already purged the leadership of some of his opponents, notably the minister of defense, Marshal Peng Teh-huai. While the Soviets could and did gloat over Chinese troubles—Khrushchev for years had criticized the Great Leap Forward as doctrinaire and un-Marxist—their own economic situation could hardly be deemed satisfactory. The rate of industrial growth, while still impressive, was slowing down. In agriculture the negative effects of the virgin lands scheme and of other hasty improvisations were now being felt. The years 1960–62 were bad ones for the Soviet consumer, especially in view of the increased expectations aroused by the post-Stalin reforms and oratory. The housing situation, with the country becoming rapidly urbanized, continued to be desperate. In 1961–62 there would be severe food shortages.

The regime's ways of dealing with internal and foreign crises still bore the imprint of Khrushchev's impetuous personality. There were new improvisations and what might be described as publicity stunts. Thus the USSR exploited to the hilt its early successes in developing the missile and space technology. To outside observers, Soviet economic troubles and the ever-widening split in the Communist world were obscured by such achievements as the spectacular rise in the production of steel and the first manned space shot, which took place in the spring of 1961. (Even Khrushchev was to say in a rueful moment that one cannot eat steel.) For all the vulnerability of the Soviet international position, the new administration of President Kennedy took office in the shadow of a deep apprehension over what was believed to be an imminent showdown over Berlin, as well as the widespread

American belief in the existence of a "missile gap" in favor of the Soviets.[5]

Despite his previous failures on this count, Khrushchev still believed he could keep West Germany and Communist China from joining the nuclear club. On China, Soviet hopes were revived by what was evidently a setback to Mao's leadership. The catastrophic consequences of the Great Leap Forward led to a strong opposition to Mao's policies, and the Liu Shao-chi faction—Liu, then president of the People's Republic, was the second person in the regime—while in no sense pro-Soviet (but without the virulent anti-Soviet feelings that Mao now displayed) succeeded in curbing the Great Helmsman's power and arresting the drift toward a complete break with Moscow.

On the Germany question, the Soviets still kept the threat of a separate peace treaty with East Germany suspended like a sword of Damocles over West Berlin. But in addition they believed they had found another lever to break down the U.S. obstinacy on the issue: Cuba.

Ever since coming to power in January 1959, Fidel Castro had drifted closer to the USSR. It would be unreasonable to describe Castro as having always been a Communist. He became one, so to speak, by adoption, hoping to find in the USSR and communism support both against the United States and for his ambition to become leader not only of the Cuban but of a general Latin American revolution. There must have been some hesitation in Moscow about assuming the burden of economic support of Cuba and even more at incurring the danger of a clash with the United States over the inclusion within the Communist bloc of a country 90 miles from the U.S. mainland. But we may be sure that, since this gamble was taken, the Kremlin must have hoped for benefits that would not be confined to the Caribbean or even Latin America as a whole.

The Kennedy administration was eager to resume the Soviet-American dialogue interrupted so drastically by Mr. Gary Powers' uninvited appearance on Soviet soil. But before another summit there intervened the debacle of the Cuban invasion sponsored by the United States in a both inept and clandestine manner—though it could not have been unanticipated by Soviet intelligence. The Bay of Pigs fiasco gave Khrushchev another opportunity to display the qualities he had evidenced on such previous occasions as the Suez crisis. *After* it be-

[5] It was only later that Western experts realized that they had been largely fooled and that, despite the famous U-2 overflights which began in the late fifties, the Soviet armament in heavy bombers and then in missiles between 1955 and 1962 was much smaller than was thought at the time. In view of the vast investments needed for industry and agriculture, the regime in those years actually skimped on armaments.

came clear that the United States had called off the venture, the Soviet message to the United States contained such bits as "aggressive bandit acts cannot save your system." But the Soviets still looked toward a deal with the United States, so the message contained also "coexistential" passages, as "We wish to build up our relations with the United States, in such a manner that the Soviet Union and the United States, as the two most powerful states in the world, would stop their saber rattling. . . ."

The bullying Khrushchev was in full evidence at the June Vienna meeting with the young American President. If there was no German treaty forthcoming he would sign with East Germany in December. West Berlin could then become a free city, but if the West wanted to keep its troops there so would the Russians. The Soviet leader combined bluff with fibbing: Russia would not be the first to resume nuclear testing. (It had been suspended on both sides by an unwritten moratorium under Eisenhower; the Russians would resume with a real bang in late August.) Russia's relations with China, said Khrushchev, with a straight face, were of the best!

The meeting must have reassured the Soviets about American susceptibility to such tactics, for on August 13 the East German authorities proceeded in clear violation of the Potsdam agreements to bar egress of their citizens to the West: The Berlin wall and similar barriers along the whole western frontier were erected. This would effectively stop further flights of East Germans, three million of whom had fled since the war. The West, fearful of future challenges over Berlin, acquiesced uncomfortably in the wall.

Predictably this acquiescence led to a further crescendo of pressure. At the end of August there began a series of Soviet nuclear tests; they continued for two months and concluded with the explosion of the most potent devices yet tested by any power. They could have tested an even more powerful bomb, said Khrushchev cheerfully, but it would have blown windows in Moscow! (The tests took place beyond the Arctic Circle.) Mindful of Khrushchev's December deadline over the German peace treaty, Western statesmen and the people of Berlin held their breath.

It was under these circumstances that the Twenty-second Party Congress met on October 17. There was momentous relief as Khrushchev once more postponed the dread deadline. Foreign Minister Gromyko was even more soothing as he described the happy times Khrushchev and Kennedy had had at Vienna and declared that if only the "two giants" united their efforts for peace, "who would dare and who would be in a position to threaten peace? Nobody."

In fact it was on internal and intra-Communist relations that the Twenty-second Congress made the biggest news. Khrushchev now openly delivered an attack on Stalin that surpassed in its comprehensiveness and violence the "secret" speech of 1956. Almost equally vitriolic were the attacks delivered upon the fallen "anti-Party group"—Molotov, Malenkov, et al.—and upon the Albanian Communists, whose vilification was to serve as a surrogate attack upon the Chinese. But this delicacy failed to prevent the most drastic manifestation of conflict within the Communist camp yet. Chou En-lai took the floor of the congress to decry Khrushchev's attack on the Albanians: "To expose openly a dispute among fraternal countries and fraternal parties for enemies to see cannot be considered as a serious Marxist-Leninist approach." And then, having deposited a wreath on Stalin's tomb inscribed "to the memory of a great Marxist-Leninist," Chou and the entire Chinese delegation left abruptly for Peking. Undaunted, the congress proceeded to order that J. V. Stalin's remains be removed from the place of honor next to Lenin, and they were reburied in the Kremlin wall with a host of lesser Communist lights.

It was easy to dislodge Stalin's mummy. It was infinitely more complicated to try to remove Stalinism from Soviet government and society. Many in the hierarchy, and this is proved by what happened in 1964 and afterward, felt that de-Stalinization had gone far enough if not indeed too far. Had Khrushchev been able to display some domestic and foreign successes, it is quite possible he could have gone on with his reforms. As it was, his position was again becoming vulnerable. He tried to obscure this by his usual pyrotechnics: The Twenty-second Congress was informed that by 1980 the Soviet Union would be entering the era of communism. As to the details of this new brave world, the First Secretary did not quite spell them out beyond promising that travel on public transportation would become free, that the state committee on sport would be abolished, and the country would produce 200 million tons of steel. Yet even such visions of a wonderful future began to rankle. It was remembered that Khrushchev had promised that soon the USSR would surpass the United States in the production of meat, milk, and butter per person, and the current state of Soviet agriculture made mockery of this promise.

Khrushchev's Decline

The foregoing is the context in which Khrushchev undertook a series of desperate improvisations in domestic and foreign policy in 1962, the failure of which was the main reason for his removal two years later.

The anti-Stalin campaign continued. There was now a spate of books: histories, memoirs, and fiction which threw lurid light on the recent past and on the behavior of Stalin and his henchmen. It was the First Secretary's personal intervention that enabled a former Soviet officer and inmate of forced labor camps to publish a book that was to become a milestone in Soviet political as well as literary history. *One Day in the Life of Ivan Denisovich,* though written within the Leninist canon of the critique of Stalinism which Solzhenitsyn was to repudiate later on, was a shattering indictment not only of the past but also by implication of much of the present. Previous accounts of life in forced labor camps had reached but a limited reading public. This one, illuminated by the greatest talent in modern Russian literature, became a world as well as Soviet best seller. The man who persuaded Khrushchev and the Presidium to authorize the publication of Solzhenitsyn's novella was Alexander Tvardovsky, the poet and editor of *Novy Mir* (*The New World*), both the best and most liberal Soviet literary magazine. (It was Tvardovsky who in 1960 published the celebrated poem on Stalin, "Beyond the Horizon" with its startling lines: "Though alive, yet cut off from life by the Kremlin Wall, he stood over us like a dread spirit.")

The search for panaceas for the economy continued. The most drastic and "harebrained" one was the bifurcation of the Party apparatus. All Party organizations up to but not including the union republic level were split into two. Thus there would be two district first secretaries, one specializing in agricultural, the other in industrial affairs, two bureaus, etc. It would have been difficult to think of a reorganization that would mess up things more thoroughly; from the beginning there were bound to be unending jurisdictional disputes. Which part of the organization would look into the problem of fertilizer, repair of agricultural machinery, and so on? Who would handle general political and propaganda work? Within days of Khrushchev's fall this bifurcation was abolished.

But the most signal improvisation and failure of Khrushchev was the famed Cuban missile crisis.

It is necessary to consider briefly the international setting in which the crisis erupted: the first several months of 1962 witnessed a certain relaxation in international tensions insofar as the USSR was concerned. Public controversy between the Chinese and the Soviets was stilled, largely on the initiative of other Communist parties, for whom the dispute was a source of embarrassment and danger. Both Communist powers worked together at the Geneva conference on Laos to produce a neutralist government in the little Southeast Asian country.[6]

[6] Laos was in 1961 the scene of a rightist coup, helped by the C.I.A., that helped push out the previous neutralist government. This in turn brought the Soviet airlift of military supplies to pro-Communist forces. Eventually the powers responsible for the original 1954 neutralization assembled again and agreed to revert to the neutralist government of Souvanna Phouma.

The Berlin crisis continued with incidents—such as Soviet military planes buzzing passenger aircraft bound for West Berlin—notes, and harassments. But incongruously Secretary of State Rusk and Gromyko, meeting in Geneva in July, engaged also in talks on nuclear disarmament. It was agreed to take up this subject at the late fall meeting of the UN Assembly.

The coincidence of greater Chinese affability, the continuing impasse over Berlin, and nuclear disarmament discussion between the United States and the USSR was highly suggestive as to the Soviet motives in establishing launching facilities for nuclear missiles in Cuba. For that is what the Soviets began to do in greatest secrecy and in a great hurry, probably as early as in July. By September, now in feverish haste which precluded efficient camouflage, they began to erect the actual missile sites and emplacements. The target date for completion was in November—at about the same time that Khrushchev had announced he would appear before the UN Assembly in New York. Rumors of any untoward Soviet activities in Cuba were being vigorously denied by official sources.

On October 14 an American overflight of Cuba revealed that the USSR was constructing forty launching pads for medium- and intermediate-range missiles which when installed could rain nuclear warheads on the U.S. mainland. With these facts already in his possession but not revealed to the public, President Kennedy received Gromyko on October 18. The Soviet foreign minister informed the President that the German problem must be solved promptly after the American congressional elections in November and that Khrushchev then might be meeting Kennedy.

On October 22 came Kennedy's speech revealing the crisis and informing the world that the United States would institute a blockade of Cuba. This was confrontation! An alert went out to the Soviet rocket, air, and submarine forces. There followed hurried communications between the President and Khrushchev. By the twenty-eighth the crisis was over: The USSR agreed to withdraw its missile installations from Cuba.

The most reasonable explanation of the whole maneuver is that the Soviets aimed to use the nuclear bases in Cuba as a bargaining counter to force the United States to sign a German peace treaty on Soviet terms. And it is likely that Khrushchev still hoped somehow to use the Cuban gambit as the means of preventing China from acquiring nuclear weapons. Quite possibly he would have demanded that the United States remove its nuclear weapons from the Pacific in return for a Chinese pledge, or perhaps he would have also demanded that America lift its protection of Taiwan. The whole package as well as the revelation that the USSR did have nuclear weapons in the Caribbean would be revealed presumably on his visit to New York and the UN in November.

It is most unlikely that the Chinese would have agreed to any deal. But now, in addition to their fury over Soviet trickery, they were also incensed over official Soviet neutrality in the frontier war that broke out in October between China and India. Peking's reaction to the lame Soviet excuse that the missiles were being placed in Cuba to protect it from an American attack won a withering rejoinder: "Without consulting anybody you willfully embarked on a reckless course and irresponsibly played with the lives of millions upon millions of people."

Mutual relief about the two superpowers' having been so close to and then having drawn back from the brink brought a kind of Soviet-American détente. Chastened, Khrushchev abandoned the Berlin gambit. In 1963 the USSR, the United States, and Great Britain would sign a test ban on all except underground nuclear explosions. The treaty was to be open to other powers for signature. West Germany would sign, China would not, and in 1964 the Chinese would explode a nuclear device.

The mere fact of the treaty brought a further escalation of the Sino-Soviet conflict. There was a public exchange of letters and of abuse between the central committees of the two "fraternal" parties. Its tone may be gauged from a passage from a Chinese missive. "The Soviet government . . . is insolent enough to say that we are able to criticize them only because China enjoys the protection of Soviet nuclear weapons. Well then, leaders of the Soviet Union, please continue to protect us awhile with your nuclear weapons. We shall continue to criticize you, and we hope you will have the courage to argue the matter out with us."

In addition to the direct challenge that the dispute posed for the Soviet Union, it loosened the hold of the USSR over world communism. A few Communist parties embraced the Chinese side entirely, following the example of Albania. Some found the quarrel between the giants a convenient occasion for trying to maneuver between the two and to extract support from both. This was the game the Communists of North Vietnam were to play with such momentous consequences. But even within the Soviet sphere Rumania was able, very largely because of Chinese support, to emancipate itself to a very considerable degree from Soviet domination and to pursue a course almost as independent of Russia as that of Yugoslavia.

But the most dangerous element of the dispute was undoubtedly its territorial aspect. Border incidents along the Sino-Soviet, the world's longest state frontier, had become quite frequent. In August 1964 Mao himself, in an interview given to a group of Japanese, branded the Soviet Union as an imperialist power: "The Russians took everything they could." And how about those vast areas in Asia that the Russian state had detached from China ever since the seventeenth century? How about Mongolia?

The fact that the Chinese attacks centered especially on Khrushchev might well have prolonged his tenure in office. Other leaders would not want to give the impression that a foreign attack could affect their decisions. And so in February 1964, at a Central Committee meeting, the senior Presidium member Mikhail Suslov declared: "The Chinese leaders, and not only they, should get it through their thick skulls that our Central Committee, headed by this faithful Leninist, Nikita Khrushchev, is more than ever united and monolithic." But this was a fib worthy of Nikita Sergeevich himself.

Cornered on both domestic and foreign issues, Khrushchev grew, from the point of view of his colleagues, increasingly irresponsible and erratic. He threw out the slogan that the USSR was on the way to becoming the "state of the whole people," which to some suggested a veiled attempt to derogate from the authority of the Party. That there might have been something to that interpretation is forcibly brought out by Khrushchev's last, and for him fatal, improvisation. Ever since 1962, meetings of the highest Soviet organs—beginning with the Central Committee, but by 1964 occasionally also of the Presidium and of the Council of Ministers—were held in the presence of outsiders, sometimes hundreds of them. These were Party activists and supposedly experts on the subjects being discussed, but there is no doubt that the main reason for this innovation, shocking to any conservative member of the Soviet establishment, was to stifle any criticism of the First Secretary by inhibiting other leaders and in a way to "pack" the highest policy-making organs.

In October Khrushchev took a vacation in the Crimea, from where he conversed with a trio of Soviet cosmonauts orbiting the earth. In his absence the plot ripened. On the fourteenth, having heard reports from Suslov and Shelepin, an erstwhile protégé of the First Secretary whom he had elevated to the head of the security apparatus, the Central Committee "acceded to the plea" of N. S. Khrushchev that on account of his advanced age and ailments (he was a vigorous seventy) he be released from his state and Party duties. Brezhnev took over as first secretary, Kosygin as prime minister. This time there was no reversal: brought from the Crimea, one assumes under guard, Khrushchev was informed both of "his" request and the decision.

For all his "harebrained" ways, Khrushchev undoubtedly pushed internal liberalization and relaxation much further than would have been the case had the Molotov or Malenkov wing of the Party remained in ascendance. He had a populistic streak in his nature that made him attack Stalinism more strongly than would have been urged by sheer political calculation. His legacy in foreign affairs was more dubious. Again he probably meant well: desired peaceful coexistence and détente but went about it in an oversubtle and truly "hare-brained" manner, which almost brought about what he feared most. His bluffs, bravado, the irresponsible sponsorship of "wars of national liberation" everywhere under the sun, as well as nuclear missile rattling, were to contribute to future fearful crises in Southeast Asia and in the Near East.

It is characteristic that the fall of the man who, for all his huge faults, helped improve both the material well-being and the feeling of personal security of the Soviet citizen aroused no discernible emotion among the population at large. For the Party oligarchs Khrushchev, who had freed them from the constant fear under which they lived in Stalin's time, had of late become an embarrassment and a threat. They now opted for a real collective leadership, without the choleric man with his continuous gambles and improvisations. In brief and paradoxically, Khrushchev, by humanizing Soviet politics, prepared the way for his own removal, and while he abolished and decried tyranny he did not advance the course of freedom.

9.
The Ascendance of Bureaucracy

Stabilization of the Political Structure

Khrushchev fell because he lost the support of the same element that enabled him to prevail in 1953–57, the local Party secretaries. The local bosses were behind him when he dismantled most of the machinery of terror and subordinated the security apparatus, as threatening to them as it was oppressive to the rank-and-file citizen. But once the First Secretary subdued the narrower oligarchy of Stalin's former henchmen he in turn became a threat to the bureaucracy. He acted erratically, vented his frustrations by firing on the spot this or that official, and seemed in his campaign against Stalinism to threaten some features of the Soviet system in which the Party bosses had a stake. Hence there was no opposition in the Central Committee when the Presidium plot unseated Khrushchev. The new pattern of leadership, though it was determined by the "big boys"—i.e., the Presidium—rather than by some three hundred members of the Central Committee, still conformed to the desires of the bureaucracy. It would be much more "collective" than before. No single person would be allowed to dominate public attention or to give the impression that he was the leader. (By 1972, however, Brezhnev's public stature would become more than that of just the first among equals.) Hence the post of head of the Party was separated from that of head of the government. Khrushchev, born in 1894, had joined the Party before the Stalin era (in 1918). His successors' formative years were spent in ascending the administrative ladder under Stalin. Brezhnev (b. 1906) had been made a member of the central Secretariat in 1952. Kosygin (b. 1904) had held a number of ministerial positions beginning in the late thirties and rose to the Politburo in 1948. Both of them had suffered temporary eclipses following Stalin's death, but by 1960 were on the Presidium. In the eyes of the typical bureaucrat, here were two "safe" men with none of the populistic impulses of their predecessor who would keep de-Stalinization and liberalization within safe limits and pursue prudent foreign policy. Two other veterans, Mikhail Suslov and Nicholas Podgorny, would also be prominent in shaping Soviet policies during the next decade. Suslov, a Party secretary since 1947, would continue in charge of ideological and propaganda affairs as well as being the principal figure in liaison with foreign Communist parties. Podgorny, who took over from Anastas Mikoyan as official head of the state in 1965, would also play an important role in decision making.

By the previous Soviet standards the transition was decorous. The fallen leader was retired on pension, with no opprobrious charges of treason or "anti-Party" activity being given out. Just incompetence! In fact his name would hardly be mentioned in public during the remaining eight years of his life. (One such occasion was the disavowal of his memoirs, which appeared in print in the West. Though undoubtedly genuine, *Khrushchev Remembers* (Vol. I, 1970; Vol. II, 1974) contains little in the way of revelation.) A few of those closest to Khrushchev were demoted, but nothing in the nature of a purge—in a way, testimony to how isolated Khrushchev had become during his last months at the top.

Public announcements stressed (not completely truthfully) that the new team would not reverse the process of liberalization nor abandon the search for peaceful coexistence. There was a short-lived détente in Sino-Soviet relations. In 1964, on the anniversary of the November Revolution, a high-ranking Chinese delegation headed by Chou En-lai arrived in Moscow. But the new leaders disappointed the Chinese hopes. Of course, for the time being the tone of the dispute became much more subdued. The meeting of several Communist parties planned by Khrushchev to lead to a resounding condemnation of Peking, if not indeed to the exclusion of China from the Communist family, was postponed. But no more than Khrushchev would Brezhnev and Kosygin appease the Chinese through pursuing more militant policies vis-à-vis the West. For some time the Soviet leaders had suspected, and said so now, that Peking's aim was nothing else than to provoke a war between the United States and the USSR—thus neatly paralleling the Chinese Communists' suspicion that the Soviets would be pleased by a confrontation between the United States and the People's Republic.

As the experience of several years had shown, any accommodation between the two Communist giants was bound to be temporary. Though China's dictator was by now staunchly anti-Russian, Soviet sources undoubtedly exaggerated in attributing all the trouble to Mao and his "clique." (The basic issues in the dispute transcended personalities and thus one must take with a grain of salt Soviet insinuations that such officials as Marshal Peng and Liu Shao-chi were disgraced because of their "internationalist"—read pro-Moscow—orientation.) Symbolic of the continued Chinese intention to needle the Russians was Chou En-lai's gesture before leaving Moscow: once more, and ostentatiously, the Prime Minister deposited a floral wreath at Stalin's tomb.

Peking's basic fear was, and remains, the possibility of a thoroughgoing accommodation between the USSR and the United States. To prevent such a turn of events, Communist China had long encouraged more militant Communist tactics throughout the world. This then put the USSR in an embarrassing position. The Kremlin, while seeking détente, at the same time proclaimed its support of "wars of liberation"—i.e., Communist and radical movements that pursued guerrilla tactics, whether in areas under outright Western domination (such as the Portugese colonies) or under Western influence (such as South Vietnam). By encouraging more militant activities from those movements, the Chinese were putting the Soviets on the spot: if the latter were to show themselves lukewarm in their support of "liberation movements," Peking had a potent propaganda argument in its rivalry with Moscow among other Communist parties and in the Third World. And Soviet *material* support for insurrectionary activities, whether in the Congo or Vietnam, was bound to frustrate attempts at a rapprochement with the United States.

Thus it cannot be a complete coincidence that 1960, the year when the Sino-Soviet dispute became acute, was also the time when the Third Congress of the Communist Party of North Vietnam stressed the importance of freeing the South from "American imperialism" and that the National Front for the Liberation of South Vietnam (NLF) was created. Vietnam was a promising place to provoke an indirect American-Soviet confrontation. In 1963–64, the tempo of guerrilla activities in the South quickened and so did the American involvement. The Soviet role in the momentous events of 1964–65 is still unclear. But the Russians may well have surmised or learned through their intelligence channels that, following the presidential election of 1964, the Americans would step up their activity in Vietnam. In January 1965, according to the Chinese, the Soviet government transmitted to North Vietnam American proposals that it stop supporting the Vietcong. In February 1965, Kosygin went to Hanoi to ascertain North Vietnam's military capacity and needs, and ap-

Kosygin calls on Mao Tse-tung, Peking, February, 1965.

parently to urge the Ho Chi Minh regime to exercise restraint in supporting the Vietcong. But as Kosygin was negotiating in Hanoi, the Americans staged their first bombing attack on North Vietnam, supposedly as a reprisal for the Vietcong raid at the American base at Pleiku in the South.

The bombings, as the Chinese had hoped, did put the Russians on the spot. Vietnam now became a testing ground not only for the Americans' theories on how to cope with wars of liberation, but also for the Soviet readiness and ability to protect a Communist regime from the superior power of the United States. Soviet failure to react sharply to the bombings would have eroded Moscow's credibility as the protector of Communist movements and states, and would have "proven" the Chinese thesis that Russia was not a fit leader of world communism.

On his way to and from Hanoi, Kosygin stopped in Peking, and on the second occasion Mao deigned to grant him an audience. But while aggravating Soviet-American relations, Vietnam did not bring about a Sino-Soviet reconciliation. Far from it! The Soviets proposed, again the Chinese sources reveal, to step up material aid to Hanoi and to try to discourage the Americans from further escalation by tough talk, including the threat of sending "volunteers" to North Vietnam. In pursuance of these goals they asked Peking for air bases on

Chinese soil in order to expedite the transit of supplies and "advisers." But to Mao and his entourage these proposals not only fell short of what was required in the emergency, but were suspect in themselves. Massive Soviet help to North Vietnam and the introduction of Russian military specialists there would increase Soviet leverage in Hanoi—and then the USSR would "sell out" North Vietnam!

As the official Chinese source, the *Peking Review*,[1] put it: "If we were to take united action on the question of Vietnam with the new leaders of the CPSU who are pursuing the Khrushchev revisionist line, wouldn't we be helping them to bring the question of Vietnam within the orbit of Soviet–U.S. collaboration?" The Russians, by giving some help to North Vietnam, were in fact trying "to keep the situation under their control, to gain a say on the North Vietnam question and to strike a bargain with U.S. imperialism on it." The Chinese position was understandable: the Soviet Union was supposed to help Hanoi through pressuring the United States elsewhere, say in Germany. As for Vietnam, this was China's bailiwick, and the extent and type of help furnished to the North and the guerrillas in the South was to be decided by China.

The Chinese allegations undoubtedly reflected the Peking regime's bitterness at the Soviet maneuvers and disappointment that the Vietnamese affair did not lead to a sharper clash between the United States and the Soviet Union. Each step in the escalation of the American involvement in the civil war in South Vietnam and in the bombing of the North brought new, if vague, threats from Moscow. But in fact Soviet help to the North would be confined to military supplies, especially a sophisticated antiaircraft missile system that would make the Americans raids increasingly costly. At the same time, Moscow kept reiterating its willingness to assist in a peaceful solution of the conflict, provided it met at least some of the postulates of North Vietnam and of the NLF.

The situation in Southeast Asia presented some potential dangers as well as actual inconveniences for the USSR. During the first phase of the crisis, one could not be sure that in their desperation the Americans would not take some action (such as an invasion of the North or mining approaches to its ports) that would put pressure on the USSR to go beyond the safe and relatively inexpensive measures of helping North Vietnam with military supplies and diplomacy-propaganda. (The total cost of military hardware for the Soviets has been estimated at $700–800 million per annum, as against American expenditures on the war on the order of $30 billion.)

[1] Issue of November 12, 1965.

Beyond this danger the Vietnam crisis put obvious restraints on any steps the Soviet Union might take in seeking a broad détente with the United States as well as in dealing more resolutely with the Chinese problem. From the vantage point of foreign Communists, this was not the moment to deepen the Sino-Soviet rift or to read China out of the Communist family of nations. The meeting of Communist parties held in Moscow between March 1 and 5, with China the main item on the agenda, was thus bound to end in failure: of the twenty-six parties invited, only eighteen attended, North Vietnam and Rumania being conspicuous by their absence. Obviously no concrete decisions could be made without incurring the risk of an irreconcilable split in world communism.

As it was, the Sino-Soviet relations did take a turn for the worse, but mainly because of Chinese actions. On March 4, 1965, the Soviet authorities organized a "spontaneous" demonstration before the American embassy in Moscow to protest the latest American bombings of North Vietnam. But then the demonstration did in fact become spontaneous, for the Chinese students who were in its forefront broke through the police cordon and manhandled Soviet militiamen, a novel spectacle for Moscow citizens. This was the last straw. The Chinese students were expelled and on their arrival home received a heroes' welcome. Trivial in itself, this incident was the portent of the tempestuous relations between Peking and Moscow during the next few years. There would be actual military clashes along the Sino-Soviet border. The tone of the Chinese press about the Soviet Union and its "revisionist" leaders would reach a level of vituperation surpassing the already considerable achievement in this respect during Khrushchev's last years.

The Sino-Soviet split colored Soviet policies toward two other major events of 1965 in Asia. Ever since 1958 the Soviet Union had supported the Congress regime in India, hoping a strong India would prove a barrier to the spread of Chinese influence in Asia. Peking, for its part, established intimate ties with Pakistan. An eruption of the Pakistan-India military conflict in August brought a Soviet offer to arbitrate the dispute, mainly to prevent China from intervening on the side of Pakistan. In January 1966, in Tashkent, Kosygin mediated the dispute between the heads of the governments of India and Pakistan and effected a reconciliation that postponed further India-Pakistan clashes for five years, a diplomatic success for the USSR and a setback for Communist China.

Even more damaging to Peking's ambition to become the arbiter of Asian politics was an event in Indonesia. On September 30 the failure of a Communist coup there led to a bloody suppression by the army. It is estimated that the number of victims of anti-Communist terror was on the order of 100,000. The army then took over, with President Sukarno, of late an ally of the Communists, first relegated to a figurehead, then dismissed and imprisoned. This, the most serious setback of Asian communism since the Korean War, was met by the Soviets with more than equanimity: the Indonesian Communists as well as Sukarno had for some time been squarely in Peking's camp. The USSR did not do as much as suspend diplomatic relations with the new Djakarta regime. Peking thus had new and ample evidence of Soviet perfidy.

When the Twenty-third Congress of the Communist Party of the Soviet Union assembled on March 29, 1966, the main lines of Soviet foreign policy in the post-Khrushchev era were firmly set. The USSR would pursue its attempts at a rapprochement with the United States, at the same time continuing its material and diplomatic-propaganda help to North Vietnam. On China, the new leaders adopted the posture of patience and restraint, but with an undertone of an unmistakable warning to Peking not to abuse Soviet patience. The invitation to the Chinese Communists to attend this festive conclave in Moscow with other fraternal parties brought forth the Chinese rejoinder that they would be glad to come at some future day after the true revolutionaries in the CPSU ejected their revisionist leaders and other "lackeys of imperialism." The Chinese were joined in their boycott by the Albanians, the Japanese Communists, and some minor Asian parties. The Soviets did not try, and wisely, to match the Chinese level of vituperation, preferring to refer to the dispute in lofty generalities. Said Brezhnev, "Life has shown that departures from Marxism-Leninism, whether of the left or right variety, become especially dangerous when they are combined with symptoms of nationalism, great power chauvinism, and striving for world hegemony." He was speaking of China!

The fissures in world communism were smoothed over but could not be quite concealed by the new leaders' prudence and restraint. (It is easy to imagine what Khrushchev's rhetoric and threats over the Americans in Vietnam or Peking's opprobrious language would have been!) To some of the foreign guests, including of course the North Vietnamese but also the Cubans (now full-fledged members of the Communist family), the USSR was *not* doing enough in the struggle against American imperialism. But to the majority of foreign Communists Soviet tactics and activity in North Vietnam represented just the right mixture of defiance of American imperialism on behalf of a fraternal Communist state and of prudence. There was, however, veiled criticism of other aspects of Soviet policy. The Italian Communists stressed their party's interest in broader intellectual freedom, a transparent reproach about the renewed Soviet campaign for ideological conformity in the arts. Rumania's leader, Ceausescu, again in Aesopian language, castigated the Soviets' interference in other Communist countries' internal affairs. Peace, he said, required the observance "of national sovereignty and independence, equality, noninterference in internal affairs . . . of the sacred right of every nation to decide for itself its own fate and to choose . . . the nature of its political, economic and social development." Rumania was still playing with gusto the role of *enfant terrible* of the Soviet bloc. Member of the Warsaw Treaty organization and of COMECON (Council for Mutual Economic Assistance—the economic organization of the Communist bloc countries in Europe plus Mongolia set up in 1949 as an answer to the Marshall Plan organization), the Balkan country was enjoying cordial relations with China as well as expanding its commercial and other links with the West. That it was cultivating such links puts in proper perspective Chinese claims that their main objection to the Soviet leadership was ideological, that is, based on the Kremlin's allegedly revisionist policies at home, as well as its sinful contacts with the West. In both these respects Rumania's leaders went far beyond Russia's. The real reason for Peking's attachment to Rumania was obviously that country's fairly independent course vis-à-vis the USSR.

One should not, however, exaggerate the extent of the disunion of the Communist bloc. Soviet power was for the ruling Communist parties a guarantee of their rule, for the nonruling ones the main ingredient of their hope of achieving power one day. Where would they all be should the Soviet Union decline as a world power, or should it publicly profess loss of interest in supporting and advancing the course of world communism? And so the Rumanians, for all their determination to be bosses in their own country, were far from daring or even wishing for a definite break with Moscow. The Italian Communists might publicly criticize the USSR for the extent of intellectual repression there (and in 1968 for the invasion of Czechoslovakia) but this was largely for the benefit of the non-Communist left in their own country whom they were wooing.

For most Communist parties, the Sino-Soviet split was an embarrassment and a potential danger, though some, as we have seen, used it to escape (Albania) or to loosen (Rumania) their ties to the USSR. By the some token, not only traditionalism but also more tangible considerations would keep the majority of them within the Soviet camp. The USSR was still vastly more powerful than its rival and in a position to do more for its foreign followers than China. The latter's partisans would be attracted by special considerations or by the fact that the Chinese brand of Communism was currently more revolutionary and, hence, exciting. This was responsible for a certain popularity it had among the youth and intellectuals even within those Communist parties that remained pro-Soviet.

On domestic affairs the Twenty-third Congress marked a year and a half of the stewardship of the new team of Brezhnev and Kosygin. (According to the Party statutes, the Congress should have been held in 1965, four years having elapsed since the last one.) Both their record and the prospects for the future outlined by the leaders must have gladdened the assembly, composed as it was for the most part of Party and state bureaucrats. The new course, the new style of leadership, partook of none of the sins of "subjectivism, voluntarism, boastfulness and 'from aboveness' " in which a certain leader—not once was Khrushchev identified by name—had indulged prior to October 1964. There were no more lurid revelations about Stalin and the "Anti-Party group"; again, it was rather a remarkable achievement that the dread name was not pronounced even once during ten days of speeches. There had evidently been some thought given before the Congress to a partial rehabilitation of Stalin. A number of leading intellectual and literary figures had been prompted to write a letter to Brezhnev imploring him not to do this and, what was more decisive, fears had been expressed at the highest Party levels that such a rehabilitation, reviving old fears and painful associations, would be most untimely. And so only very indirect and symbolic steps were taken in this direction. The highest Party official was once again named *general* secretary; it was awkwardly explained that the title was "established in 1922 on the initiative of V. I. Lenin, and used later." The Presidium reverted to its pre-1952 name of the Politburo. Such bows to the past, in themselves harmless, still signified the determination to arrest the dangerous trend started by Khrushchev. The flood of revelations about Stalinism had ceased: he himself would not be fully rehabilitated, but his official image would now be that of neither god nor beast, but of an outstanding Party leader who had committed some mistake. (There must be some suspicion that the most damaging documents from the pre-1953 era have now been put through the shredder.) This partial and discreet refurbishing of the image of the despot and of his rule was, of course, connected with an equally discreet but discernible shift in current policies.

Ideological and intellectual controls were being tightened. Some weeks before the Congress, two dissident writers, Andrei Sinyavsky and Yuli Daniel, were sentenced to several years of penal exile.[2] The

2 The two of them had for years written "underground" articles and short stories (circulated clandestinely in the USSR and published abroad), critical or satirical about various aspects of Soviet reality, under the pseudonyms Abram Tertz (Sinyavsky) and Arzhak (Daniel). The secret police must have known for some time the true identity of the writers, but decided to take steps against them only after October 1964.

Congress heard from a Party official what might be described as a classical definition of artistic freedom in the USSR: While everybody in the Soviet Union was free to say and write what he wanted, "by the same token the Party and our state organs are free to decide what to publish." And so Solzhenitsyn's future works would not be licensed for publication, and the outstanding Soviet exponent of liberalism in the arts, Alexander Tvardovsky, was dropped by the Central Committee. For some this was not enough; Mikhail Sholokhov, the dean of Soviet writers, lately known for his toadying ways toward whoever is currently in power, raved and ranted how in the old days people like Sinyavsky and Daniel would not have gotten off with a few years in a penal camp, but would have been "stood against the wall" (i.e., shot).

Cultural life in the USSR had been the main battleground of liberalization, and so tightening up of ideological and intellectual controls had a significance going far beyond its consequences for writers and artists. Political *opposition* in the sense that the term is understood in the West was, and remains, inconceivable in the Soviet Union; one cannot, for obvious reasons, start a party or movement that challenges the establishment and solicit popular support. (In the early sixties there were evidently some small clandestine student groups organized in a few universities, but almost immediately they were broken up by the KGB, with all the usual consequences.) What the death of Stalin and the consequent abolition of mass terror had made possible (but far from safe) was political *dissent:* an individual or a group (usually a handful of intellectuals) would try to propagate ideas critical of some aspects of the Soviet regime, or (much less frequently) of communism as such, not with any expectation that the activity would bring down the system or even attract wide popular support, but simply in the hope that it might incline the rulers to be less repressive and/or to put into effect what until now had been purely decorative aspects of the Soviet constitution (such as the one prohibiting imprisonment without judicial sanction and a public trial). Political dissent has been both a frustrating and a hazardous enterprise: frustrating because no sensible dissenter could believe that his activity would *force* the regime to do something, but would merely hope against hope that the more sensible members of the oligarchy would be persuaded or shamed into the realization of the absurdity and inhumanity of many restrictions on personal and intellectual freedom; hazardous because the most optimistic of dissenters had to realize that public voicing of demands, even as seemingly innocuous as that the regime should abide by some of the provisions of the constitution, might bring him consequences ranging from losing his job to exile in a penal colony or incarceration in a psychiatric institution. (The last type of political chicanery, not unheard of under the tsars, has, especially during the last decade, often been used against dissenters, people of undoubted sanity being committed to mental clinics, some allegedly run by the KGB.)

Political activism has thus been (with exceptions we shall note later on) a fairly hopeless venture, with those indulging in it fully conscious that their activities have a symbolic and at most a long-range effect. But a much more important and effective breach in the conformity was opened in the fifties and early sixties, through literature and the arts. Those who, like Solzhenitsyn in his *One Day,* tried to depict the horrors of Stalinism hoped, whether consciously or unconsciously, to humanize the regime and to make impossible a relapse into the barbarism of the thirties and forties. This genre flourished between 1956 and 1965, when it was driven underground. There were a number of memoirs by survivors of the forced-labor camps, laudatory biographies of the most prominent military figures destroyed by Stalin (such as Blyukher and Tukhachevsky) and of some of the political victims of the purge (with the notable exception of those tried in the Moscow trials and, almost superfluous to add, of Trotsky), as well as a number of novels and short stories by such popular Soviet writers as Konstantin Simonov and Victor Nekrasov, all of them in varying degree critical of the recent past. But beyond stigmatizing Stalinism, the writers also criticized by implication some of the features of the current political and cultural scene. An unspoken premise of much of this writing, as well as of parallel attempts to breach the old taboos and discard the Stalinist stereotypes in the arts, historiography, etc., was that greater intellectual and artistic freedom would erode what still remained of the repressive and obscurantist in the Soviet regime. Alas, this was precisely the reason why Khrushchev's successors decided both to curtail frankness about the past and to devise new limits to artistic and intellectual freedom. They would not want, nor would it be possible, to shut this Pandora's box as tight as it had been before 1953, but the Twenty-third Party Congress marked a clear determination of the ruling oligarchy to reverse, albeit prudently and gradually, the trend that had started at the Twentieth with the "secret" speech. Now one of the chief oligarchs was quite explicit in squashing hopes for a continued or increased tolerance. It was vile slander (sic!) said Podgorny, to talk "about 'liberalization' of our socialist society which is supposed to be developing, if you please, in the direction of convergence with the so-called free world."

The post-Khrushchev regime did not, however, propose to turn the clock back. If there was to be an end to the liberalization in the intellectual sphere and no modification in the one-party/police-state pattern of the Soviet system, then the regime proposed to pay more attention to the needs of the citizen as consumer. Khrushchev had been full of promises on that count. He had stressed the difference between the Chinese model of what might be called ascetic communism, and what he once for the benefit of his Hungarian audience called "goulash communism." But he was far from being consistent in pursuing this goal, and his administrative and policy improvisations proved counterproductive. His successors learned from his mistakes: not administrative pyrotechnics and extravagant promises but carefully thought-out schemes of reform would be the means they would employ to restore the Soviet economy to an even keel. The most "harebrained" of Khrushchev's administrative designs, his bifurcation of the Party administration, was abrogated within weeks of his overthrow. In 1965 another of the main administrative reforms of the past decade was reversed. The system of regional economic councils (*sovnarkhozy*) established in 1957 had not been functioning well. There were repeated complaints about "localism"—i.e., the economic councils, which were to a large extent based on political divisions, concentrating excessively on the needs of the given region, rather than having the overall economic problem in sight. And so the Brezhnev-Kosygin team restored the supervision of the national economy through ministries, virtually abolishing the local economic councils. This brought back a profusion of industrial ministries—about forty at present—and in a sense once again substituted the inherent defects of overcentralization for those of "localism." But there can be little question that, from the perspective of 1976, Soviet economic administration has functioned more efficiently during the past decade than before.

Bureaucratic reorganizations within the Soviet experience (barring the most "harebrained" ones!) have had an effect somewhat similar to the one a new coach has on a team in this country: buoyed up by change and a new atmosphere, things are likely to go better for a while, but then the level of performance of the team or of, say, the chemical industry reverts to the old pattern. Yet there is little doubt that the Brezhnev-Kosygin team has managed to instill greater efficiency in Soviet economic administration. The number-two man in the regime, Kosygin, had long experience as an industrial manager and minister rather than on the Party side, and many members of the ruling oligarchy had their higher education as engineers. Of course, under the Soviet system there is no room for an independent managerial class. The Party continues to control all branches of administration, including economic, through the so-called *nomenklatura* system. This means that appropriate Party organs must approve appointments of industrial managers, trade union officials, etc. For larger enterprises this power is exercised by the cadres department of the Secretariat of the Central Committee of the CPSU. But freed both from Stalinist terror and from Khrushchev's constant improvisations, the Soviet economic bureaucracy could perform more professionally.

The Twenty-third Congress exemplified the more realistic course the new rulers proposed to adopt in regard to the economy. There was to be no more attempt to obscure its basic defects through such spectaculars as space shots and new records in steel production. The Soviet space program continued, but no longer on the scale and with the emphasis which in the late fifties and early sixties contributed to the panicky feeling in the United States that America was now outdistanced technologically. Having squeezed out the last ounce of propaganda value from such "firsts" as the original Sputnik and Gagarin's space flight in 1961, the Soviets deemphasized the program, allowing that such American feats as the landings on the moon had but little scientific or technological value. It was now freely admitted that the increase in agricultural production during the past five years had failed to keep pace with the growth of population; that in some years, as in 1963, production of cattle, hogs, and milk had fallen substantially. Even before the Congress, the leadership took steps to succor this almost perennially sick sector of the Soviet economy. Investments in agriculture were doubled, prices for state purchases from the collective farms increased. At the congress it was announced that the government would soon summon a Union-wide Congress of Collective Farms to legislate a new structure for the kolkhozes. (Actually it did not meet until 1969, the delay a testimony as to how divisive an issue agriculture remains.) Following the Twenty-third Congress, the cumbersome system of remuneration of kolkhoz members based on the so-called labor day and dependent on the fluctuating production of the collective farm as a whole was abandoned in favor of the regular wage system. Another step meant to bridge the social and material gap between the industrial and farm laborer was the extension to the collective farmer of social security benefits.

The general character of economic measures adopted since Khrushchev's removal indicated that his successors proposed to continue, but in a more sober and systematic way, his "goulash communism"—i.e., without abandoning the traditional Soviet emphasis on heavy industry, they aimed to expand the production of consumers' goods; indeed they believed that at this point in the Soviet Union's development further advance on the industrial front was dependent on satisfying the consumer's needs in a more comprehensive way than had hitherto been the case. The projected rate of increase in the production of consumers' goods was to be *almost* equal to that of heavy industry. The rise of the consumer as a figure of some importance in the Soviet oligarchs' calculations was perhaps best symbolized by the decision to encourage private ownership of automobiles. Khrushchev (and rather perceptively, from the American perspective in this era of energy crisis and of concern about pollution) believed that it was preferable to stress public transportation and to provide opportunities for private citizens to rent rather than to own cars. It was announced at the Twenty-third Congress that the Soviet Union's automobile production was to be four times as great by 1970 as in 1965. Western capital and expertise (through contracts with Western automobile producers for plants in the USSR) were to be enlisted to bring the Soviet citizen into the automotive age.

Indeed one must suspect that the rulers, whether consciously or unconsciously, intended to prevent the rise of any widespread opposition to the persistence of authoritarian controls by putting more effort and resources into raising the standard of living. Beguiled by the increasing availability of motor cars, washing machines, and color television sets, the Soviet man in the street was unlikely, so this reasoning runs, to long for the forbidden fruit of Western-style freedoms. In place of mass terror as under the Stalin regime, and the revival of the Party élan as under Khrushchev's, Brezhnev and Kosygin proposed to concentrate on "consumerism" as the means of preventing any widespread pressure for political and social reforms.

In pursuit of this goal the rulers have been handicapped by certain inherent defects in the Soviet economy. It has been geared to a high level of performance on certain priorities, mainly industrial targets, hence the achievements in heavy industry, in developing a highly sophisticated level of military technology, the head start the Soviets obtained in the space competition, etc. Equally obviously the Soviet economy has lagged behind the market economies—i.e., those of the West plus Japan—in productivity of labor and especially the quality of goods in the consumer sector.

Since 1965 the Soviet regime has sought to deal with this dilemma in a twofold manner. First it has tried to enlist Western (again, also Japanese) technology and capital for economic development of the country. Thus an Italian consortium undertook in the late sixties to build an automotive factory in Kama. There is no question that the Soviets' own resources and technology would have been adequate to construct a factory on this scale. But it was believed to be cheaper to hire Western capital and expertise—that is, an equivalent amount of Soviet capital would produce more in another branch of the economy —for example, in the defense industry. In the seventies the Soviet government would intensify its efforts to engage Western and Japanese capital in the development of the country's vast resources. The Soviets have had hopes of enlisting Western technological help in the building of Russia's socialist economy since Lenin's time. Western help, such as Germany's, following Rapallo, did play a role in Russia's industrial recovery in the twenties. The thirties, with their spy mania and purges put an end to any significant economic collaboration with the West. In the sixties the USSR, no longer a backward country but the second industrial power in the world, again turned to the world market, not only to catch up to and overcome the still superior technology of the West, but also to correct the imbalance in its own economy.

Apart from hopes of a considerable infusion of foreign capital and technology, the regime placed its main wager on yet another major restructuring of industrial policy and administration. Complaints that the Soviet industrial structure is rigid and overcentralized and as such discourages initiative and innovation in individual enterprises have been constant themes in Soviet economic literature, practically from the first days of rapid industrialization. Equally insistent and usually victorious has been the counterargument that socialist planning requires centralized direction and detailed supervision of all branches of industry. Behind the latter, and probably decisive, has been the fear of the ruling Party oligarchy that any genuine decentralization of economic decision making might have untoward social and eventually political consequences, and the vested interest of top bureaucrats is always to preserve their own power and jobs. But following Stalin's death, an increasing number of Soviet economists and managers argued that the now more advanced state of the economy both allowed and made imperative a new system of industrial organization which, while preserving the ultimate control and planning prerogatives of the center, would, by bestowing greater autonomy on individual enterprises, provide a stimulus to innovation and invention. In addition to the inherent advantages of central planning, the Soviet economy thus garnered the benefits that accrue under capitalism through individual enterprises' competing for the market and thus having every incentive to reduce costs of production and to improve quality, two respects in which Soviet industry has for long been at a great disadvantage when compared with that of the West. One of the most insistent advocates of such reforms was Evsey Liberman, professor in a Ukrainian university. Liberman's rather unsensational thesis that profit should be made a more important criterion of economic performance was given prominence with the publication of an article of his in *Pravda* in 1962, an indication that his views had powerful supporters. "We should consider the use of profit as a yardstick or indicator of the effectiveness of the production activity of our enterprises."[3] The logical extension of this principle, Liberman and others of his ilk believed, should be a considerable decentralization of economic decision making, not in the sense of

[3] E. G. Liberman, *Economic Methods and the Effectiveness of Production,* New York, 1971, p. 60.

such reforms as Khrushchev's when territorial bureaucracies were partially substituted for the central one, but by giving more power to directors of individual industrial enterprises.

This economic discussion found a practical expression in a series of economic reforms announced by Kosygin in 1965, first to be applied to selective enterprises but then to be extended to the economy as a whole. Their main provision was to reduce the number of centrally determined targets for individual enterprises. Instead of about thirty categories of directives, the firm's director would now receive only eight. He would still have his quota of production-rules to be met and be told how much money he would have for wages, but it would now be up to him to decide how many workers his enterprise should employ, etc. The given firm's success in meeting and surpassing the given targets would, on a scale more generous than hitherto, bring bonuses for the director and technical personnel as well as the workers.

The 1965 reforms, which Kosygin promised at the Twenty-third Congress would be extended to all Soviet enterprises except agriculture by 1970, had as of that date been extended to a great majority of Soviet industrial firms. There were, both foreign and domestic economists agree, tangible benefits in terms of the managers' greater innovations and inventiveness. But the new system did not produce any economic miracles, and even the modest degree of decentralization inherent in it brought protests from the central bureaucracy. Thus under the reforms the managers could theoretically discharge superfluous workers, and this, many feared, would bring strains and tensions to the economy, which, according to the official creed, is not supposed to tolerate any even short-term unemployment. By 1971 the pendulum was to swing once more in the direction of centralization of economic administration.[4]

The reader might well conclude that the Soviet experience shows it is futile for a political system that represents the quintessence of bureaucracy in power to try to overcome defects inherent in bureaucratic management of a vast economy. In a sense the economic neatly parallels the political dilemma: Much as some individual members of the oligarchy are desirous of expanding the individual citizen's freedoms and of strengthening "socialist legality" against arbitrary proceedings by the KGB, they are still inhibited from carrying their reforming zeal to the point where the rule of the oligarchy itself may be threatened. The economic reforms of the sixties and their partial reversal in the early seventies represent then that cyclical pattern which will undoubtedly endure as long as the Soviet system itself.

[4] Paul R. Gregory and Robert C. Stuart, *Soviet Economic Structure and Performance,* New York, 1974, pp. 357–59.

But while acknowledging this fact, it would be unreasonable to deny that the Brezhnev–Kosygin regime has tackled the economic problems of the country in a more workmanlike fashion than its predecessors.

Following the Twenty-third Congress, the Brezhnev–Kosygin team was firmly in the saddle politically. Both men amply justified the expectation of the other oligarchs that they were "safe," unlikely to rock the boat or to exhibit inordinate passion for absolute power. Insofar as we know, the middle and late sixties were a period of virtual consensus among the top leadership as to the main lines of domestic and foreign policy. There were no basic splits such as had existed in Khrushchev's Politburo in the years 1953–57 between the Stalinist old guard and the reformers and after 1957 between the proponents of a cautious de-Stalinization and of a more basic one. Two personnel changes following the congress illustrate well the conservative policies of the recent era: added to the Politburo was Arvid Pelshe, former head of the Latvian Communist Party and a veteran of the secret police, but most characteristic from this point of view, a man in his late sixties. Marshal Voroshilov was restored to the Central Committee, a move of no direct importance in view of his venerable age, but symbolic of the new rulers' desire to appease even those still nostalgic about the Stalin era who felt outraged at the treatment meted out to Voroshilov at the Twenty-second Congress, when he was publicly humiliated by Khrushchev.

Human nature and the Soviet system being what they are, the apparent consensus within the ruling elite and the generally unadventurous character of most of its members could not preclude occasional brisk infighting and maneuverings for more influence and power. While neither desirous of nor in the position to make a bid for one-man rule, Brezhnev's first concern still had to be to curb his potential rivals for the top spot. Podgorny, who as the Central Committee secretary in charge of the crucial cadres section could have acted as a brake on Brezhnev's domination of the Party apparatus, was in 1965 transferred to the prestigious but much less influential position of official head of the state—chairman of the Presidium of the Supreme Soviet. Alexander Shelepin, another potential claimant for top leadership both on account of his relative youth (still in his forties) and his rapid advancement during the preceding few years—from head of the youth organization to that of the KGB, and then to the Politburo and the Secretariat—found himself also removed from too close a proximity to the most effective levers of power. The Party-state control committee of which he was chairman was disbanded in 1966. And in 1967 Shelepin was released as secretary of the Central Committee and appointed the boss of the trade unions, a time-consuming job but hardly promising as a power base. As between Brezhnev and Kosygin, there was for a long time a definite division of functions: the former concentrated on Party affairs as well as the world Communist movement, the latter had within his domain economic planning and administration as well as overall charge of foreign relations with non-Communist countries. It was only in the seventies that Brezhnev, with Kosygin's apparent acquiescence, assumed the ultimate direction of policies hitherto within the prime minister's sphere. The impression of continuity and stability of Soviet politics during the most recent period is strongly reinforced by the fact that about 80 percent of the previous membership of the Central Committee was reelected to the new one both at the Twenty-third Congress and at the Twenty-fourth (1971). Ways of resolving policy differences and personal rivalries have become, though it is prudent to suspend judgment as to how permanently, more civilized by contrast with those employed before 1964, not to mention the Stalin era!

Foreign Developments

The stability and "normalcy" of the Soviet political picture, if viewed in terms of its highest organs, contrasted drastically with the contemporary Chinese developments. For reasons that still are not completely clear, Mao and his partisans launched the Cultural Revolution, which between mid-1966 and 1969 plunged China into virtual anarchy. But one element in the campaign must have been Mao's conviction that he had to overcome his own oligarchy which, while promoting his "cult of personality," sought to turn the seventy-three-year-old chairman into a figurehead. While Stalin used secret police to decimate his bureaucracy, Mao's group employed fanatical youths, the Red Guards who invaded ministries and other institutions, beat and humiliated senior officials and "revisionist" Party leaders, as well as teachers, artists, and others hitherto constituting China's "establishment," and for good measure at times attacked foreign embassies, including that of the "revisionist" USSR. This was sheer anarchy, but at the instigation and on behalf of Chairman Mao and his officially designated deputy and successor, Marshal Lin Piao. (The latter may well have had his own reasons for promoting the excesses that then could be curbed only by the army under his command. In 1971 Lin died, allegedly in an airplane crash while fleeing to the USSR. Subsequently he was denounced as a traitor who had planned to overthrow the Great Helmsman.)

The upheaval led to the fall of some of the hitherto most powerful men in Communist China. Liu Shao-chi, until 1966 president of the republic and number-two figure in the regime, was denounced and arrested; several others, such as the Party's General Secretary Teng Hsiao-ping and Peking's Mayor Peng Chen, also fell. (Teng was restored to grace and high office in 1973.) In many places the local Party and state organs ceased to function, and it was only the army that preserved some semblance of authority throughout the country.

Whatever the political motivation behind this, one of the most bizarre of all revolutions, it reflected Mao's genuine conviction that a revolutionary upheaval once in a while is necessary to restore ideological purity and extirpate the noxious bourgeois and bureaucratic excrescences that are bound to develop within every successful revolution. There were touches of utter ludicrousness and of egalitarianism run wild. Schools and universities were shut down, distinguished professors and artists compelled to go to the countryside to be rehabilitated through physical labor. The supreme leader, while seen occasionally, preserved silence. His closest subordinates, including Lin and Chou En-lai (whose own position at one time was threatened by the young fanatics), would appear in public carrying the little red book of Chairman Mao's sayings.

The public reaction of the USSR to the events in China was one of amusement mixed with a certain apprehension and watchfulness. Up to a point, the developments played into the hands of the Soviet regime by baring to the world the full extent of instability and irrationality hitherto concealed behind the monolithic appearance of Mao's China. Several Communist parties until then in Peking's camp, such as Japan's, now switched back to Moscow's. By the same token, such instability in a country that was developing a stock of nuclear weapons and was acting provocatively toward the USSR—incidents continued along the Sino-Soviet border, culminating in 1969 in actual fighting between sizable military units—had to be a source of concern. We have no way of knowing whether the Soviets came close to intervening in China's internal struggles. (Some Russian sources were to claim that Liu Shao-chi and his faction represented the "internationalist" point of view—i.e., one opposed to Mao's anti-Soviet policies. But it is at least doubtful that any of the struggling factions was pro-Soviet, or that the Sino-Soviet relations were the main issue in the Cultural Revolution.) Still there must have been some temptation to profit from the trouble, perhaps even to destroy China's nuclear installations. But the risks inherent in such a policy would have been enormous and only a very close understanding with the United States—going far beyond mere détente, requiring a real alliance—would have persuaded the cautious men in the Kremlin to take such a hazardous step. But at that time, largely because of Vietnam, the United States and the USSR were hardly in a position to coordinate their policies.

While thus unable to resolve its most difficult foreign problem, the

Soviet regime still drew solid diplomatic benefits from China's internal strife, just as it was reaping them from the American overcommitment in Vietnam. China's troubles brought most of the errant foreign Communists back into Russia's fold, while the Americans' unpopular and unsuccessful war in Southeast Asia undermined confidence in the United States among its allies. General de Gaulle, who led France out of NATO, visited the USSR in 1966, the first time since President Poincaré visited Nicholas II that the head of the French Republic had stepped on Russian soil. (De Gaulle's wartime visit to the USSR had been as leader of the provisional French government.) The very flattering reception accorded de Gaulle—he was the first foreigner given the opportunity to inspect Soviet nuclear and space research facilities—reflected the Soviet leaders' satisfaction at the weakening of the Western network of alliances and at France's independent, indeed at times defiant, policy vis-à-vis the United States. To the west Europeans, including the Germans, the Soviet Union no longer appeared, as it had in the forties and fifties, as a clear and present danger which called for unity and reliance upon the United States, but as a powerful neighbor, still somewhat menacing, but one that could be propitiated and hopefully one day integrated into the European family. This shift in western Europe's stance was caused partly by its disunity and increasing social and political troubles, but also by skillful Soviet diplomacy. Thus the Kremlin was on the threshold of achieving what had been its objective ever since the end of World War II: the recognition by the West of the status quo—i.e., of Soviet domination in central and eastern Europe.

For all the formidable internal problems and foreign policy dilemmas, the fiftieth year of the Soviet regime found it in a strong position. Its main rivals were largely incapacitated—the United States by its involvement in Vietnam, China by the travails of the Cultural Revolution. Soviet influence now reached into the areas once the preserve of Western powers, but which the collapse of their empires left in a state of ferment. In practically every corner of the globe, the departure of Western rulers or the eruption of civil strife was followed by offers of aid from the USSR, often the arrival of Soviet advisers, economic "developers," and sometimes military experts. In black Africa's most populous and soon richest state, Nigeria, a civil war pitted the central government dominated by the Moslem north against an attempted secession of an ethnically and linguistically distinct southeast area, Biafra. While public opinion in the West was divided on the Nigerian issue—Biafra's struggle could be construed as a *real* war of national liberation—the Soviet government could throw its support without any compunctions to the stronger party. The northern Nigerians' victory enabled the USSR to garner the dividends of increased influence in this oil-rich country. (Communist China expressed its support for Biafra, for no other apparent reason than to be on the opposite side from Russia.) Another civil war in Yemen found two Arab countries supporting rival factions. The Egyptian army, which intervened on behalf of one, found itself unable to prevail over hostile tribesmen aided by Saudi Arabia until helped by Soviet supplies and instructors. With the British about to move out of neighboring Aden, Soviet influence now reached the Red Sea.

From the beginning of the Khrushchev era the rulers of the Soviet Union had conceived of their foreign task as consisting in a worldwide competition with the West, primarily with the United States. This competition before long transcended the traditional Soviet support for foreign Communist and radical movements. Thus in the Middle East the USSR offered at first diplomatic support and then economic and military aid to nationalist regimes that in some instances banned Communist parties and persecuted their leaders as long as these regimes were at cross-purposes with Western policy. As British and French influence in the area waned, especially after 1956, that of the Soviet Union grew. As against Washington, the great advantage Moscow enjoyed in courting the Arabs was of course that, besides giving them economic help and military supplies, it could also be unrestrainedly anti-Israel.

The Soviet stake in the Middle East grew, and by the middle sixties the area, from being what might be called a secondary theater of confrontation between the two superpowers, became a primary one. Several states there, notably Egypt, Syria and Iraq, were clients of the USSR, dependent on it for military supplies and diplomatic support to offset the power of Israel, supported by the United States. The Soviet navy established its presence in the Mediterranean, hitherto the exclusive preserve of the United States Sixth Fleet. The Soviet naval building program was vastly expanded in the 1960's, reflecting not only the lesson of the Cuban crisis of 1962, but also the Soviet Union's resolve to become a world naval power. Always strong in submarines, the Soviets now put a new emphasis on surface ships, launching new cruisers and helicopter carriers.

It would be difficult to ascertain the exact Soviet role in precipitating the 1967 Middle Eastern crisis. But it appears likely that without wanting a war in the area, the USSR desired a diplomatic victory, further attrition of U.S. prestige and influence, and a palpable proof to its Arab clients that it could protect their interests as against Israel. In the spring of 1967 Soviet intelligence sources alerted Cairo and Damascus that Israel, in the wake of repeated border incidents with Syria, planned a major blow against that country. In view of these reports President Nasser of Egypt, long taunted by Arab extremists for being lukewarm in his anti-Israel stance, demanded that the UN withdraw its emergency force, which, ever since 1956, had separated Israeli and Egyptian armies. UN Secretary U Thant incautiously complied with his request. On May 18 the entire UN force was withdrawn, including the tiny detachment that guarded the Strait of Tiran at the southern tip of the Gulf of Aqaba. The latter's presence enabled ships to and from Israel to navigate the gulf and to reach Eilat, a port of some significance for Israel since it enabled ships from Asia and Africa to bring goods into the country. But now Nasser, carried away by the momentum of his oratory, declared the Gulf of Aqaba, as he had previously the Suez Canal, banned to shipping to and from Israel.

At this point the Soviet leaders clearly forsook their prudence and let the Middle East crisis "escalate." They could have warned Egypt off, or expressed their disapproval of the blockade. But during the two weeks that preceded the actual armed conflict, the Kremlin did little to stop the Arabs' bellicose oratory or to relieve the tension. What Moscow desired and envisaged was not an Arab-Israeli war (there could be no illusions in the USSR about its likely outcome, though the speed and completeness of the Arabs' collapse was to come as a shock) but a diplomatic solution that would be a setback for Israel and its protector, the United States, and a prestigious victory for Nasser and the Soviets.

But the Israeli attack on June 5 spoiled this scenario.

The Arab states' defeat in the Six-Day War was a huge embarrassment to the Soviet Union: all the military equipment and the work of the Soviet military advisers had been wasted. The Soviets were not able to protect their allies—Egypt and Syria—from incurring territorial losses, the Suez Canal was rendered useless. But it was too readily assumed in the West and in Israel that the Soviet position in the Middle East had suffered an irreparable loss. Indeed, had the United States stepped alertly into the breach immediately after the UN-imposed cease-fire, at the time when the Arab world was disenchanted with the USSR, it is possible that American diplomacy might have recouped some of the West's former influence in the area, and possibly brought about some—even though precarious—agreement between the more moderate Arab regimes and Israel. But with the United States attention and resources again riveted on Vietnam, the opportune moment soon passed. Things in the Middle East returned to normal—i.e., a festering crisis with the ever-present danger of a violent one erupting. Much as the Soviets and the Arabs now viewed each other in a more realistic light, the Soviets had to protect their political investment, hence they resumed arms shipments to the Middle East, while the Arabs, for all the comforting and anti-Soviet messages from Communist China, had no power to turn to except the USSR.

To cover up their setback, the Soviets had engaged in a flurry of diplomatic activity while the conflict was still going on. Leaders of the European Communist countries, including Marshal Tito, gathered in Moscow to condemn Israeli aggression; subsequently the USSR and its partners, with the exception of Rumania, broke off diplomatic relations with the Jewish state. A top-ranking delegation headed by Kosygin went to New York for a special session of the General Assembly.

The Middle Eastern crisis was not a *direct* confrontation between the two superpowers. Still it had posed the danger of one or both of them becoming directly involved, with all the incalculable risks such an eventuality was bound to present in a nuclear age. (At one point Egyptian and Jordanian war communiqués alleged, in obvious hope of bringing Soviet reprisals, that American and British fliers were bombing Arab targets. Soviet sources did not for a moment lend their support to such false accusations. But the USSR adopted a menacing attitude when it appeared that Israel, in defiance of the cease-fire, might continue its offensive on the Syrian front in order to bring down the Damascus government.) And so in order to soothe their peoples' nerves, if for no other reason, Kosygin's visit to the UN (*not* to the United States) had to be used as an occasion for Russia's premier to meet the President of the United States. After some rather childish sparring about who should take the initiative and about the locale, the two potentates met in a small college town, Glassboro, New Jersey, equidistant from the UN and Washington.

Nothing momentous transpired at the meeting, though an offical Chinese source was sure that it had: "through the Glassboro talks, U.S. imperialism and Soviet revisionism have arrived at an overall coordination and collaboration in their global strategy."[5] But the era of détente was still a few years away. For the moment there was no common ground for the two powers except for their sincere desire to avoid a head-on collision. The Soviet Union, somewhat humiliated in the Middle East, was not going to help the United States out of its predicament in Vietnam.

Internally, the setback in foreign policy failed to shake the position of the ruling team. One member of the ruling group, Nikolai Yegorichev, the Moscow Party secretary, in a public speech criticized by implication his senior colleagues' policy in the Middle East. But Yegorichev was promptly fired and, though it is unlikely that he would have taken the incautious step on his own, there were no further reverberations on the Soviet Olympus. There were, however, serious consequences insofar as the Jewish problem in the USSR was concerned. The official anti-Zionist attitude was bound to enhance the

[5] *Peking Review*, July 7, 1967, p. 73.

already considerable covert anti-Semitism, while the Israeli victory had stimulated pro-Zionist feelings among many Soviet Jews. Prior to 1967, the Soviets had authorized only a trickle of migrations—mostly old people—to Israel. Now demands for permission to migrate to the Jewish state grew more numerous and insistent, and what had been an irritation would soon become a bothersome internal as well as foreign policy problem.

Domestic and Foreign Dissidence

This problem in turn became part of the larger dilemma of political dissidence. As explained above, dissidence became an observable phenomenon in the sixties: curtailment of mass terror made possible expression of dissent, whether forthcoming from ethnic groups who felt themselves persecuted, such as Jews and Crimean Tatars (the Crimean Autonomous Republic was abolished in 1944 and its Tatar inhabitants dispersed throughout the USSR as punishment for alleged collaboration with the invaders during World War II; the opprobrious charge was lifted in the wake of Stalin's death, but the surviving Crimean Tatars and their descendants were not allowed to resettle in their homeland), or from those individuals who demanded liberalization of the system and resumption of the momentum of reforms arrested in October 1964. This dissidence, while in no sense presenting a political danger to the regime, was in the late sixties a source of increasing embarrassment. With the Soviet Union no longer hermetically sealed from the rest of the world, the arrest of a prominent dissenter, the hunger strike of a Soviet Jew demanding to be allowed to emigrate to Israel, or publication of a *samizdat* would become known to correspondents and through them to wide circles abroad. (*Samizdat* was the term adopted for underground literature comprising books and stories not cleared by censorship, political pamphlets reporting trials of dissidents, and occasional journals relating information withheld by the regime, etc. Such literature would circulate in typescript or mimeographed copies, since the efficiency of the KGB made an underground press virtually unthinkable.) Prominent dissenters, like Solzhenitsyn, who received the Nobel Prize for literature, and the distinguished physicist and member of the Academy of Science Andrei Sakharov, became household names in the West, their works and political pronouncements—banned in the USSR—widely circulated abroad. For all the quantitative insignificance of dissidence, the regime could not but view it as a considerable embarrassment and a portent of potential future trouble if unchecked.

The problem of establishing the right balance between repression and a positive response to pressures for change confronted the Kremlin not only at home but in relations with other Communist countries. There was little, short of taking incalculable risks, that the USSR could do about China. And the latter's defection had enabled tiny Albania to assert independence and Rumania to gain a degree of autonomy. Again, as in the case of their domestic policies, Khrushchev's successors were too prudent to attempt to reverse drastically such lamentable results of his stewardship of the Communist camp. But by the same token they set themselves resolutely against any further loosening of ties between the USSR and its junior partners.

The test case came in 1968 in Czechoslovakia. Longer than in any other east European country, the leaders of the Czechoslovak Communist Party retained the Stalinist mentality and the methods of government appropriate thereto. By the middle sixties the resultant dissatisfaction within the rank and file and the country's economic stagnation brought pressures that the leaders could no longer ignore. There was some halfhearted and ineffectual effort to appease the proponents of change: victims of the terror were (often posthumously) rehabilitated, the most hardened Stalinists in the leading party and state organs were placed in retirement. And finally the position of the chief of them, Antonin Novotny, became untenable. After seeking Soviet help in vain (in December 1967 Brezhnev flew to Prague but decided that it would not serve Soviet interests to preserve the discredited satrap), he was forced in January to resign as first secretary, and in April was dismissed from his less important office, that of the president of the republic.

Alexander Dubcek, Novotny's successor as leader of Czechoslovak communism, seemed to possess all the qualities needed to revitalize his party, while at the same time keeping close ties to Moscow. He was young—forty-six—and popular with the rank and file. At the same time his whole background bespoke loyalty to the Soviet Union. But the pent-up pressures could not be contained by half measures. There were demands for basic reform and for fuller revelations of the Stalinist excesses of the past, as well as for freer intercourse with the West. Whether Dubcek himself and his closest collaborators shared the reforming zeal or whether they were pushed by the events, the tempo of democratization as well as the tenor of the general political debate in Czechoslovakia became deeply disturbing to the Kremlin and the more conservative of the east European Communist regimes. By late spring official censorship of the press and other media had virtually ceased. There were voices calling for an end to the monopoly of political power by the Communist Party.

In June the Warsaw Pact forces held maneuvers in Czechoslovakia and many within the country and in the West expected the Soviets to strike then. But the Kremlin's mind was not yet made up; with the end of the exercises foreign troops were withdrawn. Yet the Soviet, as well as the official Polish and East German, press was escalating its warnings to the new rulers in Prague. On July 15, 1968, representatives of the Soviet Union and of the Communist parties of Bulgaria, Hungary, East Germany, and Poland issued from their conference in Warsaw a public letter to their erring comrades: "The developments in your country have aroused profound anxiety among us. The reactionaries' offensive supported by imperialism . . . threatens to push your country off the path of socialism and consequently imperils the interests of the entire socialist system." The fact that the Rumanians did not choose to associate themselves with the warning increased in the Russians' eyes the gravity of the Czech crisis. The Kremlin must have felt that it faced, to borrow a simile from an American President, a domino situation in east Europe. Were the Czechs to get away with excessive liberalization, were the lesson learned that Communist rule could be modified through popular pressure, similar demands might be voiced in other east European capitals. The resulting convulsions could jeopardize the Soviet position in the whole area. And it was not entirely inconceivable that the Czech example might prove contagious even within the Soviet Union. Hence the explicit threat in the letter of the fraternal parties: "It is not only your task but ours, too, to deal a resolute rebuff to the anti-Communist forces and to wage a resolute struggle for the preservation of the socialist system in Czechoslovakia."

Much as they were under pressure from East German's Ulbricht and Poland's Gomulka (whose regime after enjoying genuine popularity between 1956 and 1960 had in recent years grown increasingly conservative and repressive; in the spring of 1968 it had launched a thinly disguised anti-Jewish campaign and cracked down hard on dissenting intellectuals and students) to put an end to the scandalous and dangerous situation in Czechoslovakia, the Soviets had to make the final decision whether to intervene or not. There were, it seems, voices in the Politburo pleading for restraint. It was not the fear of world public opinion, but the possibility that the Czechs might resist which must have worried some Soviet leaders. Armed resistance might lead to reverberations throughout the Communist bloc and elsewhere. The Politburo of the Soviet Party offered to meet with its Czechoslovak counterpart. The unprecedented meeting took place in the Slovak frontier town of Cierna between July 29 and August 1. What happened at the meeting must have reassured the doubters. On August 21 the forces of the Warsaw Pact countries (with the exception of

A Czechoslovak student waves national flag while standing on Soviet tank in Prague, August, 1968.

Rumania) invaded Czechoslovakia. This predominantly Soviet force of 400,000 met with no organized military resistance. But in one respect Soviet hopes were disappointed: There was universal passive resistance, and even the most conservative Czech and Slovak Communists did not dare to identify themselves with the invader. Dubcek and his principal collaborator, who were seized and flown to Moscow, had to be released and allowed to return to their posts but not before they negotiated a partial surrender: they would crack down on the "anti-socialist forces" and the Soviet army would stay to make sure they did!

The resulting chorus of worldwide protests in which some Communist parties, notably those of Yugoslavia, Rumania, and Italy, joined did not seriously disturb the Kremlin. The Soviets knew from their Hungarian experience in 1956 how short-lived and ineffectual such protests were likely to be, and on the contrary how pervasive and long-lasting the canon that you cannot with impunity defy the Soviet Union in its sphere. In April 1969 Dubcek, already discredited, was removed, soon to be followed by other makers of the "Prague spring." The new Czechoslovak regime, headed by Gustav Husak, did not turn the clock back to the Novotny days but, as the Soviets would have it, put a firm end to such "excesses" as freedom of the press and the talk about democratization. The public mood in the unhappy country turned from defiance to resignation.

In the backwash of the Czechoslovak affair the Soviet leadership reaffirmed its right, indeed its duty, to interfere in the affairs of a fellow Communist country whenever in its opinion the interests of socialism were being threatened. This was dubbed the Brezhnev doctrine, but in fact it reiterated Soviet policies going back to the end of World War II. In two years it appeared that the doctrine would have to be invoked again. Gomulka's regime compounded its long record of errors and repression by a spectacular idiocy: shortly before Christmas of 1970 it raised prices on foodstuffs. The Polish workers responded by riots and, reminiscent of 1956, party headquarters were burned in a number of cities. Again the Soviet troops were alerted. But the crisis was relieved by intraparty changes: Gomulka was replaced by a more astute politician, Edward Gierek, who rescinded the price increases and assuaged the workers by promising economic reforms. Instead of troops, the Soviet Union rushed food into Poland to tide the new leadership over the transition period.

The events of 1968–70 demonstrated convincingly the Soviet Union's determination to preserve what in effect had become its empire, eastern Europe, and beyond it not to tolerate any basic change in the character of local Communist regimes. To be sure the extent of Soviet domination had changed considerably since 1953; nowhere was it as pervasive as in Stalin's days, and it varied from country to country. The Rumanian regime was clearly master of its own house in domestic politics and occasionally acted quite independently of the Soviets in foreign policy. (At the time of the Czech invasion the regime of Ceausescu made it quite clear that it would fight were the Soviets to offer similar "fraternal help" to Rumania. Yet undoubtedly even the Rumanians were chastened by what happened in 1968; they have dropped their demand for a revision of the Warsaw Pact organization.) Despite its unpromising beginning, Kadar's regime was until quite recently more liberal than those of Poland or Bulgaria. The East German Communists, for obvious reasons, stayed closest to their Soviet protectors. Albania and Yugoslavia, though Communist, have in different ways been outside the sphere of direct Soviet influence. Albania in 1960 defied Moscow and virtually severed all relations with the USSR while continuing very close to Communist China. Soviet relations with Belgrade since 1948 have been at times quite tempestuous, at times—as recently—quite close, but Yugoslavia has resolutely followed its own path outside the two formal structures of Soviet-dominated east Europe: the Warsaw Pact and the Council for Mutual Economic Assistance. (Yugoslavia's perennial nationality problems became exacerbated in the seventies. This, in conjunction with Marshal Tito's venerable age (b. 1892), has opened the possibility of a major threat to Yugoslav unity within a few years, and with it of Soviet intervention, should one of the warring factions request it.)

While much of the old rationale of Soviet domination of east Europe is no longer valid, this domination remains of vital importance to the Kremlin. The old argument that Soviet security needs require friendly allied regimes in all those countries is much less persuasive in this era of intercontinental missiles and hydrogen bombs. Economically, though the USSR draws undoubted benefits from its control of the region, it can no longer exploit it outright as in the old days. Indeed at times, as in Czechoslovakia after the invasion in 1968 and in Poland in 1971, the shoe is on the other foot: for political reasons the USSR feels constrained to subsidize the economy of its satellites.

Ideologically, however, the existence of states that are not only dependent on the USSR but share the same political and economic system reinforces the Soviet rulers' sense of legitimacy and mission: in their own eyes they are not indulging in anachronistic imperialistic practices but are protecting and advancing the course of communism. And paradoxically many of their subjects who have no use for Marxism-Leninism and no concern about real or alleged threats to its survival in Poland or Czechoslovakia feel national pride in reflecting that the Soviet state has achieved what has been the objective of the Russian rulers for at least two centuries—hegemony in east and southeast Europe. It is noteworthy that except for what might be called a mini-demonstration by a handful of dissidents in Moscow's Red Square, the Czechoslovak affair evoked no protests within the Soviet Union. Those, mostly among the intellectuals who opposed the regime on other grounds, found the invasion another reason for their opposition, but it is fair to say that the Soviet man in the street saw nothing opprobrious in this act of force.

All in all, the Soviet leaders must have viewed their intervention as a barely qualified success. It failed to have any lasting negative effects on Soviet relations with either the Communist or non-Communist world. Of course, there may have been some indirect effects on Communist China's foreign policy. Peking, though it had but little sympathy for Dubcek's reforms and viewed them as the quintessence of "revisionism," condemned vigorously this latest and brutal example of Soviet interference in the internal affairs of a fellow socialist state. In theory at least the Brezhnev doctrine had unpleasant and threatening implications for Mao's China. The eruption of fighting at the Sino-Soviet border in 1969 added some weight to the warning. Both powers drew away from a wider conflict and in 1970 decided to start negotiations about settling the contentious frontier issues.[6] But it is likely that the escalation of the Soviet threat was instrumental in Communist China's decision to seek a rapprochement with the United States.

The Cultural Revolution ground to a halt in 1969, probably as a consequence of the realization by the ruling group that it was doing it harm both at home and abroad. With a measure of stability restored to the country, Chinese diplomacy guided by Chou En-lai established contacts with the United States which culminated in the visit of presidential assistant Henry Kissinger to Peking in 1971, and then early in 1972 in an unprecedented trip to China by America's President. This was perhaps the most dramatic turn in world politics since the end of World War II. The intensity of the U.S.–Communist China conflict had by 1970 dimmed that between the United States and the USSR: it was largely to bar the spread of Chinese influence that America had embarked on its ill-fated venture in Vietnam; it was the suspicion of U.S.–USSR collusion that set Peking on its anti-Soviet course. But now the United States, chastened by Vietnam, saw a normalization of relations with China as possibly helping to end the unfortunate war, while in Peking's eyes the Soviet threat justified this diplomatic tour de force. (This dramatic reversal of the Chinese Communist "line" on the United States, heretofore the archenemy, at least in Peking's rhetoric, may well have been due to the apprehension that in their desperate search for a face-saving solution in Vietnam the Americans might offer to make far-reaching concessions to the USSR, including giving the Kremlin a free hand vis-à-vis China.)

Détente

The U.S.–China rapprochement was bound, in turn, to speed up the Soviet resolution to seek détente with America. For Moscow this was not as dramatic a reversal as for Peking, providing that certain conditions of theirs were met, Russia's rulers have for long sought friendlier relations with the one power that could destroy the USSR.

[6] These discussions as of the beginning of 1975 had failed to produce any tangible results. The actual points of the territorial dispute are quite trivial. But the Chinese have insistently demanded that the USSR acknowledge that much of its territory in Asia was acquired from the Manchu Empire under "unequal treaties," something that the Soviets, though the Chinese do not demand its return, are never going to admit. The Soviet Union has proposed a nonaggression treaty, only to be reminded infuriatingly by Peking that, since the two countries already have a friendship pact (of 1950), such a treaty would be superfluous and that in any case the Russians could demonstrate their goodwill by withdrawing some of their armed forces currently along the Sino-Soviet border.

These conditions, as we have seen, touched on the recognition by the West of the status quo in Germany and east Europe. By the end of the sixties Soviet demands on this count were in a fair way of being satisfied: America's internal and external troubles were making Washington less rigid on the German question, and Western Europe, alarmed by the American overcommitment in Vietnam, was on its own beginning to seek accommodation with the USSR. In 1969 West Germany elected a socialist government under Willy Brandt. The latter had been for some time determined to pursue a new approach toward the USSR and its Communist partners. This new "eastern policy" of Brandt's led between 1969 and 1972 to a series of agreements which in fact, if not in the letter of law, constituted a German peace treaty. Poland's territorial acquisitions, declared by the Potsdam Conference to be provisional and subject to modification in a future peace treaty, were now through formal treaties between Bonn and Poland, as well as between the former and the USSR, recognized as permanent. Then the German Federal Republic, with the approval of other Western powers, abandoned its claim to be the only legitimate government of Germany. An agreement between the two Germanys put their relations on a new basis. And by 1975 all Western powers, including the United States, would exchange representatives with Communist Germany. If not a peace treaty, this has amounted to pretty much the same thing.

In return for the achievement of its historic aim, the Soviet government pledged to desist from harassing the Western outpost in Berlin. The Four Powers' (Britain, France, the United States, and the USSR) negotiations began in March 1970. In September 1971 they reached an agreement that was ratified in June 1972, following the Soviet-American summit in Moscow. In the protocol all parties pledged not to attempt unilaterally to change the status of West Berlin. The USSR pledged to preserve unimpeded Western access to this oft-embattled area.

It might be asked why the USSR was so eager to proclaim by formal agreements what in fact had become an unalterable feature of Europe's political landscape—the division of Germany and, largely because of it, Soviet domination of east and central Europe. The answer must be that the Kremlin still felt it of great psychological importance to legitimize what in the first instance had been secured by Soviet military power. In the second place, normalization, as they saw it, of the European situation fitted in with the Soviets' long-range diplomatic objectives. If western Europe were to lose most of its fear of the Soviet colossus, it would grow even more independent of the United States, and the impetus toward political unity of the area (originally a function of that fear) would grow weaker. Beyond virtual neutralization of western Europe (admittedly not tomorrow or the day after tomorrow), or even, as it is sometimes described, its "finlandization," the Soviets see profitable economic ties with its countries. At the Twenty-fourth Party Congress in 1971, Kosygin drew a vista of vast collaborative projects, such as a united electric grid, joint transportation network, Western credits and expertise already exemplified in the huge Kama automobile plant being built on Soviet soil by a consortium headed by Italian interests. Thus quite apart from similar hopes in respect to the United States, the Soviet Union would like various European countries to provide it with trade and help to improve its somewhat unsatisfactory rate of economic growth.

The attempt to detach western Europe from the United States has not precluded the striving for détente with the United States. On the contrary, in the Kremlin's eyes the two must go together, for any serious exacerbation of the situation in Europe leads to a conflict with the United States and vice versa. And in view of America's still continuing industrial and technological primacy, prospective benefits from a wider commercial intercourse with the United States are greater than those that would accrue from closer trade relations with France or West Germany.

A measure of cooperation between the two superpowers continued despite the war in Vietnam. In 1968 this cooperation ensured the agreement on nuclear nonproliferation. Of course, to use a fractured metaphor, the biggest horse had bolted before the barn door was locked: Communist China would not cease its development of nuclear weapons, nor, much less significantly, would France (nor India, which in 1974 would explode a bomb). But from the Soviet viewpoint the agreement had a positive value insofar as the Bonn government subscribed to this renunciation of atomic weapons along with most of the world's states. Talks between the United States and the USSR about possible ways of limiting their own nuclear race were going on at the same time that Soviet-made ground-to-air missiles were bringing down American planes over North Vietnam and other Soviet equipment was enabling the Vietcong guerrillas to fight the American army in the South to a standstill.

This paradoxical half-hostile, half-cooperative relationship was altered in 1971–72 through two developments: first, America's decision to bring its military intervention in Vietnam to an end; and second, the beginning of the Sino-American rapprochement. The first made it more possible for the Kremlin to seek détente with the United States without arousing a chorus of disapproval from the Communist world. The second made the Soviet leaders apprehensive that, unless they mollified the Americans, the United States would court Mao's regime more vigorously, conceivably offering to extend credits and technological help to Peking. For President Nixon and his soon-to-be secretary of state but already principal foreign adviser, Henry Kissinger, the road to Moscow led almost literally through Peking.

The Nixon visit was preceded by a moment of uncertainty. The North Vietnamese had launched an offensive sending sizable regular army units into the South, in a last-ditch effort to overthrow the Thieu regime, presumably in order to be in the most advantageous position for the final truce talks. President Nixon then ordered stepped-up bombing of the North and a measure the United States had previously refrained from precisely out of fear of the Soviets' reaction—mining of the North Vietnamese harbors.

This act did not cause the Soviets to disinvite Nixon. The stake the Kremlin had in a successful summit was too great—agreements on Germany and on nuclear arms hung in the balance. If rebuffed, the United States might turn even more toward Peking. There were rumors, possibly spurred by Moscow itself, that some oligarchs favored a tougher stance. On the eve of Nixon's arrival, Peter Shelest, member of the Politburo and head of the Ukrainian party, was removed from the latter position. (His fall, however, was apparently due to domestic reasons and his ineffective, in the view of his colleagues, ways of dealing with the Ukrainian nationalists.) There was no way of ascertaining whether Shelest and, as was rumored, another Politburo member, Gennadi Voronov, were really opposed to the détente or whether it was another demonstration of the Soviet negotiation gambit: "We have hard liners among us too, so hurry up and make an agreement before it is too late."

The May 1972 visit of the American President and his entourage was seen throughout the world as signifying the end of the Cold War and the beginning of Soviet-American détente. Whatever the appropriateness of these rather elusive terms, such verdicts must be at least qualified. The *intense* period of hostility between the two superpowers had ended in 1953 with Stalin's death. Since 1963, in the wake of the Cuban missile crisis and the test ban agreement, both superpowers have realized that however competitive their positions in various areas of the world may be, they must work more realistically than hitherto to minimize the horrendous possibility of a nuclear clash. And the visit's results and its sequence until 1976 have not put an end to the two countries' very basic conflict in many areas such as the Middle East or brought an agreement on basic issues of world politics. The visit in the main served as a dramatic occasion for ratifying the agreements that already had been worked out. Thus the German-Berlin one, of which we already spoke, followed the visit in June. The most important and hopeful was the provisional pact on stabilizing the two powers' nuclear armaments. SALT I—from Strategic Arms

Limitations Talks—proposed to freeze for five years the present quantity of fixed ICBM launchers on both sides, as well as to regulate other forms of nuclear vehicles and related nuclear facilities. Hardly a measure of disarmament, the agreement still aimed at preserving the delicate balance of terror: neither power, for all the fantastic means of destruction at its disposal, would be tempted to initiate a nuclear holocaust in the hope or illusion that its cities and launching sites could enjoy a measure of security against a retaliatory strike.

A number of other agreements previously prepared, which could have been quietly signed without the drama of the summit meeting, were also initialed during the historic meeting: a declaration of high-sounding principles according to which both powers would regulate their intercourse and general behavior in international relations, on collaboration on problems of environment and medicine, and on a joint space venture in 1975.

Except for the one on nuclear weapons, the formal agreements were overshadowed by two informal understandings reached during the President's visit. Both sides decided to seek wider trade relations, the President pledging to seek Congress' approval to include the USSR under the most-favored-nation category in American trade legislation. (Even before this pledge was redeemed there was to be a spectacular rise in Soviet-American trade, a widespread discussion about the possibility of—and actually some agreements on—American credits and investments to develop Soviet natural resources, such as gas deposits in Siberia, etc. The most spectacular transaction was the agreement on a huge wheat sale to the USSR. This sale, both on account of its magnitude and the favorable price and credit conditions the Soviet bargainers obtained, was subsequently widely criticized in the United States on grounds that it contributed to the considerable rise in the price of foodstuffs on the domestic market.)

There seems also to be but little question, though the whole matter was shrouded in secrecy, that the U.S.-Soviet discussions touched heavily on Vietnam, and that the USSR promised to assist in the American efforts to secure a truce. Publicly the Soviet position had always been that North Vietnam was an independent state and that it was up to Hanoi and its southern extension, the Vietcong, to accept or reject American proposals. In fact, however, the Soviet Union, as the main supplier of its arms if for no other reasons, has had a potent voice in North Vietnamese policies. It is very likely that it was discreet Soviet advice, if not indeed pressure, that prepared the way for the truce signed early in 1973 and which, though far from bringing peace to the unhappy country, enabled the United States to extricate itself from its agonizing military involvement in Southeast Asia and to retrieve the American war prisoners.

In addition to reaping the advantages already discussed, the Soviet regime could consider the results of Nixon's visit as a considerable diplomatic and propaganda success. The USSR was now formally recognized as America's equal as a nuclear power. It could be and was represented that the visit and its sequel constituted a shift in American policy: In response to the unalterable Soviet stand, Washington finally recognized the harm and fruitlessness of its Cold War tactics and grasped the proffered hand. Certainly the most inveterate opponent of the status quo in east Europe now had to recognize that, banning a miracle, no change would be forthcoming for a long time.

As to disadvantages of the new relationship with the United States and the German Federal Republic, these at most were hypothetical. The bogey of (West) German militarism and revanchism could no longer be used as readily, but then this propaganda weapon had for some time been blunted. Who in 1968 could really have believed that the "Prague spring" had been inspired by Western imperialists and that NATO forces might have pounced upon Czechoslovakia had the Soviets not acted in the nick of time? Friendlier relations with the United States carried some danger of encouraging hopes for political liberalization within the USSR. But then the Kremlin made it clear immediately that it did not propose to tolerate any "ideological coexistence." In fact, the line on dissidence hardened perceptibly in the wake of the Nixon visit.

Détente had its impact on intraoligarchy politics; 1971–72 marked the emergence of Brezhnev as more than just the first among equals on the Politburo. He was personally identified with the favorable turn of events and arrogated to himself the spotlight in international relations previously occupied by Kosygin. At sixty-six and not in very good health, Brezhnev obviously would not dream of trying to institute a personality cult of his own, or even of imitating Khrushchev's style of leadership. But he now became the dominant figure of Soviet politics rather than, as hitherto, the chief spokesman for the ruling oligarchy.

The overall international position of the Soviet Union as it emerged in the seventies must have been viewed with satisfaction by its rulers. Soviet influence and prestige throughout the world was growing, while social and economic troubles besetting the West were hampering it from translating its still enormous resources into effective policies. Détente was not intended to put an end to the competitive character of the U.S.–Soviet relations, but mainly to prevent this competition from assuming a catastrophic character. There were occasional setbacks. In 1972 President Sadat requested the Soviet Union to remove the Russian "advisers," some twenty thousand strong, from Egypt. Some of these "advisers" had previously manned Egyptian missile sites, while others had flown combat missions against Israeli raids. But then the Egyptian leader decided that this arrangement gave the USSR too strong an influence in his country's policies. He would rather play his own game. But even this setback illustrated the advantages the USSR enjoyed over its rivals in the game of international politics. Unlike America's in Vietnam, Soviet involvements in the actual fighting in the Suez Canal zone had been small and not subject to an impassioned public debate at home and throughout the world. In dealing with the rapidly changing developments and moods in the Third World, Soviet policies, unhampered by public opinion, could be flexible and responsive to the needs of the moment. And so, though set back, Soviet influence in the Arab world was to remain potent.

Even in Asia and despite the intractable nature of its largest state's hostility, the USSR could show solid gains. Though imperfect, the reconciliation with the United States had enabled Mao's China to secure recognition by Japan and to enter the United Nations. But the still unsettled internal conditions within the Asian colossus, exemplified by the mysterious death and subsequent official execration of Mao's onetime number two, Lin Piao, gravely handicapped China's international position. The Soviets took advantage of this configuration of events. In August 1971 the USSR signed a treaty of friendship with India, whose Congress regime had for years been bitterly denounced by the Chinese Communist regime. Thus encouraged, the Indians moved against Pakistan. Their army invaded East Bengal, where the local insurgents with its help proclaimed the independent republic of Bangladesh. Defeated Pakistan had to agree to this amputation of its more populous part. China proved incapable of protecting the state which in the past had relied on its support, and to a lesser extent this discomfiture was shared by the United States. It was characteristic that, after at first bitterly assailing Soviet complicity in their country's defeat and partition, Pakistan's new leaders felt compelled again to plead for Russia's friendship and assistance should India advance further territorial claims. The Soviet Union was in a fair way to become the diplomatic arbiter for the Indian subcontinent.

As suggested by the above, many of the advantages the Soviet Union has enjoyed in the game of international politics have reflected not so much its inherent strength as the continuing decline in the West's power and prestige. The USSR has proclaimed itself protector and natural ally of the nations of the Third World, the sponsor of the movements of "national liberation" against the remnants of Western imperialism (as in the Portugese colonies). Having abjured, at least in its official pronouncements, the goal of ideological expansion, it threw its support, both material and diplomatic, to those states and regimes that, no matter what their ideological character, found themselves at cross-purposes with the Western powers. While many rulers of the new states would recognize the self-serving aspects of Soviet policies (e.g., Sadat of Egypt) they still at times would be constrained to seek Soviet help. By contrast, American policies have been hamstrung by the insistent demands of at least a part of public opinion that any government the United States supported should offer continuous proofs of democratic virtue, by the revulsion reborn through the lesson of Vietnam against "foreign entanglements," and by the electorate's growing weariness with both foreign aid and defense expenditures. As against discordant voices which always accompany formulation and execution of foreign policy in a democracy, the Soviets could operate in world politics decisively and efficaciously, and with much greater flexibility: in 1948 the USSR was the first power to recognize Israel, perhaps already sensing that the Jewish state would become the apple of discord that would erode the remaining Western influence in the Middle East. Then almost immediately Soviet diplomacy shifted its support to the Arab states. Such maneuverability and the ability to subordinate everything else to considerations of power politics are not open to a democratic state. Again in 1974 the Soviet Union would give direct encouragement to the Turkish invasion of Cyprus, but in its wake offer public sympathy to the new Greek regime. The fact that the current Indonesian government has suppressed the country's Communists more thoroughly and bloodily than has been the case anywhere in the world since World War II has not been allowed to stand in the way of correct diplomatic and commercial relations between the USSR and Indonesia. The Shah of Iran, once denounced as a despot and an American puppet, has in recent years been courteously received in Moscow, and perhaps his inference that the Soviet Union no longer constitutes an immediate threat to his country was not without influence on the monarch's decision to take the initiative in quadrupling world oil prices, the step that has plunged the world into its most serious economic crisis since the Great Depression.

If the decline in the West's worldwide power and influence has enhanced the Soviet Union's international position, then the social—some might call it a spiritual—crisis that has afflicted Western societies even at the time of their continuing material prosperity has been of indirect benefit to the Communist system. Sociologists might point out that the Soviet Union has not been free of most of the troubles that are besetting advanced industrial societies: the breakdown in social discipline, the decline of the family, rising crime, sharpening ethnic and social conflicts. Yet the fact remains that the institution of liberal democratic society appears incapable of dealing with this seemingly sudden surge of social malaise and the breakdown in social values; and this fact serves to obscure the internal dilemmas and social conflicts in Soviet society, appears to strengthen the argument that communism is the wave of the future. Both the power and political and social ideas represented by the West have been in retreat, and as often before, notably in the thirties, this has served to enhance the power and influence of the USSR and of communism.

To some previous, more ideologically motivated generation of Soviet leaders, this situation, as well as the economic crisis that after a generation of unprecedented prosperity began to envelop the West in the seventies, might have appeared as a dazzling confirmation of the prophecies of Marxism-Leninism and a signal for an ideological offensive. But the present rulers have grown too realistic and cautious to dream of and perhaps even to wish for a world revolution. For one, world communism, unlike before World War II when only tiny groups of Trotskyists challenged the Soviet Union's leadership, is no longer monolithic, and it is at least problematic whether its further advances would rebound to Russia's national interest. In fact, much of the New Left throughout the world has rejected the Soviet model and is finding its inspiration in the allegedly purer communism of Mao's China. For another, the lesson of the thirties, made more emphatic by the advent of nuclear weapons, suggests forcibly that a crisis of capitalism and deepening world instability may eventually lead to a terrible danger for the Soviet Union. Confronted by the crisis, the current occupants of the Kremlin have acted less as revolutionaries, eager to snatch an opportunity for a death blow to the hostile system, than as careful rentiers, eager to increase their dividends, but unwilling to speculate on a dramatic coup that might wipe out all their investments.

In foreign policy this continuing caution of the Kremlin has been demonstrated by its effort to preserve and expand U.S.–Soviet détente. Whatever the logic and direction of social and economic forces, the United States remains the one power capable of annihilating the USSR, and in less dramatic terms of hastening the emergence of China as an industrial and nuclear power. No matter how competitive the relationship of the two countries may be in various areas of the world, this fact argues for not breaking off the pursuit of friendly relations with the United States. The logic of this situation brought Brezhnev to the United States in 1973, and led to the return visit of Nixon in 1974.[7] The subsequent meeting in Vladivostok (chosen in

[7] The Watergate crisis and Nixon's resignation were greeted in the Soviet Union first by puzzlement and then with suspicion. To the official Soviet mind, it appeared incomprehensible that a trivial case of political corruption and chicanery should cause the downfall of the President of the United States. Hence the even now not completely dispelled suspicion that he was the victim of an intrigue hatched by those who opposed his policies, notably détente. Also the deeply conservative temperament of the ruling oligarchy makes it partial to dealing with people and situations they are familiar with.

part undoubtedly to irritate the Chinese comrades: Vladivostok—its literal translation is Ruler of the East—lies in the area that had once been China's), between Brezhnev and President Ford, resulted in new guidelines for the two countries for nuclear weaponry. The alacrity with which the Soviets agreed on the SALT II arrangement, after having indicated not long before that negotiations might actually be protracted, is a good indication of the Kremlin's eagerness to involve the new President in the continuing momentum of détente.

We have seen how détente, while soothing to the nerves of citizens of both countries, has, as far as practical results are concerned, been beneficial mostly to the USSR. Yet in one respect the U.S.–Soviet diplomatic dialogue has been embarrassing and potentially dangerous to the Soviet regime. This has been on the issue of Jewish migration. From the beginning it became clear that Congress would not approve the granting of the most-favored treatment in foreign trade to the Soviet Union without the latter's offering a pledge that it would allow a sizable number of Soviet Jews to migrate to Israel. A few years ago it would have been inconceivable that the Soviet government would have agreed even to discuss the issue. It is deeply embarrassing for any regime to admit by implication that any ethnic group finds itself discriminated against in the fatherland of socialism, that a foreign power has any business intruding in its internal affairs, and to set the precedent of some group of its citizens prevailing against the government and compelling it to release them from its grip. The Soviet government *informally* apprised the American Secretary of State that he could *informally* tell Congress that the number of those allowed to emigrate would be on the order of sixty thousand for the year following the signing of the trade bill granting most-favored-nation treatment to the USSR. When this pledge was publicized in the United States and the actual linkage between the most-favored clause and emigration was written into the bill, the Kremlin *formally* denied, in October 1974, that it had made a commitment, and in January 1975 rejected the trade agreement as incompatible with Soviet sovereignty. Thus if the Soviets pledged at all, and albeit in a left-handed way, to allow some Jews to emigrate, this can be ascribed to two reasons: One, there was a realistic recognition of the strength of the pro-Zionist sentiment within Congress, and the consequent need to make a gesture to appease it if American trade, technology, and credits were to be forthcoming. Second, this concession, painful as it must be to Soviet pride, is in the Kremlin's eyes less costly than would have been some other quid pro quo the Americans could have demanded—say, a pledge to reduce the Soviet flow of arms to the Arabs or North Vietnam. Since you cannot employ mass terror, it makes sense, cooler heads in the Politburo must have argued, to ship the troublemakers out of the country. But it would be foolish not to expect further complications and conflicts arising out of this most sensitive issue.

The Jewish question epitomizes the problem the Soviet regime faces in trying to combine the totalitarian rigor of its rule with the image of a society where mass terror and other features of Stalinism are things of the past. By the official count, there are now more than two million Jews in the country. There is no question that a majority of them consider the USSR their home, and culturally at least they are assimilated into the ethnic groups that surround them, be they Russian, Ukrainian, or Georgian. At the same time, there has been since the last years of the Stalin era an undoubted undercurrent of discrimination against persons of Jewish descent. It is rather difficult for them to get into certain branches of officialdom, e.g., the diplomatic service and the army officer corps. There is now but a handful of Jews in high state or Party positions. But Jews still are amply represented in the academic world, the medical and other professions, etc. It is thus most inappropriate to liken the situation of the Soviet Jews to that of Jews in Nazi Germany, or even the situation that prevailed in tsarist Russia, where persons of the Jewish *religion* were subject to legal disabilities and where local officials at times tolerated, if indeed did not encourage, anti-Jewish pogroms. Yet by the same token there remains what might be called a shadow of discrimination, and those who publicly assert their loyalty to Israel are subject to actual persecution. The basic root of the troubles lies mainly in the Soviet system's inability to tolerate any group, or for that matter, individual, with connections and loyalties that transcend the confines of the Soviet state.

If the Jewish problem in the USSR has come to reflect partly the situation of the embattled Jewish state in the Middle East, then, as we have seen, the general Soviet attitude toward Israel has always been determined by power considerations. The commitment to the Arab side in the intractable conflict, first made to gain influence in the area and to weaken the overall position of the West, had by the late sixties grown into a major concern of Soviet foreign policy. Paradoxically, the Soviet Union, which until the 1950's had neither a stake nor a major role in the area, has become one of the arbiters of Middle Eastern politics, and the region, twenty years ago quite peripheral to Soviet concerns and aspirations, has become a crucial one in determining the Soviet role in the world and relations with the United States.

The almost inextricable and dangerous nature of the Soviet entanglement was demonstrated in the 1973 crisis. The long-expected new war began, this time with a reversal of the 1967 scenario: a sudden attack by Egypt and Syria upon Israel. After the initial setbacks,

Israel, bolstered by massive American arms airlifts, was on the verge of surrounding and destroying a large part of the Egyptian army that had crossed the Suez Canal. When Israel appeared to disregard the United Nations' resolutions ordering a cease-fire, the Soviet government proposed to the United States a joint military action to enforce the truce, intimating that should Washingon refuse and fighting continue, the USSR might intervene on its own. This brought the American response in the form of a worldwide nuclear alert. It was meant as a gesture rather than a prelude to an expected military conflict, but still the whole situation demonstrated vividly the fragility of détente. In a way the Soviet threat served its purpose: pressured by Washington, Israel stopped its counteroffensive. Hectic negotiations conducted in the following months by the secretary of state, Kissinger, resulted in as yet another of those precarious Middle Eastern truce arrangements.

By 1976 the dangerous impasse in the Middle East still continued. The enormously enhanced powers of the Arab world, only a few years ago scorned on account of its disunity and repeated military defeats, now represented a threat not only to Israel but to the whole economy of the West. Both by quadrupling the world oil prices and through the weapon of withholding oil supplies, the Arabs emerged from their previous client status and have become in effect, as long as they remain united, a world power. By the same token, a new spirit of independence entered their policy, as exemplified by friendlier relations between the United States and Egypt. It would be a mistake, however, to conclude that the Soviet Union's position in the area has been fundamentally undermined. As long as their military confrontation with Israel continues, such Arab states as Egypt, Syria, and Iraq remain dependent on actual or potential military aid from the Soviet Union. (An incidental result of the crisis has been that the USSR has considerably increased its foreign currency earnings, both because it sells arms to the Arabs for cash and due to the spectacular rise in oil prices.) The professed goals of Soviet policy do not include the liquidation of the state of Israel; indeed the Soviet leaders have at times publicly recalled how theirs was the first state to recognize Israel. Moscow has seconded the Arabs' official position that any basic settlement of the Middle Eastern conflict must be preceded by Israel's withdrawal from the territories it occupied in the 1967 war.

The Arab-Israeli conflict is in its essence not of Soviet making. But in the Middle East, just as in other regions once called "backward" and now given the less jarring appellation of "underdeveloped" or the "Third World," Soviet help, propaganda, and encouragement have often been the catalyst of political change and provided an impulse for those countries to assume independent or even frankly hostile attitudes toward the states that for a century and a half dominated their world. To an ideologue, this role of the Soviet Union may appear as fulfillment of the hopes and prophecies of the founders of the Soviet state and of communism. To a more realistic or cynical observer, this has been the means through which the USSR, still incapable of matching the West in material development, has managed to reduce drastically the West's power in world affairs and to increase its own. Yet the process has not been one of unambiguous gain for communism and the Soviet state. The latter, while a superpower with its influence extending to all corners of the earth, is no longer an unchallenged leader of world communism. In fact, communism's greatest triumph since World War II, the birth of Communist China, has posed the main challenge and the most basic dilemma for the USSR. It is those disparate historical developments that provide the background for policies of the current and future masters of the Soviet Union and must influence their decision whether and to what extent they must seek world stability rather than the advance of communism.

10.
Conclusion

While external factors have exercised a powerful influence on the development of the Soviet Union, this has obviously not been the whole story. We have seen how the earliest generation of Soviet leaders who at first thought of their country as a bridgehead of the world revolution became transferred in time into politicians for whom the development and strengthening of the Soviet state took the first and overwhelming priority. It is thus pertinent to ask, as the Soviet state approaches the sixtieth anniversary of its founding, to what extent its most recent development has adhered to the ideas of Marxism–Leninism, and conversely whether these ideas still have a hold on the minds of the ruling elite and influence the lives of its citizens. Answers to all these questions will vary according to the viewpoint of the observer, but there are certain undeniable facts. Most of the discussion of the ideological goals and of the progress toward them has been muted since the fall of Khrushchev. It was he who in 1961 projected the vision—somewhat murky in its details—of the Soviet Union entering the era of communism in 1980. Since 1964 nothing has been heard of this goal or Khrushchev's other, also rather nebulous slogan, the "state of all people"—which to some conservatives in the Soviet elite as well as to the Chinese Communists smacked of intended derogation of the role of the Party.

Ideology still colors certain areas of governmental policy. It is still the regime's long-run goal to eliminate private farming in favor of state farms, and by the same token further to restrain and eventually to abolish the private sector of agriculture, i.e., the peasant's plot. (In 1970 the private sector; though comprising but 3 percent of the total land under cultivation, produced more than one-third of the total output of meat, 40 percent of the milk, and 55 percent of the egg output.) What might be described as the mildly egalitarian thrust to wage policy initiated by Khrushchev has been continued by his successors, and the gap between the highest- and lowest-paid functionaries and workers in industry has undoubtedly narrowed. We have already spoken of the parallel effort to reduce the disparity of material rewards as between the urban and rural sectors of the working force.

For all the preceding, there is no question that Soviet society is far from being or becoming egalitarian, even in the economic sense of the term. Quite apart from the official scale of remuneration, a member of the elite, be he a minister, an academician, or a director of a major enterprise, enjoys material perquisites that, while not easily translatable into monetary terms, assure him a standard of living quite incomparable to that of a collective farmer or even a skilled worker. Furthermore, unlike in Communist China there is but little stress on the communal and egalitarian side of the socialist ideal. On the contrary, official propaganda has repeatedly pointed out how, after years of privation required for laying down the foundations of a modern industrial economy, the Soviet citizen is now beginning to enjoy the blessings of "consumerism"—television sets, washing machines, automobiles. To the plain living if not asceticism of Lenin, which was held up as an example to an earlier generation of Communists, there has succeeded an entirely new style of essentially middle-class behavior, perhaps partly epitomized by Brezhnev's hobby of collecting automobiles. That middle-class aspirations and mentality are on the increase among the population at large is corroborated by sociological surveys released by government publications. Thus a poll of young workers in a factory revealed that about 70 percent of respondents hope to advance to engineer or technician. The investigator writes: "This is true despite the fact that average earnings for engineers and technicians at the plant are lower than workers' earnings. Certainly one can welcome the young people's thirst for knowledge, but the desire to become an engineer or technician is becoming so widespread that one automatically asks: Who will be left in the workers' jobs?"[1] The same points come out forcibly from a poll of more than three thousand schoolchildren in Kiev. Hundreds named as their preferred goals and professions medicine, engineering, and teaching, with only eighty expressing a preference for industrial labor.[2]

1 "The Young Age Group," *Izvestia,* October 25, 1973.

2 "And Here We Are on the Island," *Komsomolskaya Pravda,* September 21, 1972.

Such statistics provide eloquent testimony to the fact that the realities of Soviet life—and among them must be included the effects, even if unintended, of official policies—breed values and attitudes at variance with those proclaimed by the ideology.

This increasingly materialistic orientation of Soviet society is not, however, viewed by the regime as a source of danger. On the contrary, popular expectations of and the actual rise in the general standard of living have been viewed for at least twenty years as a necessary and the most effective prophylactic against political discontent. (The need for material incentives and the inapplicability of strict egalitarianism to modern industrial society were of course already recognized in the Stalin era. But this recognition and the policies consequent upon it had then a definite elitist thrust: higher remuneration and special benefits flowed to industrial managers and designers, the "shock" workers and peasants, with the great majority of people in the last two groups—and especially the peasants—profiting little, if at all, from the country's economic growth.) The Polish workers' revolt in December 1970, which precipitated the fall of Gomulka, was a poignant lesson that even a Communist regime with its monopoly of political power cannot safely disregard the consumer's needs. The rising standard of living in the Soviet Union may well have contributed to the fact that political dissent has been confined to rather minuscule groups of intellectuals. Even among the latter there is a general recognition that their activities find practically no support or response among the population at large.

Repression has not ceased to be the government's main weapon for dealing with dissent. Of late, however, it has grown more subtle and varied in its manifestations. The most brutal means continue to be employed toward those who question the basic tenets of the Soviet system or who appear to advocate separatism for non-Russian nationalities of the USSR (notably some Ukrainian critics of the regime). Prison, the forced-labor camp (which now has the more innocuous name of corrective labor colony), confinement in mental institutions are still the lot of many who speak or write against the Soviet power, even though their punishment is no longer, as in the old days, determined by an administrative fiat of the secret police, but most often preceded by a trial. With those who eschew a direct defiance or whose arrest would create considerable stir abroad, the regime has been of late more selective in its methods of persecution. A man like the historian Roy Medvedev, who has pleaded for democratization of Soviet life but who would retain the one-party system, remains at large, his occasional statements to foreign correspondents and critical tracts published abroad viewed by the government as an advertisement for its broad-mindedness, and of the distance it has traveled since 1953. Alexander Solzhenitsyn, who has conducted a one-man campaign to educate the Soviet people about the horrifying past and the still repressive present, has been denied the crown of new martyrdom. Following his transmittal abroad of the most vivid indictment yet of the era of terror, *The Gulag Archipelago*, the great writer was expelled from the Soviet Union.

The historical record of Soviet Russia is, then, replete with paradoxes. More than in the case of any other modern state, the history of the USSR has been one of progress and yet also of privation and repression; of ideological enthusiasm and yet of widespread suffering and popular indifference to the official faith. No other ideology in modern times has been so cosmopolitan in its spirit and aims and has had such a worldwide appeal as the one officially enthroned in the Soviet Union, and yet nationalism has been the most potent force in the country's development and its salvation in moments of peril. No other government that has endured for so long has been the prey of so many crises: the intense struggle for the succession to Lenin, Stalin's decimation of the ruling elite, those recurrent struggles for the leadership which in the past have resulted in the overthrow of Beria, Malenkov, and Khrushchev, and which still determine one's membership and standing in the ruling oligarchy. The Communist regime has withstood all those traumas, any one of which might well have destroyed some other political system. In a world where drastic social and economic changes have undermined the traditional sources of political authority and legitimacy, caused the decline of ancient religions and ideologies, the Soviet Union appears as the bastion of internal stability.

Yet has the Soviet system mastered social change or has it merely managed until now to suppress such of its manifestation as would encroach on the power of the Party and the rule of a self-perpetuating oligarchy? We have been dealing with a society whose government feels constrained to expel its greatest writer, where the daughter of the erstwhile dictator-divinity finds life unendurable and chooses exile, whose recent political leader has to smuggle abroad his memoirs. More important, communism has not made Soviet society immune to social ailments and problems that afflict advanced industrial societies elsewhere: it has suppressed many of the uncomfortable statistics just as it has silenced most of the political critics. But this is hardly a new phenomenon in Russian history. For nearly a century after the end of the Napoleonic wars the tsars' empire stood immune to the process of political change which operated everywhere else in Europe; the autocracy, while sorely tried at times, still appeared unshakable. But the parallel is hardly exact. The autocratic system collapsed eventually not only because of its inherent weakness, but also because of the lesson of strength and vitality presented by societies that espoused liberal and democratic institutions. And so the future evolution of the Soviet system will be dictated not only by what happens in Russia and the Communist world.

Index